PAKISTAN

Published by Stacey International
128 Kensington Church Street, London W8 4BH

© Stacey International, 1997
All rights reserved. No part of this publication may be reproduced, stored in a retrieval system or transmitted in any form or by any means, electronic, mechanical, photographic or otherwise, without the prior permission of the copyright owners

British Library Cataloguing-in-Publication Data
A catalogue record for this book is available from the British Library
ISBN: 1 9000988 011

Editor: Irfan Husain,
Project Manager: Mela Davidson
Production Manager: Mark Petre

Printed and bound by Tien Wah Press, Singapore

The publishers gratefully acknowledge help from the following organisations and individuals:
Associated Press, Pakistan; British Museum, London; Department of Archaeology, Government of Pakistan; Habib Bank; Hameed Haroon; Harappa Museum; Hub Power Project; India Office Library and Records, London; Institute of Folk Heritage, Islamabad: National Film Development Corporation, Rawalpindi; National Book Foundation, Karachi; Quaid-e-Azam Papers Cell, Ministry of Education, Islamabad; Taxila Musuem; Victoria and Albert Museum, London; World Wildlife Fund, London

Picture Credits:
Sami-ur-Rahman title page, 12(b), 14(bc,br), 15(bl,br), 28(tl,cl), 45(r), 65, 96(b), 99(t), 100-101, 115(l,r), 118(tl,cl,b), 118-119, 119(t,bl,br), 122(t), 122-3, 123(b,t), 126(tl,tr), 139(t), 169(tl) 180 Nadeem Images 10-11(b), 14(tl,t), 28(tr), 38, 114, 122(b), 128, 129(br), 131(b), 134, 134-5, 156(bl), 148(r),156-7 Magnum 15(t), 23, 26(l), 28(cr,bl), 100(b), 154(r), 157(bl), 167(r) Popperfoto 25,26(br) Hulton Getty 64 Daanish Tapal 28(br),157(tl) Javaid A Khan 29, 33, 39(r,l), 40, 46 108(b), 113, 115(c), 124(bl), 125, 156(tl,tr,br), 156-7(t), 157(tr), 158-9(b), 164(tc), 166(r), 167(l), 168, 169(tr,b), 170, 170-171, 196(b) Pervez Ahmed Khan (Shyok Communications) Cover, half-title, 13(b,t), 14(bl), 15(bc), 26(tr), 27(tr,br), 31, 42, 45(l), 94-5, 96(t), 97, 98(t), 100(t), 120(t,b), 124 (t,br), 136, 137, 138, 142, 151, 152(t,b), 158 (l), 158-9(t), 159(r), 184(tl,tr), 201, 202-3, 194, 198 Harappa Archaeological Research Project and the Department of Archaeology, Government of Pakistan 30-31, 34(t), 35 Abbas 107(bl)(br), 111(b) 112(t,tcl,tcr,bcr) Sayyed Engineers 154(l) AW Khairi 129(t), 132(t),133(t), 155(l,r), 157(br), 166(l), 173, 175(t,bl) Sindh Wildlife Board 109 Patrick Eagar 196(t) Beaconhouse 11(t),164(t,cb), 164(b), 165(b) Irfan Husain 132(b), 175(bc,br), 176(tl) Rahat Dar 179(tr) Hub Project 12(t) PIA 160 (t,bl) Agha Khan University 165 (t,c) PNSC 160 (br) Habib Bank 162 Peter Luck 197 Asif M Khan 174 Kamil Khan 171(r) Timothy Hursley 171(b) P.A. Waheed 107 Associated Press 68 Elite Publishers 54,177 Kenneth Fink 110-111 International Advertising Ltd 194 Iqbal Archives 188 Jack Jackson 140 Javed Kazi 52, 56, 143, 183, 184 Yusuf Karsh 22 Keystone press 83, 92 M. Saeed Khan 49, 98-9, 104, 105, 137(bl,bc,br), 127 HMSO 62 Zoological Society of London 111, 108 Salam Almakky 178 Richard Ashworth 116-117 Mohamed Asrar 110, 112 (bl&bcl), 138, 184 Directorate of Research, Reference and Publications 75, 19, 186 Z.D. Barni 16,17 Pat Morris 111 Christopher Newall 176 Press and Information Department 22,19, 172 Pakistan Tourist Development Corporation 32 Quaid-e-Azam Papers Cell 69, 71, 72,73, 77, 79, 80, 83, 84, 89 Radio Times Hulton Picture Library 57, 58, 59, 60, 63,18 Hanif Raza 126 Yunus Said 71 Victoria and Albert Museum 181,182,183 P.A. Waheed 107, 143 Zoological Society of London 113
Remaining photos by Robert Harding

The contributions to this work do not represent any consensus of beliefs. It is not expected that readers will sympathise with all the sentiments they find here, for some contributors will disagree with others; but it is held that this work can do more to inform public opinion by a broad hospitality to divergent ideas than it can be identifying itself with one point of view. Neither the publishers nor editors accept responsibility for the views expressed in any contributions which appear in these pages. What they do accept is responsibility for giving them a chance to appear in print.

PAKISTAN

STACEY INTERNATIONAL
LONDON

Principal Contributors

A.F. **Asif Farrukhi** Writer of Urdu short stories and a critic and translator for Pakistani's English and Urdu press.

A.H.D. **Ahmad Hasan Dani** Former Professor of Archaeology at the University of Peshawar and Reader in History at the University of Dacca. Professor of History and Dean of the Faculty of Social Sciences, University of Islamabad. Publications include: *Gandhara Grave Culture, Muslim Architecture of Bengal,* and *Excavations in the Gomal Valley.*

A.I.H. **Agha I. Hamid** is an economist and gourmet who has closely observed Islamabad's growth.

A.K. **Azher Karim** Sports writer for leading Pakistani publications and a bridge player who has represented Pakistan in international competitions.

Ak.R. **Akhtar Riazuddin** Former columnist for *Pakistan Times* (1962-72) and travelogue writer. Founder and former president of the Behbood Association which runs a number of craft centres.

A.Q. **Abdul Qayyum** Journalist, author and diplomat, war and foreign correspondent. Former Head of the Department of Journalism, University of Punjab. Specialist in English literature and history. Author of *The Working Journalist,* and *A New History of India and Pakistan.*

A.R. **Ahmed Rashid** is Pakistan, Afghanistan and Central Asia correspondent for the *Far Eastern Economic Review* and the *Daily Telegraph* and also writes for Pakistani newspapers. He is the author of *The Resurgence of Central Asia: Islam or Nationalism.*

Ab.R. **Abbas Rashid** Former Lahore bureau chief of daily *Muslim,* and a columnist for some of Pakistan's leading publications.

A.S. **Annemarie Schimmel** Former Professor of Indo-Muslim Culture, Harvard University. Publications include *Pakistan: Einschloss mit Tausend Toren, Islamic Calligraphy, Islamic Literatures of India* and *Mystical Dimensions of Islam,*

B.A. **Babar Ayaz** is a respected writer on financial matters and heads his own firm of public relations consultants.

B.A.K. **B.A. Kureshi** Former chairman of the Board of Governors, Lahore Museum, Vice-President of the Research Society of Pakistan, and member of the Board of Governors of the Punjab Arts Council.

C.E.B. **Clifford Edmund Bosworth** Former professor of Arabic Studies, Manchester University. Publications include: *The Ghazanavids, Their Empire in Afghanistan and Eastern Iran,* and *The Islamic Dynasties, a Chronological and Genealogical Handbook.*

F.A.F. **Faiz Ahmad Faiz** Former Principal of the Haji Abdullah Haroon College, Vice-President of the Pakistan Arts Council and member of the Executive Board of the World Peace Council. Awarded the Lenin Peace Prize in 1962, and author of many collections of poetry.

F.J. **Fatima Jinnah** (d.1967). Younger sister of Quaid-e-Azam; candidate of the Combined Opposition Parties against Ayub Khan in the 1965 elections.

F.M. **Fayyaz Mahmood** Former Professor of English, Islamia College, Lahore. Editor of *Encyclopaedia of Urdu Literature* and well-known literary critic and short-story writer.

F.S.A. **F.S. Aijazuddin** Author of *Mughal Paintings and Related Miniatures, Pahari paintings and Sikh portraits in the Lahore Museum* and *Sikh portraiture by European artists.*

F.S.H. **Ferida Sher Husain** Lecturer in Social Work at Kinnaird College, Lahore, and author of *Social Characteristics of Drug Addicts.*

H.J. **Hamid Jalal** A former news editor of All-India Radio (1944-47), Radio Pakistan (1947-56), United Nations Radio (1957).

H.K. **Hamida Khuhro** Former lecturer at the University of Karachi and Fellow of St. Antony's College, Oxford (1979-73). Former Professor of History at the University of Sindh.

H.T.L. **Hugh Trevor Lambrick** Served as an officer of the Indian Civil Service in Sindh between 1927 and 1946. His publications include: *Sir Charles Napier and Sind, History of Sind, Vol.I* and *Sind before the Muslim Conquest.*

H.V.H. **Henry Vincent Hodson** Fellow of All Souls College, Oxford, and Reforms Commissioner (Constitutional adviser to the Viceroy) in India (1941-42). Editor of *The Sunday Times* (1950-61), and Editor of *The Annual Register of World Events.* His many publications include: *Economics of a Changing World, Twentieth-Century Empire* and *The Great Divide: Britain-India-Pakistan.*

I.A. **Iqbal Akhund** Former Ambassador to Egypt, Yugoslavia and France, He was Pakistan's Permanent Representative at the UN (1972-78) and president of the UN Security Council in 1976. From 1979 to 1987 he was Assistant Secretary General of the UN and was a member of Benazir Bhutto's government as Advisor on National Security and Foreign Affairs between 1988 and 1990.

I.A.R. **I. A. Rehman** is Director of the Human Rights Commission of Pakistan and a freelance columnist.

I.H. **Irfan Husain.** A weekly columnist in Pakistan's leading English-language daily he also works as a freelance journalist

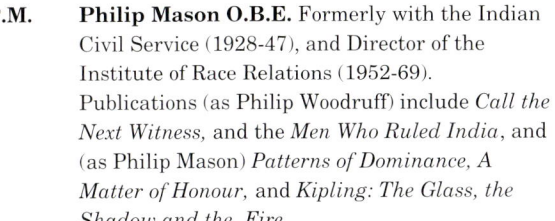

and consultant, preparing reports on population, education and conservation.

I.U.H. **Ijaz ul Hassan** is Chairman, National Artists' Association of Pakistan, a journalist and author of *Painting in Pakistan*. His paintings have been exhibited all over the world.

J.E.L.L. **J.E. van Lohuizen de Leeuw** Former Docent for Sanskrit, University of Groningen. Former Professor of Archaeology, Prehistory, History of Art and Ancient History of South and South East Asia at the University of Amsterdam.

J.F. **Jean Fairley** Worked for many years in the UN Agencies (ICAO, UNESCO, FAO). Author of *The Lion River*.

J.M.K. **Dr Jonathan Mark Kenoyer,** Associate Professor of Anthropology at the University of Wisconsin. He has been excavating at Harappa since 1986 and has worked on various sites in Pakistan since 1974, including Balakot and Mohenjodaro.

J.W.S. **James W. Spain** Former American Ambassador to Dar-es-Salaam. Publications include *The Way of the Pathans* and *The Pathan Borderland*.

K.A. **Khawaja Khurshid Anwar** Director of music programmes, All India Radio (1939). Former member of the Federal Advisory Committee for Broadcasting, and Governor of the Pakistan National Council of Arts.

K.K.M. **Kamil Khan Mumtaz** One of Pakistan's leading architects, he is the author of *Architecture in Pakistan* and the founder of the *Anjuman-e-Mimaran*, a society commited to improving design and building techniques through incorporation of traditional approaches.

K.M. **Khawar Mumtaz** Founder member of Pakistan's Women's Action Forum, women's rights activist and writer. Publications include *Women in Pakistan: Two Steps Forward One Step Back? Pakistan: Tradition and Change, The Changing Status of Women in Islamic Societies, Portraits of Working Women*.

K.U.K. **K.U. Kureshy, Colonel (Retd.)** Former President of Pakistan Geographical Association. Author of *Geography of Pakistan*, and Editor of *Pakistan Geographical Review*.

L.M. **Admiral of the Fleet The Earl Mountbatten of Burma, K.G., P.C., G.C.B., O.M., G.C.S.I., G.C.I., G.C.V.O., D.S.O., F.R.S.** (d. 1979) Last Viceroy of India (March to August 1947).

M.M. **Moni Mohsin** is a journalist and former Features Editor of *The Friday Times* and is author of a guide book to Lahore.

M.Y.B. **Muhammad Yusuf Buch.** Contributor to U.S. magazines, *Worldmark Encyclopaedia of the Nations: Asia and Australasia*; compiler of *Counsels of Peace,* 1967; author of *Kashmir: A Brief Study,* 1962 and director of Kashmir Centre, New York, 1967-72.

N.A.B. **N.A. Baloch** Former Vice-Chancellor of the University of Sindh, Hyderabad (1973-1976).

P.M. **Philip Mason O.B.E.** Formerly with the Indian Civil Service (1928-47), and Director of the Institute of Race Relations (1952-69). Publications (as Philip Woodruff) include *Call the Next Witness,* and the *Men Who Ruled India*, and (as Philip Mason) *Patterns of Dominance, A Matter of Honour,* and *Kipling: The Glass, the Shadow and the Fire*.

P.S. **Percival Spear, O.B.E.** Former Head of History, and Dean of the Faculty of Arts, University of Delhi. Leverhulme Research Fellow (1937-39). Fellow of Selwyn College Cambridge and former Chairman of the Committee of the Centre of South Asian Studies, University of Cambridge. Publications include: *The Nabobs, India, Pakistan and the West, Twilight of the Mughals* and *Master of Bengal: Clive and his India*.

Q.S. **Qaim Shah** is Chief Executive of the NWFP Barani Project and a development worker.

Q.U.S. **Q.U. Shahab** Former Secretary-General of the Pakistan Writers' Guild, and of the Pakistan Branch of International PEN. Author of several books and articles.

R.S. **Rukhsana Shah** is Economic Counsellor at Pakistan's High Commission in London and has served for many years with the Pakistani Government's Commerce and Trade Group

S.A. **Sarwat Ali** Director of the art gallery at Lahore's National College of Art and a leading writer on classical music.

S.A.R. **Sheikh Abdur Rashid**. Former Head of the Faculty of Arts and Professor of History, Aligarh Muslim University. Author of *History of Muslims of India and Pakistan*.

S.M. **Satnam Mahmood** Educationalist and authority on Punjabi literature.

S.P. **Stuart Piggott** Former Professor of Prehistoric Archaeology, University of Edinburgh. His many publications include: *Some Ancient Cities of India, Prehistoric India, Neolithic Cultures of the British Isles* and *Ancient Europe*.

T.A. **Talat Aslam** Editor of Pakistan's monthly *Herald*, and a seasoned investigative journalist on environmental issues.

S.R.W. **Syed Razi Wasti** Former Professor of History, Government College, Lahore, and Director of the Historical Research Institute, Punjab University (1965-69). Publications include *Lord Minto and the Indian Nationalist movement 1905-1910*, and *The Political Triangle in India 1858-1942*.

V.S. **Victoria Schofield** Author, *Kashmir in the Crossfire, Every Rock, Every Hill: the North-West Frontier and Afghanistan, Bhutto: Trial and Execution* and *The United Nation*.

Z.A.K. **Z.A. Khan**, Air Chief Marshall (Rtd) and former Pakistani Ambassador to Switzerland (1976-78) and the U.S. (1989).

Z.Y. **Zohra Yusuf.** Secretary General, HRCP. Founding Member, Women's Action Forum.

Contributors held these roles at the time of writing.

Contents

9	Introduction
10	**CHAPTER 1** **Pakistan in Perspective**
16	The First Fifty Years
24	Kashmir
29	**CHAPTER 2** **History**
29	The Indus Valley Civilisations
33	Discoveries at Mehrgarh
34	Recent discoveries at Harappa
35	The Kushan Era
38	Gandhara Culture
42	The Muslim Advent
45	From Arabs to Mughals
49	Mughal Ascendency
57	Confrontation with the British
61	The High Imperial Stage
64	The Cultural Encounter
66	The Struggle for Independence
70	Mohamed Ali Jinnah
85	A Sister's Recollections
92	Partition and Independence
93	**CHAPTER 3** **The Land and the People**
93	Geography and Landscape
102	The Indus
106	The Environment and Conservation
113	Islamabad
114	Punjab
121	Lahore
125	Sindh
132	Karachi
136	The North-West Frontier
141	Peshawar
143	Jammu and Kashmir
146	Balochistan
151	Quetta
152	**CHAPTER 4** **The Economy**
154	Manufacturing Industry
156	Agriculture
158	The Physical Infrastructure
162	Finance
163	The Media
164	The Social Infrastructure
166	Women

168	**CHAPTER 5**		
	Culture		**Maps**
168	Architecture		
172	Other Religions	8	*Pakistan*
173	Painting and Sculpture	16	*The Subcontinent Before Partition*
176	Miniature Painting	17	*The Subcontinent After Partition*
178	Music	24	*Jammu and Kashmir*
180	Crafts	30	*The Indus Valley & Related Civilisations*
184	Museums	36	*Alexander's March*
185	The Literary Heritage	43	*Antique Map of the Indus Valley*
187	Muhammad Iqbal	46	*The Ghaznavids*
190	Regional Literatures	50	*The Mughal Empire in the 17th Century*
192	Literature since 1947	60	*Imperial Structure: The Subcontinent*
194	Performing Arts	60	*Imperial Structure: North Western Area*
195	The Sufic Tradition	93	*Mountains and Rivers*
196	Sport	94	*Mountains*
		103	*Indus River and its Tributaries*
198	**CHAPTER 6**	115	*Punjab*
	Pakistan's Place in the World	125	*Sindh*
198	External Affairs	136	*The North-West Frontier*
200	Pakistan and Afghanistan	146	*Balochistan*
202	Defence		
204	**Bibliography**		
205	**Index**		

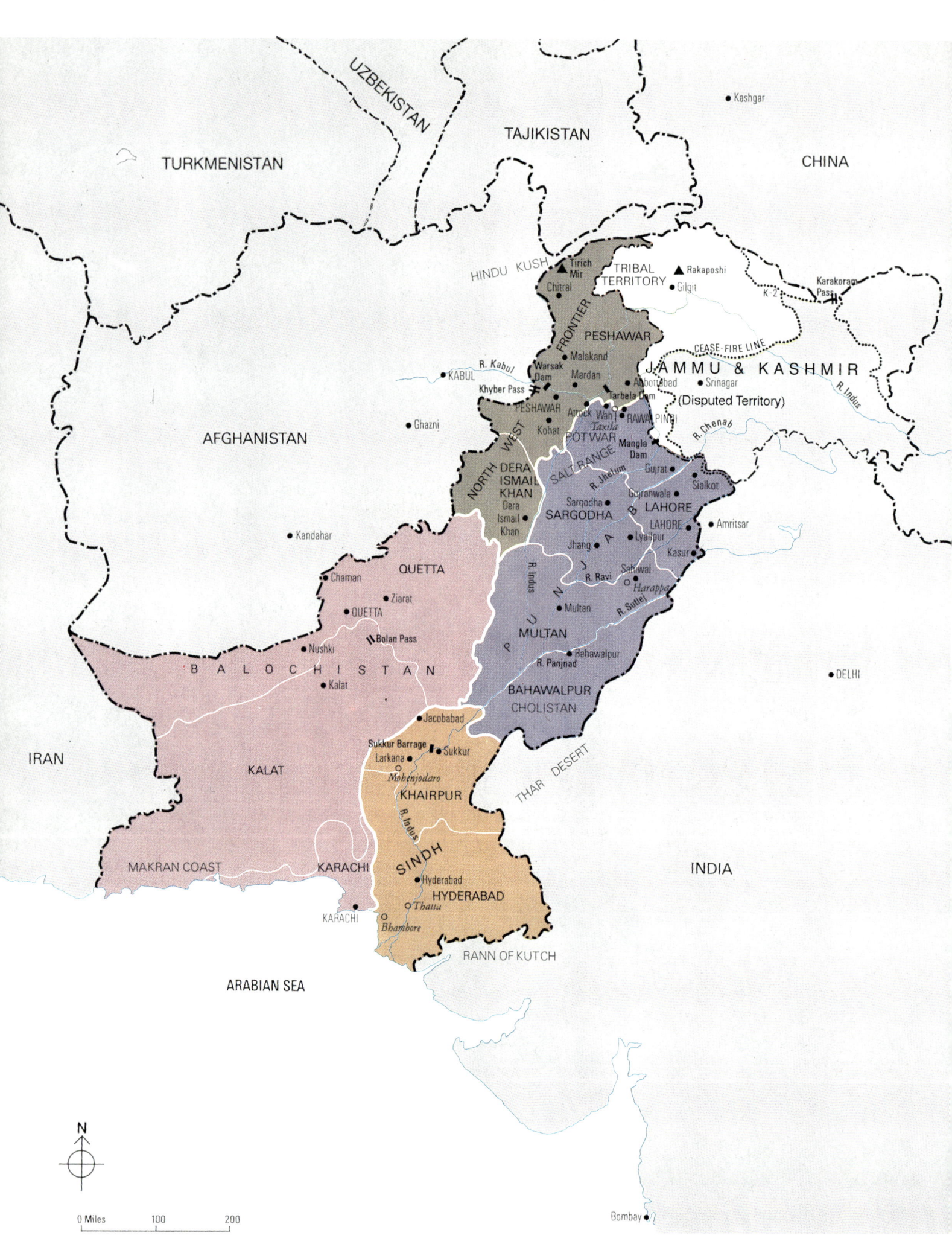

Introduction

The first edition of this work was published in 1976 to mark Jinnah's centennial. It is fitting that this second edition should mark Pakistan's Golden Jubilee. For it is a time when it may be said that Pakistan is beginning to come of age politically.

Adversity has shaped and tempered Pakistan's national character. For the country was born amid blood and fire in the partition of 1947, which proved cataclysmic. And it was an awkward birth – a realm divided by a thousand miles of what was to prove a persistently hostile territory. The infant state was soon to be bereft of the wisdom and humane vision of its creator and guiding light, Mohamed Ali Jinnah, when he died in 1948. Within three years, the assassination of the Quaid's successor, Liaqat Ali Khan, in 1951, left a constitutional vacuum. Critically vulnerable, Pakistan needed stability; and the emerging figure, General Ayub Khan, who took over in 1958, felt obliged to turn from the founder's precepts by declaring parliamentary democracy to be "against the genius of the people".

Yet the vision of the founder remained. "You are free," the Quaid had said in the Constituent Assembly in August 1947 – "You are free to go to your temples, you are free to go to your mosques or to any other place of worship in this State of Pakistan. You may belong to any religion or caste or creed – that has nothing to do with the business of the State... We are starting in the days when there is no discrimination, no distinction between one community and another, no discrimination between one caste or creed or another. We are starting with this fundamental principle that we are all citizens and equal citizens of the State... We should keep that in front of us as our ideal and you will find that in the course of time Muslims will cease to be Muslims and Hindus will cease to be Hindus, not in the religious sense, because that is the personal faith of each individual, but in the political sense, as citizens of the State."

It was to take the further trauma of the splitting off of East Pakistan in 1971 before the political freedoms and social tolerance proclaimed by Jinnah came to be promised by the elected government of the mid-1970s. But even then there was to be another convulsion, another retreat into coercion and narrowness under the weight of authoritarianism and zealotry. And again, the voice of the people demanded to be heard: the vulnerable buds of democracy were to re-appear by the late 1980s.

Beyond, and in spite of, the changeability of Pakistan's internal political fortunes and the encumbrances of its governmental structures, its people have grown rich in diversity and in creative energy – exemplified economically and in creative endeavour. The present volume has tried to draw these many strands together.

The genius of the people can be found beyond its politics – in the villages of the highland valleys and the river's edge, in the pride of heritage of the great regions of Pakistan, the Punjab and Sindh, Kashmir and North-West Frontier and Balochistan; amid its farmers and fishermen, its craftsmen and artists, its writers and poets and saints and sages, and a deep running sense of belonging to and possessing the seed-region of the subcontinent that lies beyond and in its larger part carries the name of the river that is Pakistan's. The great Urdu poet Iqbal wrote,

"Let not the sorry plight of the garden upset the gardener
Soon buds will sprout on the branches and like stars glitter.
Weeds and brambles will be swept out of the garden with a broom
And where martyrs' blood was shed red roses shall bloom.
Look, how russet leaves have tinged the eastern skies!
The horizon heralds the birth of a new sun about to rise."

The Publisher

1. Pakistan in Perspective

Until recently, even Pakistan's most ardent well-wisher could be excused for wondering where the country – born amidst so much hope and suffering – was headed for. Pakistan's first fifty years have witnessed great turbulence and institutional instability; warfare and rioting; and huge swings of the political and economic pendulum. Fortunately, Pakistan's first half-century has also seen amazing progress as an intelligent and industrious population has transformed some of South Asia's most backward and unpromising provinces into a relatively prosperous developing country. Despite setbacks – many of them self-inflicted – there have been clear and visible improvements. The physical infrastructure is being constantly expanded and improved; an elected government is striving to address an enormous backlog of unmet needs; and through privatisation and liberalisation of the economy, the country is industrialising at a rapid pace. The return of democracy – albeit with attendant din and confusion – may be seen as having heralded a new and promising chapter in the country's chequered history.

Like most developing nations, Pakistan is beset by a host of problems. But the key to a prosperous future – and a future in which Pakistan can play its rightful role in the world – lies in controlling its high growth rate and preserving stability in its erratic polity. The first factor needs little elaboration: a population that has quadrupled in size in fifty years will obviously place enormous demands on the state and great strains on the environment. This is an area finally receiving high priority from a government aware of the social and economic implications of an explosive birth rate.

The need for a stable political system is equally clear. Continuity has been a crucial element in the economic transformation of many Asian states, and this ingredient can only be provided through a broad consensus on national goals and direction. In Pakistan, however, political polarisation has made it difficult to achieve a meeting of the minds on the most important issues. The baneful Eighth Amendment to the constitution which until 1997 gave the President the power to dismiss the elected government and dissolve Parliament at his discretion is a case in point. This was a constitutional device introduced by the military dictator Zia ul Haq as a Sword of Damocles to hang over the necks of civilian governments. It was to have a destabilising effect on Pakistani politics. These powers were to be used no less than four times in less than ten years. Following the Muslim League's sweeping victory in the 1997 elections the incoming Prime Minister Nawaz Sharif expressed his intention finally to abolish the damaging clause. With the backing of the opposition Pakistan People's Party, this abolition was swiftly secured.

If a major theme has run through Pakistan's first fifty years, it has been the constant striving for a democratic order. Despite their long and sometimes bitter experience of authoritarian rule, Pakistanis have been persistent in their determination to shape their own destiny. After each military intervention, politicians and citizens obliged their rulers to concede them democratic rights, no matter how long it took. The case can be made today that in many respects, Pakistan is the freest of all Muslim nations.

The prevailing political oscillation may have prevented the nation from fully realising its social, cultural and economic potential. Pakistan's friends and foes alike tend to forget how long and bitter a struggle had to be waged by pro-democracy forces to ensure that the people won their rights. Right up to the country's fiftieth anniversary there were still voices calling for a return to authoritarian rule. Nevertheless, as Pakistan prepares to enter the 21st century, its fragile democracy gives it hope and confidence. The massive mandate won by the Muslim League in 1997 has raised hopes of a revival of the economy.

Another theme running through Pakistan's history is a search for a national identity. Created on the basis of a tolerant faith by a liberal, outward looking leader, the area that today constitutes Pakistan comprises four provinces united by Islam and federal government but enjoying their own separate and unique cultural and linguistic identities. Barely a year after Partition, the country was deprived of Mohamed Ali Jinnah's tolerance, vision and commanding leadership. Pakistan thus did not retain the strong impetus towards a self-confident nationhood it so badly needed in its infancy.

Studying for Pakistan's future:
Right *Secondary-level girls in a biology class*
Below *Children line up for lessons at an open-air school in rural Pakistan*

Above *Bringing power to the people of Pakistan: the Hub power plant supplies 13 per cent of the country's electricity*
Right *A presidential bodyguard in resplendent regalia*

This void was partly filled by a mixture of ideologies ranging from far-left communism to extreme-right, ultra-orthodox visions of a nation based on various interpretations of Islam. Immature politicians with little experience of the outside world touted their brands of instant panacea. The military strongman, Zia ul Haq, President from 1977 to his death in 1988, once declared Pakistan to be "a laboratory of Islam". He still casts a shadow.

Leaders with little understanding of history denied geographical and cultural realities. They seemed willing to turn Pakistan into a Middle Eastern rather than a South Asian nation, ignoring the contributions Muslims had made in India over a millennium. Forgetting that Mohamed Ali Jinnah had struggled so hard and so long to create a homeland for the Muslims of the subcontinent, they sought to justify the existence of Pakistan by presenting an image of a country severed from the heritage of culture and history and sealed off from the map of South Asia. All this served as a kind of deracination which left a nation orphaned of the past.

Hence the flawed sense of identity that has made the citizens of Pakistan unsure of their true selves: officially, their cultural links with South Asia were long discouraged, yet nothing of substance was fostered to fill that vacuum. As things truly are, Pakistanis have strong Persian, Arabic, Central Asian, Indian and Western influences woven through the rich texture of their cultural heritage. Going further back, the highly civilised Buddhists of the Gandhara period and the ancient Indus Valley civilisation have enriched their past. A fulfilling identity awaits. The return of democracy has witnessed a stirring of creativity as elected government strives to free the national psyche from the trammels of long years of tyranny.

Above *Water is the lifeblood of the nation: the spillway of the Tarbela Dam, North-West Frontier Province, irrigating hundreds of thousands of acres of farmland*
Below *Dancers whirl and stamp in the classic tradition of the Kathak, a dance form which graced the Mughal courts*

Pakistan's press, long gagged and manipulated, is now among the freest in the developing world. This shift from a controlled to a free press began with the return of democracy in the late Eighties, and now a number of independent newspapers are assertive and self-confident enough to launch stinging attacks – not all of them fully justified or researched – against the elected government. A whole new breed of investigative reporters and crusading editors gleefully expose wrongdoing in high places. This healthy trend, so essential to a vibrant democracy, has been supported and nurtured by a government that believes in establishing sound traditions, despite the occasional inconvenience and political pain that such an independent press inevitably causes.

Visitors to the country are often surprised by the range and quality of comments and reports, especially in the English-language press. Senior civil servants and sitting ministers are attacked mercilessly, and highly speculative news items, columns and editorials – often bordering on the libellous or seditious – appear regularly. For the most part, these damaging salvoes are accepted as a part of growing accustomed to democracy.

Culturally, too, Pakistan has grown far more open lately than in the late 1970s and 1980s. Despite periodic howls of protest from a tiny but extremely vocal minority, the state-controlled television network is exploring themes and depicting aspects of Pakistani culture and society long considered taboo. The government has proved its willingness to accept the political risks inherent in taking on the small but powerful extremist lobby.

The impetus given to the economy through liberalisation and privatisation policies initiated in the late Eighties is paying dividends in the shape of vastly increased foreign investment, both in projects and into the capital market. Pakistani entrepreneurs can look abroad to raise funding and many transnational groups have decided to invest in Pakistan, particularly in the power sector where a highly attractive policy package has generated an inflow of several billion dollars. Increased availability of power promised to lead to enhanced industrial and agricultural productivity, and make Pakistan more competitive in the global market.

Governmental efforts to reduce the budget deficit resulted in higher taxes in 1995/96. Such measures entail political risk, yet were essential for the long-term health of the economy. For too long, successive governments had borrowed and spent as it there were no tomorrow, and piled up

an external debt exceeding thirty billion dollars by the mid-1990s. Merely to service such crippling loans was taking a sizeable proportion of a government's resources. It was clear that if Pakistan were to stay solvent and control its high inflation, some unpalatable measures needed to be taken. Price rises, partly arising from inflation, added to popular unrest.

The long-neglected social sector, too, was receiving additional resources and attention from the mid-1990s. The budgetary allocations for education, family planning and health were increased, and after many years, the small family norm was being propagated on the state-controlled electronic media. This may seem a small step forward, but in a country in which the population issue had been swept under the carpet for years with disastrous results, this represented a major breakthrough requiring commitment and political courage.

Major new highways were under construction in the later 1990s which, when completed, will open up the country to faster movement of goods and people. The telecommunication system was being rapidly extended and modernised. In both key areas of the physical infrastructure, the private sector was being asked to play its role. More emphasis was being laid on oil exploration with a view to achieving greater self-reliance.

Many of these initiatives will produce tangible results only in the long term. But already, measures like freeing the economy and the press have had a measurable impact on the lives of ordinary Pakistanis. As Pakistan heads into the 21st century, it does so with many clear gains: as a functioning democracy it is a respected member of the world community; its free economy is fully integrated with the global economy; and elected governments tend to be more responsive to the needs of the people.

In fact, the main factors for rapid and sustained progress are in place as Pakistan prepares for its journey into the next century and the next millennium. What was needed to ensure the country its place in the sun was a clear sense of direction and a consensus on major issues. Once these have been achieved, there is no reason why Pakistan cannot play a major role on the world stage in the 21st century, as the exemplar of the compatibility of Islam with liberal democracy and an open, forward looking society.

I. H.

PAKISTAN IN PERSPECTIVE

Above A Pakistan People's Party (in opposition as of 1997) rally shows that democracy is alive in Pakistan
Centre (above) Carrom *is played in small towns and villages which have not yet been invaded by video games*
Opposite (above left) Chapali kebabs *are round, flat, patties made of minced meat, tomatoes, onions and marrow. They are originally from the North-West Frontier Province, but are now popular throughout Pakistan*
Below (from left to right)
A tribesman from Bannu, a settled area of the North-West Frontier Province, on the borders with Afghanistan
A namda *depicts many animals and plants; here a Kashmiri artisan adds finishing touches to a leopard*
A Punjabi craftsman concentrates on the demanding and intricate task of applying lacquer to a table top
The mountains toughen children quickly, even in Fairy Meadows where these five boys look sternly into the camera
A Sindhi folk musician travels far and wide to entertain village audiences with his skills
This Balochi girl can't make her baby sister smile for the camera

The First Fifty Years

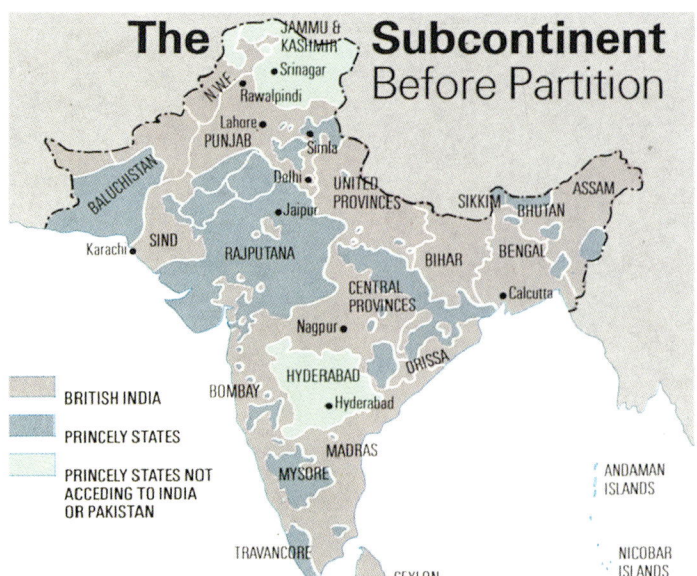

Two themes have run through Pakistan's first fifty years: the search for a lasting, stable democracy, and the repeated authoritarian interventions that have derailed democratic progress. The democratic urge has been consistent. Even the most defiant of Pakistan's military autocrats has had to pay lip-service to democratic norms. These opposing trends have been the cause of the recurring upheavals in Pakistan's political history, and the same dialectic has determined the tenuousness of today's democratic dispensation.

Democracy was never likely to come easily to the fledgling state. Consider first the peculiar geographical composition of Pakistan as it emerged from Partition. The Eastern and Western wings were ethnically, culturally and linguistically very different regions, separated by a thousand miles of Indian territory. Their only common factors were religion and the British imperial inheritance. At Independence, power was concentrated in West Pakistan; yet East Pakistan had a bigger population. To concede the universal principle of adult franchise would have meant the transfer of political control from West to East. Such a thing was unthinkable to the politicians and civil servants in Karachi, Pakistan's first, interim capital. Even in West Pakistan cohesion between the constituent peoples – Punjabis, Sindhis, Pathans, Balochis and others – needed an adequate formal constitutional framework. Thus the nation's first nine years were taken up in a futile groping for a constitution that would reflect both political and demographic realities. This constitutional lacuna proved fatal. It discredited both politicians and the democratic process and paved the way for the strongman and the opportunist.

And then, the new state was so early orphaned. Pakistan was conceived in the mould of Jinnah; Jinnah was the nation's father. But in thirteen months of its birth as a country, still without a constitution of its own making, Jinnah was dead. A firm believer in democracy and the rule of law, Mohamed Ali Jinnah's vision of Pakistan was that of a progressive, peaceful nation where all citizens were equal and would participate in the affairs of the state they had helped to create. His towering personality and unshakeable faith in parliamentary democracy set the constitutional direction for Pakistan. But direction almost proved not enough. Barely a year after his dream of a homeland for the Muslims of the subcontinent was realised, the path was lost.

We must go back in time a little, to Pakistan's emergence as an independent state on 14th August 1947, the result of the British decision to withdraw from India after dividing it into two Dominions.

Pakistan's founding father, Quaid-e-Azam Mohamed Ali Jinnah, described the event as apocalyptic. It was epoch-making in more respects than one. The South Asian subcontinent's accession to independence was the first significant expression of the global stirrings for decolonisation that had gathered pace during the war against European fascism and Japanese expansionism. Vast numbers of Muslims and Hindus were subjected to a bloodbath when partition became imminent. But the evolution of the freedom formula itself was through peaceful negotiations, and was given formal popular endorsement. A new

Leaders of the Pakistan Independence Movement came together at the new nation's first Constituent Assembly in Karachi on 11th August 1947, sealing their achievement

country was carved out of an old one that had acquired its political unity only under British imperial rule. Visualised as the national homeland of the subcontinent's Muslims, Pakistan – West and East – took its place amongst the leading Muslim states of the world.

The creation of Pakistan was the culmination of the freedom struggle of the Indian Muslims, which had branched off the broader independence movement of the people of the subcontinent. The fundamental issue was the preparation of a constitutional plan under which British India could advance to independence. The progressive introduction of the principle of representative government had led to an irresolvable disagreement between the major political parties – the All-India Congress and Jinnah's All-India Muslim League – over the safeguards demanded by the latter for the Muslim community. The federal scheme embodied in the Government of India Act of 1935 satisfied neither. Eventually in 1940 the Muslim League demanded independent homelands for the Muslims in areas where they constituted a majority of the population. The issue was clinched when, in the general election of 1945-46, specifically held to determine the representative character of the contending political parties, the Muslim voters overwhelmingly supported the Muslim League and what it stood for. After negotiations proved fruitless on proposals to accommodate the League's demand within a constitutional framework for the whole of the subcontinent, the Congress and the British conceded the principle of partition. Thus it was that the Quaid-e-Azam defended partition as the only possible solution to the subcontinent's constitutional problem.

This solution was the outcome of agreement among the principal actors; yet the process of partition was not tidy. The problems that such an operation entailed were of unprecedented nature and magnitude. The new state of Pakistan was to bring together in a new configuration the ancient land of the Indus Valley civilisation and the eastern half of Bengal. Over a thousand miles of Indian territory separated them. A cruel blow was struck to the original scheme of Pakistan by the division of the biggest two of its territorial components, Punjab and Bengal. This was turned further to Pakistan's disadvantage by the way the borders of the bifurcated provinces were drawn. The division of the provinces not only deprived Pakistan of a sizeable territory, it also affected the communal balance of its population and undermined its economic viability. Further, it contributed to the rise of the Kashmir dispute and discord over sharing of river waters. Both issues fuel tensions in the region to this very day. There were disagreements over the division of assets, including the remittance of sterling balances, cash resources and defence stores. Communal riots left unchecked, especially in Punjab and Bengal, led to a huge movement of population, with the truncated Pakistan having to absorb more than half a million refugees within the first few months of independence.

These problems made the task of establishing the new state grievously onerous. The early strains on the limited resources of Pakistan were all but unbearable, since the country comprised territories which were a lot less developed than those that came to constitute the Indian Dominion, especially in the field of industry. Nothing, however, daunted the people on the morrow of independence, buoyed as they were by their sense of achievement of statehood and of their direct role in it. The shortage of readily available resources was mitigated by faith in human potential and untapped natural resources. Compared with other states that were to emerge as independent from colonial status, Pakistan was relatively blessed with fertile land, abundance of water, a large and experienced community of farmers, two valuable raw materials (jute and cotton), an efficient irrigation network, along with a well functioning judicial, administrative, educational and health system up to the provincial level. At least in the Western Wing, Pakistan could look forward to the future with a reasonable degree of hope. What it needed most was peace and effective leadership to realise the essential goal of state building and national integration. For the better part of the first five decades this key requirement remained unmet.

A void after Jinnah

The nation's first eleven years were taken up with the search for a democratic polity and integrated nationhood, during which the custodians of power justified their failures and shortcomings with the plea of the state's infancy and its teething problems. At the beginning this was certainly true. As the years rolled by the excuse rang more and more hollow.

State formation and national integration did indeed present problems not foreseen during the short period between the adoption of the goal of a separate state and its realisation. Pakistan had inherited a scheme of representative

Below *Jinnah is acclaimed at a public meeting in Lahore, soon after Independence*

The qualities of Liaqat Ali Khan, Pakistan's first prime minister, were complementary to those of Jinnah

government modelled after the Westminster parliamentary system, and no questions were raised for eleven years about its suitability or adequacy. At local government level the people had some experience of electing their representatives, on a severely restricted franchise. At both levels this inheritance proved insufficient for coping with the problems that arose soon after independence. Parliamentary democracy implied rule by majority. Nevertheless the more populous wing of the country carried less weight in the political councils as well as in the civil and military services, and was far from the nation's centre of gravity, which remained in the Western Wing. Federalism, with substantial autonomy for the two units, had been the basic plank of the Pakistan scheme, but the practical problems faced by the new-born state demanded centralisation of resources and decision-making. The state's viability depended on a quick economic take-off, but disputes with India gave security a higher priority. Although the demand for Pakistan had been premised on the principle of self-determination, the fact that the homeland had been sought for a religious community threw up the issue of religion's place in the polity.

Amid these conflicting priorities, the record of the struggle for Pakistan offered little guidance. All that had been said was that Pakistan was not going to be a theocracy and that it would be a democratic state where the people would enjoy full sovereign rights. A strong commitment to egalitarianism was reflected, in general terms, in the arguments advanced in support of the demand for Pakistan and, more specifically, in the welfare-oriented programme adopted by the League in 1937 and the work of its economic planning unit.

Anticipating some of the problems likely to be faced in devising Pakistan's polity, the Quaid-e-Azam decided to play the anchor role in constitution-making by accepting the office of the President of the Constituent Assembly along with that of the Governor-General. More importantly, on the eve of independence he enunciated the basic assumption underlying the state. "You are free," he said in his Presidential address on 11th August, 1947: "you are free to go to your temples, you are free to go to your mosques or to any other places of worship in this land of Pakistan. You may belong to any religion or caste or creed – that has nothing to do with the business of the State." And he spoke on four themes: the total impartiality of the system of justice, the elimination of bribery and corruption, the evils of nepotism and jobbery, and the importance of working in cooperation for the benefit of his people.

With the achievement of statehood it was essential to end the regional tradition of politics followed till then. The task now was to forge a Pakistani nation of which all citizens, regardless of ethnicity, region, education or status, felt a common overriding allegiance. But Jinnah's death in September 1948 deprived Pakistan of its strongest uniting force. In those thirteen months since independence he had not finalised his constitutional blueprint.

The void caused by the Quaid-e-Azam's passing was filled by three men. The presidency of the Constituent Assembly was taken over by his deputy, Maulvi Tamizuddin Khan, and the post of the Governor-General was occupied by Khwaja Nazimuddin. The main responsibility for the nation's stewardship fell on Prime Minister Liaqat Ali Khan. The first step towards constitution-making could not be taken before March 1949. The Objectives Resolution was adopted at that time without due regard to the implications of its religious bias or the shift from the ideal the Quaid-e-Azam had given voice to with such clarity and force only two years earlier.

By the time the Basic Principles Committee Report came in September 1950, three years of improvised governance, characterised by central leadership presiding over a malnourished parliamentary system and the shift of the federation towards a unitary state, had given rise to new challenges from the provinces. The spirit of unity that had inspired them to render sacrifices for the national cause had weakened, political parties had lost their rapport with the masses, their leadership had begun to lose out to the bureaucracy, and public morale had been undermined by frustration at the stalemate in Kashmir. All these factors contributed to the shelving of the Basic Principles Report of 1950, the assassination of Prime Minister Liaqat Ali Khan in October 1951, and the reshuffle at the top – with Governor-General Khwaja Nazimuddin taking up the premiership and Finance Minister Ghulam Mohammad assuming the post of Governor-General. The second Basic Principles Committee Report was rejected in 1952, and in April 1953 the Nazimuddin Cabinet was dismissed by the Governor-General, despite the Prime Minister's command of the majority in the legislature and its recent approval of his government's budget.

The dismissal of the Nazimuddin government marked the beginning of a radical shift away from the parliamentary system of government. The first seeds of authoritarianism had been sown. Governor-General Ghulam Mohammad began wielding authority he did not rightfully enjoy. He made Mohammad Ali Bogra Prime Minister, but there was no doubt where real power lay.

Meanwhile, the people had been denied participation in democratic governance notwithstanding the grant of adult franchise – for women as well as men. The institutions of democratic rule were allowed to atrophy. The Constituent Assembly, indirectly elected in 1947, had become weaker by the allotment of state offices to a majority of its members. Provincial elections were held in the Western Wing in 1951 and these were not fair. Elections in the Eastern Wing were delayed for another three years and, when finally held in 1954, the result rocked the entire state structure. The Muslim League party was completely routed and the victorious United Front lost no time in demanding the election of a new federal legislature since the party of the sitting members from their wing of the country had been rejected. The Governor-General had no ear for democratic demands. When East Wing members of the Constituent Assembly carried out a legislative coup by stripping him of the power he had used to sack Nazimuddin, he promptly retaliated by dissolving the Constituent Assembly, on the grounds that it had failed to

Khwaja Nazimuddin, Prime Minister 1951-3

Muhammad Ali Bogra, Prime Minister 1953-5

Ghulam Muhammad, Governor-General 1951-5

Chaudri Muhammad Ali, Prime Minister 1955-6

Iskander Mirza, Governor-General 1955-6

H. S. Suhrawardy, Prime Minister 1956-7

I. I. Chundrigar, Prime Minister 1957

Feroz Khan Noon, Prime Minister 1957-8

fulfil its primary risk of framing a constitution – this at a time when the Constitution Bill was almost ready.

The dissolution of the Constituent Assembly brought the crisis of the state into the open. It confirmed the displacement of politicians by bureaucrats as superior partners in the councils of authority. The members of the cabinet the Governor-General chose for Prime Minister Bogra included not only Chaudhry Mohammad Ali, who had moved from his civil service job to ministership earlier, but also the army chief, General Ayub Khan, and Major-General Iskander Mirza, who had earlier risen from the post of Defence Secretary to that of Governor of the Eastern Wing. Another aspect of the crisis was exposed when the President of the sacked Constituent Assembly challenged its dissolution before the Sindh Chief Court. The court duly struck it down – but its decision was overturned by the Federal Court. The latter, however, did not let the Governor-General follow his own plan of constitution-making and obliged him to secure the election of a new Constituent Assembly. First, however, the ruling coterie merged the Western Wing provinces into a single province of West Pakistan. Only then, in February 1956, was Pakistan's first Constitution approved by the country's elected representatives.

The nine-year long effort to define the post-independence structure of the state shows that it had not been considered necessary significantly to deviate from or improve upon the Government of India Act of 1935 which defined the functioning of the provinces and their relationship with central government. There was more acrimonious controversy than serious reflection on the needs of a new society. No one was much concerned with the institutional requirements of sustaining a model borrowed from a country with entirely different political traditions. What occupied the constitution-makers was the search for a formula whereby the two parts of the country could be given parity in the legislature, and for a device which could keep the religious lobby at bay.

With the enactment of the Constitution on March 23rd, 1956, Pakistan acquired the title of an Islamic Republic. The Acting Governor-General, Major-General Iskander Mirza, had slipped into the Governor-General's house when Ghulam Mohammad had been declared physically unfit to hold office. Now he became the republic's first president by his own decree.

President Iskander Mirza assumed a greater role in government than even his forerunner. He also earned the dubious distinction of providing authoritarianism with a theoretical fig leaf: he decreed that the people of Pakistan were only fit for "controlled" democracy. He sired the Republican Party, helped it to acquire power in West Pakistan, and then saw it squeeze Mohammad Ali out of office (September 1956). H.S. Suhrawardy was invited to replace him but President Mirza was never at ease with him and eventually forced him to quit a year later (October 1957). He was succeeded by Ismail Ibrahim Chundrigar whose tenure lasted two months. Malik Feroz Khan Noon became the next prime minister and he survived in office until he received a letter from President Mirza (October 1958) declaring that he was imposing martial law.

The game of musical chairs that had been staged by the presidential palace from March 1956 to October 1958 caused great frustration among the people. But they had hopes of deliverance once they were asked to vote in a general election which had become due according to the constitution. This was first promised them in 1958 and again in 1959. While political parties and the people eagerly prepared for polls, the President seemed more interested in assessing the possible outcome, if not in actually determining it. Apparently guided by his own judgement, he summarily scrapped the Constitution, dissolved parliament, dismissed the government, imposed martial law, and appointed the army chief,

General Ayub Khan, as the Chief Martial Law Administrator. Thus ended eleven years of search for a post-independence polity. A people who had created a new state through the exercise of their democratic rights were told they did not qualify for democracy in the full accepted meaning of the term in the contemporary world.

Despite this slight upon their maturity and revulsion at authoritarian power, Pakistanis went about the making of their brand new nation. An industrial sector began to emerge; schools and universities were established; artists and writers were at work; and Pakistani sportsmen were winning laurels around the world.

Ayub's constitutional experiment

Describing his assumption of power on 27th October 1958 as a "revolution", General Ayub Khan moved speedily to give the illusion of such change by tempering authoritarianism with populism. Blaming the people's hardships on unscrupulous politicians and corrupt officials, he banned most of the prominent political figures from politics for six years and sacked about fifteen hundred civil servants. At the same time a series of relief and reform measures were carried out, such as provision of housing for the less affluent, price

control of consumer goods, lowering the ceiling on land holding, reform of the legal and education systems, and a new labour code. To give authority a new face, the virtues of rule by technocrats were propagated and industrialists were promoted as better qualified for public life than members of the old landed class.

These measures prepared the ground for a new political experiment that was termed "basic democracy". The country was divided into 80,000 units. Members elected to these units formed the electoral college for the election of the president. These "basic democrats" elected Ayub Khan as president by a comfortable margin in 1960. A commission was now set up to devise a new constitution "suited to the genius of the people". However, in 1962, ignoring its recommendations, Ayub Khan promulgated a constitution under his sole signature and had his presidentship regularised retrospectively. The presidential system introduced by him envisaged partyless politics, a president that was all powerful, and a legislature with little power. Other significant deviations from the 1956 basic law were that the word "Islamic" had been dropped from the state's name and the chapter on fundamental rights was no longer included.

However, members of the newly elected National Assembly, especially those elected from East Pakistan, forced Ayub Khan to review his thesis. The change in the state's designation was undone, the chapter on fundamental rights was restored, and not only was the bar to formation of political parties withdrawn, but Ayub Khan himself became the head of a Muslim League faction.

Ayub Khan's re-election to a new term in 1965 was considered a mere formality by his camp. Farm output was rising as a result of introduction of high yield seeds. Industrialisation had picked up; foreign policy was made more flexible by cultivating China, which also softened the left-leaning factions' opposition. The armed forces had been modernised. The media had largely been brought under official control. But the politicians sprang a surprise by getting together and putting up Miss Jinnah, sister of the Quaid-e-Azam, as their presidential candidate. Ayub Khan indeed managed to win the election, but complaints of large-scale interference by the administration and the police grievously tarnished his image. The people's dissatisfaction with his political system was beginning to show.

Although the seventeen-day war with India over Kashmir ended in a military stalemate, it was a political disaster for Ayub Khan as his credentials as a military commander were seriously questioned, not least when set against the heroic performance of the troops on the battlefield and the airmen in combat. The 1966 Tashkent Declaration negotiated with India, under Soviet aegis and with US concurrence, scarcely accorded with the public perceptions as shaped by official rhetoric. Suspicions of a cave-in were strengthened by the ouster of Foreign Minister Zulfikar Ali Bhutto, the architect of a markedly nationalist foreign policy. Meanwhile, throughout the September war, East Pakistan had felt defenceless and abandoned. The deep sense of grievance and political deprivation now took the form of a demand for far greater provincial autonomy, involving a capacity for its own territorial defence, enunciated in the Six Points of the Eastern Wing's dominant figure Sheikh Mujib ur-Rahman. West Pakistani politicians, however, viewed it as a formula for secession.

The government's moves to secure Bhutto's compliance in West Pakistan and Sheikh Mujib's in the Eastern Wing ignited the tinder of discontent. As the period of disqualification from political action expired, the older politicians too took to agitation. Public attention shifted from economic development to the concentration of disproportionate wealth in the hands of twenty-two families, the funnelling of the rural rents and profits into the pockets of the landed class, and the shameless rise of the President's kith and kin as master entrepreneurs. The state apparatus seemed incapable of dealing with protest and the dissidents took effectively to the streets.

Faced with an irresistible storm, Ayub Khan chose retreat, which soon turned into a rout as he first sought a compromise with the same politicians he had denounced only a few years earlier. But neither a pledge to retire at the end of his term (1970) nor acceptance of the failure of his political system could stem the tide of the movement for change. On 25th March 1969 Ayub Khan abdicated and called upon his army chief to take over. Thus he dealt a parting blow to his own handiwork, the 1962 Constitution, with its clear provision for the Speaker's succession to presidency if a President left the seat vacant. After eleven years of Ayub's rule the country found itself where it was in the early Fifties, once again in search of a democratic polity.

Despite the political stagnation, the country had made remarkable progress in virtually every field. Pakistani entrepreneurs spread the industrial base. The country's stock

General Ayub Khan went to Tashkent to sign the Agreement with India that closed the 1965 war. Zulfikar Ali Bhutto expressed his unhappiness over the terms of the Agreement

stood high abroad. Indeed, during much of this period, Pakistan was seen as a model for economic development. In the Western Wing – that which constitutes today's Pakistan – the most remote areas were connected to the rest of the country by road. The physical infrastructure was taking shape. The downside of political uncertainty may be seen as the preponderance of men of business being drawn to the quick profits of consumer goods, rather than investment in heavy industry. The country remained dependent on imports for basic engineering goods.

The nation divides

General Yahya Khan, the new Chief Martial Law Administrator, was known for the speed with which he disposed of whatever reached his desk. He came to deal with the problems accumulated by his predecessor ever more perfunctorily and with apparent lack of forethought. Within thirty-two months he had imperiously led his country to humiliating military defeat and dismemberment before it had completed its first quarter century of existence.

He adopted the Ayub formula of populist authoritarianism – making concessions to labour and broadening the base of primary education. He sacked several hundred officials on grounds of corruption. At the same time he freely used martial law regulations to suppress dissent. Constitutionally, Yahya's populism went further than that of his predecessor. Ayub had conceded a form of parliamentary government and direct election of assemblies on the basis of adult franchise. Yahya now demolished the system of parity in parliament between the two parts of the country. Henceforth West Pakistan would cease to be one unit: it would revert to its pre-1955 provincial structure. He accepted the formation of a constituent assembly to draw up a new constitution, and promised to transfer power to whoever won the general election. The only caveat to the revival of democratic rule was that the new constituent assembly, to be elected in 1970, produce a new constitution within a short time. It could be that Yahya's advisers banked upon the emergence of numerous small factions in the National Assembly so that the Chief Martial Law Administrator/President could retain his position not only as the head of state but also as the final arbiter in all key matters.

This – in December 1970 – was to be Pakistan's first general election in twenty-two years of independence. The people were seized by enthusiasm at their first ever opportunity to vote on national issues. In the Eastern Wing, voters were carried away by the prospect of autonomy, and in the Western Wing by the vision of an egalitarian levelling-up. The election itself was the culmination of the most frenzied political debate the country had witnessed. Turnout was heavy and polling free of interference. In the East, Sheikh Mujib's Awami League eclipsed all rivals, conceding them only two out of its share of 162 National Assembly seats. In the West, Zulfikar Ali Bhutto's Pakistan People's Party took a majority of the seats.

After humouring Sheikh Mujib as the Premier-designate, Yahya curiously started negotiating the sharing of power. He played simultaneously on the Eastern Wing's suspicions as to his junta's commitment to relinquishing power and on Bhutto's rejection of Mujib's "Six Points" as a thinly disguised formula for secession. Yahya allowed the parleys to drag on and failed to assess the consequences of putting off the assembly's inaugural session. Reaction in the Eastern Wing was ferocious, bringing extremists to the fore and compelling Mujib to match their militancy. Not unexpectedly the negotiations foundered and Yahya sent in troops to put down Awami League-led agitation. Clumsy use of force against the civilian population and the removal of Sheikh Mujib to West

General Yahya Khan, Commander in Chief of the Army, succeeded Ayub Khan in March 1969, clinging to power until after the secession of Bangladesh, in December 1971

Pakistan to face charges carrying the death penalty pushed East Pakistan into a bloody civil war.

India saw the opportunity to intervene decisively in East Pakistan. It opened its doors to all those who sought refuge on its territory and helped them raise militias to fight the Pakistan Army. However, it was not until the Yahya regime had lost the goodwill of the major powers, with the exception of China, and New Delhi had negotiated a treaty with Moscow, that India took its decision to attack Pakistan in what was still its Eastern zone. Pakistani forces in East Pakistan had neither the strength nor the leadership to give an honourable account of themselves. In any case, victory was probably impossible, and the plan to relieve pressure from India in the east with an offensive along the West Pakistan border failed to materialise.

The people of West Pakistan were outraged and shamed by the ignominy of surrender in Dhaka, and poured out into the streets to vent their anger. General Yahya could not resist one last fling. A new constitution drafted by his insulated experts was issued which even the officially owned newspapers could not be persuaded to publish. The junta had no option but to summon Zulfikar Ali Bhutto from New York, where he had gone on a belated mission to shore up the country's diplomatic effort. They begged him to return and assume the leadership of the nation that remained.

The brief Yahya interregnum is to be credited with the country's first free and fair election. Yet his memory is reviled for the break-up of Pakistan. To this day, the surren-

Mujib ur-Rahman became the focus of nationalist Bengali aspirations, which resulted in the formation of the separate state of Bangladesh on April 10th 1973

der ceremony in Dhaka on that fateful day in December 1971 is recalled with shame and anger.

A half-chance for democracy

In December 1971 the junta swore in Zulfikar Ali Bhutto as Chief Martial Law Administrator and President of what was left of the country. He likened his task to "picking up the pieces". The state was reeling under the shock of calamity. A sizeable chunk of its (western) territory was under Indian occupation. Over 90,000 of its soldiers were in prisoner-of-war camps and threatened with trial by a vengeful victor. The people knew not where to turn to regain their national confidence, but to the new helmsman, a charismatic leader with a liberal programme that could inspire the people to build a new Pakistan.

Bhutto began by widening the political base of authority by accommodating the parliamentary opposition in the power structure. One of the rival parties was brought into coalition at the centre, and the right of two others to run provincial governments was conceded. In a symbolic move aimed at erasing the bitterness of strife in the erstwhile Eastern Wing of the country, Sheikh Mujib's death sentence was quashed and he was flown back to Dhaka to head the new state of Bangladesh. The chiefs of the army and the air force were replaced in a decisive gesture of civilian supremacy. Another purge of the bureaucracy was considered not enough to meet the country's need for a dynamic administration and a scheme to recruit talent from the private sector was launched. The territory lost to India in the 1971 conflict was recovered and the POWs brought home. A radical redistribution policy was introduced. Banks and certain large industrial units were nationalised. The legal system was strengthened. Substantial benefits were granted to industrial workers. By August 1973 a new constitution, envisaging a parliamentary system with a strong prime minister, had been unanimously approved and enforced. Although still based largely on the Government of India Act of 1935, it constituted a signal achievement in that it represented a national consensus and the critical issue of provincial autonomy seemed to have been finally resolved. It appeared that the state's basic requirement for a framework for a stable democratic polity had at last been fulfilled.

With the domestic situation now under control, Zulfikar Ali Bhutto took bold steps to raise Pakistan's stock abroad. The oil crisis of 1973 had brought the oil-rich Arab countries a new consciousness of their strength. Seizing the opportunity for achieving the unity of Muslim states to suit the challenges of the age, Bhutto hosted an Islamic Summit. Respecting the wishes of the guests, he recognised Bangladesh: Sheikh Mujib was welcomed at the Summit. Subsequently Bhutto honoured his promise to visit Bangladesh and thus demonstrated that despite the bitterness of recent years, bonds remained among people who had jointly struggled for Pakistan in the Forties. The Islamic Summit proved to be more than a ceremonial get-together. Collective attention was focused on economic development and public welfare. But the success of the meeting and its portents also earned Bhutto some powerful enemies outside the Islamic community, as did his plans to acquire nuclear technology and address Pakistan's security concerns in the context of India's nuclear test in 1974.

Bhutto needed a respite to overhaul Pakistan's institutions and achieve a measure of Third World unity in global councils. But the common purpose seen during the drafting of the constitution did not last. Differences between the central government and the smaller provinces of the North West Frontier and Balochistan could not be sorted out, and the army was called out to deal with the strife in

Zulfikar Ali Bhutto's charisma and democratic zeal were exactly what Pakistan needed in 1971

Balochistan. As Bhutto recorded in his last testament, the bloodshed there made it difficult to resolve major issues quickly. By 1976 the economy was running into difficulties and the opposition was exploiting discontent, not least among the major industrialists and the middle class professionals.

Early in 1977, Bhutto decided to call for general elections a year before they were due. His party's position was less secure than he had calculated. The opposition surprised the government by forging an alliance capable of presenting a formidable challenge. The National Assembly election on 7th March provoked a fierce controversy over charges of vote-rigging and the opposition boycotted the provincial elections held three days later. The Bhutto government had arguably done more to satisfy the religious proclivities of the population than any of its predecessors, yet mass agitation was organized under the religious banner. When the law and order machinery had failed to restore calm, Bhutto entered into negotiations with the opposition leaders and a compromise was reached. But by then the military had made up its mind. Maybe they had not been entirely uninvolved in the violent upheavals. Emboldened by the open invitation from Bhutto's opponents to intervene, they went in for the kill. Soon after midnight on 4th July 1977, the Chief of the Army Staff, whom Bhutto had promoted out of turn, ordered the troops to carry out another putsch. Thus ended the brief interlude of democracy.

Despite his success in uniting the nation after the defeat and despair of 1971, Bhutto's rule proved to be divisive. His nationalisation of heavy industry, banking and education is still the subject of fierce controversy. But his patriotic policies and firm stance in standing up to the major powers was widely applauded in Pakistan and the rest of the Third World, and the country's stock had never been higher in the comity of Islamic nations.

Martial law returns

As the head of a new martial law regime, General Zia ul Haq realised that he had a much smaller base from which to operate than his predecessors Generals Ayub and Yahya. This time, neither democracy nor the constitution had been discredited in public eyes, and he was obliged to declare his respect for both. What was required of him was the formation of a government of elected representatives. His role must be seen as one confined to the restoration of order. He therefore presented himself as a temporary referee, determined to hold free and fair elections in ninety days. The constitution was not abrogated, it was only held in abeyance. Even the detention of the leaders of both the deposed party and the opposition alliance was described as a protective measure.

However, it soon became apparent that General Zia ul Haq had long-term personal ambitions. During those first ninety days more effort was directed towards discrediting Bhutto and his party through the release of white papers on the ousted government's working and publicising its alleged misdeeds than to preparing for the promised October elections. On the first of October the General announced postponement of elections on the grounds that the state needed to be put in order, that accountability took precedence over democracy, and that the constitution needed to be Islamicised. Plans for an open-ended extension of authoritarian rule were taken in hand. Yet the obstacle presented by a still popular Bhutto loomed large. A strategy for his elimination by judicial means was drawn up. He was charged with a political murder, and the trial culminated in his execution in April 1979 at the end of a trial whose fairness continues to be questioned to this day. Meanwhile Zia reintroduced vari-

Zia ul Haq brought in the fateful "Eighth Amendment". His rule ended abruptly when his official plane blew up in mid-air in August 1988

ous Draconian Islamic punishments and a system of *zakat*, the Islamic levy. His regime censored the press, closed newspapers and suppressed dissent. Miscreants of various categories were lashed and hanged in public, and a numbed populace was cowed by repressive measures.

Such heavy-handed theocratic rule received an unexpected boost from certain Arab and Western states, in the wake of Soviet intervention in Afghanistan in 1980. Around the same time, politicians opposed to Bhutto awoke to the hazards of the bargain they had struck with the military. Early in 1981 they joined the Pakistan People's Party, founded by Bhutto, to campaign for the restoration of democracy. General Zia retaliated with a provisional constitutional order, curtailed the judiciary's powers, dropped a number of senior judges, and resorted to large-scale arrests to quell popular protest. He promised a new political framework which he took time to spell out. Meanwhile, popular demonstrations for democracy in 1983 were harshly suppressed, especially in Sindh. To appease the opposition, Zia created an assembly of hand-picked, unelected members.

The scheme eventually unveiled by General Zia began with a referendum in December 1984, in which the people were asked whether or not they wanted an Islamic system of government. A "yes" vote was to mean that General Zia had been elected president for five years. Despite a very low turnout, this result was secured. After a partyless election in 1985, which was boycotted by all major parties, Mohammed Khan Junejo, an old Muslim Leaguer from Sindh, was nominated Prime Minister. His plea for an end to martial law could not be resisted, but before conceding this, General Zia made wide-ranging changes in the constitution which gave the President substantial powers, including the authority to dissolve the National Assembly at his discretion. This controversial provision, attacked by democratic opinion and defended by others as a safeguard against martial law, was to be used four times in the following decade to dismiss elected governments.

The framework painstakingly devised by General Zia did not in the end prove workable. Prime Minister Junejo's democratic inclinations, his decision to revive political parties in parliament, and his assertion of functional autonomy as head of government, brought him into conflict with the President. In May 1988 Zia sacked the government, dissolved the assembly and announced fresh elections. Two and a half months later he perished when his official plane

Kashmir

The Kashmir issue has caused longstanding enmity between India and Pakistan. It arose as a direct consequence of the partition and independence of the Indian subcontinent in August 1947. The state of Jammu and Kashmir, which lies strategically in the northwest of the subcontinent, bordering China and the former Soviet Union, was a princely state ruled by Maharaja Hari Singh. In geographical terms, the Maharaja could have joined either of the new Dominions. As a Hindu, he had a more natural affinity with India, but his population was predominantly Muslim. Although urged by the Viceroy, Lord Mountbatten, to determine the future of his state before the transfer of power, Hari Singh demurred. For over two months, the state created in the previous century by his great-grandfather, Gulab Singh, was independent.

There was already serious unrest amongst the Muslims, especially in the Poonch area, who were fighting for the state's accession to Pakistan. In October 1947 tribesmen from Pakistan's North-West Frontier invaded the valley of Kashmir. The Government of Pakistan maintained that the invasion was a spontaneous incursion in response to repression by the Maharaja's state forces of the local Muslim population. When the Maharaja requested assistance from the Government of India, Lord Mountbatten, who had become India's Governor-General, argued that the provision of assistance to an independent state could lead to an inter-Dominion war. He therefore advised that Hari Singh should first accede to India and recommended that the issue should be resolved by a referendum of the people. Hari Singh agreed to this suggestion but limited India's jurisdiction to external affairs, communications and currency. On 27th October 1947, Indian troops were airlifted to Srinagar. Efforts to reach a peaceful settlement through dialogue between India and Pakistan failed; resistance from the "Azad" (freedom) fighters against the Kashmiri state forces and Indian troops intensified, spreading to Ladakh, Baltistan and Gilgit. The Pakistani army officially entered the war in May 1948 on the grounds that the presence of Indian troops in Kashmir constituted a threat to Pakistan's own security.

The Indian Prime Minister, Jawaharlal Nehru, referred the dispute to the United Nations, and a cease-fire was agreed in January 1949. According to resolutions passed by the UN Security Council, both Pakistan and India agreed that a plebiscite should be held to determine the will of the people. The plebiscite has, however, never been held. The state remains divided on the ground; two-thirds of it (known as the state of Jammu and Kashmir) comprising Jammu, the valley of Kashmir and the sparsely populated Buddhist area of Ladakh are controlled by India; one-third is administered by Pakistan. This area includes a narrow strip of land, called the "Azad" state of Jammu and Kashmir, and the Northern Areas, comprising Gilgit, Baltistan and the former kingdoms of Hunza and Nagar.

Tension between the two countries over Kashmir was exacerbated by increasing Indian control of the administration of the state to the east of the ceasefire line. After the dismissal of the pro-autonomy Kashmiri leader, Sheikh Abdullah, in 1953, successive Chief Ministers acquiesced in the state's integration into the Indian Union. Attempts to resolve the issue through political discussion were unsuccessful. In September 1965 war broke out again

JAMMU AND KASHMIR
This map shows the original boundaries and the cease-fire lines that divide the areas of administrative control

between India and Pakistan. The United Nations called for a ceasefire and peace was restored following the Tashkent Declaration in 1966, by which both countries returned to their original positions along the ceasefire line. After the 1971 war and the creation of independent Bangladesh, according to the terms of the 1972 Simla agreement, Prime Minister Indira Gandhi of India and President Zulfikar Ali Bhutto of Pakistan agreed that, in the state of Jammu and Kashmir, neither side would seek to alter the ceasefire line, which was renamed the line of control, "unilaterally, irrespective of mutual differences and legal interpretations."

In 1989 Kashmiri activists, who had become disenchanted with the political process as a means of expressing dissent, mounted an armed insurgency in the valley. The movement, which gained momentum throughout 1990, was severely repressed by the Indian authorities, who substantially increased their military presence in the valley and the state was put under Governor's rule. Pakistan condemned India for human rights abuses and gave its diplomatic and moral support to the Kashmiris, urging that they should be allowed their right of self-determination. The Government of Pakistan has not, however, endorsed the "third option" of independence and the militants remain divided in their objectives. Of the major factions, the Hizb-ul Mujaheddin supports accession to Pakistan, while the Jammu and Kashmir Liberation Front is fighting for independence of the entire state as it existed prior to 1947.

The Government of India has not permitted any dialogue which contemplates the departure of the state from the union of India, pointing out that the movement is not widely supported by the people of Ladakh nor those of Jammu. It has also attempted to "normalise" the situation in the valley by holding elections to the state's legislative assembly, but the militants and political activists, who oppose union with India, insist that elections are no substitute for a plebiscite. While the issue is unresolved, the status of "Azad" Jammu and Kashmir and the Northern Areas also remains undecided, since the Government of Pakistan has not formally integrated these areas as part of Pakistan, in order not to jeopardise its demand for the future of the entire state to be decided according to the UN resolutions.

Western interest in the Kashmir issue, especially that of the US and the UK, has been heightened by the proliferation of weapons in the area as well as concern that a regional dispute, which has religious overtones, could become the flashpoint for a major conflict in the area. Both Pakistan and India are known to possess nuclear capability. Numerous violations of the line of control as well as sporadic fighting between Indian and Pakistani troops on the Siachen glacier, the most northerly point of the line of control, where both countries maintain forces at altitudes rising to 20,000 feet, add to Western concern for the stability of the region. Although the Indian Government is determined to counter the insurgency, any settlement which does not accommodate the interests of the disaffected Kashmiris seems bound to fail. Pakistan is also unlikely to relinquish its concern for an issue which directly affects its own geo-strategic and political standing.

V. S.

blew up mysteriously in mid-air.

General Zia's disappearance from the scene found Pakistan with deep problems. Pakistan's involvement in the Afghanistan war had released a flood of arms and drugs into the country. The encouragement received by ethnic groups and the fundamentalists to assert themselves outside a working of normal politics led to widespread violence and sharpened divisiveness.

Yet another beginning

The general election promised by Zia was held by his successor in the presidency, Ghulam Ishaq Khan. But hopes that the revival of civilian rule would restore a democratic system proved to be short-lived. A ding-dong battle between the democratic and the authoritarian forces ensued. In the first leg of the 1988 general election, the People's Party and its allies gained an overall majority in the National Assembly but failed to do so in the most populous province of Punjab. Allowed to form the government at the centre, Zulfikar Ali's daughter, Benazir Bhutto, became the modern world's first ever Muslim woman Prime Minister.

Benazir Bhutto and her party came in on a platform of rolling back the vestiges of military rule. But she could neither subdue Punjab, ruled by a Muslim League-led alliance, nor develop a working relationship with it, and the confrontation that developed between the Prime Minister and Punjab brought political processes to a standstill. Likewise, no working relationship was able to grow between the government and a President not willing to give up the powers the Zia amendments had granted him. After barely twenty months in office, the Benazir Bhutto government was dismissed on the charges of corruption and misrule. A fresh election was ordered under a caretaker regime headed by Ghulam Mustafa Jatoi, the leader of opposition in the outgoing assembly.

In this 1990 General Election, the Muslim League-led

Zia's successor, Ghulam Ishaq Khan, had the tough task of restoring democracy

alliance was victorious. The voting process was not accepted as fair by the PPP-led alliance. It was now the incoming Prime Minister Nawaz Sharif's turn to face agitation from Benazir Bhutto and her PPP. The government countered by taking PPP leaders to court on charges of misconduct and abuse of power. Benazir Bhutto's husband, Asif Ali Zardari, faced several corruption charges, as well as one case of kidnapping. All these lawsuits eventually failed. Meanwhile, Prime Minister Nawaz Sharif set about the privatisation of state-owned enterprises, and the development of a market economy. A major programme of motorway construction was put in hand and the building of new airports. The on-running fight between President and Prime Minister was eventually ended by the Chief of the Army Staff who persuaded both to quit and agree to a new election.

The 1993 Election was supervised by a caretaker regime

headed by Moeen Qureshi, formerly a World Bank executive, who was chosen with the concurrence of both the major parties. The PPP and its allies emerged as the single largest party and Benazir Bhutto began her second term as Prime Minister, yet without an overall majority. This disability may account for the weak record of an administration that was to be allowed to survive a mere three years. The PPP had offered a raft of reforms, including further privatisation, liberalisation of the economy, better communications, increased literacy, services for women, improved land tenure rights, a reduction of feudal power and privilege, and decentralisation of authority. The sum of its achievements, however, amounted to patchy and ineffective measures marred further by widespread allegations of corruption.

Meanwhile, the government was subjected to strong

The Muslim world's first woman prime minister, Benazir Bhutto's two terms of office ended prematurely, following the dismissal of her governments in 1990 and 1996

Nawaz Sharif was the first prime minister to emerge from a business background. His return to office with a large majority in the 1997 elections allowed him to repeal Zia ul Haq's Eighth Amendment

Farooq Leghari, earlier a minister in Benazir Bhutto's first government, was elected president in 1993. As president, he used the Eighth Amendment to dismiss Miss Bhutto and her Pakistan People's Party government in 1996, on the grounds of corruption and unrest in the country

pressure from opposition groups, who were able to mobilise public opinion against alleged corruption in high places and the freedom apparently allowed to the law-enforcing agencies to liquidate those they decided to brand as criminal. The judiciary's vigorous defence of what it saw as its right to appoint judges to the High Courts in defiance of the Prime Minister's repeated exercise of this power brought about a deadlock which was only partly resolved in a landmark judgement in the Supreme Court. It was established that the advisory role of the Chief Justice in judicial appointments would be binding, and *ad hoc* judges appointed irregularly by the government would have to stand down unless their appointments were confirmed by the Chief Justice. This was a severe setback for the PPP government which dragged its feet in implementing their ruling, thus further antagonising the higher judiciary.

On 5th November 1996, the government was dismissed on the grounds of corruption, inefficiency and abuse of authority. In a massive indictment, the Bhutto administration was charged with phone-tapping on an unprecedented scale and tarnishing the image of the judiciary. This was the second Benazir Bhutto administration to meet such a fate in seven years. The Supreme Court upheld the decision of the President, Farooq Leghari, who formed a caretaker administration until the new general election in February 1997.

This resulted in Nawaz Sharif's return to power with an unprecedented majority, albeit in a minuscule poll of less than 30 per cent of those entitled to vote. The movement launched by the admired cricketer, Imran Khan, for the elimination of corruption secured not a single Parliamentary seat. The PPP was left with a rump of 16 seats in an assembly of 210 seats. Once more, Asif Ali Zardari, his wife's former Investment Minister, faced charges of malpractice.

Among the incoming Muslim League's government's first acts were moves to repeal the notorious Eighth Amendment, rapprochement with India, specifically over the running sore of Kashmir which affects both countries, and a reduction of the strength and role of the military. In prospect was further privatisation and a widening of the tax base in such a way as to raise revenue from a wide region of trading activities hitherto escaping taxation, and in due course to curtail the agricultural landlordism which has permitted the survival of anachronistic feudal authority in Sindh and elsewhere.

The arrival of what looked like a strong government generated a mood of optimism at the 50th anniversary of Pakistan's independence. No one was minimising the gravity of the tasks ahead. Pakistan's nascent democracy still needed careful nurturing before it could throw up a culture of participatory governance. The process of accountability needed to be consolidated and the weaknesses of the system of governance removed. The "civil society" had still to find its due role.

Despite all the hazards and alarms that characterised Pakistan's return to democracy, it stands today as one of the freest Muslim countries in the world with a totally – not to say stridently – independent Press and complete freedom of association. It is a living proof of the potential compatibility between Islam and a democratic dispensation. Over fifty years, Pakistanis had paid a heavy price to ensure that they participated in their country's affairs. They were not likely to surrender this right easily, and therein lay hope of a happier political maturity over the coming decades.

I.A.R.

Above *Vigilant forces of the nation: a Pakistan Air Force F16 jet fighter patrols the skies over the snow-capped peaks of the Western Himalayas*
Below *Pakistani Army troops in a heli-borne training assault*

Above (left) *A Balochi shepherd is vigilant in guarding his precious flock: woe betide the intruding predator*
(right) *Coal-mining in Balochistan is dangerous, back-breaking work which attracts intrepid miners from the NWFP*
Left *An old man is unbowed by his heavy burden*
Right *The Arabian Sea is a rich fishing ground; a fisherman shows off his catch*
Below (left) *Pakistan's forests are dwindling but timber remains popular for furniture, construction and fuel* **(right)** *As Quetta expands, there is strong demand for bricks from kilns such as this one*

2. History

The greatest river of Pakistan, sweeping south from the highest mountains in the world, gave its name immemorially to the entire subcontinent. Along its banks and among its tributaries there grew up civilisation after civilisation, luring successive waves of conquerors – until, halfway through the 20th century AD, the land came into itself in free and modern statehood, Pakistan.

Above *The religion of the Indus Valley Civilisation is still shrouded in mystery. This statue is probably a priest-king. It was found at Mohenjodaro and is four thousand years old*

The Indus Valley Civilisations

The Indus civilisation was an urban culture, occupying a huge area largely within the modern political boundaries of Pakistan, estimated to have existed between 2600 and 1900 BC. It was centred on the river Indus and the now dry Ghaggar-Hakra in Cholistan, and at its maximum extent contained within it what is very roughly an equilateral triangle with sides of about one thousand kilometres, one of which is formed by the coast of the Arabian Sea, with its apex on the river Sutlej hardly more than two hundred kilometres south of the Himalayan foothills.

Over fifteen hundred settlements have now been discovered, from Sutagen-Dor in Makran to Rupar, where the river Sutlej leaves the foot-hills of the Himalayas, and Lothal in Gujarat. Many seem to have been commercial and industrial centres. Some were distant trade outposts, others were frontier fortresses.

Within this province there were five major cities, some 350 to 450 kilometres apart. Four of these cities, Mohenjodaro (Pakistan), Harappa (Pakistan), Mehrgarh (Pakistan) and Dholavira (India) have been extensively excavated and have had virtually identical material cultures throughout the duration of the civilisation, as well as a number of smaller urban settlements and coastal trading posts. Their architecture was consistently of burnt brick, or of mudbrick faced with firebricks; accomplished wheel-made and often painted pottery was mass-produced throughout the area; competent metallurgy produced tools and vessels (though few weapons) in pure or alloyed copper; and vigorous naturalistic art was expressed in small-scale stone, clay and bronze sculpture or on engraved stone seals. These latter also bore incised inscriptions in a non-alphabetic script which to this day scholars have been unable to decipher.

That organised authority existed is implicit not only in the uniformity of the arts and crafts of the province but in the stereotyped layout and planning of its major towns in a manner unknown elsewhere in western Asia. They had walled cities and effective wells and domestic and public drainage systems; there was also a uniform and rigorously maintained system of weights and measures.

Despite the civic identity suggested by walled cities, no palaces or temples have been identified, nor is there evidence of military power. This civilisation was maintained on the surplus of effective cultivation of cereals and pulses, melon, sesame, dates and cotton, and the domestication of cattle, buffaloes, sheep, goats, pigs and dogs and cats. The horse and camel may have been used along the borderlands but are not found in the major cities until the final phase of their existence. The Indus valley was singularly self-sufficient for all but a few imports, and while it was in touch with trade centres in Iran, the Persian Gulf and Mesopotamia, these contacts seem minimal and indirect.

Clearly the walled cities were the centres of civic authority however administered and of whatever nature. At both sites, artificial platforms six to seven metres high had been built (at Mohenjodaro on the ruins of earlier buildings). Harappa has substantial remains, Mohenjodaro, traces of fortifying walls. At the latter site, a complex group of buildings crown the citadel, difficult to interpret in detail, but including one which seems to be an assembly hall, and another a great bath with encircling rooms. Adjacent to this is the massive foundation of a large building with floor ducts to allow circulation of air, having an area of nearly 850 square metres. At Harappa few plans of buildings have survived, except for on Mound F where there is a very large structure that has twelve blocks, possibly the foundation of a large wooden building.

The implications are impressive: organisation and control are everywhere apparent, not only within the city, but over the cereal production of the surrounding countryside. Although there are defensive walls, the metal equipment of the inhabitants is, by all western Asiatic standards of the time, curiously deficient in inventiveness and effective weaponry. No building displays the power or magnificence of a despotic ruler or of the gods, and here again the contrast with the contemporary world of Akkad or Elam is apparent.

The formalised glyptic art of the engraved seal-stones is uniform through the time and space of the Indus civilisation, and with it goes the equally formal and unchanging script used on these seals, on tablets, pottery and as graffiti. Only one monumental inscription has been discovered recently at Dholavira. Consisting of about four hundred signs, the script cannot be alphabetical, and is never cursive, always consisting of formal, pictorial symbols. It can be shown to have been written from right to left, and no inscription contains more than about twenty characters and may consist of only one. Though a total of some four thousand inscriptions are known, none is bilingual with a parallel text in a known language which might aid decipherment in the manner of cuneiform or the Egyptian hieroglyphs. Many attempts have been made but none is convincing. The language is most unlikely to be Indo-European and suggested affinities with the Dravidian language group are possible but unproven.

As with the inscriptions, the visual arts represented by the seals, sculpture in stone, modelling in clay or casting in

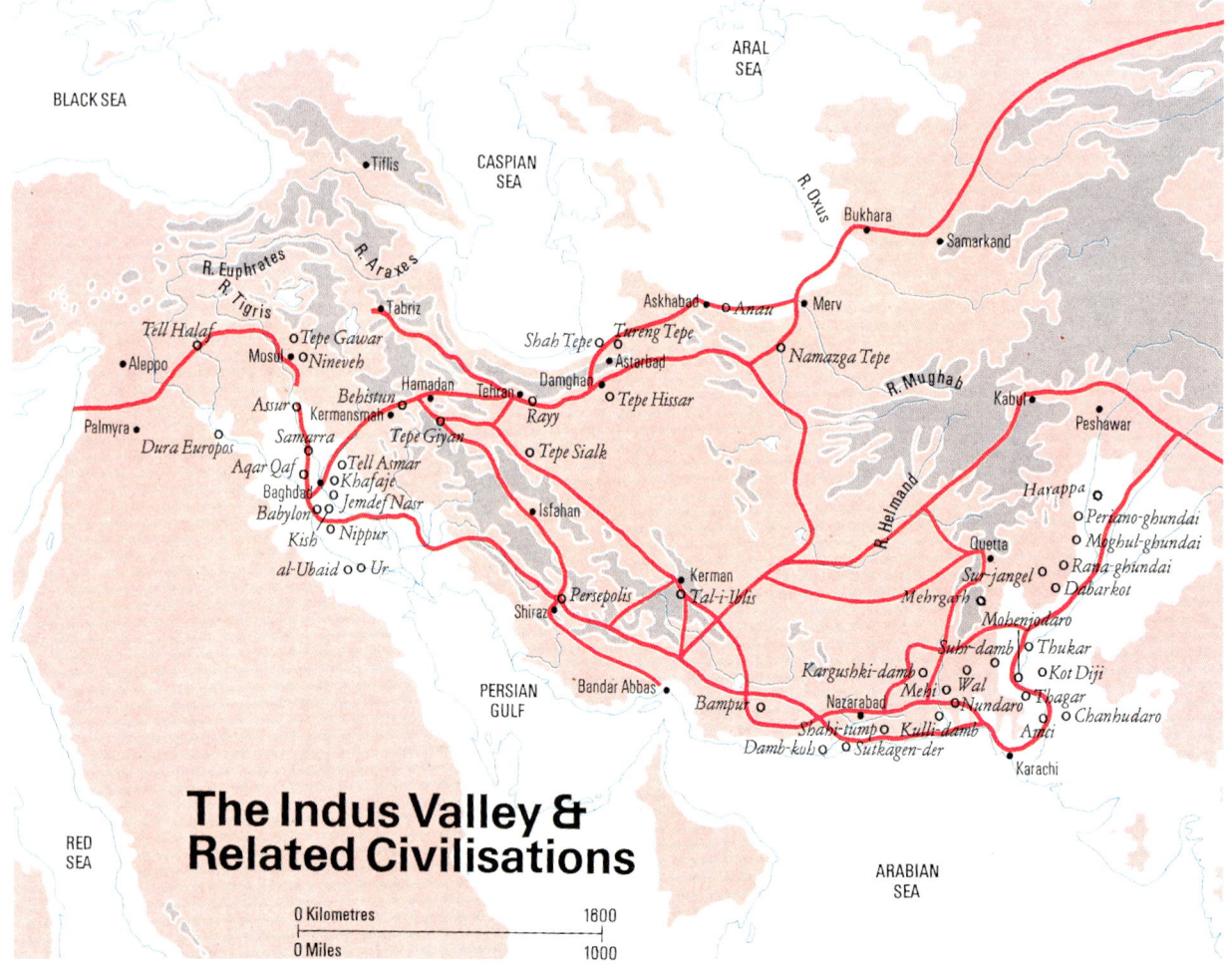

The Indus Valley & Related Civilisations

Each grave on Makli Hill at Thatta indicates by its style the dynasty of its occupant, and many bear Quranic inscriptions. Kings, queens, saints and scholars, along with many nameless individuals are buried here.

madrasahs, or schools, and mosques. Islam spread quickly in urban centres, because the political authority of the Muslims was well established there.

The expansion of Muslim rule weakened the foundations of local religions and set in motion a social revolution which prepared the way for the adoption of a universal faith. As a result, individual families and ethnic groups accepted Islam, which did not demand a violent break with the past. Its intellectual culture opened new horizons and its social and political system offered opportunities of advancement. Dr. Cantwell-Smith states the problem thus: "The environment in which the religion has had to relate its adherents to God has been a peculiarly complex and recalcitrant one. Most saliently India has been the only major part of the Islamic world in which the community has continued to be a minority; only here has the religion proved of large scale, sustained, socio-cultural creativity where its adherents' task has been to live out their lives Islamically in a society in which most members have had other visions."

The Muslim people and princes of the Indian subcontinent played an important role between 1200 and 1500 while the rest of the Islamic world was shaken to its foundations by violent convulsions and revolutions. The Delhi Sultanate in its more vigorous days was the resort of as many as fifteen unfortunate sovereigns in exile from Muslim Asia, who were often accompanied by men of learning. As a result, the court at Delhi became celebrated as the most elegant and magnificent in Islam. Cultivation of the arts was encouraged under royal patronage in Delhi and splinter states, into which the former territories of the Sultanate had been fragmented. The poet Amir Khusrau, who died in 1325, was made royal librarian, granted a state pension, and elevated to the rank of the highest amirs. He was equally at home in Persian, Turkish and Hindi.

The period 1200-1500 was also remarkable for the spread of Muslim mysticism throughout India. The influence of Muslim mystics and their teaching is important with regard to the history of the Muslims and to the conversion of Hindus. To this subcontinent Islam brought a new religion, a new civilisation, new ways of thought and new values. Its rich traditions of art and literature, of culture and refinement, of social and of political institutions were established. The Sufi presentation of Islam helped to overcome religious barriers and fired the imagination of many Hindu reformers, leading to the rise of neo-Hinduism and culminating in the Bhakti movement which prompted several Hindu and Muslim spiritual leaders to advance the theory of the unity of all religions.

"Islam introduced in India," states Pannikar, "a conception of human equality, a pride in one's religion, a legal system which in many ways was an advance on the codes of the time... The new spirit which the Hindu monarchs of Rajputana and of the Vijaynagar dynasty displayed, as champions of *dharma* and as upholders of religion, was the direct result of the contact with Islam... Religious factors became active in the secular policies of Hindu kings as a result of Islam."

Mediaeval Hindu theism, the rise of the Bhakti movement,

bronze are minor and intimate rather than of the monumental quality appropriate to temple or palace display. From their iconography inferences have been made on the religion of the civilisation, but without texts they amount to little more than guesswork. An overall impression of the culture is of traditions established, accepted and only gradually changing over time. The most likely agents for the enforcement, transmission and maintenance of such a complex of traditions might be thought to be the type of self-perpetuating corporation provided by a priesthood rather than any secular dynasty.

Transport by land and water is attested over the whole area by ubiquitous toy cart models in pottery and, very occasionally, copper, and by a few representations of boats with masts and sails. Land traction would have been by oxen, although the metal models and some of the animal figurines may indicate the occasional use of horses but the general situation in western Asia would imply this latter sophistication to have developed late in the history of the Indus civilisation.

S. P.

Indus decline

The first urban civilisation of the subcontinent gradually faded into the background as new cultures emerged at the eastern and northern edges of the Indus valley region. It took over one thousand years for the political and cultural centre of the northern subcontinent to shift from the Indus valley to the middle Ganga region. The process of change was gradual and it is unlikely that anyone living during the period between the decline of the Indus cities (1900 to 1300 BC) and the rise of the Early Historic cities (800 to 300 BC) would have been aware of the shift.

Factors that played a role in the decline of the Indus cities are as diverse as those which stimulated their growth. In the core regions of the Indus and Ghaggar-Hakra valley, the wide extension of trade networks and political alliances were highly vulnerable to relatively minor changes in the environment and agricultural base. Due to sedimentation and tectonic movement, some of the water that would normally flow into the ancient Saraswati river system was captured by two adjacent rivers; the Sutlej river of the Indus system to the west and the Yamuna river of the Gangetic system to the east. With the increase in water flow, the Indus itself began to swing east, flooding many settlements and burying them with silt. The mounds of Mohenjodaro survived because they are on slightly higher land and were protected by massive mud-brick walls and platforms, but many smaller sites were destroyed. Extensive and repeated flooding, combined with shifting rivers, had a devastating effect on the agricultural foundation and economic structure of the Indus cities. Although sites such as Harappa continued to be inhabited, the economic infrastructure for long-distance trade to the south was irreparably damaged as many less fortunate settlements along the dry bed of the ancient Saraswati river were abandoned. The refugees were forced either to develop new subsistence strategies or to move to more stable agricultural regions.

The cultivation of summer crops, such as rice, millet and sorghum made it possible to expand into the monsoon dominated regions of the Ganga-Yamuna Doab and Gujarat that were previously under-developed. During this period of change, animals that had been in use in the western highlands were adapted for transport and communications on the plains. Horse and donkey, as well as the Bactrian camel were gradually integrated into the economic sphere, as well as in the symbolic and decorative arts. Terracotta animal figurines and painted pottery styles reflecting these new developments were incorporated into the previously existent

Above *The* stupa, *or burial mound, now dominating Mohenjodaro's ancient walls was actually built two thousand years later than the city by Buddhists. The city, which was excavated in the twenties, is under threat from flooding*

Above left *Mohenjodaro, where this great bath was excavated, was one of the earliest cities in the world, boasting a covered drainage system. The bath may have been used for ritual bathing*

This athletic-looking female figure was probably a totem

The clay figurine above may have been a household god

The Mother Goddess cult of the Indus was common to Mesopotamia and to the river civilisation of the Nile

A similar Mother Goddess figure found at Harappa

This terracotta dog, found at Harappa, could be a toy

What do they tell? The pictographic scripts on these steatite seals found at Mohenjodaro have not yet been deciphered

technologies, many of which continued to be practised.

Excavations at sites such as Mehrgarh, Nausharo and Pirak provide a complete sequence of the gradual transformation that was going on in the Kachi Plain, and excavations in Swat Valley to the north provide a complementary perspective. Additional information on the nature of cultural developments outside the Indus valley come from recent work in Central Asia at sites belonging to the Bactria-Margiana Archaeological Complex. To the east, in the Ganga-Yamuna Doab and Gujarat numerous surveys and excavations have radically altered models for the decline of the Indus cities and the emergence of new cities of the Indo-Gangetic Civilisation.

Prior to these relatively recent discoveries, the introduction of new pottery styles, plants and animals, as well as "foreign" artefacts were thought to represent the intrusion of new peoples. The discovery of unburied skeletons among the latest levels of the Harappan occupation at Mohenjodaro combined with uncritical and inaccurate readings of the Vedic texts led some scholars to claim that the decline of the Indus civilisation was the result of "invasions" or "migrations" of Indo-Aryan speaking Vedic/Aryan tribes. The invasion and/or migration models assumed that the Indo-Aryan speaking Vedic communities destroyed the Indus cities and replaced the complex urban civilisation with their new rituals, language and culture.

Many scholars have tried to correct this theory, by arguing that it was based on misinterpretations of basic facts, the use of inappropriate models and an uncritical reading of Vedic texts. However, until recently, these scientific and well reasoned arguments were unsuccessful in rooting out the misinterpretations that had become entrenched in the popular literature.

Current theories on the role of Indo-Aryan speaking peoples are beyond the scope of this book, but it is important to emphasise that there is no archaeological or biological evidence for invasions or mass migrations into the Indus Valley between the end of the Harappan Phase, circa 1900 BC and the beginning of the Early Historic period around 600 BC In Central Asia and Afghanistan the Bactria-Margiana Archaeological Complex dates from around 1900 to 1700 BC and represents a complex mixture of nomadic and settled communities, some of whom may have spoke Indo-Aryan dialects and practised Indo-Aryan religion. These communities and ritual objects that they produced were distributed from the desert oases in Turkmenistan to southern Balochistan, and from the edges of the Indus valley to Iran. As nomadic herders and traders moved from the highlands to the lowlands in their annual migrations, goods would have been traded, and marriages as well as other less formal associations would have resulted in the exchange and flow of genes between the highland and lowland communities.

Recent biological studies of human skeletal remains from the northern subcontinent and Central Asia have shown that there is no evidence for new populations in the northern subcontinent during this time period, and at the same time, these regions were not isolated from one another. A limited degree of interaction is clearly demonstrated in the presence of overlapping genetic traits that would normally occur between adjacent populations. This pattern is not surprising given the fact that the highlands of Afghanistan and Central Asia had intermittent contact with the Indus valley for thousands of years prior to and during the Harappan Phase, and there is no major change in this relationship during the decline of the Indus cities.

In the absence of any direct external forces, the decline of the Indus cities can be attributed to a range of internal factors that over time undermined the economic and political power of ruling elites in the Indus cities. Over-extended networks of trade and political control were easily disrupted by changes in river patterns, flooding and crop failure. Refugees and over-crowded cities would have resulted in a legitimacy crisis for the ritual leaders and political rulers that ended with the emergence of new elites and localised polities around 1900 B.C. The previously integrated regions of the Indus valley and Gujarat broke up into three major localised cultures that can be defined by new painted motifs and ceramic styles, seals with geometric designs and new burial customs. For 600 years, until around 1300 B C the Localisation Era (commonly referred to as the Late Harappan Period) was an interlude during which a new social order was being established as new technologies and agricultural practices spread up and down the Indus valley, west into the Ganga-Yamuna valley and into the peninsular subcontinent.

J. M. K.

Discoveries at Mehrgarh

Excavations at Mehrgarh have found that the cultural sequence provides a fairly clear picture of the process of settling down and the establishment of domestic plants and animals as the major source of subsistence.

The transition to food production can be seen as an indigenous event that was probably occurring simultaneously in the highland regions and all along the piedmont zone of Balochistan. These early food-producing communities appear to have had extensive trade networks extending from the highlands to the west, out into the Indus Plains to the east and south to the Makran coast.

The earliest levels at Mehrgarh date from 6500 to 6000 BC, and because no pottery or copper tools have been found in these levels, they are referred to as the Non-ceramic or Aceramic Neolithic period. An irregular scatter of mud brick houses interspersed by refuse dumps and passageways made up the first village. Later buildings became more rectangular with numerous internal subdivisions or storage chambers at the foundation level, which may have been used for storage. The upper portions of these houses may have been made of mud bricks along with wood, branches and grass.

Although there is no evidence for pottery in the earliest levels, the earliest inhabitants were however familiar with the plastic properties of clay and they made small clay figurines and small unfired clay containers. Their subsistence was focused primarily on hunting-gathering, supplemented by some agriculture and animal husbandry. The domestic cereals found in these levels include wheat and barley that could have been cultivated either locally or brought from the highlands. Eventually as the settlement became more established they were cultivated on the Bolan River flood plain, probably after the last flooding of the Summer monsoon, or during the winter rains and harvested in the Spring. Impressions of date seeds have also been reported and this crop is still important throughout southern Pakistan and along the Makran coast and Oman.

By 5000 BC the percentage of wild animals decreases and there is an increase in the use of sheep, goat and cattle, with the humped variety of cattle, *Bos indicus*, being the most important.

The population represented at Mehrgarh during this period has been well represented through numerous burials that have been found beneath and between the mud brick structures. By carefully studying the shape of the teeth in these early burials scholars have concluded that they do not reflect peoples who have moved into the region from the west because they do not have strong genetic relationships to populations in West Asia. On the contrary, their dental morphology associates them with a distinctively Asian gene pool. This early pattern is more significant because there is a distinct change in dental shapes during the later Chalcolithic period which shows more genetic proximity to West Asian populations. This change could be explained by the increase in trade, communication and corresponding gene flow between the Indus region and West Asian cultures during the 5th to 4th millennia BC

In Mehrgarh, the dead were buried with considerable quantities of funerary offerings comprised of animal sacrifices and utilitarian objects such as tools, baskets, grinding stones and many varieties of ornaments. In several of the earliest burials dating to 6500 B.C. three or four young sheep-goat were slaughtered and buried with the dead. The ornaments in the Neolithic burials included beads and pendants made from exotic raw materials: azure blue lapis lazuli, blue-green turquoise, white and black steatite, red-orange carnelian, banded agate and white marine shell as well as various locally available yellow-brown limestone. A single copper bead is also found in one of the burials. The colours of these ornaments and the materials from which they were manufactured became the foundation for later ornaments used in the Indus cities.

Wide shell bangles made from the large conch shell, *Turbinella pyrum,* were also found in these burials. The nearest source for this species of shell is along the Makran coast near modern Karachi, some 500 km to the south. Pendants made out of mother-of-pearl (*Pinctada*) may have come from even more distant sources across the Arabian Gulf in Oman.

The exotic raw materials such as shell, lapis lazuli, turquoise and steatite can be traced to the coast or to the highland regions to the

Terracotta Mother Goddess, 3250 BC, Mehrgarh

west indicating the presence of long distance trade networks. It is interesting to note that although there was local production of limestone and soft steatite beads during this period, the other exotic ornaments, particularly the marine shell, do not appear to have been manufactured at the site. This trade in finished objects suggests that somewhere along the coast and somewhere in the highland regions, contemporaneous communities were manufacturing special status items for trade and exchange. These specialised crafts were to become of major importance during the following Indus Civilisation.

In summary the aceramic Neolithic occupation at Mehrgarh during the Early Food Producing Era shows how the basic subsistence economy of the Indus Valley became established and how the fundamentals of trade and craft specialisation were begun.

The site of Mehrgarh was excavated by the French Archaeological Mission to Pakistan under the direction of Jean-François Jarrige from 1974 to 1986.

Recent discoveries at Harappa

This terracotta tablet shows a buffalo sacrifice conducted in view of a seated figure, perhaps a deity or spiritual teacher. The unique yogic posture indicates the antiquity of human discipline involving mind-over-body.

Until the recent excavations at Harappa, urban aspects of the Indus Valley Civilisation were known primarily from discoveries made in the 1920s and 1930s at the sites of Mohenjodaro and, to a lesser extent, at Harappa. Today, careful stratigraphic and spatial recording and quantitative studies are revealing new information about development, structure, and change at Harappa and ancient Indus society.

The earliest levels of the site, prior to 3000 BC, reveal a village culture characterised by stone and bone tools, as well as copper tools. They made hand built pottery without the use of the potters wheel, that included both heavy coarse ware cooking vessels and delicate pots with polychrome decorations. These early settlers developed extensive trade contacts with surrounding resource areas to obtain copper, exotic lapis lazuli and carnelian. Their technological developments include glazed steatite (soapstone) beads, wheat and barley agriculture and animal husbandry that was dominated by the use of the Zebu or humped bull, sheep and goat.

By 2800 BC, during the Early Harappan or Kot Dijian period, the site had expanded to a large town when the basic structure of Indus cities emerged. Streets and houses were oriented along the cardinal directions, wheel-made pottery became common and the initial stages of writing in the form of graffiti on pottery became widespread. The first glazed steatite seals were produced, anticipating the later development of the distinctive Indus seals.

The full urban phase of the city is associated with the Harappan Period occupations, from 2600 to 1900 BC. By this time the settlement had developed into a complex city organized into distinct walled sectors with craft areas, bazaars, and domestic structures as well as some impressive, monumental public buildings. During this period, the city had extensive trade contacts spanning the greater Indus valley, western India, Afghanistan and Central Asia. Important new discoveries relate to massive gateways and city walls used to control access into and out of the cities and the control of craft production as an important factor in state economy. A large number of seals and inscribed objects have been discovered that will provide a new window on the use of writing and eventually may help in the deciphering of this enigmatic script.

From approximately 1900 BC to around 1730 BC. the city continued to be a major centre for regional trade and technological developments. The earliest glass beads were made, along with exquisite glazed faience ornaments, to imitate turquoise and lapis lazuli. During this period, the disappearance of the Indus script and standardised weights, along with changes in burial customs have traditionally been associated with the rise of a new culture associated with the introduction of Vedic Aryan religion and culture. It is clear however that the changes were not the result of invasion, but reflect a gradual transformation through changing social organisation and religion.

Recent excavations at Harappa undertaken by the Harappa Archaeological Research Project have been conducted in collaboration with both the Department of Archaeology and the Museums, Government of Pakistan. The excavations and related studies are directed by Drs. R. H. Meadow (Harvard University), J. Mark Kenoyer (University of Wisconsin-Madison), and Rita P. Wright (New York University).

J. M. K.

This red sandstone torso, 3ft. 9ins. high, is a realistic portrayal of the middle-aged physique

Most figurines from Harappa are female, suggesting a prevailing "Mother Goddess" cult

The Kushan Era

The history of those territories which now constitute Pakistan begins with the acquisition of the name, Sapta-Sindhu, "The Land of the Seven Rivers", of the *Rig-Veda* (c. 1500 BC), the religious hymns of the Aryans. After the decline and fall of the Indus Civilisation, the Aryan tribes emerged, their nomadic hordes gradually becoming civilised. On the plateaux and terraced fields of the hill region, they preserved their heroic tribal pattern, but in the fertile river valleys the tribes fused into one rural way of life. The Aryan language, now remembered as Sanskrit, dominated. Life was organised on a local system with a long history. The Aryan conqueror was distinguished from the conquered, who was given the servile name of *dasa* or bond slave, and their relationship led to a discriminatory social system of caste distinction. The conquerors were *arya* or nobles, and they constituted the privileged castes. They claimed the riches of the land fed by the great river, known to them as Sindhu, now surviving in the name of Indus. This name later signified the whole Indus territory, now comprising Pakistan. The Persians, in their old inscriptions, modified it to *Hind*, and in the classical account of the West it was softened to *Ind*. This name appears in an account of Alexander's campaigns.

At the beginning of the first millennium BC, bronze technology was gradually superceded by that of iron. This change helped in the concentration of military power in the hands of the few, called *rajan* or royalty, who, with the help of their collaborators, the *kahattriyas* or warrior caste, made a bid for territory. We read of the great kingdom of Gandhara with its twin capitals, Pushkalavati (modern Charsadda in the North-West Frontier Province) and Takshasila (Taxila, about twenty miles from Islamabad) and another kingdom, Sindhu-Sauvira (Sauvira meaning "the Land of the Heroes" and now surviving in Siraiki, a dialect of southern Punjab). In central Punjab, the Madra tribe, increasing in authority, founded the city of Madrapura, spelt Manda-hakur by Al-Biruni. This city was situated on the river Ravi, the ancient Iravati and its new name, Lahore, became popular in the mediaeval period. The Aryan tribes fought a great war, Mahabharat, (Bharat being one of the tribes) in Kurukshetra in eastern Punjab – the gateway to the Ganges valley – and inaugurated an age of great kingdoms. The Gandhara ruler, Pukkusati, advanced eastwards in the sixth century BC.

Internationally, still greater changes were taking place. The Persian empire had forged ahead into Iran and with the improved technology of iron, Cyrus and his successor Darius built up a mighty empire, incorporating the kingdoms of the Indus Valley and redividing them into four *satrapi* – Gandhara, Makae (Makran, i.e. Balochistan), Sattagudai (the Gomal Valley) and Hidus (i.e. the plains of Punjab and Sindh). Under Darius, Scylax of Caryanda sailed down the Indus and explored the secrets of the valley. From one province of Hidus alone, the Persian realized an annual tribute of 360 talents of gold dust (equivalent to £1,290,000 in currency before World War II). Tribute bearers from this province, leading bullocks and carrying on their shoulders poles slung with loads, are depicted on the palace walls at Persepolis.

This extension of the Persian empire's eastern dominions brought the Indus valley within the orbit of the ancient civilisations of the Orient. The imperial road ran from Persepolis to Taxila and this provincial capital reaped the fruits of Oriental learning. Princes, scholars and commoners came to the University of Taxila for higher education. A new system of alphabetic writing, called Kharoshthi, written from right to left, was evolved at this time. The syntax of Sanskrit was

This moulded terracotta tablet from Harappa portrays the struggle between human and animal power. A powerful human figure, possibly depicting a woman, grapples with two tigers, while in the foreground is an elephant. Above the figure is a script symbol that depicts a spoked wheel. The spoked wheel was used in later Buddhist art to represent the "wheel of the law"

perfected by that greatest of grammarians, Panini, who may have taught at Taxila. The local currency was linked with the new system of Persian coinage of Daric weight related to *karsha*: hence the coin named *karshapana*. Above all, the Persian administrative system secured peace and prosperity. It also made a deep impression on the minds of political thinkers such as Kautilya (also known as Chanakya), who educated Chandragupta, the future Mauryan Emperor, in his seminary at Taxila. Kautilya's book, Arthasastra, reveals the considerable influence of the Achaemenian system on him.

In the great army that Xerxes led against Greece, there was a contingent of soldiers from the territory that was to become Pakistan. Herodotus relates: "Hidus wore cotton dresses, and carried bows of cane, and arrows of cane with iron tips. Such was the equipment of the Hidus, and they marched under the command of Kharnazathres, the son of Artabates... the Paktuans wore cloaks of skin, and carried the bow of their country and the dagger. Their commander was Artyntes, the son of Ithamatres. The Utians, the Mukai (Makae, i.e. Makranis) and the Paricanians were equipped like the Paktuans. They had for leaders Arsamenes, the son of Darius, who commanded the Utians and the Mukai. They were equipped as footmen, but some were on horseback and some in chariots – the chariots drawn either by horses, or by wild asses."

Even in the battle at Arbela, Darius III was able to summon troops from his eastern territories to resist the Greek invasion of Alexander. Arian testifies that: "The Hidus were allied to the Bactrians who in turn were allied to the Sogdians who had come to the aid of Darius, all being under the command of Bessus, the viceroy of the land of Bactria... There were a few elephants, about fifteen in number, belonging to the Hidus who live this side of the Indus." The alliance of the Indus peoples prompted Alexander to advance further east and crush them in their own homes.

Actually the defeat of Darius in 331 BC created a political vacuum in the Indus region and led to conflicts among the local chiefs. Among them, Astes was supreme in the land of Pushkalavati, and Porus dominated the Jhelum and the Chenab and more. His power aroused the jealousy of Ambhi, ruler of Taxila, who allied himself with Sanjaya, the brother and opponent of Astes. They sought Alexander's help to achieve their ends. Alexander advanced further to subjugate the remainder of the Persian empire and to satisfy his pride, his advance nevertheless being resisted by every tribe that he met on the way.

In 327 BC, Alexander regrouped his forces under the shadow of the Hindu Kush in his newly-founded city of Alexandria and chose the northern route to enter the subcontinent. He divided his army into two parts, the first being led by himself through the territories which are now Nawagai, Bajaur, Dir and Swat, the second by two of his officers directly to Pushkalavati, which was captured after a siege of thirty days. Alexander himself fought many battles, but the biggest was at Massaga, not far from Chakdara in Dir, against Assakenians who resisted with 20,000 cavalry, more than 30,000 infantry and thirty elephants. Alexander himself was wounded, but he captured the city. Later he occupied Ora (Udigram) in Bazira (Rarikot) in Swat and marched over the hills to the Indus which he crossed near Hund. At Taxila, Ambhi welcomed the invader. The fiercest battle was fought against Porus, on the banks of the Jhelum. The bravery of Porus so impressed Alexander, that he appointed him governor of the area from the Jhelum to the last point of his advance on the Beas.

From here Alexander started his journey home but was unable to return along the same route. Instead, he sailed down the Indus encountering other fierce tribes. The most severe resistance was put up by a confederacy of Oxydrakai and Mallois (Malavas) who lived at Multan. Alexander was again wounded and when the rumour of his death spread, 3,000 Greek colonists, settled by him in Punjab, left for home. After recovering, Alexander advanced to the mouth of the Indus, sent part of his army home by sea and himself returned through the desert of Balochistan, hearing on the way of the murder of Philip, the satrap of the territory west of the Indus. Leading a sick and starving army, the exhausted Alexander at last reached Babylon to die in 323 BC.

Justin wrote of the end of this great campaign that the people of the Indus territory, "after the death of Alexander, had shaken as it were the yoke of servitude from their necks and put his governors to death. The author of this liberation was Sandracottus (Chandragupta). This man was of humble origin but was stimulated to aspire to regal power by super-

natural encouragement; for, having offended Alexander by his boldness of speech and orders being given to kill him, he saved himself by swiftness of foot and, while he was lying asleep after his fatigue, a lion of great size having come up to him, licked off with his tongue the sweat that was running from him, and after gently waking him, left him. Being first prompted by this prodigy to conceive hopes of royal dignity, he drew together a band of robbers and instigated the Hidus to overthrow Greek authority... Sandracottus, having thus acquired a throne was in possession of India when Seleukos was laying the foundations of his future greatness."

Taught at the University of Taxila by Kautilya, Chandragupta laid the foundation of the Mauryan empire in the Indus Valley. Later, by recruiting local forces, he defeated the Nandas, occupied the Cranges valley and pushed into the south down to Mysore in southern India, forming the first subcontinental empire. In 306-305 BC, when he successfully resisted the invasion of Seleukos, his empire extended westward up to Herat and the Hindu Kush.

He married into the family of Seleukos and received Megasthenes as the Greek ambassador at his new capital Pataliputra (modern Patna). His grandson Asoka, who as a prince came twice to Taxila, rounded off the conquests by annexing Kalinga on the eastern coast of the subcontinent. These conquests entailed much human suffering which eventually caused Asoka to become remorseful and repentant. He began to preach *dharma* (morality) and sought salvation in Buddhism.

Following the example of Darius, Asoka recorded his laws in monumental inscriptions on rock throughout his empire and had engraved on pillars his sermons of peace. At Shahbaz Garhi near Mardan and at Mansehra near Abbottabad the inscriptions proclaim the moral lessons in Kharoshthi. His practical efforts for humanity were on a similar scale. "everywhere has Priyadardin (Asoka), beloved of

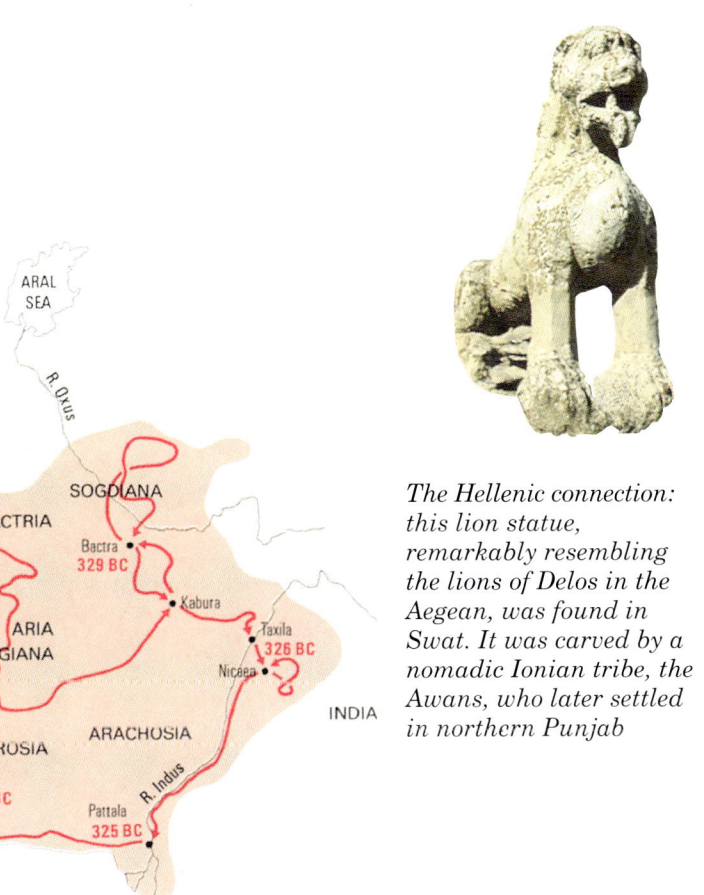

The Hellenic connection: this lion statue, remarkably resembling the lions of Delos in the Aegean, was found in Swat. It was carved by a nomadic Ionian tribe, the Awans, who later settled in northern Punjab

the gods, established medical treatment of two kinds: medical treatment for men and medical treatment for animals. Wherever medical herbs, wholesome for men and wholesome for animals, are not found, they have everywhere been caused to be imported and planted. Roots and fruits wherever they are not found, have been caused to be imported and planted. On the roads wells have been caused to be dug and trees caused to be planted for the enjoyment of man and beast."

The enduring achievement of Asoka was the spread of Buddhism and his name is associated with many Buddhist monasteries in Pakistan. But while his message of the faith lingered on, his empire could not survive his death in 231 BC. Political changes in Central Asia influenced the course of history. The Greeks who had been settled by Alexander in Bactria made a bid for independence, carving out a Central Asian Greek kingdom which incorporated the Indus Valley. The expedition itself was led by Demetrius, while Menander integrated the conquered territories into a well-knit dominion. Antialkidas held his court at Taxila. These Greeks inaugurated a new system of coinage, introduced Hellenistic city planning, popularised the Greek language and created a taste for Western classical art. Menander took a personal interest in Buddhism, which under the new rulers, made considerable headway.

In the first century BC, the Greeks were invaded by Scythians who penetrated right down to the mouth of the Indus. The Indus delta was for long after their conquest known as Scythia. They pushed as far as Gujarat and ruled there for four centuries. Their kings bore the title of *svami*, which survives in the Sindhi word *sain*. In the meantime, the Parthians advanced into the northern region. Their famous king Gondophares held his court in Taxila in the first century AD, when tradition speaks of the visit of the Christian missionary, St. Thomas. All these changes culminated in the fruition of the Central Asian empire built by the Kushans who finally established their capital in Purushapura (modern Peshawar) In the late first century AD.

The Kushan empire extended from the Caspian to the Bay of Bengal and from Urals to the Arabian Sea. Originally from the Chinese border, the Kushans imbibed the spirit of the old Persian empire and revived the glory of a mighty power. Their empire on the Indus lasted for generations and their imperial title Shao-nano-Shao survived in the "Shahanshah" of more recent times. The rule of the Shahis became proverbial and their fame is recorded in early Muslim chronicles. Their second emperor Kujul Kadphises started the Kushan gold mint and established peace and order to enable the flow of regular trade along the historic Silk Route to China. The third ruler, Kanishka, was famous as a conqueror, patron of the arts, lover of religion and benefactor of learning. He is said to have convened the fourth Buddhist council probably at Peshawar, and built there the famous Kanishka-Vihava which became a Buddhist pilgrimage centre for at least seven centuries. Buddhist monasteries were built all over the Indus region, their monks carrying the message of the Buddha into Central Asia and China. Under the Kushans, Gandhara became the second home of Buddhism.

The prosperity resulting from the Kushans' encouragement of international trade and commerce led to unprecedented urbanisation. Trade routes were opened up from the Roman world to the Chinese empire. The Bagram treasure which was unearthed in Afghanistan gives a glimpse of the luxury of the royal courts. This affluence also helped in the creation and support of the world famous Gandhara art.

Themselves far from sophisticated, the Kushans inherited the artistic tradition of the Asian Greeks and with their international contacts it reached great heights. It was on the coinage of Kanishka that the figure of Buddha is known to be represented for the first time. Since this inception, Gandhara art has been full of Buddhist legends and the life of the Buddha and Bodhisattvas. At the same time, the art still expresses a complete cross-section of the life of the time. The period of the Kushans is the Golden Age in the history of the subcontinent when the Indus empire was at its most civilized peak.

The peaceful reign of the Kushans, however, could not survive the new political challenges posed by political developments in Central Asia. First the great power of the Iranian Sassanians eroded its prosperity, and later the invasion of the Huns destroyed the empire. A new system of political hegemony took root in the sixth century AD, when petty chiefs developed a type of feudal economic order. This culminated in the dismemberment of the country and the rise of new monarchies mostly under Brahmin domination. Buddhism lost ground to Hinduism. It was then that the Brahmin Chach dynasty came to power in Sindh and Hindu rulers held sway in the northern region.

A.H.D.

Gandhara Culture

We know from inscriptions that the Emperor Asoka of the Maurya dynasty (273-236 BC) who ruled over most of the subcontinent, strongly supported Buddhism, which had already spread far and wide during preceding centuries. It now became the dominant element in the cultural life of the area of present-day Pakistan, both in the north and in the south. In fact, pilgrims from abroad considered Gandhara – the ancient name of the North-West Frontier Province – to be the second home of Buddhism after Bihar, where the Buddha was born and spent most of his life.

Hardly any art objects dating from before the beginning of the Christian era have come down to us. True, we have a large number of small terracotta figures, most of them representing the age-old autochthonic Mother Goddess or Goddess of the Earth, who remained popular at village level in spite of the introduction of Buddhism. However, these figurines are generally very difficult to date, and are usually so crude that they should rather be classified as folk art. A few small images in stone depicting this Mother Goddess have survived and are truly works of art. They were probably made for patrons wealthier than the average villager, who could afford only the cheaper, fired-clay figurines.

A Buddhist monk looks serenely inwards in the ancient monastery of Jaulian in Taxila. Buddhist imagery inspired thousands of statues in the Gandhara period from 600 BC to 1000 AD

After the introduction of Buddhism, monasteries sprang up all over the country. In the north-west, where stone was easily available as building material, many remains of monastic establishments have been discovered. Those at Taxila were so famous that the city became a great centre of learning. In the plains of Punjab and Sindh – areas without stone quarries – fired or sun-dried bricks were the standard material. Since this medium is not very durable, practically all the monasteries in the greater part of Pakistan have disappeared, and can only be rediscovered by excavation.

The principal object of worship in these religious centres was a *stupa* or burial mound containing a relic – if possible of the Buddha himself or of one of his disciples, but usually of some less important person. A few of the largest *stupa* have a core which goes back to Mauryan times. The Dharmarajika stupa at Taxila was almost certainly built by Asoka and contained a relic of the Buddha. It was a pious custom to enlarge these relic mounds continually, so the core is sometimes old, although their outer appearance suggests a date many centuries later. Apart from such brick *stupa*, many smaller ones have been discovered, sometimes in the remains of a chapel. The relic caskets enshrined in these monuments often have the shape of a miniature *stupa* in stone or metal, but many are simple round pots of stone, carefully turned on a lathe. Occasionally they were more elaborate – like, for example, the famous casket of Kanishka, excavated from the remains of the great *stupa* near Peshawar, which was erected by a well-known Scythian ruler of that name in the late first century AD.

From Achaemenian times onward there have been contacts between the subcontinent and countries further west, but in the last few centuries BC these relations increased tremendously, because of the Bactrian kingdom founded in Afghanistan by the successors of Alexander the Great, who later extended their influence into northern Pakistan. The Parthian and Scythian rulers who succeeded the Bactrian kings on this side of the border inherited their love and admiration for Hellenistic culture, as can be seen from the many excavated objects which were originally imported from the Eastern Mediterranean, and in the course of time were imitated by local artists.

As Buddhism was the backbone of life in the north-west, the art of Gandhara was basically indigenous in character, though its style soon became strongly influenced by Hellenism. However, in its initial stage, the indigenous elements were still very clear, as they are, for instance, in an early relief depicting the Buddha's descent from heaven, in which – true to tradition – the Master was not represented in human form but was merely indicated by the symbol of his footprints and other circumstantial evidence. In the first century AD this convention of using substitutive symbols was abolished and, in later reliefs showing the same event, the Buddha appears in human form, between Brahma and Indra, on the triple ladder leading down from heaven.

Although it is often claimed that Gandhara invented the Buddha image, this is not quite true. A number of very early sculptures prove that Gandharan artists began by representing the Master in almost exactly the same way as their contemporaries belonging to the school of Mathura in the Gangetic plains. However, Hellenistic influences soon made themselves felt more strongly in both architecture and

The earliest Buddhas were represented symbolically – it was the Gandharans, strongly influenced by the Greeks, who developed this beautiful figurative style

The Gandharans' admiration for Hellenistic culture is evident in their statuary, such as this of Aphrodite, the Greek Goddess of Love

sculpture, as a result of which the originally indigenous conception of the Buddha image received a stylistically new form.

In architecture the typical indigenous curved gable was soon joined by the classical triangular pediment, and though the indigenous round pilaster, crowned by a bell-shaped capital, remained in use, the flat Hellenic pilaster with a Corinthian capital became far more popular. Western motifs such as atlantes, tritons and putti carrying garlands became common decorative elements, used over and over again, while the Hellenistic influence in architectural panels became more pronounced.

In sculpture, the Western ways of representing facial expressions and the characteristic treatment of drapery were especially admired and imitated. In the early nineteenth century, these Hellenistic elements in the art of Gandhara attracted the attention of Western scholars. Indeed, until the beginning of the present century, the school of Gandhara received greater acclaim from art historians than any other style in the subcontinent.

From the early second century AD onwards, the northwestern workshops turned out sculptures by the hundreds – good, bad and indifferent. The best examples are truly beautiful. Some of the Buddhas convey an unsurpassed serene spirituality. Among the finest images are the representatives of the so-called Bodhisattvas, saviours of mankind who have renounced *nirvana* in order to be able to reincarnate and help their fellow men on the difficult path to salvation. Although many images represent Maitreya, the future Buddha, the most popular Bodhisattva was undoubtedly Avalokitesvara, Lord of Mercy, who is usually depicted with a lotus in his left hand.

The normal medium was schist, which is difficult to work as it has a tendency to split. Many sculptures, especially those decorating walls, were, however, executed in stucco which is easier to model. Occasionally laymen had themselves represented as worshippers, and thus we can recognise the pious Scythians, in pointed caps and trousers or long-sleeved dress, who commissioned most of this work.

Whereas the many images of Buddhas and of Bodhisattvas were meant for worship, the purpose of the countless narrative reliefs was edification and decoration of religious monuments. Often the scenes represent an event in one of the Buddha's previous incarnations. These so-called *jataka* stories were immensely popular in the earlier schools of art, because in these reliefs the troublesome convention of substituting symbols could be avoided. However, the artists of Gandhara, who were no longer hampered by this restriction, preferred to represent events from the Buddha's last life; so the overwhelming majority of the reliefs show incidents in the life of Prince Siddhartha and his later career as Gautama, the Buddha.

Of course, the various occasions on which Brahma and Indra, two of the most important gods of Hinduism, were

Above *Buddha blesses his disciples in this relief at Taxila. Buddhism flourished in the north-west until the middle of the fifth century AD when the white Huns invaded, destroying the monasteries and obliterating the cultural life of the area*
Opposite *The Fasting Siddartha is now in Lahore Museum and is a superb example of fourth century Gandhara work*

said to have paid homage to the Master are often depicted. Lesser deities, belonging to the realm of folk religion, were eventually incorporated into Buddhism owing to their popularity among the villagers. Thus the *yahsi*, or tree spirits, and Hariti, originally a goddess of smallpox but later a protectress of children, found their way into the Buddhist art of Gandhara. Towards the middle of the fifth century, the flourishing Buddhist culture of the north-west was destroyed by the invasion of the Hephthalites or White Huns, as a result of which the monasteries were burnt and cultural life came to a complete standstill.

The architecture and sculpture of the hilly north-west until this period of disaster are fairly well documented, but we know far less about the plains of Punjab and Sindh. There is no doubt, however, that here, too, Buddhism was the prevailing religion, for the remains of several *stupa*, occasionally decorated with beautiful stucco sculptures and dating from the late sixth or seventh century, have been discovered in both Upper and Lower Sindh.

From the early fourth until the late sixth century, the north of the subcontinent was ruled by the powerful Gupta dynasty who for a long time withstood the assaults of the White Huns, though they finally capitulated the north-west. During the Gupta period, Hinduism gained in importance, which also had an effect on Punjab and Sindh. In 1890 Sir Aurel Stein discovered the remains of a Gupta temple at Murti in the Salt Range. In Sindh, the Hindu sculptures excavated in the lower layers of Bhambore, the ancient city of Daibul, and the marvellous brass image of Brahma found near Mirpur Khas and now a prized possession of the National Museum in Karachi, confirm the emergence of Hinduism. The artistic products of this period display the refined and elegant simplicity which is typical of the Gupta and post-Gupta style.

After the conquest of Sindh by Islam, both Buddhism and Hinduism continued to flourish, thanks to the liberal attitude of the Arab governors. This peaceful co-existence with Islam lasted well into the tenth century. Some of the Buddhist votive tablets excavated in Sindh date from the eleventh century. When the White Huns overran the north-west, Buddhism took refuge in the mountainous regions. Its continued existence in the secluded valley of Swat can be seen from archaeological remains, especially bronzes discovered there. After the sixth century, when cultural life slowly recovered from the devastations of the White Huns, Hinduism became the most important religion in Punjab. A number of fine sculptures in white marble, or chocolate-brown potstone, as well as the remains of several temples in the Kunar valley and at Kafir Kot, date from the early mediaeval period (seventh to late tenth century) and show the dominance of Hinduism. Gradually the influence of Islam increased in both north and south. After the tenth century the artists – who had served Buddhism and then Hinduism so well – placed their abilities at the disposal of Islam in the subcontinent.

J.E.L.L.

The Muslim Advent

Exactly who were the first Muslims to set foot in the subcontinent is obscure, but it seems probable that Muslim traders from the coastlands of Arabia and the Persian Gulf touched at ports along the western coast of the peninsula and in Ceylon very soon after the rise of the new faith in the early seventh century AD.

The first genuinely historical data tells of Arab troops, fired by the great excess of Islamic religious enthusiasm which had just overthrown the Sassanid empire in Persia, raiding into what is now Balochistan. The coastal region of this province was, even in early Islamic times, known as Makran, and its aridity and sparse population then as now made it a formidable barrier to Muslim penetration overland to the Indus valley: communications here have always been much easier by sea. Exploratory raids into Makran from Fars and Kirman are mentioned from the Caliphate of Uthman onwards (644-656), but no lasting political authority was established over the very few settlements of the interior. We know virtually nothing of the ethnography or religious position of the indigenous population there although it is very likely that the present-day Baloch people did not arrive until the tenth or eleventh centuries.

Some of these forays reached the Indus valley, but the first permanent foothold of Islam was achieved during the opening years of the eighth century, during the Caliphate of al-Walid bin Abd al-Malik (705-715), a reign which saw other Muslim victories in places as far apart as Spain and Central Asia. About the year 711, a youthful Arab general called Muhammad bin Qasim al-Thaqafi was deputed by the great governor of Iraq and the East, al-Hajjaj bin Yusuf, to lead an expedition from Shiraz in southern Persia against Sindh. The Islamic historian, al-Yaqubi, states that al-Hajjaj encouraged Muhammad bin Qasim and the general commanding the Arab troops in Central Asia to make simultaneous attacks as the two prongs of a grand pincer movement against the Chinese empire and the Far East. In the light of the spectacular successes already achieved by the Arabs, such dreams were by no means impossible. Muhammad bin Qasim's force comprised six thousand Syrian Arab tribesmen, and the operation was carefully planned. It moved through Makran, securing the towns there as it passed.

We are ill-informed about the state of Sindh on the eve of the Arab invasion. The ruler is named as King Dahir, son of Chach (Sassa in Arabic sources). According to the thirteenth century Persian chronicle, the *Chach Nama*, he ruled over a vast empire extending as far as Kashmir and modern Uttar Pradesh in the east. In reality, he seems to have had a much more modest kingdom, comprising lower and middle Sindh, as far north as the town of Rur (modern Rohri on the Indus opposite Sukkur), with his capital at Brahmanabad and his principal port at Daibul on the Indus delta (the position of which has still not been determined with any certainty, despite excavations by the Pakistan Department of Archaeology at Bhambore and other possible sites). The Islamic sources say that after Muhammad bin Qasim's conquest, a number of local Indian princes in Sindh became vassals of the Caliphate, so that Dahir's unitary state there may only have been a temporary achievement, and fragmentation the norm.

The dominant religion in Sindh at this time was probably Buddhism, since the Arabs gave the name *budd* to every idol and temple which they found there, and they used the title *samani* (in Prakrit *samana*, meaning Buddhist monk or ascetic) for the representatives of the local people with whom they negotiated; but Brahmanism or Hinduism, which was at this time gaining over Buddhism in the subcontinent, must also have been widespread.

Daibul fell to the Arab besiegers in 711, and its great Buddhist *stupa* (*dewal*) whence Daibul, or in Arabic *manarat-al-budd*, was overthrown. Magnanimous in the hour of victory, Muhammad bin Qasim offered quarter to the local people; he then proceeded to found the first mosque ever to be built on the soil of the subcontinent, and settled four thousand Arab families in a new section of the town. He then led his army against Niran (near modern Hyderabad), whose priests surrendered the town peacefully, and against Sadusan. The Arab ranks were swollen by the addition of four thousand Zutt or Jat auxiliaries; the Indus was crossed by a bridge of boats, and a final confrontation with Dahir and his host took place in 712 near Rawar. Dahir was killed and his army scattered, after which the Arabs occupied the capital Brahmanabad (near the site where the later Muslim city of al-Mansura was to rise). Having secured that vital point, the Arab forces pushed northwards and captured Rur. Finally, the army penetrated as far as Multan, the goal set by al-Hajjaj in his instructions to his subordinate and, after a lengthy siege, Multan and its famous golden shrine, *baital-dhahab*, to the sun-god *Aditya* with all its treasures, fell into Muslim hands. Multan was for three centuries to mark the northernmost point of the Muslim advance in Sindh: the story of the *Chach Nama* that Muhammad bin Qasim conquered as far as Kashmir can hardly be true.

Within the occupied towns, Muhammad bin Qasim established a social and religious framework of life which reflected the early Islamic policy of tolerance. The conqueror proclaimed the general principle of freedom of religion, allowing Buddhists and Hindus to be included among the "People of the Book" or "Protected Peoples", as Jews and Christians had always been and as the Zoroastrians of Persia had become. This tolerance was dictated, no doubt, partly by expediency. The Muslims in Sindh were a tiny minority in a sea of alien, potentially hostile non-Muslims. The process whereby Islam became the majority faith in Sindh extended over many centuries.

Muhammad bin Qasim fell from power, and was killed when the new Caliph Sulaiman came to the throne in 715, but his pioneer work of carving a foothold in the subcontinent for Islam had been well done. It is true that the impetus of spectacular military expansion was spent for some three centuries, and that Sindh became a peripheral province of the Caliphate, where the power of the central government in Damascus or Baghdad was felt only intermittently: but the Muslim community in Sindh put down strong roots; further

An open courtyard is all that remains of the subcontinent's first mosque which was constructed during the Arab conquest of Sindh by Mohammad Bin Qasim, in the eighth century AD

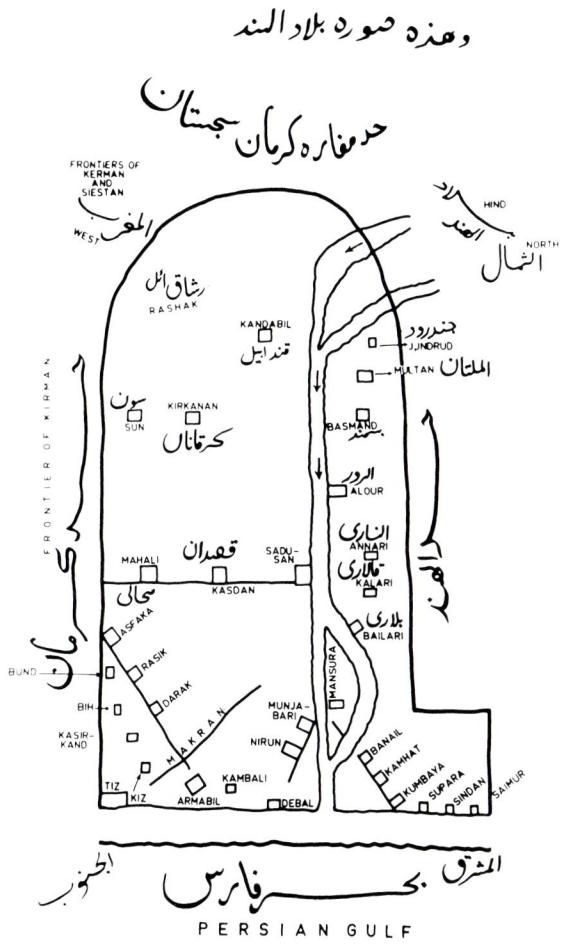

Map of the Indus Valley by Ibn Hauqal (943 - 976 AD)

contingents of Arab settlers probably arrived to reinforce the original colonists; and Islam dwelt there at peace with the indigenous faiths until the next great wave of expansion under the Ghaznavids in the eleventh century. The Italian scholar F. Gabrieli has justly said that "present-day Pakistan, holding the values of Islam and Arabism in such high esteem, should look upon the young and luckless Arab conqueror, Muhammad bin Qasim, almost as a distant *ktistes* (founding father), a "hero of Indian Islam".

Not a great deal is known about the subsequent history of the Arab presence in Sindh. Governors were sent out periodically by the caliphs, and after 750 by the new dynasty of Abbasids in Iran. Until the ninth century these governors continued to forward tribute to the Caliphate, for it is recorded that in 820, under al-Mamun, the revenue sent amounted to one million dirhams. Being so remote from the centre of power, Sindh became a favourite refuge for rebels and sectarians, who could flee there quite easily by sea from the Gulf. Control over the local Indian rulers was probably intermittent, with periods of renunciation of tribute or of lapsed adherence to Islam when the Arabs' political authority was weak. Thus we learn that the native princes of Sindh submitted to the Caliph Umar bin Abd al-Aziz in 718, having heard of his famed piety and justice, and the son of Dahir became a Muslim; under the Caliph Hisham, however, Dahir relapsed, and punitive expeditions by the Arab governors were necessary.

Rather more is known about Sindh in the tenth century, since it is described by various Muslim travellers and geographers of that period. Arab families continued to be politically dominant in the Muslim centres of power. Ibn Hauqal, whose account of the Islamic world is based on his journeys in the middle decades of the century, describes the general prosperity and the cheapness of food in Sindh. There had been cultural assimilation to the Indian ways of life, in that the dress and hair style of Muslims and infidels had become identical. They mostly wore a characteristic short tunic, though some classes, notably the merchants, had long flowing robes like the Iraqis and Persians. The languages of Sindh were the indigenous Sindhi tongue with some Arabic, and in Makran the local Makrani with some Persian.

Politically, there seem to have been governors in each principal town, virtually independent of each other, generally owing a moral and spiritual allegiance to the Abbasids in Baghdad (as evidenced by mention of the Caliph in the Friday khutba or sermon), but no longer sending revenue. The governor of the largest town, al-Mansura (named after the early Abbasid Caliph al-Mansur, 754-775), was in Ibn Hauqal's time a Qureshi, i.e. of Meccan origin, a descendant of Habbar bin Aswad, who had seized power in that town. The position in Multan was similar; at Jundur, just outside, was the military camp of the governor, a descendant of Sama bin Lu'ayy. Multan's position was an exposed one, with powerful Hindu kingdoms like that of the Hindu-Shahis or Waihand or Udabhanda on its northern flank and warlike Rajput princes to the east. Its governors nevertheless preserved it as a bastion of Islam, although deriving revenue and strength from its shrine to the sun god Aditya. They appropriated all offerings brought by Hindu pilgrims, handing on only a part of them to the idol's custodians; and when Hindu potentates menaced Multan, the governor threatened to destroy the idol, thus causing them to withdraw. The traditional Islamic sciences flourished at this time in the Muslim towns of Sindh. Zeal for the faith was sharpened by the proximity of hostile, infidel powers; Ibn Hauqal again notes how assiduously the Quran, the traditions and the Islamic law were cultivated. The later compilers of biographical dictionaries, such as al-Samani and Yaqut, note a

Excavations at Bhambore: the site lies forty miles east of Karachi at the mouth of an old channel of the River Indus. It was formerly an important inland port and may have been the town of Daibul, which fell to Muhammad bin Qasim in 712 AD

certain number of scholars with the gentilic of *al-Sindhi*.

In the course of the tenth century, some of the towns of Sindh, and particularly Multan, came to give their allegiance to Shahi rulers rather than to Baghdad. Al-Mansura at one point acknowledged the suzerainty of the great Buyid Amir in Persia, Adud al-Daula (949-983). More lasting were the links with the Fatimid Caliphs of Egypt and North Africa, the Abbasids' great rivals. The maritime connection of the Sindh ports with the Arabian and Red Sea shores had always been maintained, and Ismaili propaganda came to Sindh via the Yemen. Sindh was, in fact, the scene of one of their most successful missions in the eastern Islamic world. Sources from the end of the tenth century state that the ruler of Multan recognized as his suzerain the Fatimid in Egypt and sent presents: the descendants of Sama bin Lu'ayy had obviously changed their allegiance from the Abbasids. Ismailism struck deep roots in Multan. Although the ultra-orthodox Mahmud of Ghazni attacked the town in 1006, and in 1010 deposed the local ruler Abul Fateh Dawood, Ismailism nevertheless continued to be strong there and to retain its links with the Syrian and Egyptian centres of the sect. The present-day Ismaili or Maulani communities of the extreme north of Pakistan, in Chitral, Hunza and Gilgit, may conceivably have had connections with the Sindh groups, and there may also be a continuity with the Ismaili communities of Gujarat and Khandesh in modern India.

Sindh was thus firmly won for Islam, but there are also signs that a knowledge of Islam was at this time percolating from southern Afghanistan into what is now the North-West Frontier region of Pakistan. The rise of the Saffarid brothers Yaqub and Amr bin Laith in the later decades of the ninth century was important for the spread of Islam into eastern Afghanistan; the Zunbils or local rulers of Zamin-Dawar (the modern region of Kandahar) were humbled, and Kabul and Bamiyan, centres of the Turk-Shahi dynasty, were occupied. Quantities of Buddhist and other idols and temple treasures were captured, some of which were forwarded as presents to Baghdad, where their public display caused a sensation. Islam was thus certainly brought to the borders of modern Pakistan, and there are even signs of Muslim missionary activity at a slightly earlier date. In the Peshawar Museum is a celebrated inscription, in both Arabic and Sanskrit, attesting to the presence of Islam in the Tochi valley of Waziristan in the year 857; it records the erection of a building, presumably a mosque, and must be one of the earliest Islamic inscriptions in the subcontinent.

In both Islam and Christianity, missionary efforts on remote and dangerous frontiers have often been undertaken by unorthodox and schismatic elements, so it is possible that there were at work in the valleys running down to the middle Indus, adherents of the early Islamic Khariji sect (represented today by the Ibadis of Oman, East Africa and North Africa), for Afghanistan was one of their last refuges, and as late as 982 the inhabitants of Gardiz in the Paktiya province of modern Afghanistan are described as Kharijis. Otherwise, the only Muslims in the upper Indus valley until the Ghaznavid invasions must have been small colonies of merchants, known to have existed, for instance, in the Hindu-Shahi capital of Waihand near modern Attock.

Because of the Arab presence in India during these early centuries some knowledge of the Indian way of life percolated back to the centres of Islam. Since Islam is a complete system of belief, containing everything necessary for a man's conduct in this world and his salvation in the next, there was no reason beyond sheer intellectual curiosity why Muslims should be interested in India. But a few Muslim scholars did show some interest; for one thing, the subcontinent was popularly famed as a home of esoteric lore and magic. From the time of the Abbasid Caliph al-Mansur, missions came from Sindh to the Baghdad court, bringing native Indian scholars and certain Sanskrit texts. The Indian knowledge of

The pre-Islamic pottery shown here diplays floral patterns and stylised bird, animal and fish motifs.

Much jewellery has been found among the ruins of Bhambore: these beads are made of terracotta

medicine, mathematics, astronomy and philosophy was especially esteemed, and various translations were made into Arabic. The Barmakid Vizier, Yahya bin Khalid, sent an agent to India around the year 800 to collect medicinal herbs and drugs and to acquire knowledge of Indian religions – information used by several later Islamic authors between the ninth and eleventh centuries.

The towering figure in the introduction of Indian culture to the Islamic world is, however, a scholar from Khwarazam in central Asia, Abu Raihan al-Biruni, who died in about 1050. He was able to observe Indian customs and lore, and was the first Muslim scholar to become a competent Sanskritist. The outcome of his studies was his great book on India, *Tahqiq ma li'l Hind* ("An Enquiry into India and its Civilization"), a compendium of all the knowledge which he could collect on Indian subjects. It was written in a remarkably dispassionate vein. Abu Raihan al-Biruni's purpose was not in any way polemical, and although he remained a firm Muslim and condemned such features of Indian life as "the servitude of the caste system, the blinkered self-satisfaction of the *pandits* and the degraded Hindu view of women and marriage", he felt a certain attraction towards the pure, theoretical philosophy of the Hindus, just as he did towards that of the ancient Greeks. Al-Biruni had no successor, but his work must be regarded as one of the great achievements of inter-cultural contact in mediaeval times.

C.E.B.

From Arabs to Mughals

The decline of the centralised authority of the Abbasid caliphs of Baghdad (750-1256 AD) was followed by the emergence to power of the Turks of Central Asia.

The Turks established themselves in Afghanistan in the late ninth century, and in 962, Alptagin, a Turkish officer of the Samanids, had installed himself at Ghazni. It was one of his successors, Abu Mansur Subuktagin, who, after his accession in 976, considerably extended his kingdom. His conquest of Lamaghan after his defeat of Raja Jaipal in two battles, exposed the weakness of the Indian armies and he followed these victories with further incursions into the territory. Lamaghan and Parhawar were annexed and roads constructed for military and commercial purposes.

Abu Mansur Subuktagin's son, Mahmud, succeeded him in 977, and carried his campaigns into the heart of Aryavarta in the north and the rich Hindu kingdom of Gujarat on the western coast. The Abbasid Caliph, Qadir Billah, bestowed upon him a *khilat* and the title of *Yaminuddaulah Amirul Millat*, or "Right Hand of the State and Protector of the Believers". His authority extended from Iraq to the Ganges, and from Khwarazam to Kathiawar. Sultan Mahmud's brilliant military exploits spanning a period of thirty-three years, earned for him respect and admiration far beyond the frontiers of the subcontinent. But his preoccupation with military campaigns did not distract him from his zest for the arts and encouragement of literary activity.

Above *Mai Jindan's tomb in Uch Sharif is a wonderful example of the bright blue tiles of the Multan region*
Below left *Melas, or local festivals, are joyful occasions, held in honour of Sufi Saints who first brought Islam to Punjab*

He commissioned architects of repute to beautify Ghazni by building mosques, bridges and works of public utility. He set up a state university, equipped it with a large library and attracted to his court some of the leading men of the time, the most eminent among them being Abu Raihan al-Biruni (973-1053). Al-Biruni is regarded as one of the greatest Muslim intellectuals a philosopher, mathematician, astronomer and cultural historian.

The Ghaznavids annexed Punjab up to Hansi, and Lahore replaced Multan as the administrative, cultural and spiritual centre of Islam in the subcontinent. Their successors, the Ghuris (1148-1206), with their capital at Firuzkosh, pushed the frontiers of the empire beyond the Jumna. Muhammad Ghuri, who took the title of Shahabuddin Ghuri, had been appointed governor of Ghazni in 1173 by his elder brother Ghiyasuddin. He conquered Multan in 1175, Uchh in 1176, and finally wrested Ghaznavid Punjab from Khusrau Malik, the last of the Ghaznavids, in 1186. After the defeat of Prithvi Raj, the ruler of Ajmer, at the battlefield of Tarain in 1192. Shahabuddin Ghuri captured Ajmer and Delhi and, later, his Turkish slave officers captured Gwalior, Kalinjar, Kalpi, Badaun, Qannauj, Benares, Koil and Meerut. Bihar and Bengal fell in 1199 and 1200 respectively.

By 1206, the year of the death of Shahabuddin Ghuri, the stage was set for the expansion and consolidation of Muslim rule in India. Hindus of all classes accepted government services and worked in the fields of agriculture, trade and industry. They were granted the status of *zimmi*, or allied people entitled to protection, and complete security of life, property and freedom of worship was guaranteed both in deference to *Shariat* and to political expediency.

The Ghaznavid and the Ghuri dynasties were Central Asian by origin and outlook. Both ruled their conquered territories from capitals outside India. After the death of

Above *The gateway to Rohtas Fort, built by Sher Shah Suri, 1540 AD. Suri constructed a network of roads and forts in his brief reign*
Opposite *These monumental tombs at Chaukundi date from the pre-Islamic era all the way through to the eighteenth century*

Shahabuddin Ghuri in 1206, political and military conditions changed rapidly in Central Asia. His successors, following the cataclysmic Ghuzz and Mongol invasions, were thrown on their own resources, having been cut off from their compatriots across the northwestern mountains.

Shahabuddin left no sons. His Turkish slave-officers became his co-heirs. Thereupon there arose a triangular struggle between his three leading officers – Tajuddin Yildiz, Nasiruddin Qubacha and Qutbuddin Aibek. Aibek succeeded in maintaining his authority in Lahore and the eastern provinces. After his death in 1210, following a war of succession, he was succeeded by Shamsuddin Iltamash, one of his former slaves. In 1211, Iltamash made Delhi his capital and is justifiably regarded as the founder of the Sultanate dynasty; the city replaced Lahore as a seat of Muslim administration.

By the beginning of the thirteenth century, therefore, the foundations of Islam in India had been laid. During the later period of the Abbasids, Persian had replaced Arabic as the vehicle of Islamic learning. Muslims in the subcontinent developed their own political, economic and religious institutions and their own centres of learning and pilgrimage. Allegiance to Islam, and the idea of belonging to a worldwide Muslim community, stimulated cultural proliferation.

Between 1206, when Qutbuddin Aibek succeeded to the territories of Shahabuddin Ghuri, and 1526, there were five different dynasties with thirty-three kings. This illustrates the failure of the Turks and Afghans to establish a stable political system which could withstand both internal revolution and foreign aggression. When forced by circumstances to recede to their homeland, there was still a Muslim ruler at

Delhi and in the capitals of the Muslim provinces.

The first of the five dynasties is generally known as the Slave Dynasty, because most of the governing class were either originally the slaves of Shahabuddin Ghuri or their sons. In the tenth century, a new institution had been developed, known as the imperial slave household: first the Abbasids, and later their successors, recruited a large number of Turkish slaves, and trained them as soldiers and statesmen. Turkish slave bureaucracy, therefore, made a great contribution to the new states which were established in Central Asia and later in India.

The Slave dynasty was replaced by the nondescript Khaljis who, though originally Turks, were identified with the Afghans on account of their long residence in Afghanistan. Under the second ruler of this dynasty, Alauddin Khalji, another wave of southward expansion began, but his greatest achievement was to establish a powerful monarchy. He succeeded in making the administration efficient and honest, and in stabilising prices, even though some of his measures were not approved by the orthodox.

The fall of the Khaljis ushered in a new dynasty founded by Tughlaq, commonly known as Ghazi Malik, who later took the title of Ghayasuddin. His son, Muhammad bin Tughlaq, who succeeded him in 1325, was a most remarkable ruler. In his determination to maintain power he curbed the influence of the Hindu *rais* and *rajas*, the Muslim military aristocracy, the *ulema* and the *Sufis*, or Muslim mystics. Thus he made enemies and at last died fighting at Thatta in Sindh. His successor, Firuz Shah, was an easy-going man who tried unsuccessfully to make the government correspond to the dictates of *Shariat* and by his policy of appeasement and compromise, barely succeeded in maintaining superficial peace. He lost most of the outlying provinces and left the empire in considerable disarray. After his death there was an effort to set up independent principalities and this finally destroyed the unity of the empire. During the reign of Firuz Shah's successor, India was invaded by Amir Timur (Tamerlane), in 1398.

The Tughlaqs were succeeded by the Sayyeds who were in reality deputies of Amir Timur. The Lodhi Afghans displaced the Sayyeds and for a while re-established the supremacy of Muslims in Delhi, Bihar and Punjab. The Lodhis were good soldiers but individualists – so that their tribal disagreements wrecked their statesmanship. They patronised learning and re-established orthodoxy, but could not withstand the invasion of the Mughals under Babur in 1526. With the coming of the Mughals, a new and perhaps the most glorious epoch of Muslim rule in the subcontinent began.

The Turks and the Afghans who held sway in the subcontinent for nearly three centuries had to face the threat of foreign invasions and the growing insurgence of the conquered people, the rise of heretical movements within Islam and the disobedience of their own officers and of religious pressure groups.

The spread of Islam through the subcontinent cannot be ascribed to the use of force. During the course of centuries, military and political power was occasionally used to secure conversions, but compulsion in such cases was the exception rather than the rule. In the north, the Muslim mystics and theologians followed in the wake of armies and whenever the Muslims succeeded in establishing their authority the mystics set up their *khanqahs*, or hospices, and the *ulema* their

Mughal Ascendancy

The necropolis at Makli Hill, Thatta, six miles square, includes many masterpieces of stone carving and perforated stonework.

India in the early sixteenth century was like a turbid sea between two tides. There was energy, there was power and enterprise but no unity. There was promise rather than performance, aspiration without achievement. This situation had developed in north India since the collapse of the Delhi Sultanate under the impact of Timur's invasion in 1398 and of the Bahmini kingdom of the Deccan after the murder of Mahmud Gawan in 1481. Only the peninsula south of the river Kistna was united under the Hindu raj as of Vijayanagar.

The unity which apparently existed in the north was more apparent than real. The Delhi Sultanate had revived under the Afghan Lodhis, but its Afghan supporters were proverbial for their love of independence and dislike of authority. The empire was more a confederation of chiefs than a close-knit power unit. It was kept together by the tact of Buhlol Lodhi (1451-88) and, when Sultan Ibrahim (1518-26) was unable to sustain this quality, it was ready to dissolve. In barren Rajasthan the Rajputs had apparently revived enough to threaten the Afghans, but they too were divided into prestige and clan-conscious aristocratic units. In the Deccan the Bahmini successor states warred with each other and the southern Hindus by turns. North of the Kistna only in Gujarat was there firm government and prosperity.

It was on this scene of superficial brilliance and hidden weakness that Babur and his Mughal *baigs* erupted in 1526. Fifth in descent from Timur, Babur inherited all the Timurid claims but only the small Farghana portion (north of the Hindu Kush) of the whole Timurid heritage. His Chaghatais were of mixed Turkish and Mongolian race: he himself had Mongolian characteristics while his son Humayun was more Turkish in appearance.

Babur had been ejected from Farghana by others with equal claims but more resources. He would have become a dispossessed wanderer had he not seized Kabul and its kingdom by a lucky stroke. Thence he started to raid the Indian plains in the traditional way, soon discovering that the Delhi kingdom was seething with discontent, and that Daulat Khan, the governor of the Punjab, was ripe for revolt.

The fifth raid was decisive. Daulat Khan handed him the Punjab; Ibrahim could only collect his unenthusiastic chiefs at Panipat, forty miles north of Delhi. In the battle here in 1526, Babur's cavalry's wheeling tactics, his new Turkish artillery and the disloyalty of many Afghan chiefs won him the day. He reached Agra without opposition, where his first act was to order the layout of a Persian garden.

There followed a triangular power struggle between Mughals, Afghans and Rajputs. Rana Sangha, the hitherto victorious chief of Mewar, thought he saw an opportunity of restoring Rajput supremacy. But his hopes were dashed at Kanwaha, twenty miles west of Agra (1527) where Babur, with his new tactics, won against apparently hopeless odds. Two years later he dealt with the reformed Afghans on the banks of the Ghagra. Babur was now master of northern India from the Indus to the borders of Bengal, but he had achieved only the precarious power of a successful soldier, not yet consolidated by administration or sentiment. Before he could do more he died in 1530, at the age of forty-seven. Babur was the forerunner, rather than the founder, of the Mughal empire.

Humayun's father saved his life but could not save his

the softening of the rigours of the caste system, the release from choking religious rituals, can all be traced to the influence of Islam. Equally, the rise of vernaculars to the status of regional languages was the result of the patronage extended to writers in these languages by Muslim rulers. The impact of Islam on Hinduism was deep and far-reaching in its subsequent manifestations.

A.R. et al.

This technique of building a bridge out of boats is an ancient one. Alexander and Akbar were known to have used pontoon bridges to cross the Indus and its tributaries

fortune. This "fair and fatal king" had all the social graces and many personal gifts, but these were stultified by self-indulgence. This created long periods of inattention to public affairs, and indecision which led to mistimed actions and lost opportunities. His conquest of Gujarat was followed by a period of inaction which enabled the Afghan chief, Sher Khan, to build up his strength. His conquest of Bengal was followed by inertia which left him cut off by monsoon floods. In two battles with Sher Shah he lost all that Babur had won and became a fugitive in Persia. While Sher Shah pursued his vigorous way, until killed in front of the fortress of Kalanjar (1545), Humayun was painfully re-establishing himself in the north-west. He was assisted here by new dissension among the Afghans under Sher Shah's successors. A second battle at Panipat left Humayun master of Delhi once more, only to die within six months from the effects of a fall on his library stairs. Once more the Mughal imperial stone had rolled to the bottom of the hill of success.

Humayun's unfinished task was left to his thirteen-year-old son Akbar, then under the care of Bairam Khan. India owes much to the loyalty and ability of this royal servant. Without him, Akbar might easily have suffered the fate of the English Princes in the Tower. For while Babur was the forerunner, Humayun the "also-ran", and Sher Shah's government a prototype, Akbar was the actual creator of the Mughal empire.

One side of Akbar was the orthodox Asian military conqueror, helped by the loyalty of a small core of loyal followers and by a genius for leadership and manipulation. He was fortunate too, in that the political condition of India continued to be divided and unstable. No other leaders of great talent emerged to weld the divided forces together. The various regions had vigorous but uninspired and jealous rulers who would fall one by one before a master hand. After Bairam had defeated the Hindu general Hemu at the second battle of Panipat (1556), and Akbar had assumed direct rule as he approached manhood in 1560, there followed a series of campaigns and conquests which left his dominion, at his death in 1605, a compact territory stretching from Kandahar in the north to the Bay of Bengal in the east. Rich Gujarat, beautiful Kashmir and fertile Bengal were his. In achieving them the most crucial moments had been the defeat of the Rajputs in 1568-69, the subsequent understanding with their chiefs, and the defeat of his younger brother Muhammad Hakim's opposition in 1580.

Akbar's claim to lasting fame and to world statesmanship rests upon his conversion of these congeries of lands and peoples into an organic Indian state. He not only had the talent for leadership, but the crucial, creative ability to unite. First, he faced the political problem of balance and conciliation between conflicting elements. There was a core of his Mughal followers who were reinforced by a stream of fortune-seekers from Central Asia and Persia. These were a minority of Muslims, since Muslims were a minority in the larger population of Hindus. Beyond them were the Afghan chiefs, scattered through north India from Peshawar to Bengal, embittered by their recent loss of empire, warlike and vigorous but fortunately (for Akbar) too proud and independent to combine easily. Then there were the Hindus, whose sword arm was the Rajput chiefs of Rajasthan. Finally, there were the Muslim kingdoms of the Deccan, still vigorous in spite of the break-up of the Bahmini kingdom.

Akbar distrusted the Afghans. To balance them he used other settled Muslim chiefs of Turkish origin and the émigrés from the west. His master stroke here was the alliance with the Rajput chiefs after his capture of Chitor and Ranthambor in 1568-69. Except for Mewar they recognised Mughal sovereignty. He also arranged marriages with Rajput princesses, chiefly from Jaipur, so that later Mughal generations became increasingly Indian by blood as well as by residence. This positive Rajput support secured general Hindu acquiescence and also provided a reserve of strength against possible Muslim opposition. It was this agreement which provided a stable foundation upon which Akbar was able to build the main fabric of his empire.

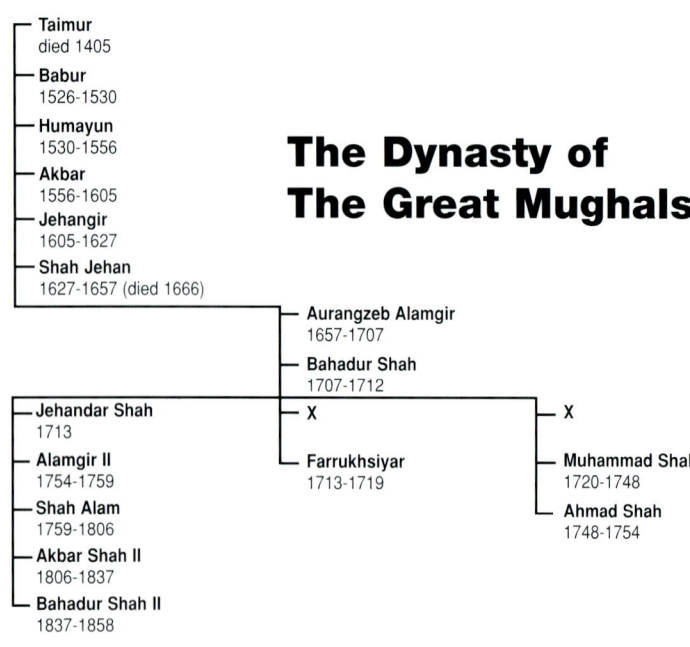

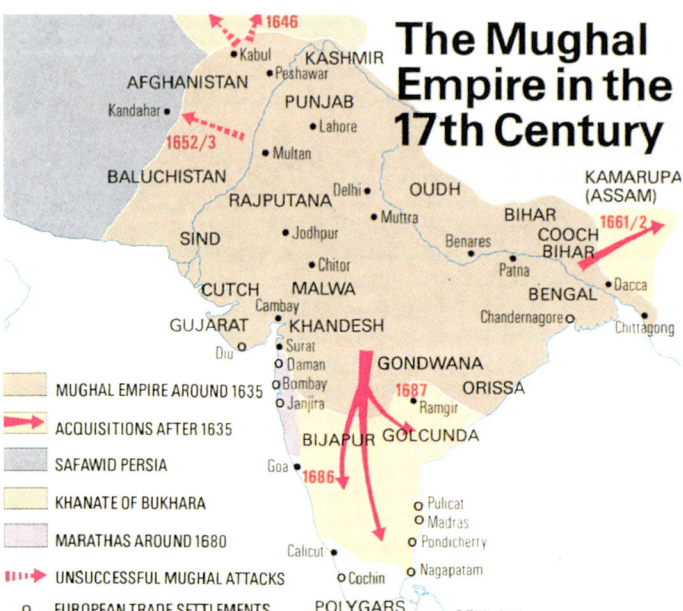

The Mughal dynasty reigned in the subcontinent from 1526 until 1858. Cultural life flourished at their imperial courts

With this secure foundation we can turn to the pillars raised upon it to support, so to speak, the canopy of empire. The first pillar was that of leadership, which was vital for success. Here again the Mughals were fortunate, for the seven great Mughals included two men of genius, two of outstanding talent, and two of above average ability; even Humayun, though erratic, was a man of parts. Akbar, however, added a new dimension to the leadership concept. In the middle of his reign he underwent some kind of inner experience, as a result of which he became what may loosely be called a freethinker. It was enough for him to be considered heretical by orthodox Muslims, but not enough for him to be claimed as a convert by hopeful Jesuit priests or keen-minded Brahmins. He established a Court cult which centred on himself, reverenced the sun and borrowed practices from varied sources. The cult collapsed soon after his death but left something permanent behind. This was a new reverence for the imperial person as God's representative on earth in temporal matters; he was surrounded with a halo of sanctity. Its symbol was the nimbus or halo with which court painters henceforth adorned Mughal imperial heads down to the nineteenth century. In this way, Akbar, without trying to make Hindus into Muslims or Muslims into Hindus, made

ister the more inaccessible parts of the empire directly.

The system, as introduced by Akbar and developed by his successors, provided a service of thirty-three grades or ranks directly appointed by the emperor, responsible to and dependent upon him. At first they were paid in cash but later by an assignment on the revenue in the form of a non-hereditary grant of land revenue, known as a *jagir*. These grants ceased with the office and might at any moment be replaced by other grants. Though appearing generous In money terms, they had to cover the upkeep of a specified number of troopers and horses.

For purposes of administration the empire was divided into twelve (later eighteen) *subah* or provinces. These in turn were sub-divided into *sarkars* or districts and *parganas* or sub-districts. In these units the principle of dual authority was enforced. Each *subah* and *sarkar* had one officer responsible for law and order and one for collecting the revenue, known in the *subah* as the *nazim* and the *diwan* respectively. The *nazim* or governor commanded a body of troops but had no local money with which to pay them, while the *diwan* had money but no troops to suborn. *Nazim* and *diwan* were appointed direct from Delhi. To minimise the risk of their collusion, each was transferred after four or five years. The

This huge, austere fortress at Attock was built by Akbar. Its impressive size tells us of the great strategic importance of this site on the Indus

the imperial office an object of reverence for all India.

The principle then, was the common employment of all Indians in the imperial service, and a common reverence by all for the emperor's person. This policy was completed by the principle of general religious toleration. Its manifestation was the abolition of the *jaziya*, or tax, on non-Muslims in 1579, which Akbar's successors maintained for a hundred years. The effect of these measures was the establishment of an Indian state embracing both communities as citizens, with a Muslim as leader and Islam as the established religion. The link between the two groups was the semi-sacred office of the emperor. The reality of this arrangement is testified by the fact that half of the Indian-born high officials were Muslim and half, Hindu. These numbered three-tenths of the whole number, the rest being foreign-born personal followers or immigrants.

To the two pillars of leadership, and communal toleration and cooperation, may now be added that of organisation. A cohesive framework was needed to replace the feudatory chiefs and an accompanying system of land grants to supporters. This need was supplied by the *mansabdari* system, which provided a civil-cum-military imperial service to admin-

system was not perfect, but it did produce the most stable and long-lived government since the times of the Guptas in the fourth and fifth centuries AD.

There remained the problem of how best to collect the revenue. Three-quarters of it came from the land, the remainder from customs duties and various local tolls. Here again, the system was made as positive as possible. Its architect was the Revenue Minister, Raja Todar Mal, and the system known as Todar Mal's *bandobast*. Land was measured and classified according to soil and crop, and then assessed for revenue at current prices. Annually thereafter, the demand was locally modified according to the season, the extent of cultivation, and the nature of the crops raised. Records were kept in the villages; the governor enjoyed the pomp, but the patwari turned the vital wheels of local administration.

A large class of middlemen involved in government service collected the revenue; central government then paid the salaries of the *mansabdars*. The remaining surplus was sometimes used productively, for example in the development of the Jumna canals, the digging of tanks and the building of roads. Much went into the financing of the great works which are the visible legacy of the Mughals to the

Lahore Fort

Top *Narrative mosaics in the wall of Lahore Fort were added by Jehangir*

Above *Tessarae reflect from the ceiling of Shah Jehan's Shish Mehal*

Above left *Mughal emperors received daily homage from their balcony*

Above *The massive steps were built for the entry of Akbar's 5,000 elephants*

Left *The fine windows are of Shah Jehan's Hall of Special Audience*

Shah Jehan presided over a golden age of the Mughals. His Taj Mahal represents Mughal architecture at its perfection

subcontinent the Taj Mahal, the Jamia Masjids of Delhi and Lahore, Wazir Khan's mosque at Lahore, and the palaces and the gardens which the Mughals loved.

In fact, only a modest amount of the national product was used constructively; it was a weak point in the whole system and helps to explain the static economics of the period. Too much was drained off and too little put back into the country. Economic levels did not rise much except in pockets of industrial activity and valuable crops such as in Gujarat with its indigo and East Bengal with its silk. The country people are thought by some economists to have been as well or better off than their western European contemporaries; but they suffered from the lethal hazards of crop failure and famine, hardly known in the west, for which there was then no remedy.

The Mughals made an important contribution to the subcontinent's cultural heritage. It may be thought of as the addition of the Persian rose to the lotus in India's cultural garden. The Turks had brought in the Persian language for official purposes and it had married with Hindi to give birth to Urdu. Babur and his successors were wedded to Persian culture in all its forms and now greatly extended its influence. The emperor Muhammad Shah gave Urdu the status of a court tongue. Todar Mal ordered all local records to be kept in Persian instead of a local dialect. Persian became the language not only of the Court and diplomacy but of the whole administration down to village level. Like French, it is an infectious language, with a captivating literature, all of whose forms took root in India. Some of its great figures, like Abul Fatal and Radayuni, were themselves Indians. Down to Ghalib and Muhammad Iqbal, poets wrote with equal ease in Persian or Urdu.

There was Persian influence not only on literature but on the arts and manners. There was a creative union of architectural styles to produce the Mughal school of architecture, still practised in the twentieth century, and the Mughal and Rajput schools of painting. Persian manners pervaded the whole of the subcontinent as the norm of social behaviour. At the coronation of Sivaji the Maratha, half the insignia used were Mughal rather than Hindu in origin. The influence was so widespread as to change the face of India, though not so penetrating as to constitute a new hybrid culture.

From Akbar the stately procession of the Great Mughals progressed to its end in the death of Bahadur Shah the First in 1712. Akbar's son Jehangir lacked his father's genius, but he was a shrewd, capable, determined if sometimes ferocious man. His achievement could have been greater had he not allowed alcohol to fuddle his brain. It would certainly have been lesser without the succour of the famous Noor Jehan. As it was, he kept the empire together and, with his capture of Kangra and aggression in the Deccan, left it a little larger than he found it. It was, however, as a patron of the arts that he achieved real distinction. His love of nature and his distinguished taste made him the creative patron of the Mughal school of painting.

Shah Jehan, impatient to succeed even at the price of rebellion, proved to be the most magnificent of Akbar's successors. His administration became a legend of just and stable rule, in retrospect something like a golden age. "Hail, O King, thou owest a thanksgiving to God," shouted a voice from the crowd as the emperor was going in procession. "The King is just, the ministers are able and the secretaries are honest. The country is prosperous and the people contented."

year 1680. Until then, his rule was a good example of Mughal statecraft, wary in the north-west, aggressive in the Deccan, internal forces carefully balanced. The one major change was that Aurangzeb saw himself as the head of an Islamic state rather than as the Muslim head of an Indian state with a Muslim state religion. This led to the reimposition of the *jaziya* tax in 1679 and a cooling of relations with the Rajputs.

The second period began with Aurangzeb's march to the Deccan to suppress the Marathas and overthrow the two surviving Muslim kingdoms. He was by now an old man, implacable in the pursuit of these aims, but increasingly pietistic and pessimistic and unable to combat the economic crises which deepened during his last years. Agrarian discontent took religious forms, such as the rising of the Sikhs and the Satnami rebellion, or tribal, such as the rising of the Jats. In the five years following Aurangzeb's death (1707-1712), his son Bahadur Shah, already an old man, strove tirelessly to solve the problems his father had bequeathed. Incessantly on the move, never setting foot in his capital, he tried to deal with the Marathas, the Rajputs, the Sikhs and the Jats in turn. In five more years he might have made a lasting impression.

At Bahadur Shah's death the empire plunged into a series of wars of succession which hastened its decline. The Sikhs were driven to the hills in 1716, but the emperor was

Hiran Minar, the "Deer Tower", was dedicated by Jehangir to Mansraj, his pet antelope

His legacy to India was the Taj and the Delhi Fort and Jamia Masjid. His perceptive patronage both guided his architects to their great achievements and encouraged portraiture among his painters. In politics he maintained the aggression towards Deccan initiated by his forebears, so that only the two Muslim kingdoms of Bijapur and Golkonda were left by the end of the reign. The loss in 1637 of Kandahar, however, was a warning signal which no-one heeded.

It was the fate of Shah Jehan to be overthrown by the same means as he had employed against his own father. He ended his days gazing across the Jumna to the Taj while his third son Aurangzeb, after defeating his brother Dara in a famous war of succession, sat in his place. Aurangzeb was a complete contrast to his father; puritanical rather than voluptuary; keenly orthodox instead of easy-going in religion; determined, relentless and a master of dissimulation His ascent to the throne cost the lives of three brothers, one son and two nephews.

Aurangzeb's long reign divides neatly into two about the

murdered soon after. When Muhammad Shah restored some dignity to the throne, his chief supporter Asaf Jah, disgusted by the Court's frivolity, established himself as the *nizam* (regulator) of the five Deccan provinces in 1724, thus founding the Hyderabad state. The next shock was the Maratha seizure of Malwa, which effectively cut the empire in two. Close upon this came Nadir Shah of Persia's famous occupation of Delhi, after defeating the Mughal forces at Karnal. He retired in 1739 with Shah Jehan's Peacock Throne and enough plunder to enable him to remit all taxes in Persia for three years.

Thereafter, the empire seemed to rally for a time and the first Afghan raid by Ahmad Shah Abdali was repulsed in 1748. Then there was a reverse and provinces began to drop away. Between 1739 and 1754 Kabul, Gujarat, Sindh, Oudh and Punjab went in this way. Only prosperous Bengal remained loyal. It was a power struggle which eventually destroyed the empire leaving Delhi the centre of a local kingdom until made a protectorate by the Marathas in 1785 and

PAKISTAN

The Badshahi Mosque was built by Aurangzeb and has the largest courtyard of any mosque in the world. Its domes and minarets dominate the north-west quarter of Lahore. The façade is of red sandstone with marble inlay in floral and geometric patterns. The arches are gilded

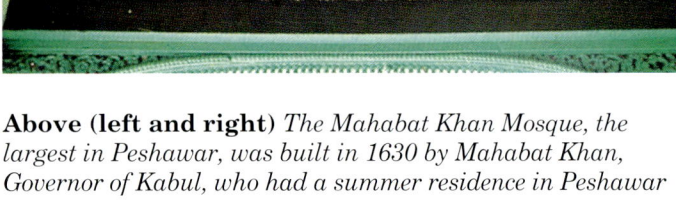

Above (left and right) *The Mahabat Khan Mosque, the largest in Peshawar, was built in 1630 by Mahabat Khan, Governor of Kabul, who had a summer residence in Peshawar*

Opposite *In the courtyard of the mosque a place is reserved for* mahfil-e-sana, *the performance of spiritual folk music*

the British in 1803. There were renewed Afghan incursions in the fifties; the imperial death knell was tolled on the fatal field of Panipat in 1761. The confrontation was between the invading Afghans, supported by Muslim elements, and the Marathas, whose nationalism had developed into aggressive imperialism under a succession of able Peshwas. The sceptre of India was now the latters' goal, and they saw their chance of it, as the saviours of the divided Mughals from the intruding Afghans. The struggle which culminated at Panipat shattered the Maratha power for ten years; but the Afghan failure of nerve, and withdrawal from India on the morrow of victory, left north India without a recognised master for forty years.

So the empire fell and historians are left with the still unsolved problem as to why it fell. In fact, the collapse can be assigned to no single cause. Rather, one must look to a combination of several factors. There was certainly a failure of leadership among the Mughals after 1712; there was perhaps too much competing leadership among the nobles. Leadership rivalry or conflict is as good a formula for anarchy as any; the abler the rivals, the quicker it works. It is a fact that Aurangzeb left a series of pressing problems behind him. To treat India as an Islamic society and the Hindu majority as a dissenting minority was a political mistake, for it eroded positive Rajput support for the empire and upset the rapport which had existed between the two communities.

While this policy may have weakened the empire's power basis, it would not in itself have overthrown the structure. A far more serious factor was the Maratha entanglement. It was a heavy drain on the empire's financial resources, but more important still, it undermined the morale of the whole Mughal nobility, causing a sense of frustration, mounting losses and prolonged absences from home. Concentrating on control of the Deccan weakened control of the north. The overthrow of the two Deccan kingdoms produced dislocation.

Above all, the prolonged conflict set in motion an economic crisis. Too large a proportion of the empire's resources was being used unproductively. Struggle and disorder in the Deccan both over-used existing resources and diminished the production of fresh ones. That is why Aurangzeb complained that he was like a physician who had only one pomegranate between a hundred sick men. This crisis steadily deepened as continued strife produced steadily increasing demands on steadily lessening resources.

Lastly there was a failure of nerve. Babur's sense of royal and cultural mission, Akbar's of creativity and Shah Jehan's of fulfilment all waned, leaving a void to be filled by self-defeating struggles for power. Aurangzeb saw salvation in the establishment of an Islamic state, but did not fully understand the economic decay at its roots. By the mid-eighteenth century Shah Waliullah, when looking for means to regenerate a threatened Muslim society, rejected the Mughal monarchy as effete and called for renaissance on the whole congregation of the Faithful.

The Mughal episode cannot, however, be abandoned on this note of disparagement. In all, the Mughals gave to India nearly two centuries of integrated rule, to Indian Islam its highest peak of cultural achievement, and to the ruling classes and their agents an overmantle of Persian culture. Finally, it produced a pattern of organised unity which, though in disarray by the time Robert Clive seized control of Bengal, was yet coherent enough to set a precedent for Indians and a model for the British in creating their version of unity. Mughal India was the harbinger of united British India, and British India of modern India and Pakistan. Without the creative work of the Mughals neither of these last two states could have been fashioned.

P.S.

Top *Shah Jehan built Shalimar Gardens in Lahore as a recreational place for his family*
Above *The tomb of Jehangir, Lahore*
Left *The Dai Anga Mosque was planned by Shah Jehan's* anga *or wetnurse, Zeb-un-Nisa, in 1635*
Below *The mosque built at Thatta by Shah Jehan is exquisitely domed*

Confrontation with the British

In 1498, Vasco da Gama landed in Calicut on the western coast, making the Portuguese the first modern Europeans to penetrate the subcontinent in search of trade. The English ship *Tyger* sailed in 1583 to open commerce with India, carrying a letter from Queen Elizabeth I to "the most invincible and most mighty Prince, Lord Zelabdim Echebar, King of Cambaia", but it was not until some years later, in 1608, that the first Englishman arrived at the court of Emperor Jehangir. Sir Thomas Roe was a distinguished ambassador at this court despite the fact that "frugality prescribed his allowance, his retinue, and even the present to the Mughal, with little conformity to the sumptuous prejudice of the most magnificent court in the Universe".

For the next 150 years, the East India Company remained a humble trading company requesting concessions from the court, in competition with the French, in Bengal and on the Coromandel coast. With the death of Emperor Aurangzeb in 1707, the Mughal Empire began its long descent into decay, but the signs of decline were as yet invisible, when, in 1715, the Company was able to obtain extra-territorial rights in Bengal from Emperor Farrukhsiyar. In the words of the writer and historian, John Strachey, these rights were "to prove nothing less than the beginning of the end of the independence of India".

The Mughals, who had been dealing with the Portuguese and the French as well as the English, could not possibly foresee that this course would lead to the conquest of a vast empire by an only moderately successful trading company, intermittently supported by the government of a small island in Europe, itself inhabited by less than six million people.

The process by which this conquest was achieved makes a strange and fascinating story, and is a subject of controversy even today. Bengal was the most prosperous province in the subcontinent in the eighteenth century, and it was here that the foundations were laid for the British Empire in India.

In April 1756, Alivardi Khan, one of the ablest governors of Bengal in the later Mughal empire died, and was succeeded by Sirajudaulah, a patriotic and impetuous young man. Sirajudaulah was surrounded by intriguing and ambitious relatives and opportunist *bania seths*, or petty merchants, ready to conspire with the East India Company servants who needed no encouragement to interfere in Bengal politics and stood to make vast fortunes out of gains from Indian territories. The inevitable confrontation came when the governor of the Company's settlement in Bengal gave refuge to one of Sirajudaulah's political enemies and, as a result, the latter attacked and captured Fort William in June 1756. The governor and half the garrison fled leaving the settlement to its fate. It was following the capture of the fort by Sirajudaulah that the so-called "Black Hole of Calcutta" outrage was committed, in which about sixty-four people were confined in a small cell where forty three of them died of suffocation. This incident was used by the Company servants to launch what might be called the first atrocity propaganda campaign of modern times. Its object was to win public support in England for a predatory venture which would otherwise have aroused little interest. The Company's employees had a great deal to gain or lose in the power stakes of Bengal: a pliant *nawab* could mean fabulous riches.

Robert Clive became first British Governor of Bengal in 1758. In a fanciful tableau, Clive is depicted with Emperor Shah Alam conferring the administration of the revenues of Bengal, Bihar and Orissa on the East India Company

The British Government responded with unusual vigour and turned over to the company the ships and armaments which had recently arrived in Madras for use against the French. Robert Clive, who had recently distinguished himself in the wars in southern India, was put in command of the British forces in Bengal. Calcutta was easily taken and within a short time, with the aid of the local enemies of the Nawab, Sirajudaulah was defeated at the Battle of Plassey on 23rd June 1757. Clive wrote of these events to the historian Orme: "fighting, tricks, chicanery, intrigues, politics and the Lord knows what, in short there will be a fine field for you to display your genius in".

Clive installed Mir Jaffer, who was in league with Sirajudaulah's enemies, as the Nawab of Bengal and from this moment "private financial greed and public policy, so intertwined themselves as to commit the British inevitably to rule in India and to compass the ruin of Bengal". From gaining Bengal it was but a small step to direct confrontation with the decaying Mughal Empire. At the Battle of

Baksar in 1765, which he won, Clive secured from the Emperor the *dewani*, or the right to the collection of revenues, of Bengal, Bihar, and Orissa. The East India Company now had formal control, and by 1818 the British were supreme in most of the subcontinent, the only areas still retaining independence being Punjab, Sindh, Balochistan and the North-West Frontier Province – areas which today form Pakistan.

The overall progress of the British in India can be divided into five easily discernible stages. In the first, up to 1785, the Company state came into existence. From 1785 to 1798 the objective was the extension and consolidation of the British position. Then came the third period, from 1798 to 1805, when Lord Wellesley pursued his forward policy, confronting and defeating Tipu Sultan of Mysore and the Maratha confederacy in south India. A peaceful interlude occurred with the British involvement in the Napoleonic Wars in Europe from 1805 to 1813. The final phase of conquest was begun between 1813 and 1818. After that the British were to desist from further expansion until the conquest of Sindh and Punjab which was complete by 1849.

In the last quarter of the eighteenth century, amidst fluctuating fortunes and wavering frontiers, there were a

Lord Wellesley, however, had to contend with a formidable adversary in the person of Tipu Sultan, the son of Haider Ali of Mysore. He combined the qualities of a warrior and an administrator, and with some justification he is regarded as a heroic figure. If Tipu Sultan realised that the British were the real danger to India, Lord Wellesley, who came to India as Governor-General in 1798, was no less aware that Tipu Sultan was the real barrier to British supremacy in central and southern India. Wellesley, with subtlety and skill, set about isolating Tipu Sultan. The Englishman neutralised the Nizam of Hyderabad with a subsidiary alliance and then attacked Mysore. Tipu Sultan met the attack with the utmost courage, but was killed fighting at the siege of Seringapatam. The British were rid of the most serious challenge to their predominance so far. In addition, Wellesley made a successful start in breaking the powerful Marathas. Although fighters, they were fatally disunited and incapable of forming a unifying force of opposition.

The years of Napoleonic domination of Europe were anxious ones for England and there was, as has been noted, little activity in India. With the retreat of Napoleon from Moscow, however, the British were once again on the offensive. By

Warren Hastings (1732-1818) became Governor-General of Bengal. He was impeached by Parliament for corruption – and acquitted

Tipu Sahib, Sultan Shaheed of Mysore (1749-1799) persevered in the struggle against the British, but was finally killed in battle

Sir Charles Napier (1782-1853) – combative, headstrong and popular – annexed Sindh in 1843 and became Governor of that province

number of potent states in India. There was Oudh, ably ruled by Shujaudaulah; there was the Sultanate of Delhi, under the Mughal Emperor, Shah Alam, which came under Maratha control in 1785 and there was the Sikh rule established at the end of the eighteenth century by the dashing Sikh adventurer Ranjit Singh in Punjab. Rajasthan had its Rajput rajas – an easy prey for the Marathas. The Kalhoras had their brilliant but brief rule in Sindh from the early eighteenth century until succeeded by the patriarchal and tribal rule of the Talpur family in the 1780s. Those with the best chance of challenging the British were the Marathas, the Nizam of Hyderabad and Balder Ali of Mysore who together effectively ruled central and southern India. Around 1780 it appeared that a coalition of the three powers would deal a decisive blow to the British, but Warren Hastings, proving himself a supremely able diplomat, bribed and bluffed his way out of the crisis, breaking the coalition and saving the Company, which remained in full possession of its territories.

1818 their hegemony was complete, with its patchwork of British-protected "native states" and directly administered provinces. The only independent states left were the Sikh kingdom of Punjab, Sindh in the lower Indus valley and towards the Frontier the undefined region of Balochistan and the Pathan tribes. Beyond that was Afghanistan, traditionally the route taken by the conquerors of India.

With Napoleon's invasion of Egypt and his possible designs on India, British fears about the safety of their Indian possessions were focused on the North-West Frontier. This menace was felt to be even more serious when the France-Russian alliance was formed in 1807. Even after the exit of Napoleon in 1815, the British viewed Russian influence at the Persian court and in Afghanistan with apprehension, and for the next half century the Russian threat was a determining factor of North-West Frontier policy.

The East India Company had treaty relations with Punjab and Sindh. The river Sutlej had been fixed as the boundary between British and Sikh dominions, and the treaty relations with the Amirs of Sindh were somewhat uneasy. An account by Dr. James Burnes who visited Sindh in 1827 aroused renewed interest in the acquisition of the country, and shortly afterwards his brother, Alexander Burnes, was sent up the Indus (on the pretext of taking a gift of horses for Ranjit Singh) in order to report on prevailing conditions. It was not until the disastrous English expedition to Afghanistan in 1839, and the subsequent retreat of the British army in 1842, that acquisition of the country was felt to be vital for the defence of British India.

Consequently, Sir Charles Napier, an excitable and ambitious general, was sent to command the British and advance on Sindh. The Talpurs, who were realistic enough to know that they did not stand a chance in any actual battle, prepared their defences but were careful to give no cause for precipitating any action by the British. James Outram, the British Resident in Sindh, protested against the proposed action, pleading that the Talpur government was benevolent and patriarchal: "I say *patriarchal*, for, however we may despise the Amirs as inferior to ourselves, either in morality or expansion of intellect, each chief certainly lives *with*, and *for*, his portion of the people; and I question whether any class of the people of Sindh, except the Hindoo traders, would prefer a change to the best government we could give them". Outram pleaded in vain. In a fiercely fought battle at Miani on 7 February 1843, Napier defeated the Talpur armies, annexed Sindh, and sent back the triumphant news in code, "Peccavi".

With the conquest of Sindh, it was inevitable that Punjab would soon be added to the British Indian territory. After the death of Ranjit Singh, Punjab's condition had become chaotic. A succession of maharajas and pretenders died violently, and the army having usurped power acted in a cruel and high-handed manner. Rani Jindan, the regent, in an effort to break the power of the army, persuaded its leaders to attack the British. The first Sikh War began in December 1845, with the British victory in a desperately fought battle which turned in their favour as a result of treachery in Sikh ranks. The subsequent treaty gave Britain the Cis-Sutlej lands and the Jullundur Doab. Kashmir was also annexed and sold to Gulab Singh, an adventurer from Ranjit Singh's army, who had become the ruler of Jammu – the man of whom Herbert Edwards wrote "he was the worst native I have ever come in contact with, and bad king, a miser and a liar."

Punjab was taken in its entirety after Lord Gough, having been humiliated in February and March 1849 at the battles of Chilianwala and Gujrat, won an overwhelming victory. The British now annexed the whole area, including Peshawar, which had been conquered by Ranjit Singh in 1829. By defeating the Sikhs, the British had won the Indus Basin; the British Empire in India stretched north to the Khyber Pass in the North-West Frontier and west beyond the Bolan Pass in Balochistan.

The next hundred years, up until the British exit from India in August 1947, was a traumatic and revolutionary era for the newly subjugated peoples of Sindh, Punjab and the Frontier.

In spite of the inevitable tyranny of colonial rule and the errors made through not understanding local customs, the British were no longer the buccaneers of the early East

Above *Ranjit Singh, whose confederacy controlled Punjab, encamped by the river Sutlej* **Top right** *He enlisted French, Italian and other officers and built up an effective army* **Right** *The* samadhi *(cremation site) of Ranjit Singh, opposite Lahore Fort*

India Company days, and they did not inflict on the Indus Valley the bitter experiences suffered by eighteenth century Bengal. British rule in these provinces was based on policies of restraint and expediency. Administrators, like John Jacob and Robert Sandeman, used not only force but diplomacy to pacify the Frontier areas. They formalised the *jirga* system, recognised the great Baloch and Pathan sardars and tribes and built up a successful frontier system for British India – although resistance was to continue in these areas for several decades. Pathan insurgence became particularly fierce when, in the face of Russian advance into central Asia, the British, fearing encroachment south towards India, sought to reinforce their defences by building forts and establishing garrisons in the tribal territories. It was in 1901 that Lord Curzon formed the North-West Frontier Province, including the settled lands beyond the Indus, with its capital at Peshawar. Quetta became the military outpost beyond the Bolan Pass and the capital of British Balochistan.

H.K. et al.

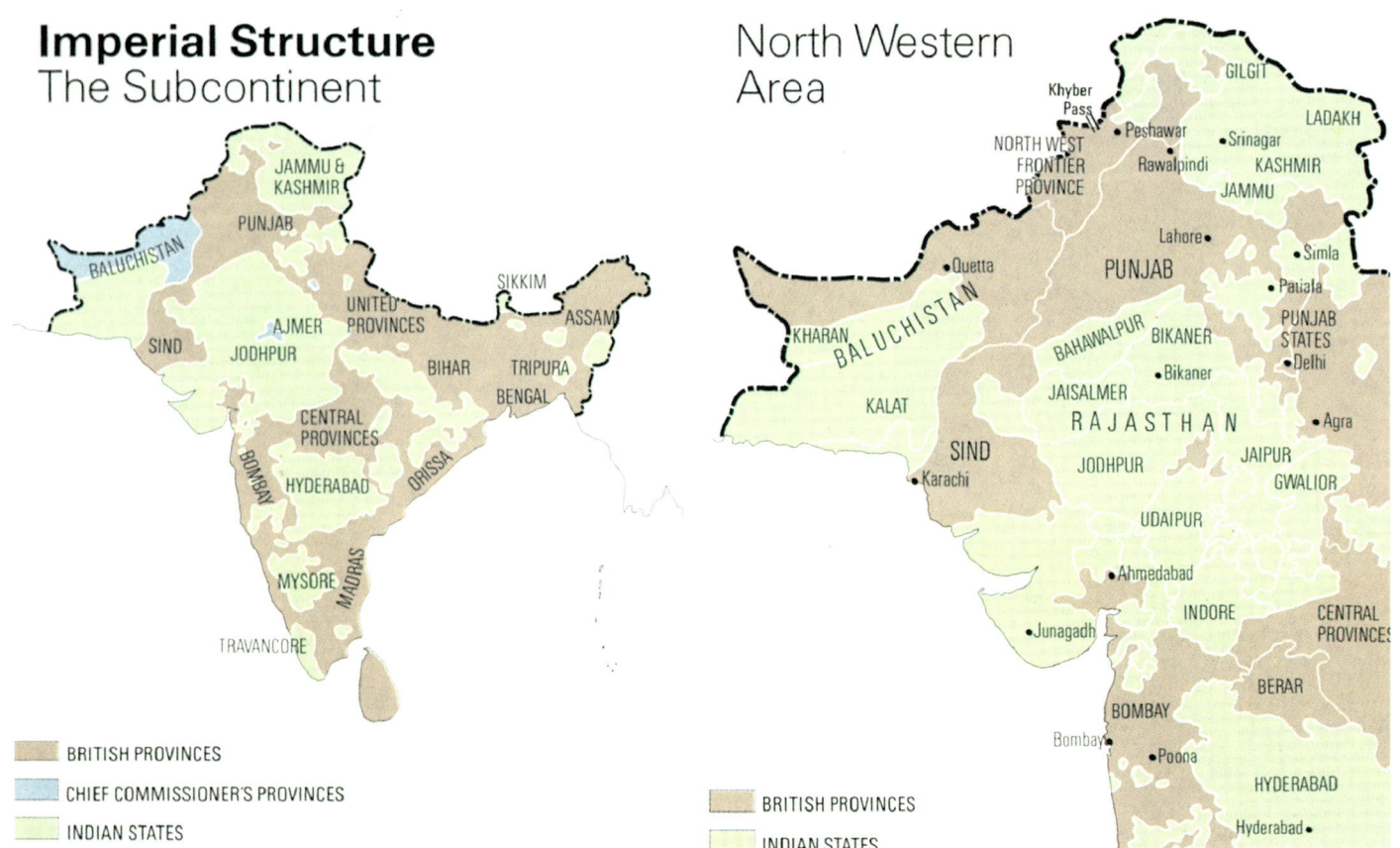

The War of Independence (or Indian Mutiny) of 1857 raised intense feeling on both sides and jolted Victorian England. It sounded the death knell for the East India Company. Lucknow – illustrated here under siege by Muslim troops – was a major centre of fighting. Muslim feeling had been outraged by the rumour that pig fat was used to grease cartridges

The High Imperial Stage

By the middle of the nineteenth century, British rule in India appeared to be secure. Supremacy as the leading power had been established by the defeat of the Marathas in 1818. After the Second Sikh War and the annexation of Punjab in 1848, there was no rival left. But there were latent weaknesses that were to surface in the Mutiny and which later had a bearing on the partition of 1947 and the birth of Pakistan.

In the first place, the tradition that the armies of the East India Company were invincible had been shattered by the First Afghan War of 1839-42 and the disastrous retreat from Kabul. The Company's *iqbal* – habitual good fortune and success – was at an end. Equally important was a new and increasing arrogance on the British side which ranged from an insensitive disregard for Indian opinion by Lord Dalhousie, the Governor-General, to occasional acts of boorish rudeness by recently-enlisted subalterns. In the first quarter of the century, the best men in the Company's service – Metcalfe, Elphinstone, Munro and Malcolm – had studied Indian languages and had respectfully enquired into the religions of the Hindus and the Muslims. In the second quarter of the century this imaginative tolerance became much less common, while an increasing number of the Company's servants professed a narrow form of evangelical Christianity.

This was one cause of the growing tension between the British and the Hindus and Muslims. As communications improved with Britain, more frequent leave was granted. English books and journals and even the more frequent presence of English women, all combined to turn the gaze of the British homeward and inward instead of helping them to accept India as their adopted land.

Finally there was the philosophical attitude summed up in the word Benthamism. In England this rational, materialist and progressive approach to public affairs was tempered by the conservatism of the landed aristocracy. The men sent out to India were in the main of the middle class, and many of them had been taught at Haileybury (the East India Company College) what was then called political economy, strongly tinged with the Benthamite creed. There were many administrators in India to whom, as for Bentham, "the greatest happiness of the greatest number" was "the foundation of morals and legislation". They regarded hereditary privilege as an anomaly and the unequal distribution of property as an evil.

The application of these principles to India seemed to many Indians an attack on both religion and property. It gave equal offence to Hindu and Muslim. If the Hindu felt it an interference with religion to make "*suttee*" murder and to permit the remarriage of Hindu widows, the orthodox Muslim was hardly less disturbed by the attitude displayed by officers of this school of thought to *waqf* – land given as an endowment to a religious charity. Both were outraged by the eagerness to disallow the title of *zamindar*, a term which in most of India meant the holder of a right to collect land revenues from the cultivator and pay a proportion of it to the state. Such rights had often been granted to officials by Mughal emperors and they were often a family's sole security for the future, but they had not always been recorded in writing and the *zamindars* were looked on by the Benthamites as parasites on the community. This attitude threatened not only the rulers of princely states and great nobles but the much smaller owners of landed property who made up the army. In the same spirit and in the interests of progress Dalhousie made it his policy to annexe any state to which there was no natural heir and also any that, by his standards, was persistently misgoverned. Such annexations were widely felt to be unjust.

This was the background to the Mutiny in the Company's army. The trigger itself was strictly military: there had been a series of grievances over pay and allowances, due to pettifogging regulations stupidly applied, and to this source of unease was added the thoughtless introduction of cartridges greased with pork fat which were offensive to Hindus and Muslims alike. The cartridges were quickly withdrawn and that mistake would have been unimportant had it not been for the general feeling in the country that the British had abandoned their traditional policy of respecting the religions and institutions of India.

The Mutiny, when it came, was fought with severity and repressed with harshness; it left ugly memories on both sides. But the point to stress here is that the insurgents needed a figurehead behind which to rally, while the British needed a theory which would account for the shattering of their cherished illusions. When the mutineers fled from Meerut to Delhi, they compelled the unwilling old Emperor Bahadur Shah II to accept the post of figurehead. This enabled the British to believe in a widespread conspiracy to restore the rule of the Mughal emperor.

The period from the Mutiny until the introduction of the Morley-Minto reforms in 1909 began in a mood of estrangement between the British and most of the inhabitants of India, whether Hindu or Muslim. Against this the Queen's proclamation of equal opportunity for all appeared a pious intention of which the fulfilment was indefinitely postponed. It was a period in which the devotion of the British administrators to their work has seldom been equalled by any ruling class in the world. Ironically, with rare exceptions on the personal level, the work was in general negative or materialist. It was the duty of the administrators to keep order, to prevent theft and murder, to keep down the taxes, to improve the roads, to build railways and canals. In this they were impressively successful, but what were later called nation-building activities, such as education and the development of local government, took a low place in their priorities.

The prevailing spirit was still Benthamite but it was a Benthamism limited by extreme caution over interfering with the religions and cultures of the subcontinent, a caution based not on understanding and respect but on pessimism about the possibility of any rapid "improvement", that is, Europeanisation. While a cold impartiality was the official creed, it was the Muslims who in the period immediately after the Mutiny were regarded with the greater suspicion. It was from the Mughal emperors that India had been won; it had been to restore the Mughal empire that the great conspiracy of 1857 had been hatched.

On the Muslim side, the realisation was only slowly growing that the Benthamite creed of progress must operate to their disadvantage. The greatest happiness of the greatest number can hardly appeal to a people who form a minority of one in four. Freedom of opportunity came more and more to mean opportunity for the man who could pass examinations, and in western education the Hindus had already a long start. Though the Hindu social structure is tightly compartmentalised, the pantheistic nature of the Hindu religion enables it to accept ideas from all sources. In Hinduism, there are two sides to every truth. Islam on the contrary is the religion of a book and a prophet; it is strictly monotheistic and its theology is exactly defined and its ethics systematised. It is not surprising that most Muslims were still resisting any approach to education that was not based on the Quran and the Islamic tradition, at a time when Raja Ram Mohan Roy was beginning to encourage Hindus to learn all they could from the West.

Ram Mohan Roy began his life's work in 1814. It was nearly fifty years later that a leader of equal intellectual stature began to give similar advice to Muslims. Before the time of Sir Syed Ahmad Khan of Delhi there had been moments of revival within Indian Islam – the Barelvi movement, led by Sayyid Ahmad Barelvi, and the Faraidhi movement but his influence was far more widespread than theirs. He taught that the Quran should be interpreted in the light of reason and science and that the security, peace and tolerance of British rule in India entitled it to be regarded as a land of peace, *Dar-ul-Islam*, as opposed to *Dar-ul-Harb*, a land of war, as the religious leaders taught. It followed that the Indian Muslims should learn all they could from the West, and the fruit of this resolve was the foundation in 1875 of the Anglo-Oriental College at Aligarh, which in 1920 became the Aligarh Muslim University. Sayyid Ahmad also taught that Muslims should stand aloof from the Indian National Congress, founded in 1885, which implicitly aimed

At the same time, throughout India, there was a shift of attitude among the British. With his new skills in the English language, it was the educated young man, frequently a Hindu, who was now regarded with suspicion as a rival. A genuine affection sometimes grew up in the army between the British officer and the frequently illiterate *jawan* (private), of whom about half were Punjabis, a major proportion of them Muslims, and nearly all of simple peasant stock. Belief in a Muslim conspiracy was replaced by belief in the martial classes. The *babus*, or clerks, might clamour for self-rule but the martial classes and the peasants would be faithful to the paternal rule of the British officer. This feeling at the level of district officer and battalion commander restored a warmth to British-Muslim relations. But agrarian debt in Punjab lent a bitterness to Hindu-Muslim feeling strong enough to survive Lord Curzon's Punjab Land Alienation Act, which aimed at keeping land in the hands of the traditional peasant classes.

This Act marked the abandonment by the British of the pure doctrine of Benthamite liberalism and a new readiness to protect certain classes against the results of unchecked economic competition. Few Britons believed that a Hindu majority would act towards the Muslim and other minorities

Zamzama, *made for Shah Wali Khan, was immortalised as Kim's Gun by Rudyard Kipling in his novel* Kim. *It was used by Ranjit Singh in 1818 against Multan*

The Koh-i-Noor was taken from Lahore and presented to QueenVictoria. It formerly belonged to the Persians, Mughals and Sikhs. It is on display in the Tower of London

at unqualified majority rule. For Sayyid Ahmad this meant all that he most feared for Muslims. Majority rule would be Hindu rule and that would transform India once more into *Dar-ul-Harb*.

One practical result of pure British liberalism was agricultural debt in Punjab. It had been the policy to make no distinctions between classes of persons, to allow the laws of supply and demand to operate unchecked, to enforce legal debts through the courts and prevent resort to violence. This gave money-lenders, almost always Hindus, the opportunity to lend money at extortionate rates to cultivators, who were frequently Muslims, to allow arrears to accumulate and in the end to get possession of the land. Individual British administrators at the district level could seldom do much to mitigate the operation of the legal system but their sympathies swung to the peasant.

with the impartiality they felt they had shown themselves. The protection of minorities was, they believed, just, and the fact that it also provided a useful argument for delaying the transfer of power was no reason for not making use of it. This new protective paternalism was a factor in the partition of Bengal, announced by Lord Curzon in 1905. The province was administratively far too large and there was much to be said for dividing it. The opportunity was taken to separate the backward and largely Muslim eastern areas from the richer and predominantly Hindu west. There was a storm of protest. The educated and highly articulate middle classes of Bengal claimed that Bengal possessed a cultural, linguistic and national unity which overrode differences of religion. The government's eventually giving way to this agitation did not reassure those who believed that the cultural and national unity of Islam would be threatened under majority rule. Constitutional development between the Mutiny and Lord Curzon's resignation in 1905 had been slow. One important step, the Local Government Acts of 1883-84, gave increased powers to District and Sub-divisional boards, which would henceforth elect a portion of their members. The intention of the Act was to educate local leaders in democratic procedure. It was a cautious move in the direction of majority rule. Again, in 1892, there was an increase in the powers of legislative councils. But by the time the next step came to be taken, the new mood of paternal protection had begun to replace the old assumption that advance, however cautious, must be in the direction of a popular involvement in which there would be no distinction of creed or caste. The Morley-Minto reforms of 1909 enlarged the legislative councils in the provinces and increased their powers. There was now an unofficial majority and most of the unofficial members were elected. The central assembly was also increased in size and powers, but here there was still an official majority, though a small one. It was another cautious step in the direction of parliamentary government, but a new principle was introduced. When discussion of these measures had begun in 1906, the Muslims had formed the All-India Muslim League and had begun to press for separate elec-

would Hindu clannishness be a danger to minorities but it would be hard for Britain to maintain ties of friendship with an India in which the Indian National Congress loomed steadily larger. On the political level, however, the honeymoon of 1909 with the Muslims was short-lived. The Sultan of Turkey was still the Caliph of Islam. In the days of Disraeli, to support Turkey had been a cornerstone of British policy. But after the Balkan War of 1912-13, it seemed that Britain had decided to acquiesce in the dismemberment of the Turkish empire. Few Indian Muslims yet realized that Turkey was on the way to becoming a secular state. Meanwhile, the confidence born in all Asians since the defeat of Russia by Japan in 1905 had brought a new urgency to Indian nationalism in all its forms. Syed Ahmad Khan had died in 1898 and Indian Muslims began to feel that his message of cooperation with the British and borrowing from the West was not sufficiently dynamic.

His place as an influential thinker was then taken by Muhammad Iqbal, who criticized the West for its superficiality and materialism, and preached the spiritual force of Islam as uniting all aspects of life and creating in Muslims a unity that was cultural as well as religious and which bound them together into one nation. It was this thinking that

Lord Curzon, Viceroy from 1899 to 1905, is pictured with His Highness the Nizam at Aina-Khana (they are seated together on the sofa). The Nizam, like most local rulers, found the growing spirit of nationalism impossible to accept

torates which would elect a specified number of Muslim representatives. The Congress opposed any such idea as divisive; the League insisted that an open electorate would be unjust. Both were right, and here, in embryo, was the argument that led to Pakistan. Separate electorates for Muslims were in fact created at the centre and in some of the provinces. It was paternal protection.

In 1909, the possibility of the British leaving still seemed absurdly remote, but talk of constitutional progress and of self-government was in the air and, at the personal level, many British administrators and soldiers continued until Partition to feel sympathy for Muslim views. They approved of the straightforward realism with which many Muslims spoke to them about the future. Such Britons felt that Islam, with its kinship with the religions of Moses and Jesus and its affiliation with Greek learning, was intelligible, while Hinduism was alien and beyond comprehension. Not only

provided the philosophy for Pakistan. But already, at the beginning of the century, there were Indian Muslims, mostly settled in areas where they were in a minority, who took the contrary view. They believed that they would have to live as neighbours with Hindus and that their best course was to cooperate with the Congress, exerting within it sufficient influence to make sure that Muslim interests should not be altogether forgotten.

The War of 1914-18 began with demonstrations of loyalty to the British by the representatives of a people who were still largely inarticulate. Indian nationalists, whether Muslim or Hindu, were bound to detest the autocracy and militarism of Germany and the unprovoked invasion of Belgium but that simple reaction was overshadowed, as the war dragged on, by the conviction that if the war was being fought for freedom they should have some say in how it was waged. For many Indian Muslims this was intensified by

Turkey's alliance with Germany. The Indian Army was fighting in Egypt, Iraq and Palestine against the Caliph of Islam; to some of the most active Indian Muslims, this outweighed other considerations to such an extent that they joined the Khilafat movement of the Ali (Muhammad Ali and Shaukat Ali) brothers and in the Lucknow Pact (1916) allied themselves with the Congress in return for recognition of the principle of separate electorates. The movement was ostensibly concerned with the safety and future of the Khilafat, that is the office of Caliph, but in the minds of the peasantry was inevitably associated with the word *Khilaf*, common in Urdu, meaning against, opposed to, on the contrary.

The movement lost its original grounds for existence in 1924 when the Caliphate was abolished in Turkey by the secular government of Ataturk. Even before that the alliance with the Congress had broken down. The announcement in 1917 by Edwin Montagu, Secretary of State, that the aim of the British Government was "the gradual development of self-governing institutions" sharpened the anxiety of Muslims, while it failed to satisfy the Congress. The delay before the inauguration of the new constitution in 1921 heightened both effects. From 1919 onwards the pace at which national aspiration would be realised was the overriding concern of political India. Under the leadership of Gandhi the decision was taken to launch a mass movement that would involve the whole people, down to village level. Such a movement under such a leader was bound to assume a religious colouring, and to most Muslims this was bound to be a cause of apprehension. From now onwards, Muslims grew in their suspicions of the Congress; they were notably increased by Gandhi's attitude to separate electorates and his claim to represent the whole of India. There was further bitterness in 1937 when the Congress refused to give seats in provincial cabinets to the Muslim League.

In the middle of the nineteenth century, attempts by the British to push India into a generalised progress irrespective of creed, caste and family had led to the Mutiny. Ninety years later, a series of steps, more cautious, but in the same direction, led to the partition of the Empire to which it had been their proud boast that they had given unity.

P.M.

The writer E. M. Forster observed the interaction of the British and the Indians in the late Imperial stage

The Cultural Encounter

The cultural interaction of the British and the Indo-Muslim community evokes many images and raises more questions. These images range from *Kim* to cricket: the camaraderie between British Army commanders and their Muslim adjutants, British colonels playing polo, Sandhurst-trained Muslim officers showing off their military slang, the English addiction to afternoon tea, the Savile Row sartorial ostentation of the Muslim aristocracy and the lively interest in sports like hockey and football among the Muslim youth. At a higher conscious level, there was the sedulous cultivation by the Muslim politicans of the quirks and practices of English parliamentary debate. More lasting has been the agonised learning and self-conscious use of the English language by Western-educated Muslims, punctilious in grammar and lacking in life.

Any listing of such examples, random or comprehensive, is bound to appear lop-sided. The Muslim community took more from the British than the British were willing or obliged to receive in turn. This was natural; in a colonial situation, there could not be a parity in the influences exerted by one culture on the other. Moreover, these examples betray the superficiality of the whole phenomenon. British influence during, or as a result of, the British raj, appears lacking in depth, if one subtracts from it the impact of Westernisation which is ubiquitous and is felt as much in societies that were never directly subjugated as in the formerly colonial ones.

An assessment of the penetration of British culture into the Indo-Muslim community will first have to answer the question: how does a Westernised (or Anglicised) Pakistani differ from, for example, his Arab counterpart? How much Westernisation is an irresistible consequence of the acquisition of science and technology and how much was brought about by the intimacy of contact between the rulers and the ruled? If the former proportion vastly exceeds the latter, what blocked the osmosis? Across what chasm were the two cultures encountering each other? If culture means the expression of a people's patterns of thought and feeling, were there no similarities between the two sets of patterns, no points of correspondence, on which some kind of a synthesis could be based? To answer the questions, one has to recapture the climate of the British raj.

The first phase of the encounter between the Indo-Muslim community and the British covers the period when there still existed Muslim sovereignties in India and the British were traders who eventually established themselves as vassals of the Mughals. Whatever were its political implications and its historical sequel, this was a phase when the governing attitudes on the two sides were conducive to some kind of learning from each other. The two main elements in the British attitude were a certain respect for the not-yet-extinct Mughal civilisation and a watchful opportunism stemming from an expansionist impulse. The Indo-Muslim attitude was one of curiosity sustained by a total ignorance of the maritime revolution. It was during this period that many an Englishman, wishing to advance his career in India, would seek to acquire a proficiency in Persian to the point of composing verses or ornate epistles in the language of the Indo-Muslim court.

However, even during this period when there were no

barriers of domination or servility, the two cultures did not interpenetrate. This was due to several factors. First, the British merchant or mercenary soldier could not be a leaven in British society upon his return home. Secondly, the Englishman brought with him bourgeois habits of thought and behaviour which, despite a common language, were incomprehensible to the Muslim feudal class with whom he had to deal. The gulf between the bourgeoisie and the landed aristocracy is unbridgeable. The one factor that could have narrowed it was religion: here was a department of life in which a sense of affinity could be established between Muslims and Christians because of the kinship of their faiths. Rut the record of British rule in India yields scant evidence that the Christian felt closer to the Muslim than to the Hindu or that the Muslim preferred the Christian to the idolators. From the English side, the explanation lay not only in the memory of the Crusades and the long historical rivalry between the Muslim and the Christian power, but also in the Englishman's entry into a social ambiance where the Muslim looked to him completely indistinguishable from

Government College, Lahore: Victorian architectural lines exemplify the imperial values prevailing under British rule. The high neo-Gothic of the Victorian heyday exemplifies the strength of British Imperial confidence. The College proved to be a major influence upon generations of the Muslim élite of the regional population

the non-Muslim. To the Muslim the Christian appeared, not as a believer in the Jesus who is revered in Islam as Allah's apostle, but as a follower of a Romanised faith garbed in an alien idiom and iconography.

If such was the gulf during the first tentative phase, it became immense during the second, when Muslim rule rapidly disintegrated and the triumphant British power convinced itself of its superiority, not only in military science, but also in standards of justice and diplomatic dealings, indeed in social and political intelligence. This coincided with the beginning of the industrial revolution in Britain, the acceleration of Britain's campaign of girdling the earth and, significantly in the subcontinental context, the coming of the evangelists and their determined assault on Islamic beliefs and sensibilities. The new temper was best expressed by Macaulay in his celebrated note on the place of English in India.

The Hindu, unburdened with a continuous literary heritage, seized the opportunity thus offered to assimilate Western science and scholarship. The Muslim, however, was still saturated with a complex tradition which had absorbed elements from Arab, Persian and Central Asian cultures as well as those drawn from the South Asian environment. In his cultural milieu, both the British missionary and the British educationalist appeared to be hostile, aggressive intruders, threatening the Muslim's intellectual displacement. Decades later, the Aligarh movement, of course, took root and the Indo-Muslim community turned to Western education. But the result was no deep and lasting transformation of sensibility. This is evidenced in the domain of literature. Poetry being the Muslim's cherished art-form, a keen interest was shown in English poetical literature; but the Muslim studied it in isolation from its social context and detached from its links with corresponding developments in music and painting. He knew his Wordsworth and Tennyson but Turner meant little to him; he was acquainted with Donne and Milton, but not with Handel. English exerted a considerable influence on the development of prose and new verse-forms in Urdu and, more importantly, on the enlargement of its vocabulary. But what happened was no more than the application of a veneer – the grain remained stubbornly native.

The illustrative aspect of the domination of British culture in India in the third phase of the maturity of the raj in the mid-nineteenth century is a still unstudied field. What it shows is how difficult it is to implant categories of thought begotten by the social, economic and intellectual life of one society upon another and what reactions such implantation produces. The participation by the Indo-Muslim and the Hindu communities in the political processes and institutions of British India and the language of political discourse in the independence movements of both (with the exception of that under Gandhian influence) gave the impression for a time that a Hindu-Muslim *élite* had thoroughly absorbed the modes of Western political thinking. Rut it was an elitist political culture and it remained fragile. This is abundantly proved by political developments in Pakistan between 1950 and 1972 and in India after 1975. Howsoever evaluated, these developments were caused by the assertion of the native mentality by the power groups which have not internalised the disciplines of corporate behaviour that are the essence of Anglo-Saxon democracy. The gulf between the common Muslim and the common Englishman (in his own habitat) was vividly demonstrated in their contrasting attitudes to two such institutions, far removed from each other, as government and medicine. The depersonalised nature of both looked logical to the English mind, a bizarre phenomenon to the Muslim.

It would be uncharitable to decry that part of the cultural effort of the Indo-Muslim community which was launched specifically to make it respectable in English eyes. Its motive was a search for anchorage. To the degree that it sought to counteract that devaluation of the past which is one of the indices of colonialism, it too was a part of the liberation struggle. This is true even of the religious expositions, written in English, which sought to vindicate Islam in terms of the Victorian or Edwardian British middle class. But to the degree that its tone was exhibitionist, it was warped by the snobbishness which reflected a confusion of values and gave it a strong colonial odour. Unsurprisingly, its appeal is now eroded. This fact, coupled with the phenomenon that the specifically British culture today bears hardly a trace of the past imperial connection with the Indo-Muslim community, serves only to show the evanescence of a symbiosis which is not brought about in freedom between two peoples.

M.Y.B.

The Struggle for Independence

The growth of British power in the subcontinent led to the progressive erosion of the socio-economic life of the Muslims. The first blow was struck in Bengal when, in 1698, the East India Company secured the *zamindari* (peasant proprietorship) rights and followed it up by depriving the Nawabs of Bengal of the prerogative to grant *jagirs* (estates) or appoint persons to high offices. The Muslim aristocracy and peasantry were the worst affected.

The next blow came when, in 1765, Clive extorted from the figure-head of a Mughal emperor, Shah Alam (1728-1806), the *dewani*, that is, the right to collect the revenue and run the civil administration of Bengal, Bihar and Orissa. The Muslims were displaced from their position in Bengal's economic life. Their deprivation was, therefore, acute. The introduction of the system of permanent settlement in Bengal in 1793 by Cornwallis (1738-1805) dealt yet another blow to Muslim proprietary interests. Under this settlement, the lands of Bengal and Bihar were made over to the new *zamindars* (landlords), mostly Hindus, without any survey of the records of landed rights or even the boundaries of the estates.

The subsidiary alliance system under Wellesley (1760-1842), enabling him to extend the Company's control over the principalities that agreed to sign the alliance, the policy of their annexation or conversion into buffer states, and the doctrine of lapse and adoption, by which heirless rulers were not allowed to adopt heirs and their princedoms lapsed to the Company, were some of the devices which caused untold hardships not only to the Muslim landed aristocracy but to all the institutions, crafts and commerce which were directly or indirectly supported by it. It became difficult, for example, for the Muslims to maintain or endow their educational institutions. The Company resumed a large portion of rent-free lands on which *madrasahs* (schools) and other Muslim educational institutions were built. In certain cases, the Company also took over the Muslim endowments and diverted the funds to other purposes.

It was against this background of political decline and economic deterioration that two outstanding social and religious reformers appeared on the scene. Shah Waliullah (1703-1761) advocated that Islam was not merely a matter of belief and worship, but also a code of conduct affecting daily life. For bringing the people into greater contact with it, he translated the Quran into Persian – the first ever in that language – and thereby opened a new chapter in the history of Islamic studies in the subcontinent. His sons later translated the Quran into Urdu.

Shah Waliullah's work was carried on by his disciples, the most illustrious among them being Sayyid Ahmad Barelvi (1786-1831). He launched a movement aimed at the renaissance of Islam in the subcontinent and resistance to foreign domination. Declaring that India was *Dar-ul-Harb* (a land of war), he migrated to Afghanistan to organise his forces, and died fighting against the Sikhs at Balakot.

Apparently there remained no danger of an armed revolt against British rule after the death of Sayyid Ahmad Barelvi in 1831. But the revolt did occur in 1857 in the shape of what is called "the Mutiny" in the West and the "War of Independence" in the subcontinent. It was attended by excessive retaliations and soured the relations between the British and the Muslims of the subcontinent for a long time to come. To the British it seemed that the Muslims were mainly responsible for the revolt, as it aimed at restoring the Mughal paramountcy. In comparison with them, their Hindu collaborators appeared more concerned with local territorial gains for themselves than with the revival of Muslim rule over the subcontinent. Consequently, Muslims were suppressed by the British in every sphere of activity in the subcontinent, while Hindus were favoured and encouraged. Leaving Muslims under this severe handicap, Hindus entered the British-run educational institutions, joined government services and took to trade, commerce and industry.

To enable Muslims to overcome the trauma of the loss of their power and their resultant alienation, Sir Syed Ahmad Khan (1817-1898) sought to bridge the gap between mediaeval and modern Islam, and counselled the acquisition of Western education and the cultivation of scientific enquiry. He set up a Translation Society in 1864 which arranged for Urdu translations of English books on history, science and literature. In 1877, he founded the Muhammadan Anglo-Oriental College at Aligarh, later to become the famous Aligarh University. While, in the political field, Syed Ahmad Khan cooperated with the Hindu leadership on certain matters affecting the subcontinent, he projected a reading of the contemporary situation which denoted a clear separation of Muslim and Hindu interests. Speaking, for example, on the Self-Government Bill, he forcefully pointed out the danger of elections, without safeguards and on the British pattern, in a country where the Hindus and the Muslims were, in effect, "two different nations". For this reason also, Syed Ahmad Khan advised Muslims not to join the Indian National Congress which a retired British civil servant, O. H. Hume, had founded in 1885, and which was later dominated by the Hindu leadership. For the Muslims, he founded the Muhammadan Educational Congress in 1886 (the word "Congress" was changed to "Conference" in 1890), which held meetings in various cities and spread the message of Aligarh to all parts of the subcontinent.

The religious prejudice of the Indian National Congress was demonstrated when the Viceroy, Lord Curzon (1859-1925), partitioned the province of Bengal in 1905 which had become an unwieldy administrative unit. The establishment of a Muslim-majority province of East Bengal provoked the hostility of the Congress which launched an all-out agitation, compelling the British to annul the partition of Bengal in 1911. The agitation owed its success to the participation in it by Hindus throughout India. But it deeply affected Muslim political opinion. This was manifested in the steps that were taken by Muslim leaders to lay the foundation of the All India Muslim League at Dacca in 1906.

In the initial stages the League confined itself primarily to safeguarding exclusively Muslim interests, such as separate electorates and weightage for minorities in the central and provincial legislatures. But, apart from the annulment of the partition of Bengal, there were other concerns pressing upon Muslim consciousness in the subcontinent, which stimulated a widespread political awareness and involvement and led to the League playing a more broad-based role. Among these were the Turko-Italian war (1911) in which the British declaration of neutrality was viewed as a betrayal of the Turks and consequently of the Muslims. the Balkan war (1912) which was regarded as an attempt by the Western powers to drive Turkey out of Europe, and the refusal to raise the

Muhammadan Anglo-Oriental College, Aligarh, to the level of an affiliating university, which was interpreted as a determined British policy to keep Muslims from the mainstream of educational and intellectual advancement in the subcontinent.

In 1913, the League revised its constitution and thus included in its objectives "the attainment under the aegis of the British Crown of a system of self-government suitable to India". The change was to serve two purposes: to bring League politics into line with the nationalist movement in India and to compel the Government to revise its policy towards Turkey. This change was widely hailed by the advanced sections of Muslim opinion and persuaded Quaid-e-Azam Mohamed Ali Jinnah that he should enrol in the League.

One of the significant achievements of the Quaid, after joining the League, was to secure an agreement between it and the Congress on a scheme of constitutional reforms leading to self-government, known as the Lucknow Pact (1916). It earned him the title of "Ambassador of Hindu-Muslim Unity" and demonstrated his eagerness to come to terms with Hindu leaders in the vital interest of securing an end to alien subjugation.

The British responded to the joint demand of the Congress and the League by promising political reforms after the First World War. However, when the War came to an end in 1918, the Treaty of Sèvres (1920) was imposed on Turkey which led to the dismemberment of the Ottoman Empire. The Muslims had looked upon the Ottoman Empire as the last bastion of Muslim power. They launched a nation-wide movement in support of the Caliphate, known as the Khilafat Movement, whose chief protagonists were the famous Ali brothers – Muhammad Ali (1878-1931) and Shaukat Ali (1863-1938). Mohandas Karamchand Gandhi (1860-1948) offered to cooperate with the Muslims on the issue of the Caliphate and started *satyagraha*, passive resistance. The Quaid-e-Azam, however, was sceptical of the relevance of the issues that had thus been brought to the fore and questioned the feasibility of the Gandhian technique of civil disobedience and non-cooperation for meaningful political action. In fact, Mahatma Gandhi eventually called off the *satyagraha* on the plea that it had turned violent instead. Meanwhile, the Turkish Government itself abolished the institution of the Caliphate.

The Muslims and the Hindus of the subcontinent had yet another opportunity to come to terms with each other when the British Government appointed the Simon Commission (1927) to review the working of the Montagu Chelmsford Reforms (1921) and to make recommendations for a new constitution for India. The Commission had no Indian members. The Congress decided to boycott it. The League was divided. Sir Muhammad Shafi (1869-1932), a prominent leader from Punjab, who had become the leader of a faction of the League, favoured cooperation, whereas the Quaid opposed it. The League session met under the Quaid at Calcutta and appointed a sub-committee to negotiate with the Congress. An All Parties Conference met in 1928 to draft a constitution for India. The report of the Conference was published in 1928. It was called the Nehru Report as the drafting sub-committees' chairman was Motilal Nehru (1861-1931). The Nehru Report came as a shock to the Muslims as its constitutional provisions virtually relegated them to the position of second-class citizens, permanently to remain a minority under the government of an unalterable Hindu majority.

Not to be deterred, Jinnah put forward his counterproposals to the Nehru Report in an attempt to give a coherent and workable shape to the constitutional scheme for the independence of the subcontinent. These, which came to he known as the historic "Fourteen Points", envisaged: a federal constitution; a uniform measure of provincial autonomy; an adequate representation of minorities in all elected bodies; including the legislatures; a system of separate electorates; not less than one-third representation of Muslims in Parliament; an assurance that any future territorial adjustment would not affect the Muslim majority in Punjab North-West Frontier Province and Bengal; a guarantee of religious freedom to all communities; a constitutional provision that a bill would not be passed if opposed by three-fourths of the members of any community in an elected body; separation of Sindh from Bombay; introduction of reforms in the North-West Frontier Province and Balochistan;, an assured share for Muslims in the services; safeguards for the protection and promotion of Muslim culture; the composition of at least one-third of the central and provincial cabinets by Muslim representatives and the condition that any change in the constitution must have the concurrence of the states forming the Indian federation. But the Congress was obdurate and rejected Jinnah's "Fourteen Points". His disappointment was acute and it was shared by Muslims throughout the subcontinent. "This is the parting of the ways," he said.

That was March 1929. In December 1930, Muhammad Iqbal (1877-1938), in his presidential address to the All-India Muslim League, articulated the proposition that Muslim-majority areas of the subcontinent should constitute a separate Muslim State. It was the first time that such an idea was put forward from the platform of a political party. Several contemporary thinkers (including some Hindu analysts) had, in some form or another, been advocating the division of the subcontinent as a solution to the Hindu-Muslim problem. Iqbal's idea of a separate state caught the imagination of the Muslims of the subcontinent. His poetry and philosophy had already kindled their enthusiasm for the pursuit of Islamic values in the context of the contemporary progressive society. Now he made them aware of the danger of the loss of their identity if, instead of lamenting the vanishing of their glorious past, they did not turn their minds to advancing their future prospects. Feeling that the Muslims of the subcontinent needed to be organised into a disciplined community and galvanised into preparing themselves for a decisive struggle, he singled out Jinnah as the one person capable of espousing their cause and leading them to their goal. Iqbal urged Jinnah to lead the nation.

Jinnah was a realist *par excellence*; he would not promote an idea unless it was translated into terms of concrete action in a specific situation. Between 1930, when Iqbal gave authentic expression to the idea of an independent Muslim State, and 1940, when Jinnah converted it into a national proposal, a number of developments occurred that promoted the idea of Hindu hegemony over the entire subcontinent.

Three Round Table Conferences were summoned in London by the British Government to work out a scheme for qualified self-government. The first ended in failure as Mahatma Gandhi, who had launched a civil disobedience movement, refused to attend. The second proved abortive as Gandhi, who came as the sole representative of the Congress, pleaded inability to accommodate Muslim demands, which were still far more modest than they eventually became. The third resulted in the British Prime Minister, Ramsay Macdonald, announcing the Communal Award (1932), which conceded separate electorates to the Muslims. It was followed by the passing of the Government of India Act of 1935 by the British Parliament.

Settling the fate of the subcontinent: Mountbatten (from the right, anti-clockwise), Nehru, Patel, Kripilani, Baldev Singh, Nishtar, Liaqat Ali and Jinnah at their meeting on 2nd June 1947 which determined the basics of Partition of the subcontinent and the procedures of handover of authority from Britain to the fledgling governments of India and Pakistan a mere two and a half months later. The decisions reached here led to the flight of population and to grievous slaughter at the time of the handover – and territorial problems, notably concerning Kashmir, which remain to this day

This British-promulgated constitution for India provided self-government in the provinces and envisaged their eventual federation, with Britain as the ultimate arbiter. Elections to the provincial legislatures were held in 1937 and contested by all parties, including the Congress and the League. The League performed well in Muslim-minority provinces, but not so well in Muslim-majority ones, where parochial parties had entrenched themselves with British support in varying degrees. Out of the eleven provinces, the Congress formed ministries in seven, while the League entered into coalition ministries in the other four.

The Congress rule in the Hindu-majority provinces accentuated the fears of Muslims. Independent inquiries confirmed reports of discrimination against Muslims and suppression of their culture. The Congress flag flew on public buildings; *Bande Matram* (a song from the anti-Muslim Bengali novel, *Anand Nath*) was made the national anthem; Hindi replaced Urdu; cow slaughter was banned; Muslim representation in the services was reduced; the *Wardha* system of education, which had pronounced overtones of Hindu revivalism, was sought to be enforced; Gandhi's portrait was worshipped and school textbooks extolled the virtues of Hindu culture. The Congress rule produced a deep sense of insecurity and resentment among Muslims. Meanwhile, the Second World War broke out in 1939, and, taking advantage of Britain's difficulties, the Congress demanded the transfer of power as a precondition to cooperation in the war effort. The British refused to concede the demand, whereupon the Congress ministries in the provinces resigned. The Muslims observed the day – 22nd December 1939 – as "the Day of Deliverance".

On 23rd March 1940, at the League session in Lahore,

the historic declaration, known as the "Pakistan Resolution", was moved by A. K. Fazlul Haq, the Chief Minister of Bengal, and adopted. "No constitutional plan would be workable in this country or acceptable to the Muslims unless it is designed on the following basic principles: namely, that geographically contiguous units are demarcated into regions which should be so constituted, with such territorial readjustment as may be necessary, that the areas in which Muslims are numerically in a majority, as in the North-Western and Eastern Zones of India, should be grouped to constitute independent states in which the constituent units shall be autonomous and sovereign." Endorsing it in his presidential address, the Quaid-e-Azam said: "To yoke together two such nations (as the Hindus and the Muslims) under a single state, one as a numerical minority and the other as a majority, must lead to growing discontent. Mussulmans are a nation according to any definition of the term and they must have their homeland, their territory and their state."

The Pakistan Resolution spurred on the Muslims of Bengal, Punjab, Sindh, Balochistan and the North-West Frontier into unprecedented political activity. They rallied round the Quaid, giving him unquestioning loyalty. A number of writers and thinkers expounded the rationale of the Muslim demand for a separate homeland. Chaudhri Rehmat Ali (1893-1951), a student at Cambridge, had coined in 1933 the word "Pakistan", by taking the letter 'P' from Punjab, 'A' from Afghania (by which name he preferred to call North-West Frontier), 'K' from Kashmir,'S' from Sindh and the suffix 'tan' from Balochistan.

The Congress reaction to the Muslim demand for a homeland was adamantly negative; Gandhi called it the "vivisection" of a sacred cow. Spurning negotiations with the League on the issue, it decided to intensify its campaign of forcing the British authorities to transfer power to the Congress alone. The war cabinet of Winston Churchill (1874-1965) sent Sir Stafford Cripps (1889-1952) to India in 1942 to negotiate with the Congress and the League leaders. Gandhi termed the Cripps proposals as "a post-dated cheque on a crashing bank". The Congress was not willing to wait until the end of the war. Since the Congress rejected the proposals, the League saw no basis in them for any practicable new arrangement. The Muslims, however, had the satisfaction that the proposals had at least implicitly recognised the possibility of a separate Muslim state through the provision by which provinces choosing to remain outside the Indian Union could form a union of their own. After the failure of the Cripps mission, the Congress launched the"Quit India" movement in 1942. The Quaid condemned the agitation and advised the Muslims to keep out of it. C. Rajagopalachari (1879-1972), a leader of standing in the Congress, attempted to convince Gandhi and the Congress to come to terms with Jinnah, but his efforts were fruitless.

Gandhi's "Quit India" campaign foundered in 1942-43, and there prevailed a kind of stalemate until the end of the World War. In the middle of 1945, however, the Viceroy was directed to convene a conference of the Indian leaders in Simla to formulate a basis for the setting up of a national government with the participation of both the League and the Congress. This too was unproductive because the Congress would not accept that the Muslim members of the proposed cabinet should be exclusively nominated by the League. Some weeks later, it was announced that general elections would be held in January 1946. The results of the elections gave striking proof that the Muslims ranged solidly behind the Quaid-e-Azam. In the Central Assembly, the League won all the Muslim seats. It also won a large majority of the Muslim seats in the provinces of Punjab, Sindh, Assam, and Bengal and a substantial proportion in the North-West Frontier Province. A few months later, the British Prime Minister, Clement Attlee (1855-1967), dispatched a three-member Cabinet Mission to India. It proposed a centre with limited powers and the setting up of three groups of provinces: the Hindu-majority provinces, the eastern, and the western Muslim-majority provinces, each group having the right to frame its own constitution. The League accepted the proposed agreement in the hope that the scheme would mean a peaceful transition to independence and a fully sovereign Pakistan would eventually emerge through a constitutional process. The Congress also at first accepted the proposals. But, later, Jawaharlal Nehru, the Congress President, said that the Congress would only enter the proposed Constituent Assembly, "completely unfettered by the agreement and free to meet all situations as they arise", and that the grouping of the provinces was not obligatory. The League's foreboding that the Congress had accepted the Cabinet Mission plan only to sabotage it, proved right. It was now compelled to revise its position and withdrew its acceptance.

On 20th February 1947, Attlee announced the British Government's "definite intentions to take necessary steps to effect the transfer of power to responsible Indian hands by a date not later than June 1948." Lord Mountbatten came out as Viceroy, changed the timeframe and declared that the British would relinquish their authority on 15th August 1947. After a series of consultations with the Hindu, Sikh and Muslim leaders, he announced what came to be called the "Partition Plan" of 3rd June 1947. Under the Plan, steps were taken to ascertain the. wishes of the elected representatives of Sindh, West Punjab and East Bengal. Plebiscites were then held in North-West Frontier and the district of Sylhet in Assam, contiguous to East Bengal, These, like the consultative procedure devised for Balochistan, yielded an overwhelming vote in favour of Pakistan.

On 11th August 1947, the Quaid-e-Azam inaugurated the Constituent Assembly of Pakistan and on 14th August Mountbatten arrived in Karachi and formally proclaimed the transfer of sovereignty over its territories to the new State.

A.Q., S.R.W. et al.

On 14th August 1947 Admiral Lord Louis Mountbatten, last Viceroy of British India, made his valedictory address to the Constituent Assembly of Pakistan; he is seen here with the Quaid-e-Azam, Fatima Jinnah and Lady Mountbatten

Mohamed Ali Jinnah: A Political Biography

Of Mohamed Ali Jinnah it can be said, as of very few other men in modern history, that without him – him alone – the map of the world, the destiny of a nation, could not have been as they became. Had there been no Mahatma Gandhi, there would still have been Indian independence; had there been no Lenin or Mao Tse-tung, the Russian and Chinese revolutions would still have happened, though differently. But had there been no Jinnah there would have been no Pakistan, certainly not in 1947, though it conceivably might have emerged much later by bloody revolt from an Indian republic. His life and character are therefore of the highest interest to every historian and student of mankind.

Mohamed Ali Jinnah was born on 25th December, Christmas Day, 1876 (according to his own testimony, the records being defective), in Karachi, the elder son of Jinnah Poonja, partner in a family export business. His ancestors were of the merchant clan of Khojahs, from Rajkot. "A keen jealous spirit of competition is the chief trait in the Khojah character," pronounced the *Bombay Gazeteer* many years ago: "the Khojahs have a great regard for their religion, the tenets of which they observe faithfully. They are neat, clean, sober, thrifty, ambitious, and in trade enterprising and cool and resourceful."

Mohamed Ali Jinnah was an outstanding exemplar of that inheritance – keenly competitive, sober, thrifty, enterprising, cool and resourceful in all emergencies, whether professional, political or physical – and ambitious? "At the root of Jinnah's activities is ambition" wrote Edwin Montagu in his diary in 1914 when Secretary of State for India; but the word needs careful definition. Jinnah was certainly ambitious in his personal career, always ambitious to lead rather than follow in politics, but he never trimmed his ideals for personal advantage. His supreme political ambition was to lead the Muslims of India to securing their proper place and rights in an increasingly democratic society and in doing so to help lead all India to national freedom. Neither friend nor foe ever questioned his personal integrity: throughout his life it was his greatest asset, whether in the courts, in political assemblies or in his influence with the masses.

The young Mohamed Ali Jinnah went to primary school in Bombay and then to the Sindh Madrasah High School in Karachi. In 1892, when he was not yet sixteen, he sailed for England where he read for the Bar at Lincolns Inn, returning four years later. As a practising lawyer Jinnah became outstanding from the Bombay High Court to the Judicial Committee of the Privy Council, commanding fees which put him far beyond not only financial anxiety but also any temptation by the material fruits of office or place. Jinnah's legal training and his practice of the law deeply affected his political views and conduct. He was always a constitutionalist, believing in the supremacy of the law and deploring both revolutionary methods against lawful government and the suppression by government of lawful rights.

Congress Leader and Legislator

Jinnah's first appearance in active politics was in 1906, when he acted as private secretary to the President of the Indian National Congress, Dadabhai Naoroji, at its Calcutta session. Naoroji, with Gokhale and other leaders, was on that wing of the Congress which stood for constitutional progress through peaceful demonstration. Opposed to them were militant social reformers like Lokmania Tilak and Lala Rajpat Rai. Earlier, (Sir) Syed Ahmad Khan, founder of Aligarh University, had ceaselessly called for educational uplift of the Muslims who had fallen far behind the Hindus in modern ideas, Western education and political consciousness – coupled with loyalty to the British Crown, which he viewed as their ultimate defence against the Hindu majority.

"He thought and spoke of Hindus and Muslims as two nations," wrote the historian D.V. Tahmankar, "with separate cultures and religions. If his theory is accepted his rhetorical question becomes unanswerable. He asked: 'Is it possible in these circumstances for two nations – Mohammedans and Hindus – to sit on the same throne and remain in power? Most certainly not. It is necessary for one of them to conquer the other and throttle it down. To hope that both could remain equal is to desire the impossible and inconceivable...' Jinnah did not openly subscribe to Sir Syed's theory until 1940, although he gradually gravitated towards it."

To those objectives and methods, for his people, Jinnah persistently adhered. The main events of that Calcutta session were the adoption of Home Rule *(Swaraj)* as the goal of Congress and the defeat of the moderates over the campaign against the partition of Bengal, which took on an increasingly revolutionary character. Immediately after the Congress meeting, on 30th December, 1906, the All-India Muslim League was founded. Its declared objects were:

> 1 To promote among the Mussulmans of India the feeling of loyalty to the British Government...
>
> 2 To protect and advance the political rights and interests of the Mussulmans of India.
>
> 3 To prevent the rise among the Mussulmans of India of any feeling of hostility towards other communities, without prejudice to the other objects of the League.

Two years later the Indian National Congress, in which Jinnah was already prominent, adopted a constitution of which Article 1 read:

> The objects of the INC are attainment by the people of India of a system of government similar to that enjoyed by the self-governing members of the British Empire and a participation by them in the rights and responsibilities of the Empire on equal terms with those members. These objects are to be achieved by constitutional means, by bringing about a steady reform in the existing system of administration, and by promoting national unity, fostering public spirit, and developing and organising the intellectual, moral, economic and industrial resources of the country.

In 1909 Jinnah was elected to the Imperial Legislative Council of India from the Muslim constituency of Bombay Presidency. Towards the system of separate communal electorates, Jinnah's attitude was for long equivocal. They had entered India's political system by a side door. The authors of the Morley-Minto Reforms of 1909 had no thought of introducing parliamentary government into India: they regarded the new legislative councils not as embryo parliaments but rather as *durbars*, means whereby the rulers could hear the pleas of their subjects and draw upon the experience of leading citizens. It was natural, therefore, to provide that the members should be chosen as spokesmen for different groups and interests, particularly the less strong or sophisticated. However, once the Muslim communal electorates were thus created they became a vested interest for the community and were regarded by most politically-minded Muslims as indispensable to their representation in due strength and by men who truly spoke for them. At the same time, communal electorates were a symbol of India's national disunity, anathema to nationalists who thought that they were bound to perpetuate divisions which must be healed if India was to become free.

The latter was Jinnah's personal view. As late as 1927 he declared: "I am personally not wedded to separate electorates, although I must say that the overwhelming majority of Mussulmans firmly and honestly believe that it is the only method by which they can be secure."

In the Legislative Assembly, Jinnah quickly made his mark as an acute parliamentarian. Among his important early interventions, he supported Gokhale's Elementary Education Bill and the Indian Criminal Law Amendment Bill, directed against illegal and violent resistance to the authority of Government. "Those men," he proclaimed, "who have a desire to disturb law and order are, in my opinion, the biggest enemies of my country and my people", a belief which became one of the root causes of his eventual break with the Congress.

and Hindu-Muslim concord as its necessary condition. Re-elected to the Imperial Legislative Council in the autumn of 1916, he joined eighteen other members in presenting to the Viceroy a memorandum, known thereafter as the Memorandum of Nineteen, on constitutional reforms to be applied after what we now call the First World War, a war in which he gave consistent if critical support to the Government, urging the Muslims of India, "notwithstanding their religious sentiments and feelings", to show "due control, restraint and moderation".

In 1915 he had invited the All-India Muslim League to hold its annual session in Bombay simultaneously with that of the Indian National Congress. This move, deliberately aimed at mutual understanding and a common front, was opposed by the League's more militant wing, but Jinnah carried the day by his personal authority, and annual sessions of the two bodies in the same place became the practice for some years. The most important occasion of all was at Lucknow in 1916, for it produced the famous Lucknow Pact recognising Muslim claims in a post-war democratic constitution.

The Pact's special provisions for Muslim representation

Jinnah at nineteen – a photograph he sent his father when he was studying for the Bar at Lincoln's Inn, London

Jinnah was the youngest Asian to be called to the Bar in London. He had by-passed university with intensive study

By 1910, Jinnah had already made his mark as an outstandingly able advocate at the Bar in Bombay

In 1913 the All-India Muslim League stated its objects afresh: "Attainment under the aegis of the British Crown of a system of self-government suitable to India through constitutional means, by bringing about, amongst other things, a steady reform of the existing system of administration, by promoting national unity, by fostering public spirit, and by cooperation with other communities for the said purpose."

The hand of Mohamed Ali Jinnah is to be distinctly seen in this: not only in the emphasis on national unity and constitutional method and in the deliberate echo of the objects of the Indian National Congress, but equally in the prescription, not of parliamentary self-government, but of "a system of government suitable to India" which might be one devised to share power between majority and minority communities – and possibly in the words "under the aegis", which implied that India's relationship to the British Crown, though unbroken, would not be one of subordination.

Jinnah's political efforts were now powerfully pursuing two interwoven lines, towards Indian national advance

included separate electorates, weightage in Muslim minority provinces, fifty per cent of the elected members in the Punjab, forty per cent in Bengal, and one-third of those in the Central Legislative Council. But the Lucknow Pact was much more than a bargain about Muslim claims; it was an agreement between League and Congress on a whole scheme of constitutional reform, moderate in character and practical in content. Had it remained, as it was intended to be, the cornerstone of Hindu-Muslim understanding on the road to *Swaraj*, the whole history of India, and Jinnah's life-story, might have taken a very different course. But, for a complex of reasons, it gradually faded and eventually vanished from the centre of Congress thinking, try as Jinnah might to keep it there.

Two key events in India happened shortly after Lucknow. In 1916 Mrs Annie Besant had founded the Home Rule League. Jinnah joined the League as its Bombay president. Explaining why, he said: "When representations were made and resolutions passed year after year by the National Congress, it was said that that was only the demand of a few educated agitators and lawyers, but that the masses were not ready for any such reforms. It was to meet that attack... to remove the misrepresentation, that they resolved that there would be an educational propaganda and that they should reach the masses and put the verdict of the masses not only before the bureaucracy but before the democracy of Great Britain."

This marks a fresh stage in the evolution of Jinnah's political philosophy. From early days his attitude had been essentially intellectual and elitist. This was partly an expression of his own nature – strongly individualist, proud, and conscious of his own forensic and political superiority. But he also feared mass propaganda as liable to excite mob hysteria and as chaining its leaders to crude popular slogans. Thus in method as well as ideology he found himself poles apart from Mahatma Gandhi, who was now beginning to be the dominant voice in the Congress. In his adherence to the Home Rule League he attempted a synthesis of the two approaches: the whole people must be enlisted, but not as mere sepoys and cannon-fodder in a cause; they must be educated to understand and share the ideas of their leaders. The Pakistan movement was later to bear the stamp of this conclusion.

In October 1920 Gandhi took over the presidency of the

By 1916, Jinnah had become the principal conciliator between the Muslim League and the Indian National Congress

All-India Home Rule League and at once set about moulding it to his own policies and aims. When he proposed to change its creed, directing it, by continuous propaganda, to "organise the people for peaceful and effective action to achieve 'complete *Swaraj*', and to take such action whenever necessary," Jinnah opposed the resolution as unconstitutional, moving that the purpose should be to "secure *Swaraj* for India in conformity with Article 1 of the constitution of the Indian National Congress" (quoted above). His amendment was defeated, whereupon he resigned from the Home Rule League. He had no intention of lending his support to a militant organisation serving Mr Gandhi's policies and methods.

The second major event was the announcement made by the new Liberal Secretary of State for India, Mr Edwin Montagu, in the House of Commons on 20th August 1917: "The policy of His Majesty's Government," he said, "is that of increasing association of Indians in every branch of the administration, and the gradual development of self-governing institutions with a view to the progressive realisation of responsible government in India as an integral part of the British Empire. They have decided that substantial steps in this direction shall be taken as soon as possible." The Secretary of State would go to India to confer with the Viceroy and others. Jinnah was among those who promptly welcomed the statement. At a joint session of their executives, the Congress and the League together called off passive resistance. When Montagu came to India he lost little time in meeting the chief political leaders. A famous passage in his diary records:

"We were face to face now with the real giants of the Indian political world... They (Surendranath Bannerjee and others) were followed by Jinnah, young, perfectly mannered, impressive looking, armed to the teeth with dialectics, and insistent upon the whole of his scheme. All its shortcomings all its drawbacks... were defended as the best makeshifts they could devise short of responsible government. Nothing else would satisfy them. They would rather have nothing if they could not get the whole lot. I was rather tired and funked him.

"Chelmsford (the Viceroy) tried to argue with him, and was tied up into knots. Jinnah is a very clever man, and it is, of course, an outrage that such a man should have no chance of running the affairs of his own country."

The Muslim League passed a resolution welcoming Mr Montagu's statement and calling for immediate introduction of a Bill embodying the Lucknow terms and a statutory time-limit within which complete responsible self-government should be established in India, "provided always that the principle of adequate and effective representation of the Muslim Community is made a *sine qua non* in any scheme of reforms". Jinnah backed a similar resolution in the Congress, and particularly stressed the need for a statutory time-limit. He strove to allay his co-religionists' fears of Hindu domination under *Swaraj*. "Do you think that the Hindu statesmen, with their intellect, with their past history, would ever think of – when they get self-government – enforcing a measure by ballot box? Then what is there to fear?" Jinnah's experience had been among men like Gokhale, Bannerjee, Motilal Nehru, Tej Bahadur Sapru, who took a wide, tolerant and historical view of politics.

The Indian political scene was now confused by two memorable developments. The first was the Khilafat movement, directed against the British Government for its complicity in the post-war threats to the Ottoman Caliphate and in the handing-over of former Turkish territory to non-Muslim rule in the shape of League of Nations Mandates. The movement was soon espoused by Gandhi, out of genuine or calculated sympathy with the Muslim cause, and became a national rather than a communal agitation. The second development was the setting-up of the Rowlatt Committee on measures to deal with "criminal conspiracies", followed by the so-called Rowlatt Bills creating new offences, providing for detention without trial, and restricting civil liberties. In Council debate Jinnah solemnly warned the Government: "If these measures are passed you will create in this country from one end to the other a discontent and agitation the like of which you have not witnessed."

The Montagu-Chelmsford constitutional reform proposals, published on 8th July 1918, were met by Jinnah with faintly approving criticism. "I for one," he said, "look more to the principles and essentials of a scheme rather than to its framework" – an attitude so markedly repeated in the claim for Pakistan between 1940 and 1947. The Lucknow Pact, Jinnah continued, "is the crystallisation of Indian national opinion." The Montagu Chelmsford proposals, he said, were weighty, well considered and could not be rejected summarily, but needed important modifications before they became acceptable to the people. When they were debated by a Select Committee of Parliament at Westminster, Jinnah gave evidence on behalf of the Muslim League, and displayed, according to historian Khalid B. Sayeed, "a knowledge of constitutional law and parliamentary institutions which has seldom been equalled by any Hindu or Muslim scholar or political leader." The new Government of India Act, large parts of which survived in the Act of 1935 and thus in the interim constitutions of both Pakistan and India, was passed in December 1919. Gandhi had earlier launched a campaign of *satyagraha*, linked both with the Khilafat movement and with the cause of *Swaraj*, which had resulted in many riots and other disturbances, particularly in the Punjab.

On 13th April 1919 there occurred the massacre of Jallianwala Bagh near Amritsar, an event which did much to change the course of Indian history. Soon afterwards the Mahatma suspended his campaign, because, he said, the people were not yet ready for *satyagraha*, but he continued to whip up Hindu support for the Khilafat agitation, which was led by Maulana Muhammad Ali and Maulana Shaukat Ali and backed by the Jamiat-ul-Ulema-i-Hind, the body of Indian Islamic scholars. In December 1919, meeting at Amritsar, the Muslim League passed a resolution calling for non-cooperation on the Khilafat issue; in September 1920 it met in special session at Calcutta, alongside the Congress, with Jinnah as President. He denounced the "outrageous" terms imposed upon Turkey, and the "plunder" of the Ottoman Empire under the guise of Mandates. But he was not ready to call for non-cooperation, whose dangers he well perceived.

In committee of the Congress, he opposed Gandhi's non-cooperation resolution, which was supported by Shaukat Ali, Fazlul Haq and other prominent Muslims and carried by a small margin. If the Muslims were in two minds, so too were the Congress leaders, but the death of Lokmania Tilak, who had led a movement for "working the Reforms for what they are worth", left Gandhi and his programme in the ascendant, and when the Congress met in full session at Nagpur in December 1920 (again alongside the League) a resolution on non-cooperation was carried by almost unanimous acclaim. Amid the tumult one man "stood up to be counted" in opposition – Mohamed Ali Jinnah. Jawaharlal Nehru wrote: "A few old leaders dropped out of the Congress after Calcutta, and among these a popular and well-known figure was Mr. M. A. Jinnah... He had been largely responsible in the past for bringing the Muslim League nearer to the Congress. But the new developments in the Congress – non-cooperation and the new constitution which made it more of a popular and mass organisation – were thoroughly disapproved of by him."

Jinnah's disbelief in non-violent non-cooperation proved all too well founded. Without a uniting cause – the Hindus seeking *Swaraj*, the Muslims revival of the Khilafat – anti-government demonstrations often became communal riots. A rebellion of the Moplahs in Malabar in 1921 cost many lives. Finally came the horror of Chuari Chaura on 5th February 1922, when twenty-two policemen were immolated by a mob in a burning police station. Gandhi called off civil disobedience, an act already demanded by an All Parties Conference in Bombay of which Jinnah was one of three secretaries.

Both Hindus and Muslims were now split over the issue of taking part in the new constitution. C. R. Das resigned as President of the Congress because it would not rescind its boycott of the Councils. In a manifesto of September 1923 for his election to the Central Legislative Assembly Jinnah declared he was more than ever convinced that the right course was to send representatives to the Assembly. "I have no desire," he said, and no one doubted him, "to seek any post or position from the Government. My sole object is to serve the cause of the country as best as I can." He was returned unopposed, as an Independent, and in the ensuing session took a leading and constructive part in debates, especially on Indianisation of the Army, civil service reform, and the penal and criminal codes. In the popular view of him, his powers as a parliamentarian have been overlooked in the shadow of his public stature.

The Muslims were at that time in political disarray. The Jamiat-ul-Ulema and the Khilafat Committee were bitterly opposed to Jinnah's line of cooperation with the Councils, Maulana Muhammad Ali, then President of the Indian National Congress, denied the representative status of the Muslim League, and Jinnah openly attacked what he called "Muhammad Ali's antics". The Punjab being the centre both of public disturbance and of Muslim divisions, with characteristic courage Jinnah put his head in the lion's mouth by deciding to hold a session of the League in Lahore in May 1924, aimed at bringing about, "through and by means of the All-India Muslim League", a complete settlement between the two main communities, as in the Lucknow Pact. Only when the League became a well-organised body with branches all over the country, he said, could the leaders speak with authority and be able to effect a settlement acceptable to the Muslim people.

One obstacle to the organised solidarity of the Muslims had been removed when in March 1924 Mustafa Kemal Pasha (Kemal Ataturk) abolished the Ottoman Caliphate,

Jinnah was always immaculately dressed, reflecting his precision of movement and mind. He always took great care of the figure he cut: long before air-conditiong he would never allow himself to appear rumpled

and the Khilafat agitation thereafter faded away. Again the Indian political leaders pursued the will-o'the-wisp of Hindu-Muslim unity. Jinnah took part in abortive All-Parties Conferences in November 1924 and January 1925. Charged, after the latter, by Srinivasa Sastri with being a communalist, he reiterated his adherence to the Lucknow Pact and the Memorandum of Nineteen.

At the 1925 session of the All-India Muslim League at Delhi he moved a long resolution defining the Muslim attitude towards reform of the constitution. It included these words:

> "The following basic and fundamental principles must be secured and guaranteed, namely,
> 1 All legislatures of the country and other elected bodies be constituted on the definite principles of an adequate and effective representation of the minorities in every province without reducing the majority in any province to a minority or even to equality;
> 2 Representation of communal groups shall continue to be by means of separate electorates as at present, provided that it shall be open to any community at any time to abandon its separate electorates in favour of a joint electorate;
> 3 Any territorial redistribution that might at any time be necessary shall not in any way affect the Muslim majority in the Punjab, Bengal and North-West Frontier Province;
> 4 Full religious liberty, that is, liberty of belief, worship, observances, propaganda, association and education shall be guaranteed to all communities;
> 5 No bill or resolution or any part thereof shall be passed in any legislature or any other elected body if three-fourths of the members of any community in that particular body oppose (it) on the ground that it would be injurious to the interests of that community or in the alternative such other method is devised as may be found feasible and practicable to deal with such a case.

The proviso to the second point hinted at the possibility of a compromise on separate electorates, and in March 1927 a conference of Muslim leaders including Jinnah made what seemed a sacrificial offer on this issue. Provided that Sindh was made a province separate from Bombay and the North-West Frontier Province and Balochistan were given full provincial status, "Muslims are prepared to accept a joint electorate in all provinces so constituted, and are further willing to make to Hindu minorities in Sindh, Balochistan and the North-West Frontier the same concessions that Hindu majorities in other provinces are prepared to make to Muslim minorities... In the Central Legislature, Muslim representation shall be not less than a third, and that also by a mixed electorate."

Jinnah's feat in securing this resolution was the highwater-mark of his concessions in the search for Hindu-Muslim accord. In a press statement he declared: "The question of separate electorates is after all a method and a means to an end. The end in view is that Muslims should be made to feel that they are secured and safeguarded against any act of oppression on the part of the majority."

The Muslim formula was unanimously accepted by the All-India Congress Committee, meeting in Bombay in May 1927. But, as had happened before in India, political attention was distracted by a new event. In November of that year the Simon Commission on Indian constitutional reform was appointed. Jinnah instantly led a move among Indian leaders of all persuasions to boycott the Commission because it included no single Indian member, drafting a manifesto which was signed, at his invitation, by almost all the most prominent of them.

The year 1928 was a fatal one for Hindu-Muslim unity and marked a turning-point in Jinnah's political life-story.

An All-Parties Conference appointed a committee under Pandit Motilal Nehru "to consider the principles of a constitution for India". On two vital points it rejected the claims of the Muslims – to one-third of the seats in the central legislature and to reposing residuary powers with the provinces. Nevertheless Jinnah appealed for calm, and saved his fire for the All-Parties Convention which was to be held in Calcutta in December to consider the Nehru Report.

There, a sub-committee first rejected all three amendments put up by the League emissaries. Nevertheless Jinnah moved them again in general session on 28th December. The sagacious if sometimes cynical old Liberal leader Tej Bahadur Sapru followed him. There was no reason, he said, why the Muslim demand for thirty-three per cent at the centre instead of the existing twenty seven per cent should be resisted. If Jinnah, whom he had known intimately for fifteen years, was "a spoilt child", he was prepared to say "give him what he wants and be finished with it. I am going to ask him to be reasonable, but we must, as practical statesmen, try to solve the problem." M. R. Jayakar latched on to Sapru's half disdainful phrase about Jinnah: "I can assure you that he comes before us today neither as a naughty boy nor as a spoilt child but as a fearless and lucid advocate of the small minority of Muslims whose claims he has put forward": his proposals would only revive the "violent and arrogant claims" of Jayakar's Hindu Mahasabha friends. After Jinnah had replied to the debate in measured terms, calling Jayakar's warning an ultimatum by the Mahasabha, his amendments were put to the vote and all rejected. "If we do not settle this question today," Jinnah had said in his peroration, "we shall have to settle it tomorrow... Let us part as friends."

Jinnah must have had great cause for despondency at this moment. Not only had his bid for unity failed, but his own Muslims were divided – some for the Nehru Report, some for Jinnah's position, others intransigent. In an effort to rally them he formulated his famous Fourteen Points. The first two called for a federal form of constitution with residuary powers vested in the provinces, and for a uniform measure of autonomy for all provinces. The next six repeated the language of the League's resolution of 1925, recorded above, with the addition of a demand that in the central legislature Muslim representation should not be less than one-third. Points 9 and 10 dealt with the separation of Sindh and provincial status for the North West Frontier and Balochistan, points 11 and 12 with safeguarding the Muslim share in state services and Muslim culture. The last two points were:

> 13 No Cabinet, either Central or Provincial, should be formed without there being a proportion of at least one-third Muslim Ministers.
> 14 No change shall be made in the constitution of the Central Legislature except with the concurrence of the States constituting the Indian Federation.

The reason for using the word "States" instead of "provinces" in the last point can only be guessed at. Perhaps it revealed a sub-conscious shift in Jinnah's mind towards heightened independence for the units of an Indian confederation. At the Calcutta conference he had described the question of residuary powers as "by far the most important from the constitutional point of view".

Now yet another external development altered the background of India's internal conflict. A Labour Government replaced the Conservatives in office in London, and the Viceroy, Lord Irwin (later Earl of Halifax), went home for consultation with the new Secretary of State. Jinnah seized the opportunity to write a long letter to Ramsay MacDonald, the incoming Prime Minister, urging him, first, to persuade his Government to affirm without delay that Britain was unequivocally pledged to grant India full responsible government with Dominion Status; and secondly to invite representatives of political India to confer with His Majesty's Government after the Simon Commission had reported.

What impact Jinnah's letter had on Mr MacDonald's mind we do not know, but the fact was that on Lord Irwin's return to India he issued an historic declaration: "I am authorised on behalf of His Majesty's Government to state clearly that in their judgement it is implicit in the declaration of 1917 that the natural issue of India's constitutional progress, as there contemplated, is the attainment of Dominion Status." The Viceroy went on to announce that in due course the Imperial and Indian Government would invite representatives of British India and the Indian States to meet them in conference. Thus it is more than possible that the idea of a Round Table Conference, as it came to be called, originated with Jinnah.

Sir Syed Ahmed Khan was a "morning star" of Muslim political awakening in the subcontinent. Unless Muslims, he recognised, acquired Western education, they must forego power. His Mohammedan Anglo-Oriental College, founded in 1877, grew into Aligarh University.

Naturally he welcomed both parts of the Viceroy's statement, and he successfully urged the Muslim League Council to do likewise. The Congress, however, under Gandhi's influence, was now on a totally different tack. Its All-India Committee had laid down four conditions for cooperation with the Government: the Round Table Conference must be on the basis of full Dominion Status for India, the Indian representation must be predominantly from the Congress, there must be a general amnesty for political prisoners, and the Government of India must forthwith be converted into a virtual Dominion Government. Jinnah, seeing that these conditions would never be accepted, tried personally to dissuade Gandhi, and joined him in a delegation to the Viceroy along with Motilal Nehru, Vithalbhai Patel and Tej Bahadur Sapru. Of all the conditions, Lord Irwin could offer only the amnesty. A few days afterwards, at the Lahore session of the Congress, Jawaharlal Nehru declared that the time-limit of one year for the Government's acceptance of the Nehru Report had expired and called for a programme of civil disobedience. This was launched in March 1930 by Gandhi's famous Salt March. Jinnah's estrangement from the Congress and its policies was now virtually complete.

Talks between the Viceroy and Gandhi early in 1931 led to the Irwin-Gandhi pact of 5th March. Civil disobedience – which had achieved nothing, as Jinnah had prophesied – was called off, and the Congress agreed to be represented at the Round Table Conference. Its Working Committee decided in June that Gandhi would be its sole representative. Three months later he joined Jinnah and the other Indian spokesmen in London. Very soon he announced "with deep sorrow and deeper humiliation... the utter failure on my part to secure an agreed solution of the communal question through informal conversations" – which was hardly surprising when Jinnah's minimal claims on behalf of the Muslims were so incompatible with Gandhi's own ideas and those of the Mahasabha and Liberal representatives. At Ramsay MacDonald's invitation, all the Indian members of the conference agreed to abide by the Prime Minister's arbitral decision. The fact that the ensuing Communal Award went most of the way to granting the Muslim demands – in particular, one-third representation at the centre – was surely a tribute to the skill with which Jinnah had presented his case at the conference, in which he was from the start one of three or four outstanding figures.

An Interval of Disillusionment

At the end of this first session of the Conference Jinnah decided to remain in London, making his home there, practising his profession of law and "fighting India's battle in England"; he hoped to enter Parliament. Years afterwards, speaking at Aligarh University in February 1938, he explained his reasons thus:

"Many efforts had been made since 1924 to settle the Hindu-Muslim question. At that time, I knew no pride and used to beg from the Congress. I worked incessantly to bring about a rapprochement. But I received the shock of my life at the meetings of the Round Table Conference. In the face of danger the Hindu sentiment, the Hindu mind, the Hindu attitude led me to the conclusion that there was no hope of unity. I felt very pessimistic about my country. The Mussulmans were led either by the flunkeys of the British Government or the camp followers of the Congress. Whenever attempts were made to organise the Muslims, toadies and flunkeys on the one hand, and traitors in the Congress camp in the other, frustrated the efforts. I began to feel that neither could I help India, nor change the Hindu mentality, nor could I make the Mussulmans realise their precarious position. I felt so disappointed and so depressed that I decided to settle down in London. Not that I did not love India, but I felt utterly hopeless."

There were, however, other reasons, of which he never spoke. For the first time in this narrative, Jinnah's private life becomes a key to his public career. In 1918, at the age of forty-one, he had married a beautiful, dashing Parsi girl, Rattenbai (Ruttie), daughter of Sir Dinshaw Petit. So far as one can use the words of one so rational and self-possessed, he was deeply in love. But the incompatibility of temperaments was too great. Ruttie was extravagant and wilful, her husband austere and single-minded. His political ambitions could have meant no more to her than her social pleasures meant to him. "It is my fault," he told a friend: "we both need some sort of understanding we cannot give." After ten years of marriage, the two separated, and in the following year she died. (They had had one child, a daughter, who married a Christian Parsi and so forsook Islam.) Between his wife's departure and her death, Jinnah had suffered, with the passage of the Nehru Report, not only the greatest political setback of his life but also a blow to his private pride and contentment.

The Muslim political cause

Among Jinnah's visitors in London were Nawabzada Liaqat Ali Khan, who was destined to become his right-hand man and first Prime Minister of Pakistan, and his wife, who was also to play a valuable part. They and others pleaded with him to return and rescue his community, and the Muslim League, which in the Begum's words was "in a degraded state". Jinnah was also influenced by realising his inability to help India and the Muslims when isolated from his power base, and undoubtedly by reflecting on the need for far stronger organisation of his community, which he alone had the authority to inspire. But let him tell the story in his own words, again in 1938 at Aligarh:

"I kept in touch with India. At the end of four years I found that the Muslims were in the greatest danger. I made up my mind to come back to India, as I could not do them any good from London... Then in 1935 I entered into negotiations with the President of the Congress. A formula was evolved but the Hindus wouldn't look at it. When I felt I had exploited every method of bringing about unity I turned round to see what the actual situation demanded. I saw that the new constitution was coming... We in India have been brought up in the traditions of the British parliamentary democracy. The constitution foisted on us is also modelled more or less on the British pattern. But there is an essential difference between the body politic of this country and that of Britain. The majority and minority parties in Britain are alterable... But such is not the case with India. Here we have a permanent Hindu majority and the rest are minorities which cannot within any conceivable period of time hope to become majorities... The only hope for minorities is to organise themselves and receive definite and statutory safeguards for their rights and interests... If Muslims are united the settlement will come sooner than you think."

Now, with the Government of India Act 1935 about to go into force, the leader toured the provinces to study how Muslim political unity could be won. The task was formidable. In the strongholds of Punjab and Bengal, Muslims were participating in non-communal majority parties, the Unionist Party created by Sir Fazl-i-Husain and afterwards headed by Sir Sikander Hyat Khan, and the Krishak Proja Party led by Fazlul Haq. In the North-West Frontier Province the Khan brothers were leading the majority of the Muslims into the Congress. In Sindh they were split into many factions. The Muslim League everywhere was largely a party of few leaders rather than many electors. Nevertheless, in the provincial elections of 1937, League candidates had more success overall than might have been expected. Of the 450 Muslim seats, only twenty-six were won by the Congress, though a minority of the other successful candidates fought under the banner of the League.

At this juncture, with Congress Governments being formed in seven out of the eleven provinces, two strategic errors committed by the Congress leadership played into Jinnah's hands. First, Jawaharlal Nehru, then President of the Congress, claiming that the only parties which mattered in India were the Congress and the British, launched a "Muslim Mass Contact" movement to enlist Muslims into its ranks. Such action produced an opposite reaction. Every non-Congress Muslim group was incensed. Jinnah's response fell on ready ears. "There is a third party," he declared, "namely, the Muslims. We are not going to be dictated to by anybody. We are not going to be camp followers of any party. We are ready to work *as equal partners* for the welfare of India." (The italics are ours.) Those words mark a new stage in the Quaid-e-Azam's thinking. Equality between Muslims and Hindus in politics had clear implications. Majorities and minorities can never be equal, but nations are equal as nations, however large and however small. Not only was political equality to become thereafter Jinnah's tactical demand, but strategically the concept of two equal nations was already implicit in his outlook.

The second Congress *faux pas* was to insist that any Muslim brought into a Congress provincial government should sign the Congress pledge and take orders from the Congress. This produced a particularly bitter reaction in the United Provinces, but everywhere it signalled a determination by the Congress "High Command" that the League should be reduced either to a powerless fringe-group or to a communal subsidiary of the Congress. Again solidarity behind the League was seen as the necessary and only retort. In office, Congress Governments took, or more often countenanced, a number of administrative measures inimical to the Muslims. A cool if communally interested summary is that of Chaudhri Muhammad Ali:

"Muslims were denied equality of opportunity and were deprived of their rightful place in the administration. Symbols of Hindu raj and Hindu culture were adopted in government institutions... Schools began the day by saluting the Congress flag, by singing the *"Bande Matram"*, a notoriously anti-Muslim song, and by *puja*, or worshipping of Gandhi's portrait – a practice deeply obnoxious to the Muslims. Insistence on the protection of cows took forms which inflicted economic injury upon the poorer Muslims... A systematic effort was made to replace Urdu, which was the common cultural heritage of Muslims and Hindus, with Hindi."

It was typical of Jinnah, however, that at the Patna session of the League in 1938 he opposed a resolution which called for direct action against the "atrocities" by Congress Governments, and instead secured the vesting of authority for any emergency action in the Working Committee. He did not want a national movement to disintegrate in futile local disorders. The time for national demonstration came when, at the behest of the party's "High Command", the Congress Governments resigned towards the end of 1939. Jinnah called on all Muslims to celebrate 22nd December as "a day of deliverance and thanksgiving". The *hartal*, which very few Muslims refrained from observing, was also joined by many members of other minorities.

At the Lucknow session of the League in October 1937 Jinnah had an ecstatic reception. The following April, the League was claiming "...complete equality with the Congress or any other organisation." That claim was very soon to be asserted. In the same month Gandhi talked with Jinnah in Bombay but pleaded his lack of authority to commit the Congress to the pact with the League which the Quaid-e-Azam still sought, and recommended negotiation with the Congress President-elect, Subhas Chandra Bose. Jinnah's mannerly and incisive correspondence with Bose ended in deadlock. One cannot but reflect that there was reason and logic on both sides. The League stance implied that the Congress would negotiate only on behalf of the Hindus. The Congress said in effect: "We agree to negotiate a Hindu-Muslim settlement with the League, acknowledging its powerful status among the Muslims, but not as a Hindu organisation, which the Congress is not and never has been." This confrontation of incompatible claims was to bedevil all later negotiations.

Provincial Muslim Leagues were now being built up. A vital advance towards all-India Muslim unity had been made at the Lucknow session when Sikander Hyat Khan announced that he was advising all his Muslim supporters in the Punjab to join the League; and, in Bengal, Fazlul Haq followed suit. A provincial League conference in Karachi in October 1938 recommended the All-India Muslim League to review the entire question of a suitable constitution for India, suggesting that the Hindus and the Muslims were two different nations.

The annual session at Patna in December 1938 marked a complete and final break with the Congress. In an extempore presidential address, Jinnah, who again had a tremendous reception, declared: "The Congress has now killed every hope of a Hindu-Muslim settlement... The Congress High Command makes the preposterous claim that they are entitled to speak on behalf of the whole of India... Others are asked to accept the gift as from a mighty sovereign... We Muslims have made up our minds to have our fullest rights but we shall have them as rights, not as gifts or concessions."

In national politics Jinnah and the League concentrated their attack upon Federation, which many Muslims feared might be accepted by the Congress as a means to eventual majority government and as a preferable alternative to the two-nation concept. It was therefore a distinct gain for the Jinnah campaign when the federal part of the constitution was put into indefinite cold storage on the outbreak of the Second World War.

The war brought new opportunities as well as problems for Jinnah and the League. The attitude of the Congress drove it into the wilderness, leaving the political field wide open to the League and other smaller parties. The fact that nearly half the Army were Muslims, and Punjab was its main recruiting ground, gave the Muslim leaders extra leverage with the Government. Moreover, under pressure from many directions, the British, in desperate straits at home, were anxious to hasten a settlement of the Indian problem and therefore ready to make concessions both to the majority and to obdurate minorities.

While the Congress Working Committee, on the outbreak of war demanded as the price of cooperation with the Government that India be immediately declared independent and a constitution be framed by a constituent assembly based on adult franchise, the Working Committee of the Muslim League adopted a far less all-or-nothing attitude. It pronounced:

"Muslim India... is irrevocably opposed to any 'federal

In the late 1930s, Jinnah began to bring together central Muslim leaders under the Muslim League. He was already proving to be the political catalyst. Here, at Simla, he is seen with Shaukat Ali on his right

By the Lucknow session of All-India Muslim League in 1937, Jinnah had already won the personal allegiance of Liaqat Ali Khan (back row, one from the right). To the left of the picture is Khwaja Nazimuddin

objective' which must necessarily result in a majority community rule under the guise of democracy... Such a constitution is totally unsuited to the genius of the peoples of the country, which is composed of different nationalities and does not constitute a national state... The Muslim League condemns unprovoked aggression and the doctrine that 'might is right'... The Committee feel, however, that real and solid Muslim cooperation and support to Great Britain in this hour of her trial cannot be secured successfully if His Majesty's Government and the Viceroy are unable to secure to the Muslims justice and fair-play in the Congress-governed provinces... No declaration regarding the question of constitutional advance for India should be made without the consent and approval of the All-India Muslim League nor any constitution be framed and finally adopted... without such consent and approval."

When Jinnah met the Viceroy, Lord Linlithgow, early in 1940 he asked for five assurances: that Indian troops should not be used against any Muslim power, that the Act of 1935 should be declared obsolete, that no new constitution should be promulgated unless the consent of the Muslims had been obtained, that the Palestine question should be settled forthwith, and, finally that a Royal Commission should report on

Jinnah took great pleasure in the company of young people. Here he is with Punjabi Muslim students at Islamic College

the oppression of Muslims in Congress-governed provinces and Congress governments should never be reinstated. The Viceroy replied politely, but in effect negatively, or in vague terms. It was about this time that the honorific title Quaid-e Azam (great leader) became popularly attached to Mohamed Ali Jinnah's name. According to Maulana Abul Kalam Azad, its use was inadvertently propagated by Mahatma Gandhi himself. In a letter of 1st January 1940 to Gandhi, who had so addressed him, Jinnah wrote: "I thank you for your anxiety to respect my wishes in the matter of the prefix you should use with my name. What is in a prefix after all? A rose by any other name smells just as sweet. So I leave the matter entirely to you, and have no particular wish in the matter."

While titles meant nothing to Jinnah, power meant a great deal, and his consciousness of rapidly growing power led him to increasing hauteur in his dealings with others, whether the Viceroy or a British emissary, Congress leaders or Muslim figures whose pretensions he disdained.

On 22nd March 1940, the historic session of the Muslim League opened at Lahore – none had been held in 1939. In his presidential address Jinnah began by praising the work of the League's Ladies' Committee (which had been appointed at the Patna session on his initiative) in arousing political consciousness among Muslim women, who could play a vital part in the uplift of Muslim society. Jinnah believed implicitly in the emancipation of women, though he was careful not to force the pace for those Muslims reared in a different tradition. "Rapidly women were becoming politically conscious", Begum Shaista Ikramullah has written. "This was... directly encouraged by Quaid-e-Azam. He did it without saying much but in little ways, such as making Miss Jinnah his sister, always sit on the dais... The audience gradually got used to the idea of women being present and participating in public meetings."

In his speech at Lahore, after attacking the concept of a constituent assembly, Jinnah declared: "It has always been taken for granted, mistakenly, that the Muslims are a minority, and... these settled notions are very difficult to remove. The Mussulmans are not a minority. The Mussulmans are a nation by any definition... The problem in India is not of an inter-communal but manifestly of an international character... The only course open to us all is to allow the major nations separate homelands by dividing India into autonomous national states. There is no reason why these states should be antagonistic to each other."

Yet the dream of a common Indian nationality had occupied Jinnah's mind for half a century, before this awakening. As late as September 1939, only six months before Lahore, he was saying (in a speech to Osmania University graduates): "I still remain a nationalist. I have always believed in a Hindu-Muslim pact... One does not see much light at present but you never can say when the two communities would unite." The Muslim League proceeded at Lahore to carry, on the motion, ironically, of Fazlul Haq – the famous "Pakistan Resolution":

"Resolved that it is the considered view of this Session of the A.-I.M.L. that no constitutional plan would be workable in this country or acceptable to the Muslims unless it is designed on the following basic principle, viz., that geographically contiguous units are demarcated into regions which should be so constituted with such territorial adjustments as may be necessary that the areas in which the Muslims are in a majority, as in the north-western and eastern zones of India, should be grouped to constitute 'independent States' in which the constituent units shall be autonomous and sovereign... This session further authorises the Working Committee to frame a scheme of constitution in accordance with these basic principles, providing for the assumption finally by the respective regions of all powers such as defence, external affairs, communications, customs and such other matters as may be necessary."

The language of that resolution deserves close scrutiny. In the first place, it was not an ultimatum, but an expression of "considered view". It clearly envisaged a constitution in the singular for India as a whole providing for central conduct of major powers until they were "finally assumed" by the regions. It called for territorial adjustments. It contemplated at least two Muslim majority "Independent States" in the plural. Lastly, and most importantly, the looseness of the wording and even of the syntax must have been deliberate. Jinnah and his colleagues evidently did not want to be tied down to too precise a formula for "Pakistan". This is borne out by the fact that the mandate given to the Working Committee to prepare a constitutional scheme in accordance with the proclaimed principles, if privately attempted, was never discharged. Jinnah had no intention of diverting support for the main scheme into criticism of its details, which could only give ammunition to its opponents.

The Viceroy and other British authorities, therefore, viewed the resolution more as a political gambit than as an adamant demand, and in this belief they were encouraged by the openly expressed opinions of some leading Muslims who had formally subscribed to the resolution, but who regarded it as open to many interpretations. Prominent among them was Sikander Hyat Khan, who continued to promote ideas of Indian federation with minimal central powers.

On 8th August 1940 Lord Linlithgow issued a statement which became known as the August Offer. He intended, he said, despite the differences obstructing national unity, not to delay any longer the expansion of his Executive Council to include more Indian members and the establishment of a body which would associate Indian public opinion more closely with the conduct of the war. As to the constitutional future, no part of the Act of 1935 or its underlying policy was Viceroy, at the latter's request, certain "tentative proposals" for the immediate future. After flying his flag for the Lahore resolution and claiming that dividing India and creating Muslim States had become "the universal faith of Muslim India", Jinnah urged that the fullest war effort in India could be achieved only if the Muslim leaders were brought into the Government "as equal partners".

Those were terms which the Viceroy could not accept, but he came out bruised from the second important event of 1940-41 which concerned the last of them. Among those who accepted his invitation to join a new, advisory National Defence Council (Jinnah's proposed "War Council") were the

This rare photograph shows Jinnah with his sister, Fatima (left), and his only child, Dina. Jinnah's marriage with Dina's mother had been a true love match, but his dedication to political life put an unbearable strain on his much younger wife. Though they parted, after her death Jinnah endured a period of private desolation. His affection for his daughter and grandchildren was sustained to the end of his life: his delight in the company of children was evident

excluded from examination, full weight being given to the views of minorities in any revision. The British Government, Lord Linlithgow declared, "could not contemplate transfer of their present responsibility for the peace and welfare of India to any system of government whose authority is directly denied by large and powerful elements in India's national life. Nor could they be parties to the coercion of such elements into submission to such a Government." The British Government would assent as soon as possible after the end of the war to the setting up of a representative Indian body to devise the framework of a new constitution.

Jinnah and the Muslim League, despite their opposition to a constituent assembly, felt that they had gained two vital points. The whole plan of the constitution was open to change, and as a "large and powerful element" they had been given in effect a veto on any system fundamentally hostile to their claims. Points once gained were, for Jinnah, points never lost.

A few weeks before the August Offer he had sent to the Muslim Premiers of the Punjab, Bengal and Assam. A meeting of the League's Working Committee in Bombay, at which Sir Sikander was present, decided that they should resign. He protested that they had been invited as Premiers of their provinces, but Lord Linlithgow had made the tactical slip of writing, in a message to Jinnah, that he had asked them because it was essential "that the great Muslim community should be represented by persons of the highest prominence and capacity". Confronted with those words in a cat-and mouse interview with Jinnah, Sir Sikander accepted the League's ruling and resigned from the Defence Council. So, too, did Sir Muhammad Saadullah of Assam and, after a delay, Fazlul Haq, who in protest resigned from the League's Working Committee and Council; in December 1941 he was expelled from the League for forming a new Bengal party in coalition with the Congress and other Hindu groups.

One of Jinnah's devoted admirers, M. A. H. Ispahani, wrote many years later: "It is difficult to realise now what a tremendously bold and courageous step it was for Quaid-e-

Azam to take. Fazlul Haq was one of the giants of the Indian subcontinent. He maintained that he was every bit as good as Quaid-e-Azam himself and was not going to take orders from him. The same point of view was held by many other prominent men with the same personal vanity... This was unfortunate as it deprived the League of the advice and counsel of men eminently fitted to give it, and accounts today for there being so few to carry on the work now that the Quaid-e-Azam is gone. Quaid-e-Azam's point of view was that you could not have an effective organisation unless it was disciplined, and the organisation could not be disciplined if its members, no matter how prominent they might be, refused to abide by its rules. It was in its trial of strength with Fazlul Haq that the League really proved its mettle."

Thus Bombay, 1941, saw the emergence, by a decisive tactical coup, of Jinnah as the sole, unchallenged monarch of the Muslim League, indeed of Muslim India. The next major event to tax Jinnah's skill was the Cripps Mission of March/April 1942. The Cripps offer included the promise that immediately the war was over steps would be taken to set up in India an elected body to frame a new constitution for an Indian Union with full Dominion Status. The British Government undertook to implement such a constitution, subject to: "the right of any province of British India that is not prepared to accept the new constitution to retain its present constitutional position, provision being made for its subsequent accession, if it so decides. With such non-acceding provinces, should they so desire, His Majesty's Government will be prepared to agree upon a new constitution, giving them the same full status as the Indian Union..."

This was immediately seen by Muslims as a virtual promise of Pakistan if Muslim-majority provinces opted out. Moreover it was Pakistan composed of the historic provinces, which thereafter became Jinnah's claim.

Sir Stafford Cripps's negotiations were conducted mainly with the Congress leaders, who eventually rejected the offer. Jinnah bided his time, and when the Congress rejection was announced the Muslim League Working Committee followed suit, but in vaguer terms, and with attack concentrated on the long-term plan aimed at an all-India Union through a constituent assembly.

In August 1942, under Gandhi's inspiration, the All-India Congress Committee endorsed resolutions for a "Quit India" campaign, demanding that British rule must cease immediately, otherwise the Congress would use all its strength in a widespread struggle. Jinnah described this as "blackmailing the British and coercing them to concede a system of government which would establish a Hindu raj immediately under the aegis of the British bayonet". The Government immediately arrested Gandhi and all the chief Congress leaders and proscribed Congress committees throughout India. A few militant spirits in the Working Committee of the Muslim League wanted to follow the Congress into revolt against British rule, and presumably into gaol: Jinnah was at great pains not merely to defeat them but to convince them they were wrong – the League was not yet strong enough, he said. They soon had to admit their error. "Quit India", indeed, proved another fatal move for the Congress, for the League was left virtually in command of the main political terrain for the next three years.

In September 1944 Jinnah and Gandhi (who had been released on medical grounds) met in Jinnah's house in Bombay, at Gandhi's suggestion. In the exchange of letters which followed, Gandhi wrote that he was willing to recommend acceptance of the claim for separation in the League's Lahore resolution, subject to certain conditions. Areas in the north-west and north-east, where it appeared that Muslims wished to separate from the rest of the Indian family, should be demarcated by a Congress-League commission, and the wishes of the inhabitants then ascertained by a plebiscite. If they voted for separation, an independent State would be formed as soon as possible after India was free. Jinnah rejected this plan because it refused to acknowledge that the Muslims were a nation with a right of self-determination, required that all the inhabitants even of admitted Muslim-majority areas should vote on separation, and deferred separation until after India was free. No doubt Jinnah thought that he could get better terms from the British by holding out than by compromising with the Mahatma and perhaps having even that compromise whittled down because Gandhi alone could not "deliver the goods". He had gained not only national prestige as the equal whom the Mahatma had to visit and appease, but also the tactical advantage of having separation taken seriously by the Congress leaders as well as the British. With Jinnah, every salient won was held tenaciously as the base for the

"You have mesmerised the Muslims" quipped Gandhi to Jinnah, during their famous meeting in 1944. "You have hypnotised the Hindus" was Jinnah's reply

next advance.

Between the release of the Congress leaders after the end of the war in Europe in May 1945 and the arrival of Lord Mountbatten as Viceroy in March 1947, Jinnah's three-cornered struggle with the Congress and the British Government takes the form, in retrospect, of an essay in tactics. At Lord Wavell's Simla conference of June 1945, designed to set up an "Interim Government" with "equal proportions of caste Hindus and Muslims", Jinnah insisted that he should nominate, on behalf of the League, all the Muslim Ministers. Lord Wavell, refusing this because he wanted to include a Punjab Unionist, at once abandoned his efforts. Congress leaders were flabbergasted. The Viceroy, who in tactical boldness was no match for Jinnah, had sacrificed to the latter another vantage point: Jinnah's demonstration of imperious strength at the Simla conference was a shot in the arm for the League and a serious blow for its Muslim opponents, especially in Punjab.

The next tactical encounter came with the Cabinet Mission in March 1946. Meanwhile, Jinnah's power base had been vastly strengthened by the elections of 1945–46, thanks to prodigious efforts on his own part. Though the Congress won a clear majority in the central assembly, the League swept the board with all 30 Muslim seats. In the provinces, while the Congress had majorities in two of the claimed provinces, NWFP and Assam, the League won 442 Muslim seats out of 509 in the eleven provinces combined, and in the Punjab, reduced the Muslim Unionists to a rump of only seven members, against 79 for the League. Although a Unionist-Sikh Congress coalition continued in office in Lahore until Governor's rule was imposed in March 1947, the election results had fully vindicated Jinnah's claim that the League was the sole genuine spokesman of Indian Muslim opinion, even in Punjab. The Pakistan bandwagon was rolling, and shifts of allegiance after the provincial elections showed that more and more Mussulmans were ready to jump on it.

The Cabinet Mission's negotiations over three months were complicated and tedious, and need not be rehearsed here, save for one incident. Early in their course, the Mission confronted Jinnah with possible alternative solutions, as a basis for discussion with others: either a separate State of Pakistan, shorn of the non-Muslim majority areas of the Punjab, Bengal and Assam; or a minimal Indian Union, with equality for the Muslims, within which the five claimed provinces could form a federation of their own. Jinnah refused to commit himself, saying: "Let the Congress make a suggestion to me, and I will consider it." When it became clear that no Congress-League agreement could be established, on 16th May the Mission issued its own plan. This came down against handing over power to two entirely separate sovereign States, but envisaged a three-tier constitution, in which three geographical groups of provinces (North Western, North-Eastern and the rest) would frame their own provincial constitutions, and permissibly group constitutions, under the umbrella of an all-India constituent assembly.

The reaction of the Muslim League to the statement of 16th May and to the Mission's subsequent statement of 16th June which nominated a Government of six members from the Congress, five from the League and three others (non-Hindus), was motivated by careful tactical calculation. The League was the first to accept the May statement on the constitution (claiming that the basis of Pakistan was inherent in it) but waited to accept the June statement on the make-up of the Interim Government until the Congress had rejected it. The first manoeuvre threw upon the Congress the onus of rejecting the Mission's scheme, with its grant of a democratic constituent assembly; the second threw upon the Viceroy, so they thought, the onus of forming a Government which in the self-imposed absence of the Congress would be dominated by the League.

The Congress duly obliged. Not only was their acceptance hedged about with damaging footnotes, but Jawaharlal Nehru torpedoed the scheme when he publicly proclaimed that the Congress had committed itself only to the constituent assembly, which would be free to alter the plan, including the grouping, as it thought best. Jinnah at once protested against this "complete repudiation of the basic form on which the long-term scheme rests", and the League revoked its acceptance of the scheme.

If the first manoeuvre thus succeeded, the second failed, because the Viceroy put a different interpretation from Jinnah's on a promise about the Interim Government, and proceeded to try again for a Congress-League coalition. Jinnah and Nehru were unable to agree on the basis of the coalition, and Nehru formed a Congress-dominated Government, but in October 1946 the League Working Committee decided to join it, on the 6:5:3 formula. M. A. H. Ispahani has captured the critical moment: "It felt that ... it would be fatal to leave the entire field of administration in the hands of the Congress. The League's entry ... was a strategic triumph. The Quaid succeeded in putting the League into the Interim Government in its own right and without any commitment to join the Constituent Assembly in the way the Congress wanted it to join ... The Quaid-e-Azam told us that he had extracted the last ounce of concession from the Viceroy in difficult circumstances."

Thus an initial tactical setback was turned into a victory. When the League revoked its acceptance of the Cabinet Mission's plan and called for a programme of "direct action" and the renouncing of any titles received from the Government, Jinnah proclaimed: "Never before have we in the League done anything except by constitutional means. Now we are forced into this position. This day we bid good-bye to constitutional methods."

Direct Action Day was called for 16th August, when meetings would be held all over the country to explain the League's attitude. In Bengal Mr Shaheed Suhrawardy's Government went further than had been intended by Jinnah, who hated the risk of bloody violence, and declared 16th August a public holiday. Communal riots broke out and some 20,000 people were killed or gravely injured in Calcutta, the majority of them being Muslims.

The events of 1947 are too well-known and well chronicled to need recounting in detail here. Dramatic as they were, in a sense they were an anti-climax. The battle for Pakistan had in truth already been won. Not only were some powerful leaders of the Congress already reconciled to partition of India, but British Government policy itself made it inevitable. That both those facts were due to the implacable force of Jinnah's will is beyond dispute.

A statement of 20th February 1947, announcing the appointment of Lord Mountbatten as Viceroy, contained two vital points:

> 1 It was the Government's definite intention to take the necessary steps to effect the transfer of power into responsible Indian hands not later than June 14.
> 2 If by that time it appeared that such a constitution as had been proposed by the Cabinet Mission had not been worked out by a fully representative constituent assembly, the Government would have to consider handing over power either to some form of central government or in some areas to provincial governments or in some other reasonable way in the interests of the Indian people.

Those terms meant, in effect, that if the Muslim League continued to boycott the constituent assembly, and the Cabinet Mission's scheme fell to the ground, and if the Muslim attitude ruled out "some form of central government", the only road open would be partition, either by devolution of national power to provinces or otherwise. The trump cards were in Jinnah's hands. The time-limit was not the only change from the position in 1946. The Cabinet Mission had authority only to negotiate a settlement between the Indian parties: the new Viceroy had power to decide. That made a radical difference to the tactical requirements. Jinnah need no longer think of settlement with the Congress: his task was to convince the British rulers.

When Mountbatten came to Delhi he very soon perceived two crucial facts: the Cabinet Mission's scheme, which he had been instructed to resurrect, could not be revived, and, secondly, both at the centre and in disputed provinces, the authority of government was disintegrating so fast that a very quick solution was urgently necessary. His personal impressions of Jinnah, contributed at the request of the present author, are printed elsewhere in this book. "It was clear," he wrote in his *Report on the Last Viceroyalty*, "that this was the man who held the key to the whole situation."

After Mountbatten had drafted and referred to London his first plan for the transfer of power, he had his famous

Muslim leaders confer with Mohamed Ali Jinnah at Lahore on the Pakistan Resolution which first mooted the idea of Muslim independence

"hunch" that he ought to show it in strict confidence to Pandit Nehru, who exploded, protesting that it meant "the balkanisation of India". The fact that only Nehru was shown it, not Jinnah, has been seen by some as evidence of the Viceroy's bias and of his making unilateral last-minute concessions to the Congress. But, in the first place, it was pointless to show Jinnah a plan which Nehru had already vehemently rejected; in the second place, and more importantly, not only was the new plan inherently sounder than the first, but it was better in effect for the secure establishment of Pakistan, which might otherwise have been a bundle of fragments.

Mountbatten revealed the revised plan to a gathering of Indian leaders on 2nd June. He had taken it to London himself on 18th May and returned with Cabinet approval of it on 30th May. At the meeting on 2nd June Jinnah insisted on referring back to the Working Committee and Council of the League. Lord Mountbatten, who saw that the assent of the Congress was absolutely dependent on that of the League, could not wait for their decision. When he met the leaders the next day, he enacted a pre-arranged scene. Telling them he was satisfied with the assurances he had received from Jinnah, he turned towards the Quaid-e-Azam, whom he had asked thereupon to nod his head. This, with the faintest possible motion, Jinnah did.

Jinnah's silence was more pregnant than words. He knew that the last fateful moment had come when in the name of the Muslims of India he could either take the Pakistan for which he and they had fought such a hard fight, but on certain terms which heightened the tremendous problems of launching a new nation, or resume the battle with all its ardours and risks. The responsibility must have weighed heavily, as he looked back over the half-century of his struggle and theirs. Had he been right to lead them to this climax with its fresh ordeals? His indomitable courage could have given only one answer. The late Aga Khan said of Jinnah: "He and I never saw eye to eye, but I regard him as a very great man indeed. I say this because you get one or two opportunities in life when you have to take major decisions. Quaid-e-Azam had the choice of saying whether the Muslims of India should or should not have Pakistan, and he said, 'They will have nothing but Pakistan'. He took the right decision, at the right time. You can see his breadth of vision, how great he was, a man of tremendous determination and sense of purpose."

In the hectic days leading up to partition and independence the chief issue that concerns us here is the Governor-Generalship of Pakistan. Lord Mountbatten believed he had good reason to think that both the new Dominions would accept him as their common Governor-General for a transitional period while the dissection was completed and the new governments established themselves. It was a bombshell, therefore, when Jinnah told him on 2nd July that he had unwillingly decided that he himself must become Governor-General, though he urged the Viceroy to stay on as a sort of super-Governor-General for both countries. Lord Mountbatten's reactions are on record, as is Jinnah's cordial approval of his becoming Governor-General of India alone, when the super-Governor-General idea had been discarded as not constitutionally viable.

As for Jinnah's reasons, they are best given in the words of M. H. Saiyid, his principal official aide at that time: "Jinnah, who by temperament and lifelong training had a constitutional bent of mind, could not see how a common constitutional Governor-General faced with conflicting advice from two Dominion Cabinets could discharge his responsibilities properly. There was an even stronger political aspect. The powerful propaganda machine of the Congress concentrated on the theme that Pakistan was nothing but a temporary secession of certain territories from India that would soon be reabsorbed. A common head of state for India and Pakistan ... would strengthen this belief in India and Pakistan and throughout the world ... If the Quaid-e-Azam himself became Governor-General of Pakistan, he would be a living symbol of Pakistan's independent status. His towering figure would overshadow everything else. Perhaps Pakistan would lose some millions worth of assets, which the good offices of Mountbatten might have secured for it, but, in the struggle for survival that lay ahead, the moral factors would count far more than material losses."

There must surely also have been present to Jinnah's mind two other reasons, neither, for obvious reasons, ever mentioned by him or canvassed at the time. His political experience and skill had been those of a top leader, and he

Jinnah's relationship with Nehru was coloured by difference in temperament and their wholly divergent perceptions

Britain's penultimate Viceroy, Field Marshal Wavell, faced a tangled and difficult situation during the Second World War

Sir Stafford Cripps, first despatched to India in 1942 by Churchill's war cabinet, speeded plans for Independence

Jinnah addressing an Eid gathering in Bombay in 1946. He is accompanied by his sister, Fatima

could deploy them much better from the supreme post, driving and counselling Ministers, than as a Prime Minister involved in daily administrative problems and managing an awkward new Cabinet. The second reason reinforced the first. Jinnah was seventy years of age. During his last fatal illness he told his physician that he had been aware of certain symptoms of ill-health, including loss of weight, for a couple of years. In July 1947 he may have realised that something serious was wrong with him, but even if he thought only of the inevitably declining powers of one of his age he would have felt that a younger man should carry the day-to-day burdens of political office, while he employed all his remaining strength as constitutional head of state and father of his people.

Pakistan Achieved

So, on 14th August 1947, Jinnah took the oath as first Governor-General of free Pakistan. He and his Ministers were at once faced with immense tasks: setting up a governmental machine, finding and equipping the men to run it, completing territorial, administrative and financial partition, negotiating with Princely States, starting or fostering sections of industry and commerce, including state industry, which had previously been branches of all-India concerns or in departing Hindu hands. From the very first day he had to shoulder the major weight of administrative responsibility. At the Cabinet's own request, he presided over its meetings. Those tasks were the inevitable consequence of establishing a new national state. To them was added another of horrific character and proportions, that of coping with the flood of Muslim refugees from India and the counter-flood of Hindu and Sikh refugees from Pakistan. How far that result of Partition was due to the haste and the detail of the Boundary Award can only be a matter for fruitless speculation, as is the still-debated question whether inter-communal disorder and violence would have become less or greater if the date of the transfer of power had been deferred for some weeks or even months. Here all that need be said is that Lord Mountbatten himself had no hand in the Award.

On top of all that came the tribal invasion of Kashmir, the Maharaja's accession to India and the dispatch of Indian troops, and Pakistan's response, with all that followed. The available evidence shows that Jinnah did not know in advance of the movement of tribesmen through Pakistan territory to Kashmir, although his Prime Minister connivingly did, apparently seeing it as a means of coercing the Maharaja into acceding to Pakistan. It had been a grave

The Quaid was ill and dying when he attended his last public function, opening Pakistan's State Bank at Karachi

miscalculation, quite out of character for a far-seeing political strategist like the Quaid-e-Azam; for it foresaw neither the nature and speed of the Indian reaction nor the fact that if Pakistani troops were sent to confront Indian forces – or State forces if the Maharaja had acceded to India – British officers would have to be withdrawn from both sides, since it was out of the question for them to take part in war against each other or between two Dominions of the British Crown. It seems that Jinnah, who upon hearing of the tribal movement had urgently invited a Kashmir Government emissary to Karachi to seek an amicable solution, was shaken when he learnt the full story. The outcome of the Kashmir Confrontation of 1947 was disastrous for Pakistan and for Indo-Pakistani relations, and poisoned the Pakistan view of Lord Mountbatten and the British – though the British Government's attitude on Kashmir at the United Nations was regarded by Nehru and his Indian Cabinet as hostile and unfairly pro-Pakistan.

Kashmir and all the other problems of the time must have placed an intolerable strain on Jinnah's failing health. But he worked on without respite, as he had worked all his life. "For several years before his death," wrote his sister, Fatima, "there was a constant tug-of-war between his physicians and the Quaid-e-Azam. His physicians warned him to take long intervals of rest and short hours of hard work, but he did exactly the opposite, knowing full well the risk he was running, but cheerfully pursuing the task he had set himself, the attainment of Pakistan during his lifetime. After the establishment of Pakistan and the events that followed, he worked harder still... His frail body could bear the burden no longer. His unconquerable spirit helped him to ignore the dark forebodings, writ large in his failing health".

When at last he submitted to intensive medical care he was found to weigh only 5 stone (70 lbs). His normal weight in health, he said, had been 8 stone (112 lbs) itself extraordinarily little for a man of his height (close on 5 ft 11 ins). He had worn himself to a shadow. The diagnosis of the disease that was gnawing at him was ominous, but his sister had no hesitation in advising the doctors that he should be told. His fortitude was adamant. He fought to regain strength, at least enough to return to Government House in Karachi on his feet. But it was in vain. On 13th September 1948, Mohamed Ali Jinnah was laid to rest.

H.V.H.

Hidden Sadness

Jinnah has been described by many as cold. Those who worked closely with him knew differently. A former chauffeur, Mohammad Hussain Azad, (who later became a film actor) recalls of Jinnah: "... sometimes my sahib would give orders that a big cabin trunk be opened. It contained his dead wife's clothes and those of his daughter when she was a child. They would be taken out of the trunk and spread out in an airy room. He would look at them in silence, and grief would crease his fine and sensitive face. Suddenly he would remove his monocle from his right eye and, with both eyes moist, would murmur to himself, 'It's all right... It's all right...' and polishing his monocle with his handkerchief walk out of the room."

He married Ruttie when he was forty-one and she nineteen. A Parsi by birth, Ruttie took the formal name of Rattanbai on her conversion to Islam. Their love was deep enough for her to walk out of her multi-millionaire father's house taking only the clothes that she was wearing. Jinnah saw to it that she lived in the style to which she was accustomed. His papers listing his gifts to her – nearly a hundred items of jewellery with diamonds, emeralds pearls, rubies and agates.

Jinnah and his wife separated after nine years. She died a year later. She had fallen ill in Paris. Jinnah's close friend Chaman Lal telephoned Jinnah in Dublin. Jinnah was at her bedside two days later. He stayed with her nearly three hours, and arranged for her transfer to another clinic where specialist care would be available. Ruttie appeared to recover.

It was the last time the couple were together. For shortly afterwards back in New Delhi, a trunk call came through from Paris. It was Ruttie's father – the first time he and Jinnah had spoken since the marriage. Ruttie's condition was critical; Jinnah left the next morning for Bombay to board ship. But Ruttie was by then already dead.

Ruttie's last letter to her husband was written about two months before she died. The last sentence in the letter reads: "I have loved you my darling as it is given to few men to be loved. I only beseech you that the tragedy which commenced with love should also end with it. Darling, goodnight and goodbye."

H. J.

Rattenbai "the flower of Bombay" was eighteen when she married Jinnah, a celebrated barrister. Sadly, the couple's differences were too great and they separated after nine years

A Sister's Recollections

By Fatima Jinnah, who was the Quaid-e-Azam's constant companion in the last forty years of his life.

I have wondered at times if my family was datemarked by history. That my brother, Mohamed Ali Jinnah, was born on 25th December 1876 is known to all. What may be known only to our family is that his father was born in 1857, the year of what to us was our War of Independence but what the British dismiss as the Indian Mutiny.

At that time our family lived in Gondal, a princely state in Kathiawar. It was one of India's most placid spots. The Takhur Saheb of Gondal, in return for his loyalty to the British, continued to rule in all his splendour. It paid him to keep the freedom fighters out of Gondal, lest they should tarnish his glittering *durbar* and reduce his power over his subjects. So under his protective umbrella, the people of Gondal went about their daily business undisturbed by the political upsurge that had affected most of India.

The ancestral village of my grandfather, Poonja, was Paneli with a population of less than a thousand. He was one of the few in Paneli who were not agriculturalists. He owned some handlooms, on which he and a small number of workers produced coarse cotton cloth. His income placed him and his family among the well-to-do of that village.

He had three sons, Valji, Kathoo and Jinnah, and a daughter, Manbai. Jinnah, the youngest, was more energetic and imaginative than his two older brothers. He heard about Gondal where city life was brisk and business big. The prospect of working on the family handlooms did not attract him, the city did. His mind was made up.

Poonja gave his son little cash but much advice about circumspection in business. And my father was off to Gondal. It did not take him long to find a few profitable lines in which quick buying and selling helped him to add substantially to his original capital.

When he returned from Gondal to Paneli after some months, Poonja was happy that his son had done well in a big city. They decided that it was time for him to get married as were their two other sons and daughter. They looked for a suitable bride in their own Ismaili Khojah community and their choice fell on Mithibai, whose family they liked. A match-maker was called in, and in 1874 the wedding took place in Dhaffa where the bride's parents lived.

My father's business prospered and soon he was looking beyond Gondal. He had heard of Bombay where enormous fortunes were being made by big business families, and also about the growing port of Karachi, which he selected. There he rented a modest two-room apartment on Newnham Road in Kharadhar, which was the business centre of the city. The apartment was on the first floor and had a spacious balcony of wood and iron above the pavement, exposed to the cool sea breeze which came from the west throughout most of the year.

The new businessman from Gondal prospered, especially in transactions with a British firm, Grahams Trading Company, one of the leading import and export houses. With Grahams, my father did business mainly in isinglass and gum arabic. As his business spread abroad he also learnt how to read and write English, which was the language of the commercial houses he dealt with in Hong Kong and England.

The oral history of my family, as it is preserved by aunts and uncles, relates how my father devoted his full attention and care to Mithibai when he knew that she was going to have a baby. Both were excited and happy. My father's first child came into the world, a boy. It was Sunday, 25th December 1876.

My mother was devoted to Mohamed Ali, and although six other children were born to her, he remained her favourite child. Rahmat, Maryam, Ahmad Ali, Shireen, Bundeh Ali and I were her other children; three sons and four daughters.

Running a flourishing business demanded my father's full attention, but my mother was determined that the two of them should take Mohamed Ali to the shrine (*dargah*) of Hassan Pir in Ganod, ten miles from Paneli, for the *aquiqua* ceremony. As a child, my mother had heard stories about the supernatural powers of this holy man. She believed that a great future awaited her Mohamed Ali and she wanted the *aquiqua* to take place at an auspicious place like Hassan Pir's *dargah*, where, in traditional ceremony, her son's head would be shaved, and she, his mother, would make a wish, invoking the blessings of the saintly Pir for its fulfilment. My father said he could not afford to be away from Karachi for a month, but he soon gave in to his young wife's pleading.

And so, with their baby a few months old, they sailed from Karachi, to Verawal, a port in Kathiawar. The frail boat ran into a storm and it was with great difficulty that it reached Verawal. Days later, my mother told my father that in those anxious moments she had made a vow, that if the ocean did not swallow them she would stay a day longer in Ganod, to pray and thank God for His mercy.

At Verawal they hired a bullock-cart to take them there, a distance of a few miles. After the stormy sea voyage and a journey by bullock-cart the baby arrived in Ganod safely with my parents. Many of our numerous relatives attended the ceremony at the *dargah,* where his head was shaved.

After the *aquiqua* ceremony my father and mother took their child to Paneli. There my mother decided to celebrate the occasion by inviting the entire village to a community dinner. I learnt about the feast when I was a child: "On that day in Paneli not a single family lit a fire in their homes; their pots and pans rested on the kitchen shelves, and all because tiny Mohamed Ali was visiting his ancestral village."

After staying in Paneli and Gondal for a few weeks, my father and mother made the journey back to Karachi, where my father once again got absorbed in his business and my mother gave all her time and attention to her baby.

Such outbursts of extravagance as at Paneli were rare and usually instigated by my mother. My father was careful with his money, his family lived a simple life in which a close and warm relationship existed among its members. Although my father had quite a flourishing business, he thought of fortune – in the idiom of Paneli – as a capricious deity. It was on this principle that my father ran his family budget. This left a lasting impression on our minds as we grew up.

When Mohamed Ali was about six years old my parents engaged a tutor to teach him Gujarati at home. They thought that he was still too young to be sent to school, and the nearest school was at quite a distance from our house, a distance which they thought was too much to be covered on foot by a boy of his age. He was indifferent to his studies and he positively loathed arithmetic. He liked playing in the neighbourhood with boys of his own age, and was good at games. Through this proficiency, he became their leader.

However, when he was about nine, he was put in a primary school, where his confidence wilted when other boys secured better marks than he did. He developed an aversion to books and school, much to the disappointment of my father, who was anxious to give his son a good education. Mohamed Ali was gently asked by his mother to attend school regularly and to give serious attention to his studies. His father asked him why he did not devote sufficient time to his books. "Bapa," said little Mohamed Ali, "I don't like school."

"What would you like to do, then?"

"I would like to be with you in the office, and learn to do business."

"But you are too young for that, Mohamed Ali."

"I would do better in your office than at school." My father was a tactful person. He said, "Mohamed Ali, in my office there is strict discipline. You would have to go with me to the office early in the morning at eight, return for lunch from two to four, and then be again at the office from four to nine at night."

"I will do that, Bapa."

"But that will give you no time at all for play."

"I don't mind."

And so young Mohamed Ali started going to his father's office. He soon realised that all work there depended on reading and writing; all that he was fit for were minor chores which he did not like. Important decisions were taken by his father in consultation with his business executives. Nobody bothered to ask for his opinion. And he had no time to take part in games, which he missed.

After about two months, he announced to his father that he would like to go back to school.

My father replied, "You see, my boy, there are only two ways of learning."

"What are they, Bapa?"

"One is to trust the wisdom of your elders and to accept their advice."

"And what is the other way, Bapa?"

"The other way is to go your own way and learn from your mistakes."

Mohamed Ali listened attentively. He seemed to have made up his mind both to learn from his mistakes at school and to go his own way. His attitude to studies changed. At school he was no longer inattentive, indifferent – nor did he lag behind his class-mates. He was at his books till late at night. My father was impressed and asked Mohamed Ali's class teacher how his son was faring. He was told, "He is catching up fast, but is weak in arithmetic."

This worried my father as accounts were the backbone of business, and he wanted Jinnah Poonja & Co. to keep forging ahead when his son took over from him.

"Without arithmetic what will be my boy's future?" asked Father.

But my mother's faith in Mohamed Ali was unshaken. She said: "You wait. My Mohamed Ali will do well, he will be the envy of all we know."

When Mohamed Ali was fifteen my father decided to send him to Grahams Trading Company in London, to work as an apprentice for three years. There he would learn practical business administration, which on his return would qualify him to join his father.

The total cost involved was quite substantial, but my father decided that he could afford it. In fact, he prudently deposited the estimated expenses for three years with Grahams in London, so that Mohamed Ali should not be dependent on periodic remittances from a business which had its up and downs.

My mother was against Mohamed Ali going away for three years. After much persuasion she gave her consent, but with one condition: England, she said, was a dangerous country to send an unmarried and handsome young man like her son. Some English girl might lure him into marriage and that would be a tragedy for the Jinnah Poonja family. My father agreed and the quest for a bride began.

My mother knew of an Ismaili Khojah family of Paneli who were distantly related to her; their Emi Bai would be a good bride for Mohamed Ali. My father thought it advisable to consult their son. He agreed.

This was probably the only important decision in Mohamed Ali's life that he allowed others to make for him. He loved his mother as much as he trusted his father's practical wisdom. He behaved like an obedient son, as was the custom in those days, and in this way came to be engaged to Emi Bai.

Marriage followed; so, before his departure for Paneli, he left Sindh Madrasah on 30th January 1892, when he was in the Fifth Grade, and the school register records: Mohamed Ali Jinnahbhai left school to go to Cutch to be married.

The family returned to Paneli, where they hosted a lavish wedding. In this festivity the bridegroom played a minor role. The elders had greater prominence. Mohamed Ali was hardly sixteen and had never seen the girl he was to marry. He was moved to the centre of the stage only on the day of the wedding. The village *maulvi* performed the *nikah* ceremony, recited appropriate verses from the Holy Quran, and Mohamed Ali and Emi Bai were now husband and wife. Emi Bai returned to Karachi to live with the Jinnahbhai family there.

My mother grew quieter as the time approached for her son to leave for England. She had, of course, reconciled herself to his going. When he was leaving, she told Mohamed Ali that she had given her consent because "I am sure this visit to England will do you good and help make you an important man. This has been my vision for your future. I will not live to see you return from England, but God will look after you. He will make my wishes come true." And she broke down, sobbing.

Mohamed Ali, too, was overcome, and he quietly held his mother in a farewell embrace for a long time.

Grahams Trading Company, which had its office near Threadneedle Street, looked after its young apprentice as the son of one of their business friends in Karachi. Mohamed Ali found a room, as a paying guest, with Mrs F. E. Page-Drake, at 35 Russell Road, Kensington, opposite the site on which the Olympia building was constructed half a century later. The London County Council, some years ago, put a plaque on this building, stating that Mohamed Ali Jinnah, Founder of Pakistan, lived there.

My brother wanted to learn as much as he could in England, apart from his work at Grahams. He went through his morning paper before breakfast, reading avidly about the activities of the leaders who dominated the political scene in England, and their speeches in and outside Parliament. Wherever he went, he heard people talk about these leaders. But he was buried under the ledgers and invoices at Grahams and he was not now looking forward to the drabness of his father's business after such a dull apprenticeship. It was not a challenge he would rise to meet. Money, he agreed, was important in life, but that alone would not equip him for the fuller life he wanted to lead.

He began to think about preparing for another career in which he would be independent. As he read about the lives of the great contemporary and past leaders in English public life he noted that many of them had studied for the Bar, and that their knowledge of law had stood them in good stead in public life.

He began to waver between two alternatives; to continue as an apprentice with Grahams or to become a barrister. "It did not take me long to decide that I should prepare myself for the Bar," he told me. "Fortunately for me, that year was the last when one could obtain admission to the Inns of Court by passing an examination known at that time as 'Little Go'. If I did not take my chance immediately, it would take me two additional years to be called to the Bar. So I decided to give up my apprenticeship with Graham's and, pass 'Little Go', and I began to study hard to get through the examination."

This was a turning point in his life. From ledgers he turned to law books. He must have worked hard (to live down his past record) because he passed 'Little Go' with credit and enrolled at Lincoln's Inn.

But why Lincoln's Inn, I had asked. He said, "I was so sure that I would get through 'Little Go' that I started visiting the Inns of Court and meeting students studying there. After my enquiries and discussions with them I decided on an Inn other than Lincoln's. But then I saw the name of our great Prophet engraved on the main entrance of Lincoln's Inn among the greatest law-givers of the world. So I made a *minnat* that I would join Lincoln's Inn if I got through 'Little Go'. This vow strengthened my resolve to pass the examination."

When my father had learnt from his son that he was joining Lincoln's Inn, and that it would take him three years to be a fully-fledged barrister, he ordered him to abandon this career and to return home immediately. Mohamed Ali wrote back, pleading with his father to allow him to remain in London and to complete his studies for the Bar. He even said that he would not ask for any more money; he would work while studying, and spend as little as possible. Although my father was not happy at the action of his headstrong son, he reconciled himself to the situation and hoped and prayed for the best.

Not long after Mohamed Ali left Karachi for England, his wife, Emi Bai, died. He had not known his child-wife for very long, so he could not have been overcome with as much grief as he was when my mother died, while giving birth to my youngest brother, Bundeh Ali. He was then at Lincoln's Inn and I know that he broke down and wept for hours for his tender mother, whom he loved more than anything else in the world. He was sensitive by nature, and because he tried to hide his emotions, he suffered intensely. Her premonition had come true; she had died before his return from London.

After the death of my mother nothing seemed to go right for my father. He suffered one business setback after another. He aged prematurely, and he had six children, some still very young, to look after. He wrote to Mohamed Ali hinting that things were going badly. In reply, Mohamed Ali said his father should not worry, he would retrieve everything on his return.

Mohamed Ali had decided that without completing his studies he could not restore his family's fortunes. He drove himself harder to start life anew for himself and his family. Perhaps, as a gesture of defiance, or acceptance of contemporary realities which demanded a break with the past, he changed his name to M. A. Jinnah.

By working hard, he passed his Bar examinations in two years, and at the age of eighteen he came to be the youngest Asian student then to be called to the Bar. But he still had to stay in London for some time to obtain his barrister's wig and gown, as he had to complete the formality of attending the prescribed number of dinners.

In London, he also took part in activities originated by Indian students there. In the year of his arrival in London, there was great excitement among Indian students, as Dadabhai Naoroji, a veteran Parsi leader from Bombay, who had settled in London for many years as a businessman, sought election to the House of Commons from the Central Finsbury constituency. Naoroji was the first Indian ever to attempt this, and Indian students worked enthusiastically for his election. Mohamed Ali threw himself heart and soul into this election campaign and won the esteem of Dadabhai Naoroji.

My brother's extensive reading had acquainted him with the works of many writers and poets in the English language, but the one who held the greatest fascination for him was Shakespeare. Despite a tight budget, he sometimes went to see Shakespearean plays at the Old Vic, where he fell under the spell of the great Shakespearean actors of those days. For some time he toyed with the idea of going on the stage, but the only offer he got was to play a minor part with an unimportant theatrical company.

So, when the formalities of dinners at Lincoln's Inn were over, he set sail to join his family in Karachi. He was received by his father, brothers and sisters, and a few relatives. If only his mother had been there, how proud she would have been of her Mohamed Ali.

My father was soon in conference with him, explaining that the family business was in a shambles and that he had to pay large sums of money to several business houses, some of whom had filed suits to recover their money in court. "My son," his father said, "all my dreams have been shattered, and I don't know what will happen to you and your younger brothers and sisters. My health is gone and I don't know how long I have to live."

"Bapa," Mohamed Ali replied, "don't worry. I will work hard and look after you and the family. I am young and my whole life is before me. I will pay all our debts."

My father thought it best to get him fixed up as a junior in the office of a flourishing advocate of Karachi, and in this connection he spoke to two firms who were also his lawyers, Harchandrai Vishandao and Co., and Lalachand and Co. The heads of both these firms were only too willing to take this young Muslim barrister into their firms. But my brother's mind was already made up; he had decided much earlier to try his luck in Bombay, a city that offered greater opportunities.

In Bombay he took a room, on a long-term basis, at the Apollo Hotel and got himself enrolled in the Bombay High Court. But this was easy. The real difficulty was to set up an office, secure briefs, and do well in the courts. This would take time. Expectantly he waited in his small one-room office in the port area for a client to come to him. He did not get one for months.

Even after three years he was not earning much and was agonising over his inability to help his distressed family in Karachi. But he kept up the appearance of being a busy barrister, daily making the rounds of the courts, making social contacts and frequenting some of the best clubs of Bombay. In his early twenties, my brother was a very attractive young man, slim and tall, with a commanding personality, a sensitive face, and always impeccably dressed.

His social contacts did help. A friend of his, who held his talent and ability in high esteem, introduced him to Mr John Molesworth MacPherson, who was at that time the Advocate-General of Bombay. He was impressed with the young barrister, and invited him to work in his office where he could use the facilities of his chambers. My brother never forgot this gesture, particularly as it was rare in those days for a Briton to extend such courtesies to an Indian barrister.

Mr MacPherson soon discovered the new recruit's ability and integrity. He passed on some cases to "the young Mr Jinnah". At this time my brother considered taking a government job, so that he could be financially more stable. Mr. MacPherson was willing to help and spoke to Sir Charles

Ollivant, the member in charge of the Judicial Department, and within a couple of weeks my brother was appointed a temporary Presidency Magistrate.

His exemplary conduct as a magistrate earned him praise from his colleagues, and when the period of the temporary appointment was over, Sir Charles Ollivant offered him another and better judicial appointment at Rs 1,500 a month, which in those days was a princely salary. "No thank you," replied Mohamed Ali, "I hope that soon I will be able to earn that much in a single day."

As soon as he left his post as Presidency Magistrate, he was approached by a number of clients. He gave up his small room in the Apollo Hotel and took a modest apartment in the Apollo Bunder area, furnished it well and also rented a new office. He spared no expense within his limited means in converting his office into an elegant and attractive chamber, which any lawyer would have been proud to call his own. His feet were set firmly on the ladder of success, and he sent letters and telegrams to my father to come over to Bombay with the family.

My father was by now unhappy in Karachi and so agreed to come to Bombay and leave the city which held many bitter memories for him. So we all went to Bombay and rented an apartment in Khoja Mohalla at Khajak, where my brother often came to visit us. He was now making enough money in his profession to live well, to support his family and also bear the expense of educating his brothers and sisters.

My brother's reputation grew and he led a life of complete independence, impervious to patronage or bullying from his seniors. My father was often told that his son was arrogant and quick-tempered with members of the Bar and the Bench, and that this would hinder his career, especially because he behaved in the same manner with Englishmen. But my father's earlier scepticism about Mohamed Ali had vanished, and he was confident that his son knew exactly what he was doing, for he had charted his own course and it seemed best to let him follow it.

As the centrality of Mohamed Ali Jinnah's political role became more evident, his sister Fatima moved closer to his side, as his companion and as manager of his domestic life. Here she takes up her narrative from a decade or so before the Quaid's triumph, and his encroaching final illness.

In establishing himself, first as a lawyer and then as a political leader, my brother was to show that Nature had gifted him with unusually strong willpower to achieve the tasks that he set himself, but it had encased that will in too frail a body. His health could not stand the rigours of a tumultuous life, but this was balanced by a tenacity which enabled him to overcome all obstacles and to lead his people.

I sometimes begged him to cut down the frequent tours which carried him like a whirlwind from one end of India to the other. He would say, "Have you ever heard of a general taking a holiday when his army is fighting for its very survival?"

When the general elections were being held in February 1937 all over India, the Muslim League put up its own candidates for the first time. At that time the League was not well organised and its message had not yet reached the Muslim masses. The main burden of organisation, of rallying public opinion in favour of the League, fell on his shoulders.

When the Muslim League session in Lahore in 1940 passed what has come to be known as the Pakistan Resolution, his health was already poor, but somehow he kept pace with his increasing work. With a following not yet organised, he began from that year to travel even more, to translate his party's mandate into action. He was five feet ten and a half inches tall and normally weighed about 112 pounds. He began to lose weight, ounce by ounce, but he refused my requests that he should consult a good doctor.

He was not only President of the Muslim League, but also the Leader of the Muslim League Party in the Central Legislative Assembly. In the year of the Pakistan Resolution, as we travelled from Bombay to New Delhi, he had a slight temperature. After dinner, as he lay on his berth, suddenly he gasped with pain and moaned loud enough for me to hear above the noise of the rattling train. I sat up and went to his side. He was in such pain that he could not speak. He pointed with his finger to a spot in the middle of his back, to the right of the spinal cord. His face was contorted with pain, and since we were in a compartmented train I could not rush out for medical aid. I first massaged the spot which he had indicated, but my ministration seemed to do him little good. The train was slowing down for a stop, so there was no point in applying the emergency brakes and halting the train away from a station and the medical facilities that it might afford. As the train stopped, I leaned out and called for the guard. He quickly brought a hot water bottle which I wrapped in a napkin and applied to the area of pain. Soon my brother was able to speak. He said he was better.

The train steamed into Delhi station in the early hours of the morning and soon we were at 10 Aurangzeb Road, which was our New Delhi home. I phoned his doctor whose diagnosis was that my brother had pleurisy and that he must stay in bed for about a fortnight. As soon as the doctor left, my brother said, "What bad luck. It is an important session. My participation is essential. And here I am, confined to bed."

Two restless days later he was up and at work.

It was in this session of the Central Assembly that he explained the stand of the League on India's participation in the war effort. As I watched him, from the Visitor's Gallery, taking the floor, I wondered if he would be able to speak for more than a few minutes. He began in a voice that betrayed fatigue, but as he developed his arguments, all traces of weakness disappeared. He was soon in his element, ridiculing the Government for their insidious propaganda to beguile the Muslims of India.

As we drove home from the Assembly, I saw that his hands were trembling and that he could hardly light his cigarette. On reaching home, he went to bed straight away, without so much as taking off his shoes or his tie.

That attack of pleurisy in the train was, I think, the beginning of the illness that ultimately claimed his life. He could have got over it, if he had taken proper care, kept regular hours and given up exposing himself to all kinds of weather as he incessantly toured the subcontinent. After that bout of pleurisy, he was always susceptible to cold weather and even a mild cold would develop into days of fever and painful coughing.

The seven years before the establishment of Pakistan were the busiest and the stormiest in his life. He worked ceaselessly. How vividly I remember those years! And to my mind comes a picture of him dragging himself out of bed, looking exhausted. As we drove to public meetings he would maintain silence, not to arrange his thoughts, but to conserve every ounce of his energy. He arrived nodding and acknowledging the applause with which he was greeted. His step was firm, his eyes bright and glistening as he mounted the dais.

Back home, in the solitude of his room, he would lie prostrate on his bed, gasping for breath. Fortunately, he had the ability to sleep at will. A good night's rest gave him enough energy to cope with the daily crop of letters, requests and important problems for which solutions had to be found. He kept up this tempo throughout the crucial years of the

Pakistan Movement in spite of recurring fever which emaciated his body.

Pakistan was born on 14th August 1947.

As we drove through cheering crowds on the streets of Karachi, to the Governor-General's House, even in his hour of triumph the Quaid-e-Azam was gravely ill. A new state had emerged on the map of the world, but many and gigantic were the problems it had to face in those formative days. I watched with sorrow and pain. He had little or no appetite and had even lost his ability to will himself to sleep. All this coincided with reports from both sides of the border of harrowing tales of massacre, rape, arson and looting. He began his day discussing these mass killings with me at breakfast and his handkerchief furtively often went to his moist eyes, and I pretended not to notice.

The Constitution had to be framed, and he applied his mind to this as often as he could find time from the immediate problems of rehabilitating millions of uprooted people. And there were other pressing problems that took precedence: the problem of Kashmir Muslims, who had been betrayed by a tyrannical ruler, distressed him deeply. Pakistan had taken its place on the map of the world, but it had yet to take root in all of its own soil. These problems robbed him of his peace of mind.

He worked in a frenzy to consolidate Pakistan. And, of course, he totally neglected his health, and his coughing and slight temperature were beginning to worry me more and more. At my insistence, he agreed to be examined by Colonel Rahman, his personal physician, who diagnosed a slight attack of malaria. The Quaid, who had an aversion to

At a meeting in Cunningham Park, Peshawar, on 20th April 1948, Jinnah caught the chill from which he never recovered

medicine, said to Colonel Rahman, "I don't have malaria. I am just run down." Asked to rest, he replied flatly, "I am not exhausted. I have too much to do."

He had promised the people of the Frontier Province that he would visit them to congratulate them on their great efforts during the referendum, in which they voted that the North-West frontier be part of Pakistan. To fulfil his promise he went, despite ill-health, in April 1948 to Peshawar where a heavy programme awaited him.

At an open-air meeting in Peshawar it began to drizzle. But the thousands who had come to hear their Quaid stayed even when the drizzle became rain. My brother, ignoring my advice to cut the meeting short, stayed until the meeting ended. He was drenched to the bone. That night it was obvious that he had caught a chill, but he refused to send for a doctor. "It's nothing," he said to me, "just a cold."

This cold was the beginning of the end. In Karachi, his cough continued, and only when I forced a doctor on him did we learn that he had bronchitis. He stayed in bed for a few days but continued to work on files that came to him in a steady stream.

Six weeks later he was a little better, although still weak.

I constantly entreated him to leave Karachi. My arguments were supported by Colonel Rahman, who warned that, unless he gave up work completely for at least two months, he would be doing irreparable damage to his health. One day in June he agreed and suggested that we should go to Quetta, which would be cooler.

Within a few days of our arrival in Quetta, there was a marked improvement in his health. He was able to sleep and eat well; the coughing subsided and his temperature came down to normal. Only the very important files which required his immediate attention were presented to him, and for the first time in many years he seemed relaxed. Sometimes he attended public functions in Quetta, and used them to make his views known on current issues.

The Quaid had agreed to inaugurate the State Bank of Pakistan on 1st July 1948 in Karachi. Afraid that this might affect his health adversely, I tried to dissuade him from undertaking the journey. He replied, "You know, the Congress prophesied that Pakistan would be a bankrupt State, and that our people would not know how to handle commerce, industry, banking, shipping or insurance. The State Bank is a symbol of our independence in finance and banking. I should be there. We'll be back in Quetta in a few days."

The air journey from Quetta to Karachi exhausted him and, on the day of the opening of the State Bank he was so weak he could hardly get out of bed. Through sheer willpower he went to inaugurate the State Bank. Those who saw and heard him must have realised that he was not in good health; his voice was scarcely audible and he paused and coughed his way through his speech. When we returned home he collapsed into bed with his shoes on.

He had accepted an invitation for the same evening to attend a reception given by the Canadian Trade Commissioner to commemorate the eighty-first anniversary of the Dominion of Canada. It was no use attempting to talk him out of this engagement. He showed no trace of fatigue as he smiled and chatted to other guests at the party, which was the last social function that he was ever to attend.

After five days in Karachi, we returned to Quetta by air. Although he withstood the air journey well, the next day he felt weak and had a slight fever, which made him uncomfortable. Requests began to pour in from various organisations in Quetta asking him to visit them. He had to refuse them and this depressed him so much that he decided that we should move to Ziarat, a few miles from Quetta, where it would be cooler and decidedly more restful.

The Residency at Ziarat, where we stayed, is a picturesque, old, double-storeyed building, standing like an outpost on a hillock. It has spacious lawns and gardens. A cluster of fruit trees and beds of flowers add to the beauty of the place, and the Quaid liked its quiet charm.

It was here that he at last agreed that he needed good medical advice. I wasted no time and asked Mr Farrukh Amin, Private Secretary to the Quaid, to phone Chaudhri Mohammad Ali, the Secretary General, to arrange for Colonel Ilahi Bukhsh, an eminent physician of Lahore, to come to Ziarat. This was on 21st July 1948.

After Colonel Ilahi Bukhsh had thoroughly examined him, he said, "Sir, your abdomen is all right, but I am not sure about your chest and lungs. I will have your blood and sputum examined by experts."

That afternoon I learnt the fateful news that the result was positive. The world began to slip from under my feet. I thought it best that Colonel Ilahi Bukhsh should give the report to the Quaid. "Sir," he said, "the results of the clinical tests show that you have an infection of the lungs." The Quaid heard this quietly and said, "This means I have tuberculosis. Since when have I had it?"

"I think, sir, for at least two years. But I would like to have an X-ray of the chest before giving any definite opinion on that point. It may not be very serious, and if your system responds well to treatment you will soon be well again."

When I was alone with my brother, his pale face wore a wry smile as he said, "Fati, you were right... I should have consulted specialists earlier... But I am not sorry... I will fight my illness... it is my duty to do so... I have never blindly accepted the advice of others... I have always learnt the hard way... for me there never has been any other."

They decided that it was necessary to have a night nurse. At first the Quaid refused, saying that he was being well looked after, but ultimately he agreed, saying, "My sister has been by my bedside day and night for many weeks. She must be tired. Yes, engage a night nurse."

And so Sister Phyllis Dunham from the Civil Hospital, Quetta, came to Ziarat. She proved to be an efficient nurse and the Quaid liked her professional manner. She followed the regimen prescribed by the doctors. Soon I had reason to hope when we found that he was more restful, slept longer hours, and was able to take more food than before.

As Pakistan prepared to celebrate the first anniversary of its Independence, the Quaid, against his doctors' advice, wrote out his message to the nation for that occasion. Even this effort was a strain on his health. The Quaid agreed to move to Quetta, but only after the Independence celebrations on 14th August when the people expected him to appear in public. The doctors insisted on an early move and it was arranged that he should motor down a day earlier.

He insisted that he would not travel in pyjamas. Happy that he was showing more interest in life, I put out for him a brand new suit with a tie to match, and put a handkerchief in his vanity pocket. I helped him put on his polished pump shoes. He was brought down on a stretcher and was placed in a semi-reclining position on the back seat of the big Humber car in which we travelled to Quetta. I sat next to him with Sister Dunham on the folding seat; his ADC sat in front with the chauffeur.

The car moved slowly to avoid jolts and bumps. We stopped twice for him to have tea and biscuits. It took us four hours to reach Quetta. In the Residency, the doctors examined him and said he had withstood the journey well. After a few hours he told them, "I feel better here. At Ziarat it was difficult to breathe."

He began to improve and Dr. Ilahi Bukhsh said that the Quaid might look at files for about an hour a day to divert his active mind from thinking about his health. He enjoyed this concession. After a few days he was allowed to leave his bed, and with some help, walk a few steps to improve his blood circulation. He liked this too. It was heartening to see that he was still full of fight.

The Quaid then commented, "Doctor, I like smoking. I haven't had a cigarette for days."

Colonel Ilahi Bukhsh agreed, "Yes, sir, but only one a day and don't inhale."

I brought him a tin of his favourite Craven A cigarettes, of which he had been used to smoking about fifty a day.

In the evening, the doctor saw five cigarette stubs in he ashtray. He looked pointedly at the ashtray and at the Quaid, who smiled: "Yes, I had five, but I didn't inhale."

Eid-ul-Fitr was on 27th August, and he was busy again preparing his Eid day message. This was to be his last communication to the people. He wrote,

"It is only with united effort and faith in our destiny that we shall be able to translate the Pakistan of our dreams into reality... My Eid message to our brother Muslim states is one of friendship and goodwill. We are all passing through perilous times. The drama of power politics that is being staged in Palestine, Indonesia and Kashmir should serve as an eye opener... It is only by maintaining a united front that we can make our voice felt in the counsels of the world..."

Towards the end of August he suddenly became depressed and said, "Fati, I am no longer interested in living. The sooner I go the better."

I was shocked and wondered what had brought about this change. I managed to keep calm and said, "Jin, you will soon be all right. The doctors are hopeful."

"No," he insisted, "I don't want to live."

On the first of September, Colonel Ilahi Bukhsh looking gloomy, said to me, "The Quaid has had a haemorrhage. I am worried. We must take him to Karachi. Now even Quetta's altitude is not good for him."

His health began to deteriorate, and on 6th September, the doctors said he had pneumonia, for his blood tests showed an acute infection. He was put on oxygen. On 7th September, I sent a cable to Mr. Isphahani, our Ambassador in Washington, to fly out American specialists whose names had been suggested by Dr Riaz Shah, and on the following day I phoned Dr Mohammad Ali Mistry of Karachi to come immediately to Quetta. There was another conference among the doctors and they decided that it was necessary that the Quaid be moved to Karachi at once, because Quetta's height was affecting his weak heart.

They told me that only a miracle could save his life. When I informed my brother of our impending move, he said, "Yes, take me to Karachi. I was born there... I want to be buried there." He closed his eyes and I just could not leave his bedside. He was soon asleep but restless, and occasionally, from him came sounds like muffled drum-beats, he was mumbling: "Ma... Bapa... Kashmir... refugees... Bapa... Fati".

His Viking was ordered to fly immediately to Quetta and the doctors decided on 11th September that we should be at the airport at 2 pm to go to Karachi. As his stretcher was taken into the Viking's cabin, the pilot and the crew lined up and saluted him. He in turn lifted his hand feebly to acknowledge them.

A bed had been improvised in the front cabin and I sat with him, along with Dr Mistry and Sister Dunham. The pilot warned us that he would have to fly at about 7,000 feet for some time, but that as soon as he had cleared the hilly area he would come down to 5,000 feet. Oxygen cylinders and a gas mask were ready. As the Viking began its ascent, the Quaid found it difficult to breathe, and I covered his mouth and nose with the gas mask. He inhaled oxygen for some time, then brushed it away, as if to say, "It is useless". I asked Dr Mistry to call Colonel Ilahi Bukhsh and I was happy to see that he succeeded in replacing the oxygen mask over the Quaid's mouth and nose.

After about two hours' flying, we landed at the Air Force base at Mauripur at 4.15 pm. Here he had landed just over a year ago, full of hope and confidence that he would help build Pakistan into a great nation. Then thousands had thronged to welcome him. But today, as instructed in advance, there was no-one at the airport. Colonel Knowles, as the Governor-General's Military Secretary, was there and greeted us as we came out of the plane. The Quaid was carried on a stretcher to a military ambulance that was to drive him to his official residence. Sister Dunham and I were with him in the ambulance, which moved forward very slowly. Other members of our party left in cars. Only Colonel Ilahi Bukhsh, Dr Mistry, and the Military Secretary followed the ambulance in the Governor-General's Cadillac.

After we had covered about four or five miles, the ambulance coughed and came to a sudden stop. Five minutes later, I got out only to be told that it had run out of petrol, but the

HISTORY

Left *"Tall and stately, but thin to the point of emaciation", was how Sarojini Naidu, the Indian woman leader and poet, described Jinnah. These characteristics are captured in the portrait now hanging in Quetta Staff College*
Right *From well before Independence, Jinnah had been ill. In his final months he was visibly consumed by fatigue and tuberculosis*

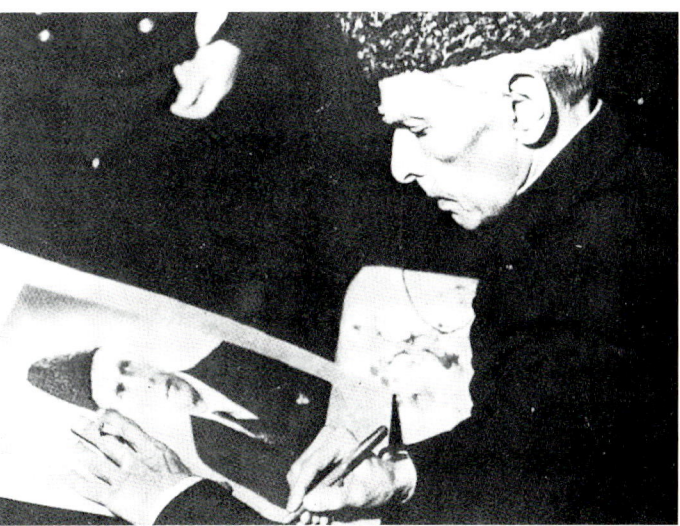

Above *Jinnah's official residence as Governor-General of Pakistan was Governor's House, Karachi*
Left *The Summer Residency at Ziarat, where Jinnah struggled with his mortal illness, is today preserved as it was when he was alive*

Left *The design of the Quaid's Mausoleum in Karachi was approved by his sister, Fatima. The tomb itself lies below ground, beneath its own replica*

driver was also fidgeting with the engine. As I re-entered the ambulance the Quaid's eyebrows moved imperceptibly, as did his hands. I bent over him and said, "The engine's stopped."

He simply closed his eyes.

Usually in September there is a strong breeze blowing into Karachi from the sea and this keeps the temperature down. But that day there was no breeze, and the humid heat was oppressive. To add to his discomfort, scores of flies buzzed around his face, and he did not have the strength to brush them away. He could hardly have been conscious of the fact that he was quite near Kharadhar, where, as a boy, his long slim hands had been so dextrous at flicking marbles, playing cricket and spinning peg-tops.

Sister Dunham and I fanned him in turns, waiting for another ambulance to arrive to carry us to the Governor-General's house. Every minute was an eternity of agony. He could not be shifted to the Cadillac as it was not big enough for the stretcher. And in a mood of resignation, we waited.

Nearby stood hundreds of huts belonging to the refugees, who went about their business, not knowing that their Quaid, who had given them a homeland, was in their midst, lying helpless. Cars honked their way past, buses and trucks rumbled by, and we stood there immobilised in an ambulance that refused to move an inch, with the Quaid's precious life ebbing away.

We waited for over one hour, and no hour in my life has been so long and full of anguish. Finally another ambulance came. His stretcher was moved to it and we drove to the Governor-General's House. When he was removed from the stretcher to the bed, my watch told me that it had taken us more than two hours from Mauripur to the Governor-General's House!

The doctors examined him and said that he had borne the journey well. He was soon fast asleep, and the doctors left saying that they would be back in a short while. I was now alone with my brother who slept peacefully; too peacefully, I felt. He slept for about two hours, undisturbed. And then he opened his eyes, saw me, and nodded his head slightly for me to come closer to him. He shocked me as he whispered, "Fati, Khuda Hafiz... La ilaha ill-Allah Muhammad Rasulullah" (Farewell, Fati... There is no god but Allah and Mohammed is his Prophet). His head dropped slightly to the right, his eyes closed.

I ran out of the room crying, "Doctor, doctor. Come quickly. My brother is dying. Where are the doctors?"

In a few moments they were there, examining him and giving him injections. I stood there, motionless, speechless. Then I saw them cover his body, head to foot, with the sheet.

Colonel Ilahi Bukhsh walked heavily towards me, put his right palm, gently, on my left shoulder, and wept. I searched for tears, but they had dried up. I dragged myself to his bedside and fainted on the floor.

The news of his death must have spread fast. The huge iron gates of the Governor General's House, which normally were kept closed, for visitors entered through the reception office, were flung wide open by an endless stream of people who came in from all directions.

Soon some of them were in the room where their Quaid lay in eternal sleep. There was sobbing and weeping all over the room. I had been revived but I refused to leave the room, where I sat in a daze. I cannot recall how long I remained there, staring at the white sheet that covered my brother's body. But I remember that an elderly lady, whom I had never seen before, put her arms round me and quietly whispered into my ear: "To God we belong and to Him is our return."

F.J.

The above was extracted from papers left by Miss Fatima Jinnah after her death. She had written them with the assistance of G. A. Allana.

Partition and Independence

The fateful weeks leading to Pakistan's Partition and Independence, recollected by the late Admiral Lord Louis Mountbatten, last Viceroy of India.

Early in 1947 I was briefed at the India office on the various leaders I should be dealing with when I became the last Viceroy of India. I was told that for all practicable purposes Mohamed Ali Jinnah was the Muslim League and that no solution to the problems of transferring power in India could be implemented without his willing consent and support. It was thought in London that partition would be fatal to the continued greatness of an undivided India and I was urged to try and get all parties to accept the Cabinet Mission Plan of 1946 with semi-autonomous provinces held together by a loose form of federation at the centre. It did not sound an impossible proposition.

When I arrived in Delhi I at once started a regular series of *tête-à-tête* meetings with the Indian leaders, and was brought up with a shock to the true situation. All parties, including Government officials, agreed on only one major point – extreme speed in the transfer of power had become vitally necessary. I fully accepted the need but it only made my task more difficult.

I began by having three meetings a week with Jinnah and although he was correct, even friendly, his mind was clearly set on Pakistan and none of my efforts to find any other solution met with the slightest success. His unshakeable willpower prevailed and within three weeks of my arrival I had to admit that I would not get him to change his mind, and that any attempt to force a unitary solution on him could only lead to the Muslim League's taking further direct action, with all that that would entail all over the whole subcontinent.

So the Quaid-e-Azam won his Pakistan and now I had the serious job of convincing all the other leaders that the price of independence would be partition. I succeeded with all except Gandhi, who objected to the bitter end, but had no acceptable alternative solution to offer. Once Jinnah knew I accepted Pakistan in principle he became far more friendly and easier to work with, though we did have a misunderstanding about the post-independence role he wanted me to play. He urged me to remain in India in a position which would be above the Governors-General of the two new Dominions, with power to enforce the fair distribution of assets and particularly the sterling balances. I told him that since he and Nehru would presumably be the Prime Ministers and that their Governors-General would only act on their constitutional advice, the simplest thing would be for him to agree with Nehru that I should act in a joint capacity as Governor-General of each Dominion, pending the transfer of assets but retaining certain rights over the assets until the transfer was completed.

It was a surprise when he suddenly announced that he intended to be Governor-General of Pakistan himself, with Liaqat Ali Khan as his Prime Minister. He explained that in the special case of Pakistan the Prime Minister would act in accordance with the Governor-General's wishes and not vice versa. But I did not personally resent his decision, as has been the common opinion, for it saved me from the daunting task of having to try and ride two separate horses simultaneously. The dilemma for me was not personal but political, in view of the commitment I had made to Pandit Nehru, but Jinnah largely solved my problem for me by urging me to continue to accept the invitation of the Indian leaders to become their Governor-General on the transfer of power, stating that my acknowledged probity would be greatly in Pakistan's favour.

I did my best to see that assets were fairly divided, but after the troubles in Kashmir started, the Indian Government held on to the remaining share of the sterling balances and nothing I could say to Ministers would induce them to send over the many millions of pounds sterling which it had been agreed belonged to Pakistan. So I had recourse to Gandhi. He agreed that the Indian Government had no right to withhold what belonged to Pakistan and finally induced them to release the sterling balances to Pakistan, by means of his most potent weapon, a fast.

The last twenty-four hours I spent with Jinnah in Karachi from 13th to 14th August 1947 were dramatic. I had flown down from Delhi to transfer power to Pakistan on 14th

Despite their differences, Mountbatten had great admiration for Jinnah's single-mindedness and gift of leadership

August. On arrival the head of my Criminal Investigation Department (for I was still Viceroy) reported that a plot to throw one or more bombs at Jinnah when he drove in an open car in a state procession from the Assembly Hall back to Government House was definitely on. He urged me to advise Mr Jinnah to abandon the drive. I did my best but he adamantly refused.

Jinnah then urged me to give up the idea of driving with him, but I said I would take the same risk as him. I won't pretend that I wasn't scared. I was, and did my best not to show it, but the new Governor-General of Pakistan did not seem in the least bit frightened. I was deeply impressed by his calm courage and high sense of duty. Nevertheless the drive was nerve-racking until the sight of the gates to Government House broke the tension. Never had my feelings been warmer towards the man with whom I shared this traumatic experience. His own gaunt face, which had been so expressionless, lit up with a warm, sunny smile. Laying a hand affectionately on my knee, he said: "Thank God I have brought you back alive."

Feeling that my presence could have halted a Hindu or Sikh assassin, I could not restrain myself from replying, "You brought me back alive? It's I who brought you back alive."

But what did it matter who had brought whom back alive? What mattered was that we had both come back alive with the ice broken and a warm-hearted evening in front of us.

L.M.

3. The Land and the People

The ancestors of the people came by the caprice of history. They were held by the bounty of the land and its mighty rivers. Yet the nation is shaped not only by those from the fertile plainlands but from great deserts and the valleys of remote mountains, from coastal villages and delta swamps – and the daily disciplines and sanctions they impose.

Geography and Landscape

The very names of Pakistan's remarkable landscapes enter the legends and histories of many people throughout the world. The Himalayan and Karakoram ranges are linked with many climbing expeditions – but, long before the days of climbing, with perhaps the most geographically hazardous trading route on the face of the earth.

The Hindu Kush, Little Pamirs and Baltistan have been perennial attractions to the more hardy traveller, but have recently become more generally accessible. Hunza, in the far north on the Silk Route from China, has long been admired by the tourist for the beauty of its landscape and is additionally fascinating to the gerontologist for the longevity and tranquillity of its isolated inhabitants. The complex of valleys further to the south, including such as Swat and Chitral, are equally, though differently, impressive.

No less renowned are the five great rivers that combine to form the lower Indus, and the great fertile lowlands that surround them. Few people in the West or East are ignorant of the Khyber Pass, but not many know of the Bolan Pass, of the barren ranges of Balochistan or of the wild coastland of Makran.

In only a handful of countries has the geography shaped so decisively the history and character of the people. It is a land that has repeatedly lured invaders, each of whom has left his mark, Thus it is a land of individual diversity – there is the hardiness and endurance of the desert dwellers, the stalwart humility of the mountain people, the skills and ingenuity of those who have made their homes, generation after generation, in the fertile plains and valleys and who have founded great cities, the restless energies of those inhabiting the highland steppes.

Pakistan comprises a remarkable variety of landscape and climate – ice fields and the Himalayan massif, verdant valleys and pasture lands, riverine plainlands, deserts, and the great Indus delta

PAKISTAN

Pakistan is a vast country, with an area of 310,403 square miles and a population of 64.9 million (34.4 million males and 30.5 million females), according to the 1972 census – increasing at over three per cent per annum. Islamabad is the federal capital, The country comprises four provinces – Balochistan, the North-West Frontier, Punjab and Sindh. The provincial capitals respectively are Quetta, Peshawar, Lahore and Karachi.

The land of Pakistan ranges from lofty mountains, through dissected plateaux, to dead-level plains. Mountains and plateaux together form about three-fifths of the total area, the remaining two-fifths being an alluvial plain, formed by the Indus system of rivers.

The north is dominated by the Himalayas, running from north-west to south-east to a depth of some 200 miles. They converge, in the Pamir complex, with their offshoots which run roughly north-south. These offshoots form the western borderland of Pakistan. The lofty Himalayas, rising to an average height of 20,000 feet, include such towering peaks as Nanga Parbat (26,660 feet) and K-2 (28,251 feet). Beyond the Karakoram Range lies the Chinese province of Sinkiang. Across the Hindu Kush are the Pamirs – the "Roof of the World" – where a narrow strip of Afghan territory separates Pakistan from Tajikistan.

Our main interest in the Himalayas lies in its glaciology, which is one of the principal sources of Pakistan's lifeblood – the waters of the Indus system. However, no detailed scientific study has yet been undertaken of the Himalayan glaciers. The outer ranges of the Himalayan system include the lesser Himalayas and the sub-Himalayas. The former lie in northern Hazara and Murree, the latter include the southern ranges of Hazara, Murree and Rawalpindi, and the Pubbihills of Gujrat. The rocks of the sub-Himalayan ranges are rich in animal fossils.

The Hindu Kush, constituting the main range of the western border mountains in the north, sends off a number of branches south towards Chitral, Dir and Swat. Trich Mir peak, in the north, is 25,263 feet high, and the ranges round about are capped with perpetual snow and ice. Their height decreases southward in Mohmand territory and the

Left *K-2 (28,250 ft.) is the second highest peak in the world. It was first attempted in 1903, but not finally climbed until 31st July 1954, when Achille Campagnoni and Lino Lacedelli conquered what climbers consider the world's most difficult mountain*

Mountains
Of all the great peaks of northern Pakistan, including K2 and Rakaposhi, none has had a more fearful reputation than Nanga Parbat, which defeated six expeditions and 31 climbers before it was conquered in 1953 by Herman Buhl. For centuries the high mountain valleys have bred tribesman of exceptional hardiness and courage, extracting a livelihood by channelling river water and making orchards and grain fields in the high rainless valleys.

Malakand hills to only 5,000-6,000 feet. South of the Kabul river, the north-south strike changes to the west-east aligned Kohi Sofed Range, whose average height is about 13,000 feet. Its lower slopes move into Kohat district. The area of ranges running west-east is bounded in the south by the Gomal river, beyond which the Sulaiman mountains run for a distance of about three hundred miles, again in a roughly north-south direction. At the southern end of the Sulaimans, are the Marri and Bugti hills. The low Kirthar Range forms the western boundary of the plain in the province of Sindhh.

Although the main Himalayas historically acted as a barrier to human movement the offshoots remained "half-open", occasionally letting foreign influences into the otherwise hermit subcontinent. The western border mountains are high

THE LAND AND PEOPLE

Centre *The massive fortress of the Thum's (ruler's) castle in Baltit (8,000 ft.) was built in the fifteenth century by the rulers of Hunza*
Left *A log bridge spans the River Shyok (8,400 ft.) in Ladakh, at Khaplu – the most fertile area of Baltistan. The jagged East Karakorams lie beyond*
Below *Askole porters face a blizzard crossing a glacier on the way to K-2. Askole is the last village before the Karakoram heights. The hooked beak of Mungo Gusor (30,632 ft.) is hidden in the clouds*

enough in the north not to permit large-scale movement. The increase in aridity makes movement as difficult as the height itself. A few broad Passes (Khyber, Khurram, Tochi, Gomal and Bolan) furnish the only "openings" into the subcontinent, which were negotiated a number of times by invading armies and immigrant hordes. Backed by adequate forces, the western border is a stable frontier.

The plateau of Balochistan is quite extensive. Its average altitude is over 2,000 feet. Within Balochistan there is a variety of physical features, ranging from tangled masses of mountains to hill-girt basin plains. In the north-eastern part of Balochistan, the Zhob-Loralai Basin is completely surrounded by mountains, as is the small Quetta plateau. Central and southern Balochistan include the Sarawan region in the north, with north-south ranges flanking narrow valleys, and a vast wilderness of ranges in the south. The backbone of the mountain systems of Balochistan is the Central Brahui Range, which runs in a north-east to south-west direction. North-western Balochistan is a true desert of lowlying plateaux, with inland drainage and a number of *hamuns* (dry lakes). Large areas of mudflats are found on the Balochistan coast.

The Potwar plateau, lying at a height of 1,200-1,900 feet and covering an area of 5,000 square miles in Punjab, is bounded on the east by the Jhelum and on the west by the Indus. In the north the plateau extends to the northern slopes of the Kala Chitta range and Margalla hills. On the south lies the Salt Range. The plateau generally is a poor

Above *The magnificent Jamia Mosque in Chitral with the Tirich Mir towering over the valley from 25,256 ft.*
Below *Crossing the Swat River: when the snow melts in spring, the river swells with icy water streaming down from the mountains*

agricultural area dissected by deep ravines. The slope of the land is in the direction of the flow of the Soan river, from north-east to south-west. The Salt Range is an area of special interest to the geologist. It has an orthoclinal outline which suggests that these mountains are the result of a monoclinal uplift combined with vertical dislocation along their southern border. The southern face of the range presents a complete geological sequence with rocks from the Cambrian Period to the Pleistocene Epoch.

About twenty-five million years ago, during the geological period known as Late Tertiary, a series of violent volcanic eruptions shook the area where the Himalayas now stand. At the time of the formation of the Himalayas, a great rift valley, nearly two thousand miles in length, lay along their southern edge. In places, the bed of this valley may have been as much as 70,000 feet below the highest peaks. In the succeeding epochs, gigantic rivers and innumerable streams rushing down from the mountains filled the valley with alluvium. The plain of the Indus and Ganges which we know today is that same alluvium-filled rift valley which acted as a gulf between the Himalayas and the main subcontinental peninsula.

The trans-Indus basins include the vale of Peshawar, Kohat valley and the Bannu plain. The vale of Peshawar is spread over the districts of Peshawar and Mardan, covering an area of 2,500 square miles. Once a flourishing centre of Graeco-Buddhist culture, it is most fertile and nearly half of the population of North-West Frontier live in this region which has a total area of 39,000 square miles.

The Indus plain is featureless terrain, with a gentle gradient averaging one foot to the mile, running south or south-west to the Arabian Sea, an area of 200,000 square miles. Its relief is of micro scale, and presents several distinct land forms, including an active flood plain (low-lying land adjacent to a river bed), a meander flood plain (the land of old river channels), a cover flood plain (where old riverain features have been covered by recent alluvium deposited by sheet floodings), scalloped interfluves (central higher part of a *doab* or interfluve), and the delta (triangular formation of river deposits near the coast). Of these land forms, the more extensive are the cover and meander flood plains.

The Indus plain supports thriving agriculture. It is divided into the upper and lower Indus plains. The upper Indus plain, in which Punjab is situated, comprises a number of interfluves formed by the Indus and its major tributaries; while the lower Indus plain, in which lies Sindh, has the Indus as the single dominant river. The upper and lower Indus plains are connected with each other through a narrow strip of plain south of the district Rahimyar Khan, which is sometimes termed the "Indus Corridor". The desert areas in the Indus plain include the steppes of the Sindh Sagar Doab, situated between the Indus and the Chenab rivers (at the centre of which is Thal, Cholistan in Bahawalpur (Punjab), Nara or Rajasthan in Khairpur (Sindh) and the Thar Desert in the Tharparkar district of Sindh.

The soils of Pakistan are classified as pedocals which have been formed under semi-arid and arid conditions and contain little organic matter. In the mountainous areas shallow residual soils have developed, which are generally strongly calcareous. The plains are formed of thick alluvial soils, also mostly calcareous. Dominant textures are silt loam, silty clay and clay loam. When irrigated and fertilised these soils are very productive. In ill-drained areas the soils are affected by water-logging and salinity, and in the delta they are loamy and clayey. The clayey soils are suitable for rice cultivation under irrigation. Aeoline deposits occur under arid conditions.

The water reserves of the land are being tapped for irrigation. The Indus system of rivers has an average annual flow of about 168 million acre-feet. The ground water reserves are estimated to be 300 million acre-feet in the upper 100 feet of aquifer.

Located on a great land mass, north of the Tropic of Cancer, between latitudes 24° and 37° North, Pakistan has a continental type of climate with extreme variations of temperature, modified in different regions by the quantum of rainfall and the extent of irrigation. The areas closer to the snow-covered mountains are characterised by a comparatively cold climate, those along the

Wakhis ride yak-back on little Pamir (13,000 ft) on the "Roof of the World" bordering Afghanistan and Tajikistan

In spring in Miandam, in the Swat Valley, apricot trees burst into blossom and streams rush in torrents down the hillsides

coastal strip are affected by sea breezes, and the rest are generally dry, dust storms and thunderstorms occasionally lowering the temperature.

The all-pervasive aridity over most of Pakistan, the predominant influence on the life and habitat of the people, coupled with the climatic rhythm, characteristic of a monsoon climate, are conducive to homogeneity of the land.

K.U.K.

Top left *Volcanic fissures score this mountainside in Balochistan*
Above *Shigar Valley with its serene river is deceptive: when the snow melts in the upper reaches of the valley, the river rampages to the plains*

Far left *The salt mines at Khewra, and its neighbourhood, once supplied all Central Asia. This small village is largely supported by mining in the forbidding environs of the Salt Range*
Left *After the wheat crop is winnowed on the small farms in Swat, straw is used for mulch and bedding for the animals*

Pictures overleaf
Top left *Village shrine in the Kharmang Valley of Baltistan*
Below left *Punjabi villagers gather buffalo dung for fuel*
Main picture *The River Jhelum in Punjab provides a livelihood to thousands of farmers and fishermen*

The Indus

The river, said the ancient Hindus, flowed from *Sinh-kabab*, that is, the mouth of a lion. The river itself they described in Sanskrit as the *Sindhu*. The Greeks called it *Sinthus*, the Romans *Sindhus*, the Chinese *Sintow* and the Persians *Abisindh*. It was Pliny who first called it *Indus* and the name stuck. The Indus in turn gave its name to India, and through accidents in navigation to Indonesia and to the West Indies, to the "Red Indians" and now to the world's largest single water development programme.

Over 60 per cent of the total area of the Indus basin lies in Pakistan and Azad Kashmir, India-occupied Kashmir, has about 15 per cent, Tibet has about 10 per cent, and India and Afghanistan each have about 7 per cent of the Indus basin catchment area. The Indus system of rivers comprises the main Indus and its major tributaries: the Kabul and Kurram on the right bank, and the Jbelum, Chenab, Ravi, Beas and Sutlej on the left. The first two join the Indus soon after it debouches from the mountains, and the others lower down in the plains. The whole of the Beas and the head reaches of the Ravi and Sutlej are in India, while those of the Chenab and Jhelum lie mostly in the disputed Kashmir state. The entire basin covers an area of about 348,000 square miles, of which 204,000 lie in Pakistan. In addition, there are about 29,000 square miles which lie outside the Indus basin but are dependent on the Indus river system for their water requirements and irrigation supplies.

But for Indus waters, the fate of agriculture in Pakistan would have been very uncertain. Even now when Pakistan is being rapidly industrialised, it cannot do without its water resources, for a very big percentage of its existing and proposed industry has to draw upon the agricultural produce for its raw materials. Almost all of the basin in Pakistan receives an overall rainfall of less than 15 inches, 60 per cent of its area receiving less than 10 inches, while 16 per cent receives less than 5 inches. The rainfall is not evenly distributed throughout the year but is concentrated during the monsoons.

Rising in Western Tibet, the Indus runs at first across a

high plateau, then the ground falls away and the river, dropping rapidly, gathering momentum and rushing north-west, collects the waters from innumerable glacier-fed streams, and runs north-west between the world's greatest mountain ranges, the Karakorams and the Himalayas. In Kashmir it crosses the United Nations cease-fire line and, in Baltistan, enters Pakistan. From here on it is Pakistan's river.

Pakistan's first town on the upper Indus, Skardu, at 7,500 feet above sea level, stands on a bluff near the junction of the Indus and one of its great right-bank tributaries, the Shigar. The majority of the people live in Skardu town; others inhabit small and scattered villages along the Indus and Shigar valleys, or tiny hamlets high on the surrounding mountains beside tributary streams or springs. Walnuts grow along the Indus near Skardu, and poplars and apples; there are delicious melons and nectarines and apricots in the valley of the Shigar, but it is difficult to send them "down-country" because they are easily spoilt in transit. Potatoes, maize and other crops need unremitting attention; the patchwork of fields must be fed by small water-channels led off from the upper streams of the Indus, sometimes for hundreds of yards. This means endless, back-breaking work in moving boulders to dam icy water, in continually checking, adjusting and repairing the flimsy clay dykes. Strong winds funnel along the river, and the fine soil blows away and must be replaced. At this height, the growing season is short, and every man, woman and child is pressed into service.

Below Skardu, the Karakorams and Himalayas close in towards the Indus. A deep, relentless, dark-grey torrent, it hurls itself through ravines of naked rock. In a brief widening of its valley, the clear, jade-green Gilgit River foams down to meet it from the Hindu Kush. These mountains stand across the Indus's path, and the river is forced to turn to the south-west. The Astor joins it from the east. Reinforced, the Indus twists and swirls down a trough between the Hindu Kush to the west, and the huge rampart of Nanga Parbat to the east.

In all these upper reaches of the Indus, narrow alluvial fans spill down the occasional cracks in the mountain rock. Good soil is rare here, and perched on their mud platforms, the few villages have to fight an endless battle against erosion by wind and climate. Some villages never see the sun in

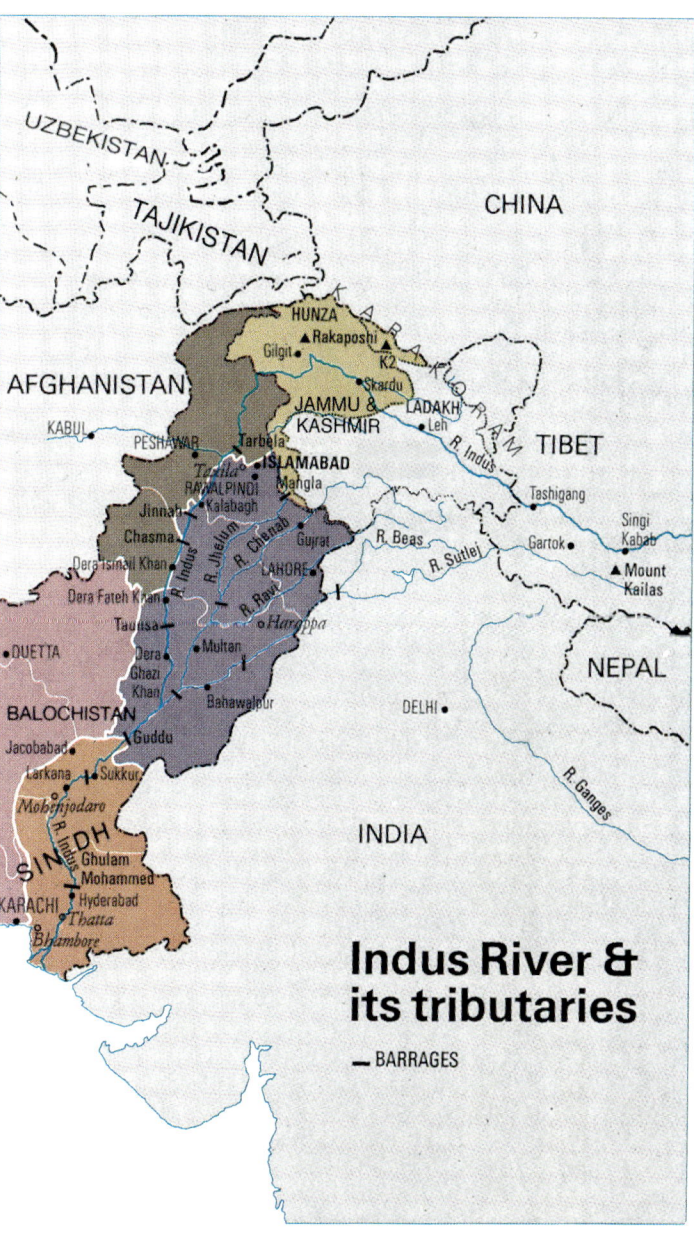

The great brown Indus takes in the blue waters of Kabul River just north of Attock, where it breaks into the plains. Together with its tributaries, the Indus spreads its network throughout Pakistan, the immemorial source of life

River Communities
The Indus in Punjab and Sindh has supported river communities for thousands of years. The Mohanas still live by fishing and trading. Their boats are their homes, each adorned and carved vessel having been built for a family.

winter, others are so scorched in summer that the inhabitants must migrate to the uplands. Every village lives under threat. Appalling storms are commonplace, especially where the Indus begins to reach the monsoon area. Sometimes, in the high mountains, a glacier will slide across a tributary river and hold it back to form a lake; when the ice-dam breaks, it releases a great gush of water that reaches high up the cliffs in the Indus narrows. A landslide from the foothills of Nanga Parbat has even been known to block the Indus itself, temporarily, and the destruction downstream, when the implacable river eventually forced its way through, was catastrophic. Avalanches of mud and boulders suddenly poured down the mountainside, overwhelming people and crops in their path. Most terrible of all are the earthquakes. This is a geologically unstable area, and there have been many earthquakes, the most recent being in the winter of 1974.

At last, just above a village called Tarbela, the Indus breaks out of the Hindu Kush. Here one of the largest dams in the world has been built to hold and control water for irrigation, and to generate electricity. It holds the river back into its gorges for some fifty miles, and contains more than eleven million acre-feet of water. The effects of the great dam, when completely concluded, are almost incalculable – for, in Pakistan, everything, in the last resort, depends on the Indus.

For a short breathing-space after Tarbela the river runs wide and shallow across the Potwar Plateau. This is a very ancient habitation of Man: 400,000 years ago people were making implements and weapons of stone here. It has also been, for thousands of years, the place where invaders entered the subcontinent: Aryans, Persians, Greeks, Central Asians. From the west, from the valley that some of the invaders followed, the Kabul River brings its brown water to mingle with the Indus grey. Then, at Attock, under the walls of the fort that Akbar built in 1586, the Indus gathers itself together again to force yet another mountain obstacle in its path, the Salt Range.

But this is the last. At Kalabagh, a thousand miles from its source, with a thousand miles still to cover to the sea, the Indus emerges on to the plains of Punjab.

The second half of the river's course is as dramatic as the first, but in a different way. Instead of being narrowly confined within walls of mountains, the Indus can now spread itself; and its bed is soon so wide that, from one bank, the other is invisible. In summer, when the snows and ice melt in the north, the great river, spumey and grey, fills its bed to the brim. In winter, when the river is low, islands and sandbanks surface, and the clear water flows in a maze of channels at the bottom of sloping mudbanks. From some of the islands men float pitchers of milk to market on reedy rafts. In every direction stretch the enormous sandy plains, lemony and brown and reddish, and patched with salt, asterisked with palm trees, shimmering with light. Different animals appear: camels, linked nose-to-tail, paniered with bales of fluffy cotton, and water-buffaloes, pink-nostrilled, wallowing in every pond. Kites scream overhead, hoopoes poke the ground with their long thin bills. Towns beautifully sky-lined with mosques and minarets stand near the river. But not too near.

For the Indus is still dangerous. The average gradient from Kalabagh to the sea is less than 9 inches per mile. When the river slows, as it must, in the plains, it drops the silt it has carried at speed through the upper gorges, and its bed gradually rises. In a heavy flood – perhaps a glacier-dam has been breached, or the monsoon has arrived before the end of the summer snow-melt – it may charge out of its bed and cut a new channel across the plains. Over the years the sands of

Punjab and Sindh have been worn down to pinhead-size by the manoeuvres of the river. Only one or two relatively unimportant tributaries flow into the Indus at the beginning of its journey across the plains; they come from the western mountains near Afghanistan. But, halfway to the sea, the Indus is joined by the greatest of all tributaries, from the east: the Panjnad, the Five Rivers of the Jhelum, Chenab, Ravi, Beas, and Sutlej.

Each of the five has travelled a different path from the Himalayas; they unite only some fifty miles before they meet – as an equal – with the Indus. The ancient civilisation of Mohenjodaro and Harappa was based on the Panjnad and the Indus; nearly a hundred towns have been identified between Punjab and the coast. Much of their commerce was carried by water and a peasant, tilling his flat fields of corn and sugar cane, must often have seen the great square sails of the river cargo boats bellying out before the monsoon. The few trading boats that work on the Indus today, carrying what occasional cargoes they can find, are of much the same pattern as the ancient boats, heavily built, clumsy to steer; they are engined now but still carry sails to harness the monsoon, when possible, against the river current.

People who live in a waste of sand veined with great rivers, which seasonally flood and are also liable to unpredictable changes of course, must try to control the waters. From earliest times men, in their battle against inundation and for irrigation, have banked the Indus, built walls to direct it, dug channels to take – and use – its overflow. Later they constructed weirs, barrages and dams, and hundreds of miles of canals. Mangoes now grow in the desert, and wide acres of cotton, and orchards of citrus where the oranges glow in the glossy dark. Below the twin towns of Hyderabad

Below *The islands of the Indus – such as the island of Bukkar – are protected by the river. For thousands of years, successive invaders and rulers have regarded these as strongholds*
Bottom left *The Sukkur barrage feeds seven great irrigation canals*
Bottom right *In spate, Indus waters reach the carriageway of the six-mile Thatta-Sujawal bridge*

PAKISTAN

and Kotri, the Indus runs south to a delta of tamarisks, scrub and saltwater rushes. For many hundreds of years the estuary seems to have been an important harbour and staging post. But a series of coastal earthquakes – the worst in recent years was in the early nineteenth century – have thrown the river back on itself and divided the navigable channels into a dozen creeks and ditches, shallow and meandering. The great river that is the life-line of Pakistan now spreads out in a green and scrubby confusion, and Pakistan's sea-port lies at Karachi, 40 miles west of the Indus delta.

For ten miles beyond the coast the Arabian Sea is discoloured by the silt of the Indus, and beneath its waters a deep canyon continues the channel of the river. The Indus, cutting through great mountains, driving across enormous sands, has carved a last gorge in the sea bed.

J.F.

The Environment and Conservation

Travellers hungry for adventure can choose from a feast of landscapes in Pakistan. A tangled knot of some of the highest peaks in the world, vast empty stretches of scrubby desert, endless miles of fertile table-flat plains, badlands pitted with ravines, sandy beaches, Alpine pastures – all these and more form the contours of Pakistan's topography. It is this very geographical diversity which accounts for the complex range of environmental issues Pakistan faces. The beauty of these

Above, right and far right
As the river runs south of Hyderabad it divides into a multitude of muddy creeks, ever shifting and separating with the seasonal floods. Fisherman make their living in the delta by catching palla *in traps hung from floating pitchers*

landscapes is being eroded by one of the highest population growth rates in the world accompanied by rapid social and economic change. Traditional land management practices often break down in the face of the demands for space, resources and new industry. The country's landscape today is being blighted by the impact of population growth, leaving slopes denuded of vegetation and rivers discoloured with chemicals.

The scale of Pakistan's environmental crisis has at last come to be recognised. Concern for the environment, once viewed as a luxury or even a conspiracy imposed on poor nations by the West, is beginning to find its place on the agenda of bureaucrats and politicians in Islamabad. Donor agencies are now laying down stricter conditions before funding projects and government departments find themselves obliged to take the subject seriously. More encouraging still is the emergence of environmental pressure groups at every level. In March 1992, Pakistan endorsed the National Conservation Strategy and, "joined a handful of countries that have pledged to balance their economic development with the conservation and use of their natural resources." More recently a high-powered National Environment Council was set up, to oversee the implementation of environmental laws and regulations.

Despite the diversity of problems, not to mention the varied social and cultural settings in which they occur, a number of common themes have began to emerge from this response to environmental degradation. The single most important lesson learnt over the years is that well-meaning conservation efforts imposed from above have little or no chance of succeeding without the active participation of the communities affected by such policies.

Perhaps the most telling example of this kind of response came when the government decided in to carve out a large tract of land in the Northern Areas and declare it as a National Park. The intentions behind this move were admirable. The park was to serve as a sanctuary for all kinds of wildlife, including the Marco Polo sheep, snow leopard, Himalayan ibex and the brown bear, all threatened by the rapid disappearance of their natural habitat. Good intentions, however, were clearly not enough. Arbitrary restrictions suddenly placed on local people, provoked an unexpected outcry. As the Park degenerated into a hunting ground for VIPs, people became so incensed that they actually went out of their way to sabotage the project. In nearby areas, people slaughtered animals out of fear that the government might take over their lands and declare it a Park. Better sense, however, soon prevailed. With the help of the World Wildlife Fund a new management plan was drawn up in 1990 with the active participation of local representatives. This new arrangement not only allowed certain legitimate rights to the locals but also provided a number of benefits to them if they chose to actively pursue conservation. Today, the people of the area have a stake in protecting the Park rather than viewing it as a threat to their already impoverished existence. A number of conservation projects with local involvement are under way in the Northern Areas and Chitral.

Above *Nature's beauty: meadows of Alpine flowers make northern Pakistan a paradise for lovers of wild flora*
Below (left and right) *Nature red in tooth and claw: marsh crocodiles at the Haleji Lake wildlife sanctuary*

It would be romantic to claim that local people always know how best to manage their natural resources. But, equally, there is an arrogance inherent in certain kinds of environmental advocacy – where experts knowing best are appointed to spread awareness among those at best unaware and at worst greedy. The lesson has been learned that such advocacy must be tempered with humility. After all, most local people have lived in close proximity with their environment for centuries, depending on it for their survival. Most

Above *The small and frequently solitary* Argali *is found in the remote valleys of northern Pakistan. Like many species it is in danger of extinction from poaching*

people have been long aware that some of their practices were doing long-term harm yet felt unable to seek an alternative solution. In the past, communities set aside certain tracts of land as pastures. Traditional land tenure and management carried over their own wisdom. Under pressure of population, penetration of market forces into once self-sustaining agricultural communities and massive migration of men to the cities, the old system has virtually collapsed. In its place is a free-for-all that has helped denude forests at an alarming rate.

People have become trapped in a vicious cycle. Let us take the environmental degradation of the country's northern mountains. Barely a generation ago, many of the less arid regions in the north were covered by a canopy of green foliage. Today, the slopes are a dusty grey-brown. Every day, an ant-like file of women, children and goats can be see trudging wearily towards the higher reaches where the few clusters of green still remain. With every passing day, they are forced to walk further to collect firewood to protect themselves against the cold winters and to cook meals for their families. Their livestock, which once had abundant pastures readily available nearby, now have to be taken to pastures at great distances. The scarcity of fodder means that animals are less productive, hence a desire to own a larger number. This in turn, means further overgrazing – the vicious cycle is complete. Attempts at afforestation have failed to solve the problem. While millions of saplings are planted every year, forest officials complain that the growing number of goats and cattle negate their efforts. People, meanwhile, view forest officials as their foes.

Successful schemes need to take into account the views of the people, understand the processes that have caused environmental problems and give the local population a stake in the initiative. The World Wildlife Fund, by taking local people into its confidence, has had great success in the fight to save rare Chilghoza forests in Balochistan. The threatened juniper forests of the province, the oldest in the world, now seem likely to survive.

While the pressure of population, overgrazing, poverty, and the lack of alternative forms of fuel have all combined to cause deforestation, other more pernicious forces are also at work. Traditionally, people exploited the forest for their own personal needs allowing regeneration to take its course. With the arrival of the British, timber was harvested as a precious commodity and was floated downstream to be used mainly for railway sleepers and construction. Colonial forest departments, however, undertook large-scale plantation drives and made sure that logging and replenishing both took place simultaneously. Today, the ravages of change have reduced the global stock of timber available and pushed up prices. Enter the timber mafia. Short-sighted and avaricious commercial interests, backed by powerful political clout, are making massive inroads into the country's forest wealth. Pakistan's forest cover today is less than 4.5 per cent. The

Opposite *The* urial's *magnificent horns have proved to be its downfall as trophy-hunters have shot the species to near-extinction*

Below *Gazelles are under growing pressure from hunting, deforestation and a rapidly increasing human population*

emergence of Non-governmental Organisations, particularly in Hazara, Malakand and Northern Areas, which have taken issue with such interests, is a welcome new development. In 1993 the government imposed a blanket ban on all kinds of cutting. Although a positive step, it was doomed to abuse given the lack of participation and poor policing.

As a result of deforestation many of the animals and birds that once shared these mountains with the people have long since forsaken the area. The more resilient have survived by moving further away from the encroaching human settlements. The less fortunate species have simply disappeared. This bleak picture is equally true for the plains. In the past, hyenas, wolves, crocodiles and even rhinos were common in parts of the Punjab and Sindh. The relentless increase in cultivation and the growth in population drove out many of these species. Others were simply hunted into oblivion.

The *houbara* bustard, a rare migratory bird that winters in southern and central Pakistan, has been the most celebrated victim of such hunting sprees. Despite various laws to protect the bird, it has been ruthlessly hunted mainly by Arab sheikhs from the Gulf. Large groups of these visitors organise elaborate hi-tech hunting parties in winter with devastating results. An outcry in the media and among NGOs has made governments sensitive to the problem but diplomatic pressures from friendly countries have pushed the species to the brink of extinction.

On the face of it, Pakistan has an impressive number of national parks and wildlife sanctuaries. No less than 7.2 million hectares have been designated for this purpose. However, the picture on the ground is less rosy. Many of these parks and sanctuaries are poorly policed and run, and tales of poaching and hunting in their confines are legion.

The rapid deforestation in the northern mountains has also had a devastating effect on the plains. As slopes become increasingly denuded, topsoil is washed away by torrential rains and the rivers carry an added load of silt. This silt has reduced the lives of the country's large dams such as Tarbela and Mangla. The former lost fourteen per cent of its storage capacity in the first decade of its construction and is expected to lose similar amounts every decade. The Mangla dam has done better thanks to the innovative work by a multi-disciplinary team working with farmers in the Mangla watershed area. As elsewhere, community participation was the key to success.

The link between felling trees and floods, though long part of folk wisdom, came home most clearly, and literally, during the 1992 floods. When torrential rains in the north caused the rivers to overflow in Hazara and Azad Kashmir, they carried away thousands of logs that were being stored along the banks for transportation downstream. These logs then became lethal missiles, knocking down homes, bridges and everything that came in their path. In Hazara, villagers told horrifying tales of how these logs caused more damage than even the furious waters.

Apart from deforestation, the effects of social and economic change can be as serious as floods or even droughts. Floods have long been a feature of life in Punjab and Sindh's plains, and riverine communities have actually thrived on the annual cycle of ebb and flow. However, in recent years floods have grown in fury, causing increasing amounts of damage in terms of life and property. Part of the reason for this greater devastation is that marginal communities, displaced due to rapid population growth as well as the far-reaching changes that have disrupted rural life since the Fifties, have been forced to make their homes on the banks, and even the dry beds, of rivers.

This same line of reasoning also explains why droughts in arid areas such as Tharparkar and Cholistan cause increasing hardships. Changes in agriculture, including the emergence of markets, have transformed cropping patterns and killed off the old subsistence economy. Along with this, land is brought under canal cultivation in the neighbouring barrage areas and animals from the desert are deprived of access to pasture, a sure recipe for growing suffering and rapid desertification.

Further land is lost through river erosion, especially by the notoriously wayward Indus which has swallowed up large tracts of land and, as in Leiah and Dera Ghazi Khan districts, even entire settlements. More land still is lost every year through waterlogging and salinity and from widespread use of tubewells raising the water level and making cultivation impossible. The extensive canal system laid down by the British in the last century further increased waterlogging of precious cultivable land. Parts of Faisalabad district in Punjab and Thatta and Badin districts in lower Sindh have been devastated by waterlogging and salinity. The canal colonies in Punjab transformed what was largely an arid tract of land into the breadbasket of India. Yet the arrival of

Left *The snow leopard lives in high altitude ranges in the Himalayas, Pamirs and Hindu Kush. There are only an estimated one hundred left in Pakistan*
Above *The* Astor markhor, *with its remarkable spiralled horns, is found in remote valleys of the North. It is in danger of extinction from poaching*
Below *The hog-deer is an elusive animal as it tries to survive in a world crowded with two-legged and four-legged predators*

hardy agriculturists from the crowded eastern districts forced a large number of the original pastoral people of the area to live on the margins as vagrants and "criminal" tribes, wiping out the wildlife and many indigenous shrubs and trees. Even the climate underwent a radical change due to colonisation.

In the Sixties, the so-called green revolution introduced new varieties of seed plus fertilisers and pesticides. For those who could afford it, productivity leaped. But a large number of farmers were reduced to penury, unable to pay for these new methods. Furthermore, this double-edged revolution pushed a large pool of labour, rendered surplus, into the cities. Largely uneducated farmers began to misuse these toxic chemicals and damaged soils across the country, also polluting water courses and streams, and introducing pesticides into the food chain. Many varieties of pests developed an immunity to particular chemicals producing a greater demand for new poisons. Already, water-borne diseases were the primary cause of death across the country. Now pollution through pesticides made matters worse.

The green revolution of the Sixties brought about a flood of rural migrants to the cities from the Sixties onwards. Unplanned squatter settlements have placed tremendous pressure on city infrastructures. Today a large proportion of Karachi's population lives in such settlements. The same applies to Lahore, Multan, Hyderabad, Faisalabad and others, while Peshawar has seen a huge influx of Afghan refugees in the wake of the war. The growth of unplanned development lacking any infrastructure such as sewerage is the source of many diseases in the low income settlements – consequences impressively countered by the Orangi Pilot Project (see also *Karachi*).

Green spaces set aside for parks have been ruthlessly appropriated by land grabbers for housing and commercial projects. The level of urban pollution has also risen dramatically, due to the growing number of motor vehicles emitting poisonous gases. In 1996 the government announced National Environmental Quality Standards, which define limits of various kinds of pollution – a useful move, provided offenders are actually penalised.

Daily, Pakistan generates 47,920 tonnes of solid waste, dumped either in low-lying land or in rivers. Rivers close to urban areas have degenerated into sewage carriers, bereft of most forms of marine life. Meanwhile, industries continue to dump their waste, (which includes toxic chemicals) irresponsibly. The wanton disposal of hazardous chemicals has also had a severe impact on Karachi's coastline, damaging marine life and fisheries. Inhabitants of the old fishing villages in Karachi must now travel far into the open seas to make a reasonable catch.

Marine nurseries are also under threat. Some 90 per cent of tropical marine species pass part of their life cycle in mangrove forests; these forests are endangered by pollution and also from grazing and cutting and, in the Indus delta, as a consequence of the canal system that deprives the area of adequate sweet water. The government, in conjunction with local and international agencies, is currently involved in efforts to save the threatened mangroves as well as to carry out new plantation drives.

Despite all this, there is growing awareness among government, voluntary organisations and citizens that unless prompt and firm action is taken immediately, the quality of life in Pakistan will fall to unacceptable levels. This sense of crisis could conceivably lead to concerted action which will restore ecological equilibrium between people, wildlife, land and water.

T. A.

Denizens of the Sanctuary at Haleji Lake **(top, left, above and below)** *As many as 220 different species of birds have been recorded in the wetlands around Haleji Lake. the sanctuary is one of the most important areas of migratory waterfowl in Eurasia*
Bottom of page *The Eastern Rosella is sold as a pet all over Pakistan*
Below left *The Western Tragopan is strictly protected*

Islamabad

Islamabad was created out of the wild as the capital Pakistan, a new capital being part of the vision of the makers of the new state. It is the newest, and also the northernmost, of Pakistan's major cities. It is situated on the edge of the Potohar plateau in Punjab Province at an altitude of 1,600 feet. To the north of the city rises the Margalla Range (3,000-5,000 feet) which merges in its easterly stretches with the Murree Hills at 5,000 to 9,900 feet. The Murree Hills themselves form the southwestern edge of the massive mountain region that dominates Northern Pakistan, Kashmir, Eastern Afghanistan, Tibet and the northern borderlands of India. To the south and west of the city lies the broken terrain of the Potohar Plateau.

Islamabad's hot summers are broken by monsoon rains in July and August. It receives more rain than most of the surrounding plateau. In winter, the temperature unfailingly drops below freezing at night between mid-December to early February. Islamabad summers are shorter and winters longer than in the Punjab plains. Islamabad's micro-climate is moderated by three man-made lakes that surround it, the Rawal, Simli and Khanpur reservoirs.

For the first twelve years following Independence, the capital of Pakistan was the port city of Karachi in the far south, now amongst the largest cities in the world. Pakistani planners felt that the concentration of investment and development activities in Karachi combined with it being the seat of political and administrative authority could relegate the rest of the country into a vast, undeveloped hinterland. A pivotal site for the country's capital, favouring no particular region, was the answer. The regime of Ayub Khan (1958-69) made the selection of a site for a new capital one of its earliest priorities. The place chosen was adjacent to the northern cantonment city of Rawalpindi, which became the interim capital. Significantly, only the narrow width of the Margallas separates Islamabad from the site of the ancient Buddhist city of Taxila. For several years the pace of development of Islamabad was fairly slow. A master plan of the city was completed by the early Sixties by the internationally renowned Greek architect and planner Doxiade s. The main feature of this design was a grid-like layout of sectors, each divided into four sub-sectors separated by parks and green belts, the whole lying roughly parallel and adjacent to the Margalla Hills. Strict building codes were applied to the new city, the ratio of built-up area to open space reflecting the emphasis on an open, spacious aspect.

Other well-known architects including Robert Matthew, Gio Ponti and Edward Stone also contributed designs for individual structures or complexes, but few of these designs have been realised without alteration – generally for the worse. The city advanced slowly during the Sixties, Seventies and early Eighties, in widely separated patches. The pace of development was dictated by administrative decisions like the shift of particular branches of government and diplomatic missions from Karachi or Rawalpindi, rather than by a spontaneous, commercially generated growth. The heads of state and government did not relocate to Islamabad from Rawalpindi until well into the 1980s.

The population of Islamabad was estimated in the mid-Eighties as below 250,000. However this was soon to change dramatically. With the shift of government completed and the Rawalpindi-Islamabad region showing some of the highest rates of commercial growth from the mid-Seventies onwards, the city expanded rapidly and as the century approached its close the population was estimated at well above 600,000. The Capital Development Authority, the main municipal body of Islamabad, was at first slow to respond to this growth by developing new sectors; however, this began to occur in the Nineties. Today, real estate prices in Islamabad are among the highest in Pakistan. The main direction of new growth in the city has been westwards towards the Grand Trunk road and south-westwards towards Rawalpindi. Once separated from Rawalpindi by open spaces, Islamabad has now expanded to meet that city, foreshadowing a far greater urban concentration in the decades to come.

The new sectors of Islamabad present a more crowded

The Presidency and the National Assembly building in Islamabad are Pakistan's proudest symbols of democracy

The strikingly modern Faisal Mosque nestles under the Margalla Hills amidst the capital's much-praised greenery

aspect, show less attention to detail and have looser building codes than the older sectors. One of the major successes of Islamabad has been the afforestation and greening of what was formerly scrub forest and open ground. A marvellous variety of exotic plants and trees from different parts of the world have been successfully introduced to the area. The climate permits a wide diversity of flora ranging from temperate pines to tropical creepers. There is ample migratory and permanent bird life – a declining feature of urban life elsewhere in Pakistan. The designation of the Margallas as a national park has also brought about a regeneration of wildlife, including wild boar and jackals (which are frequent nocturnal visitors to the city itself), monkeys, wildcats, deer, pangolins and other smaller species. Leopards have also occasionally been sighted in the Margallas.

A combination of climate, open spaces, greenery and the finest municipal infrastructure in Pakistan (including underground wiring and well-planned sewerage) make Islamabad a comfortable and attractive city to live in. There is still a sense of order that has become only a memory in Pakistan's other rapidly growing cities. Islamabad is also within easy range of a number of popular hill-stations in the nearby mountains. There is more than a tinge of envy in outsiders' descriptions of Islamabad as a bland, characterless city populated mainly by bureaucrats and diplomats. Indeed, the city has been irreverently described as being "half the size of Arlington Cemetery and twice as dead". In truth, given its relative newness, the city has not done badly at all. If it still lacks a certain cultural yeast, that may reflect, in part, the somewhat deadening effect of the Zia years which touched the whole country with its blight.

The architecture of most recent commercial and public buildings can best be described as pedestrian. Architecturally, the squat National Assembly Building and the florid neo-Mughal Prime Minister's Secretariat have few enthusiasts. On the other hand, the large tent-like structure of the Faisal Mosque, and the clean, uncluttered lines of the Saudi-Pak Tower dominating Islamabad's main commercial boulevard, are distinctive and often admired.

As the new century approaches, the challenge for planners in the coming decade will be to manage the inevitable growth of the city without compromising its high civic standards and to restore the earlier, more balanced aesthetic to Islamabad's layout and architecture.

A. I.

Punjab

Nearly sixty per cent of Pakistan's population lives in Punjab. It is the nation's only province that touches Balochistan, NWFP, Sindh and Azad Kashmir, and contains the federal enclave of the national capital at Islamabad. This geographical position and a large multi-ethnic population strongly influence Punjab's outlook on national affairs and induce in Punjab a keen awareness of the problems of Pakistan's other provinces and territories. In the acronym P-a-k-i-s-t-a-n, the P is for Punjab.

Punjab's historical ties with Jammu and Kashmir and areas adjoining the disputed territory reach back some two millennia. Their political histories interpenetrate, but, more than their mutual conquests, it was the mingling of the people of these two regions that established a deep kinship between them.

The word Punjab derives from two Persian words: *punj* for five, and *ab* for water. Probably a coinage of the Persian-speaking Ghaznavids it is a variation of an ancient name given to the land when Punjab was a satrapy of the Persian empire of Darius. In Pakistan, the quintet of rivers that provide the basis for Punjab's name are the Indus, Jhelum, Chenab, Ravi and Sutlej. The rivers, with the richness of land they bring, define the character of the place, which has outlined all the variations of political boundary-drawing. And yet, however much Punjab may be identified for its rivers, the region can claim distinction on account of the religions that originated from or flourished among its people, and for political decisions and events of great importance that took place in its *doabs*.

Hinduism developed in Punjab. The *Rig-Veda*, the most ancient of the Hindu *shastras*, was composed in Punjab. It deals with the life of the Aryan people who settled in the Indus basin about 5,000 years ago and with their struggle against the race which had developed the civilization of Harappa and Mohenjodaro. Of the two famous Hindu epics, *Mahabharta* places its action in Punjab. After the battle of Kurukshetra, Arjun, the conqueror, subdued the upper Indus plains and Gandharas (later known as Kandahar). The other epic, *Ramayana*, locates a pregnant Sita in the Ravi area during her second exile; in fact, her twin sons, Loh and Kash are said to be the founders of Lahore and Kasur, According to some writers, *Ramayana* was composed in Lahore by Valmiki.

Punjab also played a prominent role in the spread of Buddhism. This was through a native of Punjab, Chandragupta Maurya, grandfather of Asoka. When Alexander's ally, Porus, was murdered by the Greeks in 318 BC, there was a revolt in Punjab against the Macedonian invaders. Chandragupta organized the tribes of the northwest frontier against the Greeks and made himself master of Punjab and the lower Indus Valley. Under his son Bindusara and his grandson Asoka, Buddhism became the state religion of the Punjab.

Sikhism too originated in Punjab. The founder of the Sikh religion, Nanak, who was born in 1469 at Talwandi on the Ravi, in the Sharkpur area, was deeply influenced by sufis, and advised his followers to respect both the Quran and the Puranas. He never claimed to be a prophet, It was his tenth successor, Guru Gobind Singh, who converted the Sikhs from a quietist, reforming group into fanatical warriors.

This is one aspect of Punjab's past. Politically and militarily, Punjab's history tells of a sequence of invasions, the result of its location and terrain. The first conqueror of Punjab and also its first agriculturist and vinegrower is

THE LAND AND PEOPLE

reputed to have been King Osiris of Egypt.

Later, early in the second millennium BC, Sesotries, also of Egypt, introduced into Punjab the practice of observing the stars and a religion prefiguring Buddhism. Nearly a millennium later, in about 900 BC, Queen Semiramis of Babylon, thrusting eastwards and afraid only of the Indus and of elephants, was routed by Staurbates at the north-west border of Punjab. The Tartars and the Huns of Massagetae followed – the latter, known as Gates, spreading to inhabit the whole valley of the Indus. They are believed to be the Jats, perhaps the most numerous of all ethnic groups of today's Punjab; sharing the territory with Rajputs, Gujars, Arains, Chakkars and Kashmiris.

In 327 BC Alexander reached the Punjab at the head of his Macedonian army. The Greeks decreed that Pentapotamia would be their name for the Land for the Five Rivers, its King, Paurava, they knew as Porus. Alexander fought him on the east bank of the Hydaspes (now called Jhelum) – and after capturing him, asked how he should treat him. "Like a king," replied Porus, over seven feet tall, severely wounded and ready to fall. "That I would do for my own sake," said Alexander as he took a precautionary step backwards. "But what should I do for you?" A man of few words, by Greek standards, Porus said, "All my wishes are summed up in my first reply." Much impressed, Alexander declared that Porus would be his friend, and would remain king of the territories of his ancestors and of new regions that the Greeks would assign him. In the same battle Alexander lost his favourite horse, Bucephalus. The town of Phalia in the Gujrat district, founded by Alexander, is the Punjabi name for his steed.

Having crossed three more rivers – Acesines (Chenab), Hydraotes (Ravi) and Hyphasis (Reas) – the Greek soldiers refused to advance further east. They decided to take the south-west route through the remaining part of Punjab and Sindh, and thence along the Makran coast and through the western mountain passes of Balochistan. Alexander had touched the boundary points of what, 2,272 years later, was to be Pakistan. Only when he crossed the Ravi, to enforce the surrender of the ruler of Pimprama near Gurdaspur, did he enter what is now, but so easily might not have been, India.

In recorded history, the longest period of rule with a measure of continuity that continuity being the factor of Islam – comprised the successive Muslim dynasties of Ghaznis,

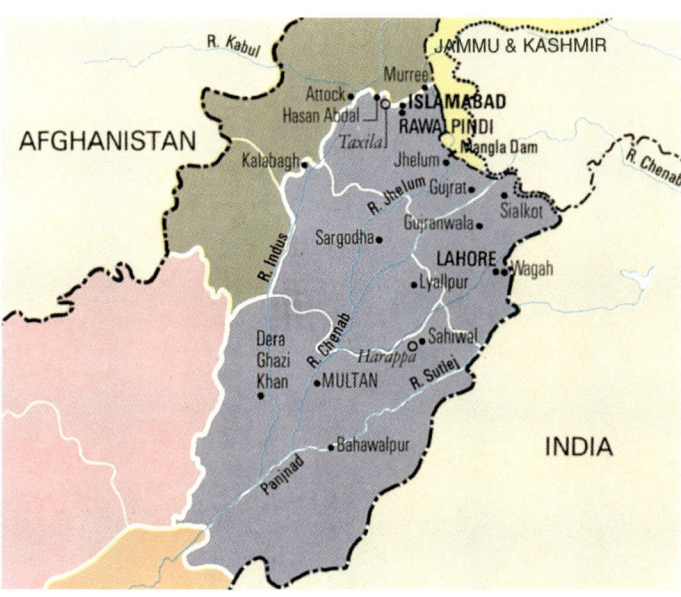

Ghuris, Tartar Slave Kings, Khiljis, Tughleqs, Lodis, Suris and Mughals. Muslim rule of one kind or another lasted for about 800 years up to 1821. It was from Lahore that the Mughal empire was ruled by Akbar for about fifteen years, and by Jehangir for about five. Shah Jehan was born in Lahore and to him and Noor Jehan, Punjab owes the splendour of its architecture.

The first mosque to be built in Punjab was a thousand years ago in 977 AD when Raja Jaipal of Lahore was defeated by the armies from Ghazni under Subuktagin, father of the famous Sultan Mahmud. The coming of Islam inaugurated a phase of Punjab's history which is of infinitely more lasting importance than the temporal rule of kings. The continuous sway of great Sufi divines has shaped the story of Punjab. Foremost among them is Hazrat Data Ganj Bakhsh al-Hujweri, whose mausoleum is in Lahore and Baba Fariduddin Shaker Ganj who is buried in Pakpattan. There are other shrines of famous saints at Taunsa, Multan, Bahawalpur, Kasur and Rawalpindi. While the Muslim kings seldom showed any interest in proselytising, it is these Sufic saints who, by example and exhortation, converted the majority of Punjabis to Islam and made possible the ultimate establishment of Pakistan. After the Muslim dynasties, the

Far from the city centres, Punjabi people have their own way of doing things, their own strong values and discipline of life
Left *A Punjabi woman in traditional* Dupatta *headgear*
Right *Girls in their brightly coloured Eid festival dress*

Top of page *Punjab – "Land of Five Rivers" – plays a central role in Pakistani affairs*
Below *This Punjabi village barber plies his trade with a "cut-throat" razor*

Sikhs came to power in 1799 with Ranjit Singh as their first maharaja. Three maharajas later, the Sikhs fought two wars with the British. After the Sikh defeats at Chilianwala and Gujrat in 1848, Punjab was annexed by the British on 29 March 1849.

Because of a bellicose Afghanistan and an expansionist Czarist Russia, the British paid particular military attention to Punjab. It was in the first place for strategic reasons that they built a railway through Punjab almost up to the Afghan border at Torkham and also a network of roads. The coming of the railway resulted in the river steam boats plying between Punjab and Sindh losing their trade: development of Punjab came to a halt. The absence of boat locks in the Indus barrages made long-distance river transport between Punjab and Sindh an impossibility. While this loosened traditional contacts in one way, the roads and railway resulted in greater mobility and rapid urbanisation. Society began to change. The *biradari* system sanctioned by tribal conventions began to erode. The introduction of modern education momentous political decisions: the resolution of the Indian National Congress in 1929 which for the first time demanded independence, and that of the Muslim League which demanded the setting-up of independent Muslim states in the north-west and north-east of the subcontinent, The objectives of both resolutions were achieved to the extent described in the historical sections of this work.

Punjab is very conscious of its history and Punjabis take pride in their lineage. There is among Punjabis a native pride, a consciousness of human dignity, a sense of loyalty, a steadiness of purpose, a spirit of hardiness, which makes them good soldiers, good farmers, good workers, and good friends. Their open-heartedness and hospitality to new ideas perhaps springs from an innate sense of equality, of a feeling of brotherhood among them. The people of Lahore will call each other *Bhaiji*, or "Brother", in everyday greeting. Punjab has escaped the taint of social stratification or courtly sycophancy.

This independence has its obverse, adding to the Punjabi

Above *An Alipur woman carries her well-water gracefully home*
Right *Farm-workers' homes, built from the earth on which they stand, in the mustard fields*

established new professional classes. Changes in the old tribal pattern of Punjabi rural and urban society was helped by the profession of soldiering. "Mercenary" soldiering – and the term did not always have the odour it sometimes has today – had a tradition of several centuries. Punjabi soldiers joined armies and saw the world; they returned to their villages with new ideas and experiences and broadened the outlook of the common man. After the Second World War, Punjabi Muslims formed 44 per cent of the Indian army and almost invariably formed the vanguard of the three-line attack which was the basic British Army strategy.

In the twentieth century, Punjab has been the site of character a strain of marked individualism. And yet, this is a simplification, because the Punjabi psyche is also nurtured on a complex value system, such as emerges so vividly in the folk legends incorporated in the great metrical romances of *Heer-Ranjha* and *Sassi-Punnu*. All these poems of folk romance emerged from the regions which now constitute Pakistani Punjab. The spiritual exaltation of Puran, the romantic idealism of Ranjha, the gallantry of Mirza, the self-immolation of Punnu and Manhiwal, the grand passion of Heer, the utter devotion of Sohni and Sussi, are archetypal patterns of Punjabi behaviour. By the time the poems came to be written down, characters like Heer and Ranjha had become symbols – Ranjha of the eternal lover and Heer of the yearning soul. Such legendary figures not only represent eternal types, but reveal most vividly the Punjabi ideals of honour, loyalty, steadfastness, courage and fortitude.

If we add to this the ecstatic utterances of the great Punjabi mystical poets (who form the largest group in the subcontinent), we gain further insight into the Punjabi character. Lal Husain, Shah Hashim, Sultan Bahuu, Bullhe Shah and Khwaja Ghulam Farid are all living voices speaking to the Infinite. They are sung daily, and induce in their hearers spiritual exaltation or rapturous yearning. The works of the Romance writers, the celebrants of ecstatic experiences, the spinners of war-poems called *Varan*, the anonymous song-writers, all such give evidence of the vigorous mental life of the people.

One of the elements in the spiritual and moral life of the people has been the devotion given to spiritual mentors and guides, known as *pirs*. These saintly men have been a prominent factor in the subcontinent. They preached and popularized the word of Islam. Many left behind systems of devotion which were built into Spiritual Orders (*silajat*) that gave cohesion to the nascent Muslim community in the vast new land of the faithful. From Punjab came, for example, Sayyid Ali Hujweri, who died in 1072 or 1088. Known popularly as Data Ganj Bakhsh, he came to Lahore during early Ghaznavid times. He and his disciples did not set up an Order, but his influence on the spiritual life of Punjabis has been enormous. Khwaja Bahauddin Zakaria of Multan (d. 1262) belonged to the Suhrwardia Order. He and his family have had tremendous effect on the moral and social behaviour of the people of south Punjab. An earlier saint, Sayyid Sakhi Sarwar (d. 1181) of Dera Ghazi Khan (d. 1181), Baba Fariduddin Shakar Ganj of Pakpattan (d. 1265), Makhdum Jahanian Jahangusht of Uch (d. 1384), and many others have left a mark on the psyche of the Punjabis that neither the political nor the intellectual whirligigs of the last five centuries have been able to efface.

The post-Mughal and even the British periods did not make for the confident evolution of Punjabi society. There was, in the rural areas, social stagnation and a draining of self-esteem. On the other hand the bulk of Punjabis had always been living far from the centres of Indo-Muslim culture, and this gave them the advantage of evolving their own cultural patterns, their own literary forms, their own songs and dances, their own values, their own dress and deportment, and their own dour philosophy of life. The virus of court intrigue hardly affected them, and if they were seldom in the thick of the subcontinent's political life, at least during the eighteenth and nineteenth centuries, it conserved their potential and saved them from becoming effete.

Above *In a pattern of existence that is thousands of years old, walls of sun-baked clay and dung preserve the intimate security of village life in Punjab*

Punjab stock, as it has emerged over the centuries, comprises five identifiable social groups. The Sayyids, with their collaterals the Quraishis, all named after their particular ancestors, were mostly prominent in the learned professions and in religious affairs. They were made Qazis, Muftis and heads of endowed seminaries. The Turks, Mughals and Afghans formed the military and administrative aristocracy. The Rajputs and their collaterals the Jats comprised the yeomanry. The neo-Muslims kept their own castes or were called Shaikh Qanungo or Khwajas (corrupted to Khojas). They were confined mostly to the commercial classes.

In the smaller towns there is usually a separate *mohalla*

Tradespeople are organised into Mohallas, *a Guild System*
Top *The potter at his wheel fashions vessels from local clay*
Above *The brick maker labours on his production line*
Below *Oils for cooking are extracted locally by camel-power*

THE LAND AND PEOPLE

Centre *A Punjabi village woman spins wool into yarn*
Above *A rural musician plays* Bhangra *music*
Below (left) *Operating the* khaddi *(hand operated loom)*
(right) *vivid designs are painted on camel skin vases*

(quarter) for most trades. There is likely to be a *Mohalla Qazis* (that is, of qazia or judges), a *Mohalla Muftian*, a *Mohalla Hamdanian* (that is of Hamdani Sayyids), a *Mian Mohalla* (that is of Imams or mosques), one of potters, another of butchers, others of weavers, tanners, coppersmiths, blacksmiths, artisans, and so on. Such segregation, though a legacy of the old Guild System, betokens a stable social order and is not necessarily a sign of rigid differences of social levels, or inherited snobbery or inferiority on any side. In a changing society like that of Punjab today, the occupational castes have the upper hand.

An interesting symptom of this change is the adoption or rejection of purdah, in urban areas. The upper classes abandoned it quite some time ago. The working classes never had any use for it. In the rural areas, the generality of women have worked with their men in the fields. They have cut grass, tended flocks, taken food to their people in the fields, helped in reaping harvests, and on the threshing floor. Now in the towns the first sign that a working-class girl has social pretentions is that she adopts purdah. It means that she has entered the lower middle class.

Most cities and towns are divided into old and new areas. Lahore that exists within the old wall rises vertically, its houses having three to five storeys and built along narrow winding lanes. The grid system used by town planners of the Harappa-Mohenjodaro era was, perhaps deliberately discarded for security reasons, and many of the tall houses had secret chambers where young women were hidden during invasions and civil wars. The newer parts of Punjab's cities are better planned with roads wide enough for wheeled traffic.

With the spreading network of canals in the last fifty years, new villages have sprouted so rapidly beside the squared-off farmland, that Punjabis – historically name-conscious – have numbered rather than named them. Called *chaks*, they are generally better laid out than the older villages. In their own way, they reflect another of the successive changes which have transformed the social landscape of Punjab throughout its history.

F.M., H.J. et al.

Above *A mosque dedicated to a local Sufi saint, Shah Rukine Alam, at Multan*
Below *Multan is famed for its antiquity (some say as old as Mohenjodaro) but today it is a busy, enterprising city*

Eid prayer at the Badshahi Mosque in Lahore is joined by thousands of the faithful, reasserting their commitment to Islam. This beautiful mosque, with its three great marble domes and four towering minarets, was built by Aurangzeb

Lahore

Lahore, the capital city of Punjab, has a distinguished lineage. Some scholars maintain that Lahore is actually Lohavar, the city founded by Loh, son of the Hindu god Rama. While that claim may be tenuous, it is probable that the Chinese traveller Hieuen Tsang, who passed through the Punjab in 630 AD spoke of Lahore when he described a large prosperous city near Jalandhra (Jallundur). However by the tenth century Lahore was very much on the map. The city was ruled by Raja Jaipal whose forces were defeated by Sabuktagin, the Muslim Governor of Khorasan. In 1022, Sabuktagin's son Mahmud of Ghazni completed his father's expansionist design by routing Raja Jaipal's successors and installing a Muslim government in Lahore.

By dint of geographical location alone, Lahore was destined for historical prominence. Located on the banks of the Ravi, the city was the point where roads intersected with navigable river routes in the vast plain of the Punjab. Favourably sited to exploit trade routes, it was from the start a rich city. Hence from a strategic point of view Lahore was a valuable prize for any would-be invader with his sights set on Punjab or even Delhi.

Lahore has seen more than its fair share of invasions. From the Ghaznavis to the Ghakkars and the terrible and persistent scourge of the Mongols, Lahore was invaded repeatedly. Sometimes it was devastated, as by Changez Khan's general Turtai when the destruction was so complete that for thirty years only owls and jackal inhabited the ruined city. On other occasions it bought off invaders. In 1398 Timur's lieutenant spared the city settling instead for a vast ransom. Again his descendant Babar let his rowdy troops loose on the city.

It is ironic, therefore, that it was Babar's descendants, the Mughals, who raised Lahore to heights of glory. The Mughals brought peace and prosperity in the three centuries of their reign and endowed Lahore with palaces, pleasure gardens and mausoleums that rival Delhi's imperial monuments in grandeur of scale and purity of form. Its strategic importance made it the fulcrum of government along with Delhi and Agra. Indeed, for twelve continuous years Lahore was the capital of Akbar, the third Mughal emperor.

The peace brought by the Mughals was shattered in 1707 with the death of Aurangzeb, sixth Mughal emperor. Thereafter until the end of the century when the Sikh chieftain Ranjit Singh seized control of the city, Lahore was pillaged repeatedly by Afghan Durranis. It enjoyed security but little cultural prominence under Ranjit Singh but all order evaporated with his death in 1839. for the next seven years Lahore witnessed internecine conflict as Ranjit Singh's successors battled it out. In 1846, using the First Sikh War as a pretext, the British moved in and three years later formally annexed Punjab.

The British moved the centre of government from the old walled city out towards the north. They built a new cantonment at Mian Mir linked to the walled city by a tree-lined boulevard which they fondly named The Mall. Along the Mall they built their high court buildings, cathedral, assembly hall, museum, university and general post office. In the design of these colonial buildings they employed a new architectural vernacular, now known as Anglo-Saracenic. Though

lacking the finesse of Mughal architecture, these colonial edifices were imposing nevertheless and added another layer to Lahore's onion-like growth.

At Independence Lahore was a city of about a million people, easily the largest in the new state of Pakistan. It was the natural candidate for the capital but its proximity to the Indian border made the choice unfeasible. Lahore remains the capital of Punjab, Pakistan's most populous and wealthy province, and continues to exercise great political clout. Until recently it was reliant mainly on agricultural revenues, but is now building an industrial base. Lahore is ringed by modern factories producing pharmaceuticals, garments, packaging and paper, textiles, sugar and processed foods. In addition the old crafts of jewellery making, carpet weaving, embroidery and leather work still survive in the old bazaars.

The real pulse of Lahore can be felt in the labyrinthine bazaars of the walled city. Here in smoky tea houses academics and journalists sit over endless cups of tea mulling over the state of the nation. In the dim interiors of adjacent shops cobblers, taxidermists, apothecaries, bookbinders and embroiderers ply their ancient crafts. The aroma of piping hot samosas and kebabs grilled over charcoal braziers wafts out from roadside cafes while fresh pomegranate juice and milk scented with cardamom and pistachio is sold from rickety stands lining the streets.

The alleys are a driver's nightmare. Already narrow they are congested with horse-drawn carts piled high with sacks

Top Left *At the annual National Horse and Cattle Show*
Above *Lahore's Mughal fort* **Below** *Shalimar Gardens*

of grain, gaudily painted rickshaws, motorcycles with families of five or six perched on them, fruit wallahs atop shaky bicycles with huge baskets of mangoes, melons and lychees strapped to the back carrier and even the odd milkman driving his reluctant cow through the traffic.

High above the bazaars, the crumbling ramparts of the walled city are the domain of pigeon fanciers and kite flyers. Here they pit their favourite racing pigeons against one another or participate in long drawn-out, dramatic duels in

Top right *Punjabi drummer and bagpiper at the fair*
Below *Jehangir's tomb, built by his son, Shah Jehan*

which one kite flyer pits his skill and endurance against another. The other great sport of the walled city is wrestling, Punjabi style. While this sport has all but disappeared in the modern, recently built cities, it lingers in Lahore's old quarters where wrestlers or *pehelwans* are still regarded as the strong men of the community.

With Islamabad the capital and Karachi the financial centre, Lahore has evolved as Pakistan's cultural leader. The adopted city of Pakistan's two greatest poets, Allamah Iqbal and Faiz Ahmed Faiz, Lahore has been a literary crucible throughout the twentieth century. It has produced literary heavyweights such as Patras Bokhari, Habib Jalib, Manto, and Ahmed Nadeem Qasmi. Lahore's National College of Arts has also contributed a bevy of artistic talent, notably Shakir Ali, Zahur-ul-Akhlaq, Ejaz-ul-Hassan and Nayyar Ali Dada. As the locus of Punjab University and a plethora of colleges, Lahore has long held the reputation of an academic centre. With the recent addition of several new institutes of higher learning, pre-eminent among which is the Lahore University of Management Sciences, Lahore looks set to hold that reputation. With its literary and academic activity, it is but natural that Lahore should have a flourishing publishing tradition. Aside from established papers such as the *Pakistan Times* and *Nawa-e-Waqt*, in recent years new national publications such as *The Friday Times*, *The Nation*, *Aaj Kal* and *Khabrein* have emerged from Lahore.

Today Lahore has an estimated population of about five million, the overwhelming majority of which is Punjabi. The city has expanded rapidly over the past ten years, subsuming villages and spilling out into farm land south towards

Above *Minarets of the Wazir Khan Mosque in inner Lahore*
Below *Zamzama –"Kim's Gun" – cast in 1760*
Right *Delhi Gate, one of the 14 gates of the walled city*

Raiwind. This sudden growth has led to a degree of urban congestion. Old residents frequently complain that Lahore is not what it was. While this is certainly true, Lahore is still a very green city with lofty trees, spacious parks and a lovely canal flowing through its length. And in its beautiful old buildings and teeming bazaars, it retains a palpable sense of history. In fact, Lahore is still moored very strongly to its traditions. While this has produced a climate of economic and social conservatism it has also bred the Lahoris' resilience, strong sense of identity and insouciant confidence.

M. M.

Sindh

The name Sindh, deriving from Sindhu, the river Indus, properly designates the plains on either side of its middle and lower course, from Attock to the sea. That is appropriate for these plains have been created by the river from the characteristic alluvial action of its overspill over many thousand years. However, to the world in general "Sindh" denotes the country below the point where the flood-plain of the Indus – between the mountains of Balochistan and the Thar, or great desert of India – is narrowest, about 450 miles from the sea. Sindh, too, has always included within its boundaries varying portions of the western hill-country and of the desert lying eastward. The three distinct tracts – rocky uplands adjoining Balochistan, the flat alluvial plains through which the Indus takes its capricious course, and the huge sandhills of the Thar – have one feature in common: very scanty and erratic rainfall. Without the bounty of its river, Sindh could never have advanced beyond the precarious pastoral economy of the neighbouring regions. The striking resemblance of the country to Egypt was noticed long before the existence in it of a comparable great prehistoric civilisation was even suspected; the idiosyncrasy of its people, when compared with Indians, is very marked.

Sindh has been a Muslim country since 712 AD when the Arab general, Muhammad bin Qasim, overcame the Brahmin ruler, Dahir. A succession of Muslim dynasties ruled it until 1843 AD, when it was annexed to British India and so remained for a little over a century before becoming a province of Pakistan, in 1947.

The aboriginal inhabitants of Sindh prior to the emergence of the Indus civilisation were probably hunters, fishers and fowlers, perhaps already in the stage of transition towards animal husbandry, with a little rudimentary subsistence agriculture. The growing of crops sporadically in the riverain tracts of Sindh was by no means a difficult process, owing to the annual flooding of the Indus which deposited fertile silt. Seed grain was simply cast haphazardly on the muddy ground from which the flood had just receded; no embanking or manuring was required, nor any attention beyond securing the crop from beasts and birds as well as possible while it was ripening. This is still the practice in the *kachha* tracts abutting the river.

It is possible that the Mohanas of the Manchar Lake, fisherfolk who live for the most part in their boats, may be the direct descendants of the lake-dwellers who we know existed in the dawn of Indus civilisation. They were probably among the indigenous primitive peoples subjugated by those

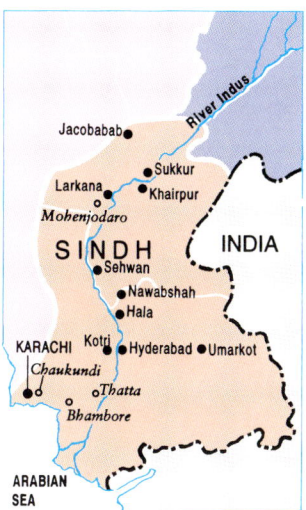

The region of Sindh is dominated by the river (whose name, in origin, it shares) and the great city of Karachi, which is the country's principal port and commercial centre. The province of Sindh itself is fertile and productive

The camel plays an important part in life in Sindh: certain tribes live largely on the milk of their she-camels

Above and right *The Indus valley of Sindh has played host to many civilisations, using Thatta as their capital. Islam came to Sindh in 711, with Muhammad Bin Qasim. The necropolis at Makli, Thatta is the largest in the world*

first bearers of true civilisation from the west. Another class of Sindhi, whose way of life may have continued virtually unchanged since primaeval days, are the camel-rearing Jats of the Indus delta country, who subsist almost entirely on the milk of their she-camels. It is well to bear in mind that the land of Sindh has been subject, at intervals throughout the entire period of which we possess knowledge, inclusive of those eras which are legendary if not mythical, to influxes of other races, mostly from the west, north and north-east. The latest great immigration, which took place in 1947 and following years, was of an altogether different nature from any that had preceded it.

Most of the Sindhi Muslims of modern times belong either to the indigenous stock or are of Arab or Baloch origin. Those who tend to classify themselves as Sammat, by race descended from the Samma, Rajput, Lakha, Lohana and Jat inhabitants of the country at the time of its conquest by Muhammad bin Qasim. Those remote forebears were predominantly Buddhist in religion, with a minority of Brahmin Hindus and Jains. The conversion to Islam of the great majority of their descendants was probably a continuous process during the succeeding eleven centuries of rule by Muslim dynasties. It is generally held to have been particularly rapid in the fifteenth century under the Sammas, and again in the eighteenth under the Kalhoras.

The occupation of the vast majority of the inhabitants of

Above *Sindhis hunt Indus cranes for food, with the help of a decoy perched on the head*
Below *Villages of the Dadu district are blessed with fertile soil and good irrigation*
Right *Sindhi women wearing hand-blocked* ajrak *cloth gather for a chat as they fetch the day's water in urns*

The Tanga horse and carriage takes tourists on the "Victoria Ride" around Karachi and is also a taxi service

Sindh is agriculture; next comes the herding of camels, cattle, water-buffaloes, goats and sheep; inland fishing and fowling are much less important than formerly, and the plying of boats on the river has all but ceased. There are two seasons for cultivation; in the autumn comes the harvest of rice, millet, Indian corn, sesame and *bajru*, with cotton much the most important crop other than food-grains, while wheat, gram, oil-seeds, mustard and chick-pea are reaped in the spring. Land producing rice, which requires heavier irrigation than any other crop during its growing season, is often cropped again for the spring harvest, usually with chick-pea, which has some fertilising effect on the soil, and the very best rice-land can thus be double-cropped year after year without any fallows. This procedure was fairly common in lands dependent on the best of the old inundation canals, many of which were adaptations or extensions of bye-rivers and former courses of the Indus, and flowed to a greater or lesser extent for four or even five months from late May onwards. Those semi-natural water courses have been superceded almost everywhere by irrigation canals deriving their supply from three barrages built across the Indus in appropriate locations, affording a perennial flow. It was in consequence of the introduction of the first such system in Sindh, from the magnificent structure at Sukkur, that a vast increase in cotton-growing began. The characteristic chronic variations in the volume and length of the annual inundations of the Indus, which formerly produced corresponding variations in the extent and quality of cultivation, no longer exert such influence. Agricultural expansion has naturally been accompanied by considerable development in all the ancillary industries and occupations, milling, processing, transport and the like. Another important effect has been much redistribution of population, leading to greater stability, the former fluctuations in means of livelihood from one year to another having been largely eliminated.

The system of land tenure in the province has of late years been subjected to long-overdue reforms designed to confer a quasi-proprietary stake in the soil on its actual cultivators. Hitherto, the predominant organisation of agriculture has been by *zamindars*; that is, the landlord, being the person responsible for payment of the annual government tax on a given area, employed cultivators who were merely his tenants-at-will, remunerated on a crop-sharing basis which by long standing custom had acquired statutory force. These arrangements tended to perpetuate the prevailing feudal character of society in rural Sindh. The peasantry were landless labourers, employed or dismissed at will by the landlords. They had no rights over the land they tilled – merely the right to the customary share of the crop they had raised. The most effective sanction these ploughmen possessed against ill-treatment by their landlords was to desert them and their holding and obtain employment elsewhere; and this move, or even the threat of it, was generally effective at times when there was a widespread shortage of cultivators. Such shortages occurred whenever large areas of virgin land had been brought under irrigation "command". Then came the opportunity for landless labourers themselves to become peasant proprietors; but a constant obstacle in their way would be the indebtedness which was endemic among them, and not uncommon amongst landlords.

These debts were incurred mostly with the *banias*, the Hindu shopkeepers and moneylenders, who, before the emergence of Pakistan, were to be found in small numbers in all but the smallest villages in every corner of agricultural Sindh. Their ordinary interest rates were so high that modest sums borrowed for purchase of seed-grain or necessities such as cloth or household articles of all kinds, if not repaid quickly, could grow into crushing burdens. And Sindhi Muslims in all ranks of life have a tendency towards improvidence. Sharp and cautious individuals of course exist, but they are somewhat untypical of the general easy-going attitude to life. A good deal of the new land under the Sukkur Barrage made available for peasant proprietors after 1932 was taken up by Brahui and other migrant labourers, often on a family basis, out of savings from their wages. They at least were not in debt to the local *banias*.

The Muslim peasantry of Sindh do not, for the most part, live in old-established villages, but in thousands of hamlets and isolated huts scattered all over the region, chosen for their convenience for cultivation or grazing. The typical dwelling of the cultivator is a single or two-roomed hut, the walls made of mud – which is baked almost as hard as burnt brick by Sindh's torrid sun (and could only be employed so universally for building in a virtually rainless climate) – and the roof of jungle grass or twigs and matting often coated with that same Sindhi "cement". Alternatively the walls may be of wattle, and the roof of branches, the whole hardly superior to the adjoining cattle-shed. Such huts sometimes cluster round the high walls which enclose the mansion, separate guest-house, and dependants' quarters of a large landowner. The permanent villages and towns of Sindh are conglomerations of flat-roofed houses, built of sun-dried brick made of mud mixed with straw. It is in the permanent villages, or in distinct quarters in the towns that one may look for the workshops and houses of handloom weavers, potters, blacksmiths, and other artisans.

Sindh's cultural life has been shaped, to a large extent, by its comparative isolation in the past from the rest of the subcontinent. A long stretch of desert to its east and a

Karachi is Pakistan's main port and home to a thriving fishing industry **Above** *The busy fishing harbour*
Left *A fisherman mends his nets before going out to sea again*
Below *The catch is auctioned morning and evening*

mountainous terrain to the west served as barriers, while the Arabian Sea in the south and the Indus in the north prevented easy access. As a result, the people of Sindh developed their own exclusive artistic tradition. Their arts and crafts, music and literature, games and sports have retained their original flavour. Sindh is rich in exquisite pottery, variegated glazed tiles, lacquerwork, leather and straw products, needlework, quilts, embroidery, hand print making and textile design.

Melas (fairs) and *malahharas* (wrestling festivals) are popular, and falconry, *malh*, (the distinctive style of Sindhi wrestling) horse and camel breeding and racing are characteristic pastimes. Sindhi fishermen float earthen pots to catch the *palla* fish in the Indus, and bullock-cart racing and cockfighting are also typical of the province.

Early professional minstrels, the Loras, carried Sindhi music to ancient Iran and the large number of indigenous instruments confirms the existence of a long-standing musical tradition. Shah Abdul Latif Bhitai (d. 1752), a renowned poet, founded a new musical tradition of *Shah jo Raga* in which thematic music primarily based on popular themes was interspersed by folk melodies.

The Baloch, a Muslim people distinct racially from the Sindhis, have been of importance in Sindh ever since making their appearance in the country some four or five centuries ago. They are, in general, a hardy, athletic, brave and honest people. In their earlier years in Sindh they continued the pastoral way of life, to some extent nomadic, which they had pursued in their former habitat. The characteristic organisation of the Baloch is tribal which continues to be the pattern in the Kachhi district of Kalat (Balochistan) and in the Punjab district of Dera Ghazi Khan; but in Sindh only two clans, the Chandias and the Burdis or Buledhis, remain identified with distinct *illaqas*, and only that of the Chandias is compact, adjoining the western border of the province.

The tribal system bears a close resemblance to that of the Scottish highland clans about three centuries ago. In Sindh, the former organisation of the Balochis has become greatly relaxed since they turned to agriculture, for which such widespread facilities exist – incomparably better than in the typical *illaqas*. The heads of tribal subsections may no longer recognize the authority of a single hereditary chief, and rank-and-file clansmen are inclined to look up to some local magnate of their name, or assume virtual independence of clan-obligations. But they will adhere to Baloch custom in their individual lives – for instance, they may accept a bride from a Sindhi family, but will never give a daughter of their own in marriage to a Sindhi. The Baloch living in the western hills of Sindh, or in the adjoining Izachho (piedmont) are still predominantly pastoral; some of them are nomadic like their forefathers, pitching their black goat-hair blanket tents (*gidans*) or pish-mat shelters wherever they find grazing for their flocks and moving on when the neighbourhood is bare.

Above *Karachi Municipal Corporation is one of the biggest permanent bazaars in South Asia*
Opposite (top) *Soldiers pay tribute at the Mausoleum of the Quaid-e-Azam on his birthday (25th December)* **(below)** *Mohatta Palace, built by a magnate, was later home to Fatima Jinnah*

Through the Western hills passes also the regular seasonal migration of Brahuis belonging to the province of Jhalawan in Kalat territory. Whole families come to Sindh to work every winter, with most of their household belongings loaded on bullocks and donkeys, accompanied by cattle, goats and dogs. They, too, encamp in tents or mat shelters wherever they find work, and return to their upland homes towards the end of March. There is a good deal of seasonal migration from other quarters to obtain work in Sindh; western Baloch are regular labourers in the cotton-ginning factories.

In the eastern desert, the manner of life of its inhabitants is dictated by the peculiar environment. In most parts of this wasteland there are wells every twelve or fifteen miles, and everything depends on them. Beside each well is a large trough at which the animals – mostly cattle, goats and sheep – have to be watered every morning and evening. The water is often brackish, and may lie a hundred feet or more beneath the surface. After good rainfall the people cultivate a little *bajru*, but their livelihood is derived from their flocks and herds. The desert grass is reckoned to be superior to any in the plains and, when at its best, cattle are driven in to be pastured for a fee. The inhabitants – Sodha Rajputs, Bhils and a variety of Muslims – live in well-built huts of wattle and

THE LAND AND PEOPLE

brushwood, the majority of them shaped like the old-fashioned beehive, and located near the wells.

The provincial capital of Sindh is Karachi, which, because of the vital importance of its port, has acquired prominence as the most cosmopolitan city in the country. There are the Borahs and Khojahs, Muslim communities engaged in trade, and Memons, a few of whom may also be landowners in Lower Sindh. Then there are the Parsis, business and professional men, Zoroastrians by religion; Jews and Goanese; Sindhis, Pathans, Punjabis and many other groups of people from beyond the province who have come to make their living in Karachi. Since the establishment of Pakistan, the city of Karachi has received the main bulk of the Muslim migration from all parts of India, gradually raising its population to more than three million. Karachi is now a metropolis comparable with the bigger cities of the world. It is difficult to believe that one hundred and fifty years ago the population of this immense city was only eight thousand souls. Karachi is the symbol of a new Sindh, a prosperous and lively region which faces its challenging future with confidence.

H.T.L.

Karachi

Among the major cities of the world, Karachi has the distinction of voting against the winning political party or grouping in every single recorded election. This contrariness has cost the city dear in terms of development funds and political clout. But it has also produced an independent breed of free-wheeling, hard-driving, cosmopolitan entrepreneurs who do business in several languages, and whose word is their bond. Its pressing problems have bred a number of individuals who have accepted the challenge of change, and have devised imaginative initiatives to meet at least some of the civic needs of the people.

Above *Karachi was developed by the British. The city's Empress Market appears to have been transplanted from a northern English market town*
Left *Dr Akhtar Hameed Khan's Orangi Pilot Project has helped to transform the lives of over 800,000 Karachi inhabitants, through self-help*

Despite years of neglect, Karachi has expanded at a phenomenal rate, growing from 200,000 in 1947 to over ten million fifty years later. Not surprisingly, such helter-skelter growth has resulted in a chaotic, largely-unplanned megalopolis that somehow still manages to function. More than a miracle, Karachi today represents a victory of the survival instinct over bureaucratic inertia. Initially designated Pakistan's first capital, Karachi was a sleepy port city before the Second World War. Most of its small population was concentrated around the harbour, and gracious stone buildings lined its wide avenues. But despite its handsome colonial architecture, nobody pretended that this remote seaside town was the pride of British India.

Although Alexander the Great once traversed the sprawling area that today comprises Karachi, it was not until the eighteenth century that the fortified town of Kalachi-jo-Ghote was established. Following his exploratory trip down the Indus and along the coast of the Persian Gulf in 1774-5, Lieutenant John Porter reported that "Crochey Town was fortified by a slight mud wall and flanked by round towers". It was not until a quarter century later that the British first established their presence in this part of India. In 1799, Lord Wellesley sent Agha Abul Hasan to negotiate with the Talpur rulers of Sindh on behalf of the East India Company. He found Karachi under [port] on the seaside "a place of immense trade... through which all merchandise for Kabul and Kandhar finds vent". Soon after this preliminary visit, Nathan Crow of the Bombay Civil Service arrived aboard *The Drake* and landed at "Currachee, the only sea port of

Taking a stroll in the Bagh-e-Jinnah (Jinnah Gardens). Karachi is the birthplace of Mohamed Ali Jinnah, the country's founder, and was Pakistan's first capital following Partition in 1947

Sindh with a population of ten thousand". Crow successfully negotiated with the Talpurs and obtained permission for the Company to open factories at Karachi and Thatta, thus ushering in the colonial presence in Sindh. But Crow was not to remain in Karachi for long: barely a year after his arrival, he was ordered to close his business and move to Thatta. Crow was convinced that his unceremonious eviction "was due to the jealousy of the native merchants at Kurrachee". Such self-protective business attitudes have not entirely died out.

During the nineteenth century, the city expanded gradually as the British developed it as an alternative port to Bombay for Western India, but it was not until the railway linked it to Punjab that it came into its own. By 1899 it had outstripped Bombay as a wheat exporter. Karachi's European population swelled to include civil servants, traders and engineers. The Karachi Gymkhana and the Sindh Club provided the focal points for the Anglo-Indian community, and the Civil Lines housed the European elite. The city's most ambitious project was Frere Hall on which the princely sum of Rs 180,000 was spent. The ground floor of this neo-Gothic building housed the city's first museum, and a library and reading room were located on the first floor. This striking edifice was built as a tribute to Bartle Frere, the energetic "Commissioner-in-Sinde" about whom *The Illustrated London News* said in 1866: "...the growing prosperity of Scinde is a monument to the good efforts of his rule".

The tempo of this sleepy port city quickened during the Second World War when it served as an entrepôt for soldiers and equipment heading towards the Middle Eastern and Western theatres. The airfield on the outskirts of the city – briefly home to Lawrence of Arabia during the First World War – was a staging point for military aircraft.

But it was not until Independence in 1947 that Karachi acquired its paramount position in the new state of Pakistan.

Right and below *Glazed pottery and tilework have been made since the thirteenth century in Hala near Hyerabad*

Left *Rilli is a colourful patchwork quilt made of dyed pieces of cloth. The basic design is a check* tukir,

So far, its major claim to fame during the freedom movement had been that the founder of the country, Mohamed Ali Jinnah, was born there in 1876. It was now catapulted into the limelight by the decision to name it Pakistan's capital city. Overnight, its population of 200,000 was swollen by hundreds of thousands of Muslim refugees who flooded into a city most of them had barely heard of. Karachi – indeed, all of Sindh – responded magnificently and welcomed this influx of humanity with open arms. Desperately, the fledgling administration battled to avert a major disaster and somehow managed to settle this multitude of refugees, most of them destitute. From out of this fraught yet still hopeful beginning was to grow the bitter discord that would later divide the city and lead to much tragedy and upheaval.

Although most of the newcomers had lost whatever they possessed in India, some of them brought precious entrepreneurial skills and capital. From Bombay came traders and industrialists, and from Delhi and other parts of North India came civil servants who filled an administrative vacuum and took the levers of power. Soon enough, their very success bred resentment, and their share in power declined. Then, in the early Sixties, the capital shifted to Islamabad. Karachi's political role was greatly diminished, and although the city grew relatively prosperous as an industrial and commercial powerhouse, the refugees and their descendants – collectively known as *mohajirs* – nursed a feeling of deprivation rooted largely in the quota system that had originally been designed to give the local population access to government jobs in ratio to their share of the population.

Apart from Sindhis and *mohajirs*, Karachi had become home to millions of Pathans and Punjabis who flocked to Pakistan's industrial capital in search of work, and Biharis who had fled Bangladesh after the conclusion of the civil war in Pakistan's erstwhile Eastern Wing. This ethnic cocktail often proved an explosive mix, and all too frequently an accident or a newspaper headline caused tempers to flare and riots to break out. With the flood of modern weapons into the city after the outbreak of the Afghan war, these conflicts reached horrifying proportions. It was against this backdrop that the Mohajir Qaumi [National] Movement was established in 1985, and over the next decade was to play a pivotal and often divisive role in the city's politics of violence. The MQM had overwhelming support among urban *mohajirs*, and in spite of a strong parliamentary presence, it was the ethnic party's shadowy armed wing that triggered a virtual civil war in Karachi in which thousands of citizens as well as security personnel were killed in a decade of sporadic but vicious urban gunfights. However, hope returned with the MQM joining the political mainstream after its performance in the 1993 elections and its alliance with Nawaz Sharif's Muslim League in Sindh and at the centre.

To a considerable extent, this disenchantment is rooted in the inability of the city's administration and the captains of industry to provide adequate jobs, electricity, water and most other services associated with urban life. Growing at around five per cent a year, Karachi has been inundated by waves of immigrants from up-country, as well as hundreds of thousands of job-seekers from Bangladesh, Sri Lanka, Afghanistan and even Burma. This surge of humanity has placed an intolerable strain on the city's stretched resources. At the same time, Karachi's random violence has caused the business community to oversee a flight of capital (and in many cases, families) to the relative safety of Punjab. Fresh investment has dried up, further reducing the number of new jobs, with the consequences that unemployed youth form the bulk of the gangs that turn Karachi's mean streets into killing fields.

In contrast, there has been the emergence of individuals and NGOs to fill the vacuum caused by the virtual paralysis

Above *Paradise Point marks the culmination of miles of beaches, many of them delightful and busy local resorts*
Opposite *Habib Bank Plaza – the headquarters of Pakistan's largest bank, in Karachi*

of state institutions and power in large parts of the city. the Edhi Trust, established by Abdul Sattar Edhi, runs a fleet of hundreds of ambulances together with clinics, hospitals and homes for the destitute. At the time of writing this, it may be said that Edhi's ambulances are the first on the scene of any emergency. This remarkable operation – now extended to many parts of the country – is financed entirely by private donations. Dr Adeeb Rizvi's Institute of Urology provides free state-of-the-art specialised care to thousands of patients, again largely through financial help from philanthropists. *Shehri*, an NGO dedicated to improving the urban environment, takes on developers in court battles to prevent further illegal high-rises from blighting the cityscape. The Citizens-Police Liaison Committee is a model of cooperation in the battle against crime. The CPLC has been remarkably successful in sharply reducing the kidnappings that once plagued the city.

Although many other NGOs have made life more bearable for Karachi's citizens, perhaps the most successful and widely admired and emulated private initiative is the Orangi Pilot Project (OPP) that was established in the depressed settlement of Orangi by the charismatic Dr. Akhtar Hameed Khan. A sociologist who has thought deeply about development, he brings a rare mix of theory and practical experience to bear on the task of helping the poor to help themselves. After resigning from the prestigious Indian Civil Service in the Forties, he has devoted himself to studying the dynamics of change. Now in his early eighties, Dr Khan's mind is as incisive as ever, and his close study of history and human behaviour is central to his philosophy of development.

Following a stint as director of the Rural Development Academy in Comilla in the sixties, Dr Khan established the Orangi Pilot Project in the late Seventies with financial assistance from the BCCI Foundation and the World Bank. Initially, he and his team undertook the task of helping the low-income inhabitants of Orangi to develop their own covered sewage system to replace the unhygenic open drains that lined the streets. The OPP technical team designed a low-cost system that was installed by the people themselves by using their own money and labour. Indeed, self-help is at the heart of OPP's programme which has been steadily expanded to encompass health, education, housing and credit for small enterprises. OPP's success can be gauged by the fact that at no cost to the government, over eighty per cent of Orangi Township – which has a million inhabitants – has built its own sanitation system, and infant mortality had fallen from 130 per thousand in 1984 to 37 by 1991. And entirely through OPP's initiative and the efforts of the local population, literacy in Orangi is nearly 80 per cent as against 62 per cent for Karachi overall and 35 per cent for the rest of the country.

Perhaps even more important than these statistics is the message of hope the Project carries for the rest of the city, and for much of the third world. Already, the experience gained in Orangi is being transplanted to other parts of Pakistan. When faced with official neglect and a breakdown of the most basic services, the people of Karachi have responded with imagination and resourcefulness: instead of waiting apathetically for government agencies to help them, they have shown that given technical support and advice, the common people can evolve their own leadership to solve civic problems through cooperation and hard work.

Although Karachi today is beset with ethnic, social and financial problems, it has come a long way in the last half century. As Pakistan's trend setter, it has evolved creative solutions that may serve as models for the rest of the country in the 21st century. Once it has resolved its inner conflicts, it is poised to lead Pakistan into the next millennium.

I. H.

The North-West Frontier

There are approximately seven million Pathans living in Pakistan. All of them are Muslim. More than half live in or on the fringes of the Indus Plain. These constitute the "settled districts" of Peshawar, Mardan, Kohat, Bannu, Dera Ismail Khan, Swat, Dir and Hazara.

The other three million or so Pakistani Pushtu-speakers inhabit "tribal territory" in the hills and mountains to the north and west of the Indus. The political agencies, running from south to north are South Waziristan, North Waziristan, Kurram, Orakzai, Khyber, Mohmand and Bajaur. The former princely states of Dir, Swat, and Chitral have now been turned into districts of the North-West Frontier Province. Further north and east, and with only a minority Pathan population is the Gilgit Agency, of which Hunza, Nagar and Baltistan are parts, now called the Northern Areas.

The land of the Pathans has been a frontier since history first recorded it. Its climate and geography are harsh; its natural resources, few and its location strategic. More than most, the Pathans' character has been shaped by their land.

The Pushtu-speaking area begins at the western end of the Himalayas where the mighty massif breaks up into a jumble of great peaks and ranges: the Karakorams, the Pamirs, the Hindu Kush. The main range of the Hindu Kush runs south and west into Afghanistan. Another spur drops more directly south into Pakistan, becoming successively the Safed Koh Mountains, the Sulaiman Range and eventually the Chagai Hills which fade away into the deserts bordering the Indian Ocean.

Running along the crest of the mountain ranges is the Durand Line, laid out in 1893 by the British to fence off their Indian Empire from its western and northern neighbours. On the east and south of the Durand Line is Pakistan's North-West Frontier area, some four hundred miles from north to south and about one hundred miles from east to west. On the other side of the Durand Line are Afghanistan's

Pathans, perhaps five million in number, again all Muslims. This political division of the Pushtu-speaking people, who are proud of their common language, heritage, and religion, has been a sporadic source of strain between Afghanistan on the one hand and British India and Pakistan on the other, since the Durand Line was established. This was in spite of the fact that the Durand Line was recognized by all the successive rulers of Afghanistan as a valid international boundary between the two neighbouring countries.

The vigorous Pathan tribal structure is far more complex than the mere division of their residences into 'tribal territory" and "settled districts" would indicate. All Pathans belong to one of the three great branches of the race. Each branch, the Sarbani, the Bitanni (with Ghilzai as its descendant) and the Ghurghushti, traces its descent from a son of their common ancestor, Qais, whose exact date and identity are unknown. Each branch has dozens of tribes: to name only a few of the best known, the Shinwari and the Yusufzai are Sarbanis; the great semi-nomad sects of Sulaiman Khel and Aka Khel are Ghilzai, and the Afridis and Wazirs are Ghurghushti. All of the tribes named have members resident in Afghanistan as well as Pakistan.

The tribal system of the Pathans is complex. Each tribe has several *khels*, clans; the *khels* break up into extended family systems of varying degrees of magnitude. Some of these subdivisions are also known as *khels*, some are called *kors* or *kahols*. However, an individual *khel* may have lost all connection with its parent tribe and may be larger than other tribes which have several *khels*, and two unconnected groups may have the same name. There is a Sepah clan among both the Afridis and Shinwaris, and Usman Khel among both Mohmands and Mahsuds.

Identity is closely associated with blood relationship, real or fancied. This is most compelling in tribal territory where a man will describe himself, for example, as "the second son of Malik Shahbaz Khan Shahbaz Khel of the *Galai kahol* of the Adam Khel Afridis". Among the long settled tribes in the districts, geographic identification is often important too, as in, "Jehangir, son of Isa Khan, of Tehkal village, a Khalil living in Peshawar *tehsil* of Peshawar District".

Despite the awareness of all Pathans of their common religion, language, and history, customs, dress, and even physical appearance may vary considerably from family to family, *khel* to *khel*, and tribe to tribe.

The Yusufzai are perhaps the largest, oldest, and most sophisticated of Pakistani Pathans. They live both in the mountains of Dir and Swat and in the fertile plains of Mardan district in North-West Frontier, (N-WF), which is a "settled district", They are tall, hard-working agriculturalists, clean and neat, aristocratic in bearing, traditionally individual free-holders

The Mohmands have two distinct sections. One, the Kuz (Lower) Mohmands are vigorous, land-hungry farmers living in and around the settled districts north of the Kabul River. The Bar (Hill) Mohmands occupy a patch of barren, inaccessible hills abutting on the Durand Line in a separate tribal agency. Their *khans*, *maliks*, and *mullahs* have more influence than is the case among the more individualistic Yusufzai. They tend to be somewhat shorter, sturdier and more quick-tempered than many of the other tribes.

The Afridis are archetypal Pathans, having collected a whole catalogue of contradictory adjectives from those who have studied them – brave, cautious, honourable, treacherous, cruel, gallant, superstitious, courteous, suspicious, and proud. Pleasant-looking men, light-skinned, often with blue eyes, they are as a rule slim and graceful. A Semitic cast of features and a partiality for full beards, added to the dignity with which the older men wear their flowing garments and light blue turban cloths, convey an impression of an assembly of Old Testament prophets. Their heartland centres on the Khyber and Dara Passes.

The Turis of the Kurram Valley are Shia rather than Sunni Muslims. They have definite well-developed social, religious and legal frameworks, with various *khels* following – four different families of Sayyids who have long dwelt among them. Though living in tribal territory, they have generally been cooperative with government administrators, perhaps in part to protect their relatively fertile lands and in part because of their quarrels with their Sunni neighbours.

Of the hill tribes, there is room here for mention of only two more: the Wazirs and the Mahsuds. Though often at enmity with each other, these two tribes dominate the entire southern part of tribal territory. Their land is particularly barren and their history and reputation especially fierce.

Above *Trout fishing is renowned at Saiful Muluk Lake, named after a legendary prince who met and courted his fairy love, Badar Jamal, at the lakeside*
Far left *Pathan tribespeople are fiercely independent, persistently opposing imperial rule before 1947*
Centre *Terraced farms overlook the Shangla Pass at Swat, a valley of some 4,700 square miles*

They gave the government of British India more trouble than any other tribe, and produced such notable "hostiles" as the Fakir of Ipi, and as late as 1937-38 took on several British divisions in what amounted to almost full-scale war.

In contrast to their northern neighbours, the Wazirs and Mahsuds speak the soft Pushtu of the south and dress largely in black and darker colours. Their population has been increasing rapidly in recent years and many, especially Mahsuds, have left their home territories to join the military and to work at road building and construction in other parts of Pakistan. They are a vigorous and dynamic people, and some emerge in such unlikely occupations as timber merchants in Karachi, deck hands on coastal steamers, soldiers, policemen and truck drivers as far away as Rome and Singapore.

As has been noted, many of the hill tribes have members living in the plains of the N-WF. Some tribes and groups, however, dwell exclusively in the N-WF. Their tribal structure has broken down somewhat but they maintain their Pathan heritage and customs. The Daudzai, Muhammadzai, and Khalils constitute the hard-working yeomanry of the

Peshawar Valley. The Bannuchis who occupy Bannu city and the area around it are very active economically. Their bazaars are clearing houses for goods from all over the Frontier. Their fields and orchards provide much of the food for the people of the nearby hills.

The Khattaks, whose lands run along the east bank of the Indus from above Attock to just north of Kalabagh, historically have come closer to being a nation than any of the other tribes. Since the thirteenth century, the whole tribe has been led more or less consistently by one chief, and the equality which each man claimed did not lead to the semi-anarchy that often prevailed within and among the other tribes. In Khushhal Khan Khatak (1613-89 AD), they had a great warrior, statesman and poet, whose achievements compared well with the other great Muslim and Indian leaders of his time.

Today, the Khattaks are a sturdy, light-skinned lot, noted for their cleanliness, restraint, straightforwardness and industry, as well as for their bravery and initiative. They are particularly adept in the Frontier and in all of Pakistan at the twin careers of warrior and farmer. Some of them are contructors and others occupy high positions in the Army.

There are, of course, other fascinating and important groups which are not properly Pathan, some functional, some racial: e.g., Sayyids and mians, Gujjars and Awans, Peshawaris (as mixed and cosmopolitan but also as integrated a city population as any in the world), Mongols and Qizilbash. In the far north live the Kohistanis ("People of the Mountains"). Among them are many different dialects and racial groups, the result of a mingling over the centuries of Mongol, Chinese, Iranian, Turkish, and Pathan blood with that of the original invaders of the subcontinent. Some of them, such as the ruling family of Hunza and the Kafirs of Chitral, claim, not without some plausibility, to be direct descendants of Alexander's Greeks. All of these other peoples, to varying degrees, have today come under the influence of the dominant Pathan society and culture.

If the Pathans' land is harsh and their tribal structure complex, their history is both. Peshawar first appears in the records of the Arochosian satrapy of the Persian Empire of Darius' Hystapes, as capital of Gandhara, the "Garden Land", now the districts of Peshawar and Mardan, part of Kohat, the Mohmand country, Swat Bajaur, and Buner. Alexander the Great appeared there in the spring. of 327 BC, to be followed as ruler in a few score years by Chandragupta Maurya and Asoka. Then came Seleucid Greek dynasties, the residue of Alexander's great march. About the beginning of the Christian era, these gave way first to the Kushans then to the Ephthalites or White Huns, sweeping down from Central Asia.

By the tenth century Islam had reached the Frontier Hills, and for the next several hundred years some of the greatest of the Islamic conquerors held sway over the Frontier: Mahmud of Ghazni, Muhammad Ghuri, Timur, Babur, Sher Shah Suri, Akbar, Aurangzeb, and Nadir Shah. The Sikh Empire of Ranjit Singh replaced the Islamic rulers early in the nineteenth century, itself replaced by British suzerainty in 1847. One hundred years later, the British too went their way and, on 14th August, 1947, the Frontier became part of Pakistan.

All of this contributed to the shaping of the Pathans. There is little doubt that the indigenous peoples of the area, in religion Zoroastrian, Hindu, Buddhist, Hellenic, and animist, contributed to the bloodstream of today's Pathans. But it was only after the coming of Islam that the tribal structure, customs and culture we know today began to emerge. At the core was a fierce love of independence which even in the days of the great Muslim rulers caused the Frontier to be

Above *Two Chitrali girls: they are speakers of Khowar, a dialect written in both Urdu and Roman scripts*

Above *Homes at Bahrain, Swat, are safe from spring torrents* **Below** *Chapli kebabs – a delicacy at Landi Kotal*

Kafiristan's Kalash hold to their unique religion

Tug-of-war is a popular sport among these Tajik and Wakhi boys in Little Pamir, south of the Oxus Mountains

THE LAND AND PEOPLE

Passing through harsh territories: Kashmiri Nomads in the North-West Frontier Province, with all their worldly goods

A Tajik bride wears henna, and jewels

A Tajik lady wearing a Chumona *necklace*

An ancient mosque stands near Saidu Sharif, the divisional headquarters of the former Malakand Agency

A Kohistani man wearing shalwar *(loose trousers)*

A Pathan stands at the entrance of the Khyber Pass

called "Yaghistan", or "Land of the Unruled". Growing out of the harshness of the land and the need of other peoples to pass through it, came a warlike tradition coupled with industry and ingenuity in the production of food. With this, there developed a rigorous code of honour and a set of institutions for defence, protection of the weak and strangers, and relations between individuals. When outside authority was imposed too strongly on the Pathan way of life, there was revolt. Indeed, the main reaction of the Pathans to every ruler before 1947 was rebellion: against Afghans, Mughals, Sikhs and British.

At the heart of the Pathan way of life for hundreds of years and until today is *pukhtunwali*, "the Pathan Code", or, colloquially, "The Way of the Pathans". Its three main requirements are in accord with the Pathans' history and land: *badal*, revenge, regardless of consequence; *melmastia*, hospitality and protection to anyone who seeks shelter under a Pathan roof; and *nanawati*, the right of anyone, even an enemy, to sanctuary and support. Though now supplemented by and occasionally subordinated to the laws of Pakistan, *pukhtunwali* has its own institutions: the *jirga*, a tribal assembly which decides matters in dispute, the *rewaj* and the *Shariat*, indigenous customs and Islamic rules of behaviour, the *lashkar*, or war party, by which the tribe fights, and the *hujra* or guest house or community centre found in almost every village.

Individuals, too, are important. Perhaps foremost is the ordinary tribesman who holds his status as a result of being a *daftari*, one who in fact or in theory is entitled to a share in tribal lands and a voice in tribal councils. An accepted leader and spokesman and a head of a clan is called *malik* in the tribal areas and *khan* in the settled districts. These titles can be hereditary or not, according to local custom. Playing a varying but often important role as counsellors and sometimes as actual leaders are persons of religious distinction. Sayyids are revered as descendants of the Holy Prophet. Interestingly, these religious personages are often not of the tribe which they serve and sometimes are not, by blood Pathans at all.

The Pathans' vigorous devotion to Islam and lack of the raw materials of the fine arts have narrowly limited their graphic production. They lavish their ornamentation almost exclusively on their weapons and their swords, daggers and guns are often works of art in themselves. The songs and dances are those of warriors, stirring and sometimes complex in execution but simple in theme.

In language and literature, however, the Pathans can claim considerable achievement. Pushtu is a vigorous, flexible and well-developed language and there have been dozens of writers of note since the sixteenth century. Khushhal Khan Khatak, the great warrior poet and savant of the seventeenth century, wrote in prose (both in Pushtu and Persian) on medicine, ethics, religion, jurisprudence, philosophy, falconry and an autobiography.

The Pathans today have changed little. Consider, for instance, that the average tribesman, even if illiterate, would know, and promptly explain, all of the rather exotic material set forth above, and more. In the tribal areas, he wears a turban to protect his head from the heat of the sun, and perhaps a sword cut. The turban is wound round in a particular way with a cloth of a particular colour, to show his tribe and to emphasise his individual tastes. He carries the best weapon he can afford, to defend his honour and to impress his companions. He would kill his last sheep and boil up his last handful of tea leaves because you were a stranger and became a guest when you spoke to him. This is not to suggest that change is not taking place in the Frontier. It is and at an ever accelerating pace since 1947. There are hospitals

PAKISTAN

The children of the North-West Frontier region enjoy robust health in a sharp highland climate. They will grow up to inherit a remarkable culture, warlike and vigorous, with a strong literary and poetic tradition

and schools within reach of even the most remote hill villages. New industries dot the Frontier towns, extending into tribal territory. Modern office blocks and hotels have added to Peshawar's services without disturbing its charm. Peshawar University has risen at the foot of the Khyber Pass. Opening in 1952 with a few hundred students, it now has thousands students on its roll, marrying with other tribes and with non-Pathans. For women, the veil is much less ubiquitous than fifty years ago. Urdu and English are now common in areas where not long ago communication was exclusively in Pushtu. More and more Pathans are finding their way from tribal territory into the Province and from both into other parts of Pakistan. Their numbers in the ranks of the civil and military services are growing. Despite the bitter battles that still go on between political parties and leaders, the Pathans' sense of being part of a large nation is clearer and greater than ever before.

Nevertheless, the Pathans' pride and vigour, their sense of honour and love of freedom have not changed, The Quaid-e-Azam, Mohamed Ali Jinnah, at whose behest they willingly threw in their lot with the new state of Pakistan, would, in the hundredth year after his birth, have no trouble at all recognising them as his staunch followers, always prepared to lay down their lives for the defence of the country in whose creation they played a dominant role.

J. W. S.

Peshawar

Peshawar lies at the crossing point between South Asia and Central Asia. It has long held the key to the subcontinent. The city and its valley have played host – usually unwillingly – to many of the great conquerors of Asia. Porus, Alexander the Great, Chandragupta Maurya, the first Emperor of India, and his son Asoka Babar, first of the Great Mughals, and a succession of adventurers and kings have all camped here over the millennia.

It is a beautiful place, the so-called "Paris of the Pukhtoons". On the south it is bounded by the river Bara, on the north by the Budni, the southernmost offshoot of the Kabul river, and on the west by the Khyber hills. The hills and rivers of the Peshawar plain wend their way eastward to meet the Indus. The city has gone through three distinct stages of development which are reflected in three separate areas: the old city, the British Cantonment, and the University of Peshawar around the nucleus of the old Islamia College.

The old city consists of Bala Hisar fort built on the high ground and its surrounding area which contains relics of the Kushan period (1st century AD) and even earlier. It was protected by a wall, still standing, with sixteen gates built during the Sikh regime, which marks the extent of the pre-colonial town. Ancient caravansarais nestle along the crumbling city walls where the great caravans from Bokhara, Samarkand, Herat, Meshed and Kashgar once unloaded and camped.

Increased traffic has demanded wider streets and removal of the old city gates. The houses and shops, once contained within the walled city, can now be seen outside and in many places the old walls have been incorporated into new houses. The British added very little to this part of the city, so it still holds the appearance and charm of its medieval character. The caravanserais at Gor-kathri and bazaars like the Bazazan (cloth-merchants), Misgaran (bronze articles) and the famous Qissa Khwani (story tellers' bazaar) are known throughout the Frontier, Afghanistan and even far beyond in Central Asia.

The hill in the centre of the old city called the "Gor Khatri" was mentioned by the Buddhist Chinese pilgrims, Fa Hien and Hiuen Tsang, who passed through in the fifth and seventh centuries A.D. Timur-e-lang (Tamerlane) and Babur camped here too. Most of the crumbling buildings on its top were built by the Sikhs when they ruled the city.

The Mahabat Khan Mosque is one of the city's most splendid sights and is approached from the central square of the old city, Chowk Yadgar. The Street of the Silversmiths, a dozen feet wide at the most, winds up a steep hill. Turbaned men with black, white and henna-red beards move sedately about, stopping to kneel and bow in prayer on the rich red carpets scattered on the floor of the mosque.

From the minarets of the mosque one can look at the colour and movement through the jumbled roofs and balconies below. A group of men drink tea and take their turn at the *chilum*, the simple Pakhtoon hubble-bubble pipe. A knot of women chatter as they sort spices. The rapid beat of the little wooden mallets used to pound the tissue-thin silver foil that decorates sweets can be heard from a nearby balcony. The throbbing of the drum and the soft wail of Pakhtoon pipes drift from behind half-drawn curtains, through which swaying figures can be glimpsed.

The bazaars of the city are crowded with men of many tribes, nations and languages – Peshawari and Qazilbash, Wazir, Afridi, Mohmand, and Mohammadzai; almost a third of the passers-by consist of Hazaras, Tajiks, Turkomans, Kirghiz and Uzbeks – all refugees driven from their homes by the war in Afghanistan.

All the luxuries of the East are displayed in the bazaar next to the Chowk Yadgar: brightly painted china from Russia, exquisite carpets from dozens of Oriental cities, precious metals and gems from all over Asia, the skins of rare beasts from the Himalayas, green tea from China, saffron from Kashmir, lush green melons and other fruit from the Afghan highlands, blood oranges from nearby groves. Side-by-side with exotic merchandise are also Western goods: American, Japanese and Korean tyres, German cameras, Czech rifles, Japanese radios, and British tweed. Dried fruit and nuts, bread, meat, boots, shoes, saddles, bales of cloth, hardware, ready-made clothes, and books are for sale.

In the streets, vendors carry fresh vegetables, curds, toys, and clothes. With these locals stride visitors in large white or dark blue frocks, and others in sheepskin coats, Persians and Afghans in brown woollen tunics or sheepskin hats, Khyberees with straw sandals and the wild dress and air of their mountain abodes, and the Hazaras, distinctive with their broad faces, eyes narrowed against the glare, and smooth-shaven faces. A few women can be seen in the old bazaars with long white veils that reach their feet.

The business streets of Peshawar each have their speciality. One is for shoes, another for headgear, yet another for fabrics, a fourth for silver, a fifth for carpets, and so on for a seemingly infinite variety of goods. However, interspersed among all of them are the ubiquitous tea-stalls. Most of these are similar in appearance: perhaps six feet wide, of roughly the same depth, with a narrow ledge open to the street. Each has the same equipment: a large brass samovar, an iron or stone bed for piles of burning charcoal, and racks along both walls for cups and pots of red and blue china patterned after the famous Gardener china of imperial Russia. The proprietor sits benignly with legs crossed among his gear, wearing a smile for his many customers.

The tea-shops cater to a variety of tastes. Some offer a strong black brew with a heavy component of buffalo milk and sugar all boiled together. Most, however, serve only

PAKISTAN

Above *Peshawar, surrounded by a high wall, is still very much a frontier town, full of tribesmen, traders and tourists*

qahwa, the light, delicate, cardamom-scented Chinese green tea which is the city's most popular beverage. The price of a cup is half a rupee: there are few better bargains in the world.

In sharp contrast to the old city, the Peshawar cantonment is laid on a grid pattern. Set far back from the streets, with thick walls, high ceilings and small, high, deep-set windows (to make sniping difficult) are massive bungalows. Most have colorful local histories of their own. Groups of Afridis drink tea in the shade of the verandah of the Political Agent's imposing residence while they wait for their turn to petition him. This picture has changed little in almost a century. Ponies pulling high two-wheeled tongas, identical to those illustrated in early editions of Kipling's *Plain Tales from the Hills*, still trot down the streets of the Cantonment.

Today the charm of the city is combined with the convenience of Western-style shops along the Mall in an atmosphere which is very Peshawari. The Saddar Bazaar is full of hustle and bustle, and the churches and double-storied barracks are reminders of the old British days.

Q. S.

Baltistan
For over five centuries Islam has prevailed in high Baltistan, although the region is fringed with adherents to Buddhism towards Ladakh; and the capricious spirits of rivers, winds and mountains in some of the wildest inhabited territory on earth cannot easily be ignored. Agriculture is pursued by laboriously irrigated detrital fans, especially near Baltistan's capital of Skardu, where water is tapped from the Indus before it bursts forth from the Baltistan plateau through a tremendous gorge

Top *At Khaplu, the Baltis are influenced by Ladakhi culture and language. Many are of ancient Greek ancestry*
Left *Prayer flags flutter on a saint's grave at Skardu. Beyond Queen Mindok's fortress lie stark mountains*

Left *An Askole turns to Mecca for evening prayer. Askole people speak a Tibetan dialect*
Below *Baltis saw timber at Katchura. Nearby Skardu lies on the banks of the Indus, just above its confluence with the Shigar*

Jammu and Kashmir

Bounded by Pakistan, China, Afghanistan and, over a mere thirty-mile strip of land in the south-east, by India, the State of Jammu and Kashmir is a territory of 86,023 square miles with a population of nearly six million of whom more than three-quarters are Muslims.

The conjunction of the two names is a product of nineteenth century history. Actually, the State is a conglomeration of about half a dozen regions, all disparate in topography, climate and language. These include the Jammu in the south-east, the Punjabi-speaking south-western region, the western part which blends with Hazara in Pakistan, Dardistan and Baltistan in the north and Ladakh comprising the eastern part.

In the middle, guarded by range after range of great mountains, nestles the Vale of Kashmir (called Kasheer by its inhabitants). Shaped like an elliptic saucer, it is a plateau, about 6,000 feet above the sea, eighty-four miles in length and twenty-three miles in average breadth. Here the language is Koshur (called Kashmiri by foreigners) which owes its skeleton to an ancient Dardic tongue, its flesh to Sanskrit and its life to Persian and Arabic. The language stands midway between the Indo-Aryan and Iranian branches of the parent Aryan stock; Kashmiri is the only member of this group with a developed literature of its own. The spread of this language to Kishtwar and Bhadrawah to the south-east and parts of Poonch to the west has socially, if not physically, integrated these neighbouring areas in the Vales.

Kashmir's own writers have been joined by Persian poets, notably Urfi and Faizi, and European travellers in hymning praise to the Vale's landscape: the first group with some narcissistic pride, the second in rhapsodic utterance and the third in prose which hardly conceals their wonderment at an Alpine scenery magically set apart from most of its surroundings. Francis Bernier, who visited Kashmir in 1659 during the reign of Jehangir, quotes the Mughal Emperor as having said that he would rather be deprived of every province of his kingdom than lose Kashmir. His father, Akbar, had called Kashmir *Bagh-i-Khass* (the Chosen Garden). Two centuries earlier, the great travelling saint, Syed Ali Hamdani (1314-1384) had termed it *Bagh-i-Suleiman* (the Garden of Solomon). Later writers like G. T. Vigne, Francis Younghusband and Walter Lawrence in the nineteenth century were so struck by the individuality of the place that they focused on the special ethnic characteristics of its people; Vigne called them the Neapolitans of the East, Lawrence likened them to the Irish and both Younghusband and Lawrence found pronounced Hebraic features in them. Even that most perceptive observer, al-Biruni (973-1048) who accompanied the unsuccessful expedition of Mahmud of Ghazni to Kashmir in 1021 noted that the Kashmiris did "not allow any Hindu to enter" their land. A small group, with some pretensions to being historians, still existing in both Kashmir and Pakistan, uses meagre evidence and much fanciful imagining in tracing the ancestry of Kashmiris to one of the lost tribes of Israel. All this attests to the fact that the Vale, a vast amphitheatre of six thousand square miles, interspersed with lakes and woodland, tranquil in appearance but dramatically surrounded by the grandeur of mountains like Nanga Parbat (26,620 feet) and the lesser but majestic Haramukh and Amarnath, each with a demeanour of its own, possesses a personality that stamps itself on the psyche of its natives.

In Azad Kashmir suspension bridges span several rivers

A legend as picturesque as the Vale itself holds Kashmir to have been once a vast lake. While the theory of this lacustrine origin has obtained some uncertain geological support, the poetry of the myth about Kashmir having been recovered in a struggle against demons seems to have permeated the Kashmiri consciousness. There has been diverse speculation about the origin of the name *Kashmir* with attempts to relate it to a quasi-historical figure *Kashyapa* or to a semitic tribe called *Kash* (who are supposed to have also populated *Kashgar* in China and *Kashan* in Iran). All that is certain from a continuous chain of documents for more than twenty-three centuries is that the name is very ancient. It is not, therefore, fanciful to suppose that, of all the regional societies of South Asia, Kashmir can claim the oldest settled continuity. Antiquity apart, Kashmir has the further distinction of being the only region in this part of the world which chronicled its history before the Muslim advent. The sole attempt at historiography made by the pre-Islamic Hindu mind is the work entitled *Rajatarangini*. Originally composed by the Kashmiri Pandit Kalhana, in 1148, it is a narrative in Sanskrit verse of Kashmir's ruling dynasties from the earliest period which was supplemented by successive authors (notably Jonaraja in the early fifteenth century) and updated after the Mughal Conquest in 1586. Though the antique Hindu orientation shows itself in erasing the boundaries between mythology and historical fact and in a wild chronological confusion, the work is a continuous account unlike any possessed by other parts of the subcontinent.

From *Rajatarangini* down to the profusion of later historical expositions, one fact emerges startlingly: Kashmir's sheltered location is not matched by a quietly insular development; in contrast to its placid scenic beauty, its history has been tempestuous. This is apparent from the two motifs which are discernible in the whole fabric of Kashmir's historical experience. One is the alternation of long epochs of autonomy, assertion and cultural efflorescence with the briefer but devastating periods of turbulence, tyranny and mental submergence. The other is Kashmir's implication in those movements of religious origin and social significance which have shaped the development of the Indo-Muslim community in the adjacent areas now included in Pakistan.

In broad political chronology, the history can be briefly summarized. The pre-Muslim period extends to 1320. From that year to 1560 (except for an anarchic interlude between 1323 and 1338) stretches the long period of Kashmir's independence under its own Sultanate. Its decline promoted the ascendancy of the Chaks, who were of northern ancestry,

earlier produced a succession of philosophers, including the great sage Samdhimati (a contemporary of Christ) and Nagarjuna; one of the founders of Mahayana Buddhism. Hiuen Tsiang, the Chinese traveller, visited Kashmir around 632 and was impressed by the natives "love of learning"; the common Kashmiri surname "Bhatta" denoted a scholar. Out of the sixteen great rhetoricians of ancient India, fourteen came from Kashmir. Now, a philosophical movement reached its fruition in the establishment of Kashmiri Shaivism in the eighth century. Systematised in the ninth century by Somananda, it was a distinctive branch of Hinduism, infused with an idealistic monism and temperamentally akin to Islam in its denunciation of self-mortifying, fantastic ritual. But this philosophy became effete through the intrigues and exactions of the Brahmin priestly class. The last centuries of the pre-Islamic period are replete not only with assassinations and internecine warfare, probably stemming from the ethnic heterogeneity of Kashmir's dominions, but also with the conflict between Buddhism and Hinduism and an intense, inner turmoil in Hinduism itself. The burning down of Buddhist monasteries was not so significant as the destruction of Hindu temples under King Harsha (reigned 1089-1101), himself a Hindu.

The heart of Kashmir cleaves to Muslim Pakistan. Yet the Kashmiris' traditional territory is divided by war and international dispute. In regions under the flag of Pakistan live various groups, such as this Leepa girl (**far left**) *and the Kashmiri bride and man* (**centre left and left**). *Sheep and goat rearing, for "Cashmere" wool, occupies many families* (**right**)

till 1586. Civil unrest under the Chaks invited Mughal intervention; Kashmir was the ornament of the Mughal empire from 1586 to 1752. Then came Afghan rule which lasted until 1819. In the latter year, Kashmir was annexed by the Sikhs of Punjab who ravaged the land until they were ousted by the British in 1846. The British handed over Jammu and Kashmir to a Dogra freebooter through a sale deed miscalled a treaty; the ignominy persisted through Dogra rule from 1846 to 1947. The current era has seen Kashmir as a disputed territory, a theatre of insurrection and war; until its status is decided by its own volition, the State will remain a scene of strife and potential explosion.

There are chapters of the pre-Islamic part of this history which are identical with that of Pakistan. Including the rule of Mauryas (third century BC) and Kushans (first century AD), the seizure of Kashmir in 515 by the White Huns ruling from Sialkot and the consequent reign of terror by Mehrakula (the name is still familiar in Kashmir), they are singularly unrevealing about Kashmir itself. Kashmir's personality is more clearly silhouetted under the earlier indigenous reign of the Pandus, to which period it owes the still fragrant romantic legend of Heemal and Nagrai and in the much later period of the Karakota dynasty from 627 to 980. The powerful figure of this epoch is Lalitaditya (697-738) whose domain included Tibet, Hazara and Punjab down to Multan. The Karakota expansion had not only a political dimension; there was also a cultural explosion. Kashmir had

This impasse and exhaustion of Hinduism in its intellectual stronghold set the stage for the entry of Islam. For centuries since Arab armies had marched into Gilgit in 751, Kashmir had enclosed itself in its spiritual and political shell. It had remained sequestrated despite the expedition of Mahmud of Ghazni in 1015 and the Dardic conversion to Islam in the twelfth century. Marco Polo had noted a meagre presence of Muslims in Kashmir on his visit around 1277. Now the shell was broken, not by soldiers, but by saints and friars. Islam penetrated peacefully into Kashmir when Rinchan (d. 1323), a commander from Ladakh who had conquered Kashmir, started his personal quest for religion, was baffled by the mutually contradictory answers he received from Brahmins, happened to watch Sayyid Bilal (d. 1327) at prayer, was enchanted by the simplicity of the Sayyid's faith and embraced it with fervour.

This inaugurated a renaissance in Kashmir which had its political, spiritual and cultural expressions. Politically, it begot the reign of the Shahmiri dynasty comparable in quality if not in scale with the Seljuks and the Mughals in their patronage of culture and a succession of illustrious monarchs. The representative figures are Sultan Shahabuddin (reigned 1354-1373), conqueror and builder, whose rule extended to Kabul, Kashgar and Kangra on three sides, and Sultan Zainul Abedin (reigned 1420-1470) who was a forerunner of Akbar in his tolerance and eclecticism, though, unlike Akbar, he was an accomplished scholar and no believer in an ersatz faith. In the spiritual realm, Sayyid Bilal, called Bulbul Shah, an immigrant from Turkestan, was followed by a long line of saints from Central Asia and Iran who propagated Islam in Kashmir; the most illustrious among them was Syed Ali Hamdani (1314-1384) called Amir-i-Kabir, author, poet, traveller, a leader of the Kubrawi mystic order, to whose memory the mosque Khanqah-i-Mualla (erected in 1395) stands as a monument in Srinagar. The movement was furthered by the native *Rishis* of Kashmir, notably Shaikh Nuruddin (1377-1438) and Shaikh Hamza Makhdum (1494-1576); they fostered an intense religious sensibility with a focus on inwardness and a Vedantist overlay on Islamic material. One can perceive the cultural matrix in which this spirituality was embedded from the utterances of the hermitess-poet Lalla Arifa (b. 1335) owned by both Hindus and Muslims, the contemporaneous Sanskrit jargon full of Arabic and Persian words which became a vehicle of the Islamic message and the Sanskrit inscriptions on graves of Muslim saints.

At the same time, however, there was a massive absorption by Kashmir during this phase of the learning and the arts of Bukhara, Samarkand and Hamdan. First imported by Syed Ali Hamdani and his followers, they gave a stimulus to

Kashmir's artistic genius and made Srinagar (historically known, like the Vale, as Kashmir) rank with Damascus and Isfahan as a centre of craftsmanship. Woodcarving, silver work and woollen embroidery, particularly on the shawl, handwoven of the underfleece of an Asian goat, and fine carpet-making became its specialities. The residential colleges founded by the Shahmiri Sultans and later patronised by the Mughals earned Kashmir the title of *Iran-i-Sagheer* (Little Iran); their alumni included the famous Mulla Ahmad Kashmiri (c. 1450) Shaikh Yaqub Sarfi (1521-1594) Mulla Kamal (d. 1608) the teacher of Shaikh Ahmed Sirhindi and Muhsin Fani (1615-1671). Medicine was an esteemed branch of learning. Poetry flourished. Mullah Tahir Ghani (d. 1668) is only the best-known in a galaxy of Kashmiri poets writing in Persian. While, in these respects, Kashmir became a lively contributor to the Islamic Indo-Persian culture, it also developed its indigenous literature. Habba Khatun, a peasant girl, then the Queen of Yusuf Shah Chak (reigned 1580-1586) and finally a recluse, invented the authentically Kashmiri ten-line lyrical form known as Lol which means a longing and a tugging at the heart. Her successors were Khwaja Habibullah Nawshehri (d. 1617), the Hindu Rupa Bhawani (1624-1720) and Arani Mal (c. 1750). There was also the development of an individual architectural style, which resembles the timber construction of the Scandinavian and Alpine regions and is characterized by sloping roofs waterproofed with layers of birch-bark overspread with turf and flowers, projecting upper storeys and casement windows

resembling the chalets of the Austrian Tyrol. The open work traceries of window screens and balustrades and the *Khatamband* ceilings made of panels of pinewood arranged in geometrical designs are some of its distinctive features. A parallel development occurred in music with a blend of native, Turanian and Persian elements; *Rast* Kashmiri, invented by Habba Khatun, is its most striking expression.

In sum, Kashmir blossomed under the Sultanate. The Mughals loved Kashmir which owes its exquisite gardens to them; statesmen like Khwaja Inayatullah (eighteenth century) and calligraphists like Muhammad Husain Zareen Qalam (d. 1611) rose to eminence in the Mughal court.

After the Mughals, there is a steep descent into darkness. Kashmir's institutions withered. Misrule, famine and epidemics characterised the Afghan era. However, Afghan rule seems healthy when compared to the pestilential Sikh period. Sayyid Ahmed Barelvi died in battle at Balakot in 1831 while engaged in a mission to liberate Kashmir. The rule of Dogras was vouchsafed to the State by the mere circumstance of the East India Company's need for ready cash. Kashmir, Kulu, Mandi, and Kangra were ceded by the Sikhs to the British in lieu of an indemnity of ten million rupees; the Dogra chieftain from Jammu, Gulab Singh (d. 1857)

made payment of seven and a half million *nanakshahi* (equivalent to $680,000) and through the infamous Treaty of Amritsar (1846) obtained possession of Jammu and Kashmir. Apart from the simulation of modernity under British influence, the Dogra period was but a continuation of the chapter which began with the Sikhs. The tale is of sordid exploitation. India's present claim to the State derives solely from the signing of the instrument of accession by a Maharaja who had been involved in scandals in Britain and described by an eminent British judge (Lord Simon), as "a poor, green, shivering, abject wretch".

Kashmir's current history starts from 13th July 1931 when the Muslims started a mass agitation against Dogra rule. As at the time of Sayyid Ahmed Barelvi, they were supported by the Muslims of the subcontinent; nearly 30,000 people from Punjab alone filled the Maharaja's prisons. The resistance movement reached its climax in 1946-47 with a "Quit Kashmir" campaign and with the adoption by the principal political party of the Azad (free) Kashmir resolution. Subsequent events are listed elsewhere in this volume. What needs to be said here is that the occupation by India of 53,665 square miles, including the Vale of Kashmir, leaving only Azad Kashmir, the area of highlands (32,358 square miles) free is an unnatural dispensation, designed to cut Kashmir away from its moorings, reverse its history and denature its being. International justice may not yet be a reality but the workings of power politics notwithstanding, such an arrangement cannot endure for long.

M.Y.B. and Q.U.S.

Balochistan

Balochistan, which covers about forty per cent of the area of Pakistan, has had a long and eventful history. Traces of primitive man have been found in Balochistan, dating back to 4000 BC, through the Stone and Bronze Ages, and in part contemporary with the Indus valley civilization. In early history, the armies of the Assyrians and the Meds probably visited the area. Later, Aryans from Iran made their intermediary home in Balochistan, which was earlier identified as Gedrosia because of the Gedor River, known also as the Hingol.

The first invading army of Cyrus (558-520 B.C.) perished in Gedrosia, but the land was later conquered by the Persians under Darius I (522-486 BC). The main column of Alexander, after leaving the Sindh area of the Indus valley, marched through southern Las Bela and eastern Makran. The Indo-Greeks, the Parthians and the Scythians successively established their power there. Later, Sassanid Persia dominated the scene and the area came under its suzerainty. When Sassanid power waned,

Except for a coastal strip and triangular embayment of flat, sandy country, Balochistan consists of plateaux or Mountains. It is sparsely populated by five main groups – Makranis, Brahuis, Balochis, Hazaras and Pathans

Left *A Balochi woman in the Bolan Pass feeds her camel with dough. Camels serve as pack animals, transport and a source of meat and milk*
Right *A procession of people and animals following the age-old route up the Bolan Pass, stretches for miles. In the spring, many tribes move to pastures in northern Balochistan from their warmer winter grazing in the south of the province or in Sindh*
Below right *A nomadic group rests near Quetta, having erected their tent and fed and watered their animals*

the Brahmins emerged from Sindh to rule Makran and the adjoining western areas of Balochistan. The Hephthalite Turks, however, maintained their hold outside Makran over the two states of Kaikanan (central Balochistan) and Bukan (north-eastern Balochistan). Muslim Arabs conquered the region in 711 AD.

The Ghaznavid and the Ghuri kings gained ascendancy of the area, until the great migration of the Rind-Lashar tribes laid the foundations of Brahui-Baluchi power, which later crystallised in the Khanate of Kalat (1686-1955).

British domination began with Robert Sandeman's mission to Kalat in 1875 and the recognition of Kalat's independence in 1876. Subsequently, the province of British Balochistan came into existence in 1891. After 14th August 1947, the states of Las Bela, Kharan, Makran and Kalat acceded to Pakistan. The Balochistan States' Union was formed in 1952 but shortly afterwards the whole of Balochistan, along with the provinces of Punjab, Sindh and North-West Frontier, was amalgamated into one province. When the unitary government in West Pakistan was dissolved and provinces restored, Balochistan was given the status, but not the administrative structure, of the other provinces. Balochistan became a fully-fledged province, with a directly elected assembly, only in April 1972, and under the Pakistan Constitution adopted in 1973, it was then accorded the same measure of provincial autonomy as the other three provinces.

Ethnically, Balochistan is pluralistic. The main groups, each with its own language and traditions, are the Baloch, the Brahuis and the Pathans. There are also Sindhis and smaller groups of Meds, Jats, Loris and others of mixed origin. The ethnic origin of the Baloch remains obscure. The scholarly view that they are probably the Chaldean descendants of the Belus dynasty of Babylonia (2100 BC) finds support in the universal Baloch tradition which locates their original homeland in Aleppo in Syria. The historical march of the Baloch from Babylonia to Balochistan took more than two millennia. Iran became their second homeland, where for more than a thousand years they first inhabited the northern parts in ancient Medea and the Caspian region, and later the south-eastern regions of Seistan and Kirman. They were in the soldiery of Iran under both the Achaemenian and the Sassanian emperors, and also acted as a buffer between the Iranians and the Turks. Firdausi in his *Shah Nama* pays tribute to their martial valour.

early converts to Islam and remained fortified in the Kirman and Seistan regions until the middle of the tenth century. After encounters with the strong armies of two kings, the Buwaihid Azad-ud-Daulah and the Ghaznavid Sultan Mahmud, the eleventh century saw the second Baloch migration eastward. Marris, Kurds, Dodais and others formed part of this migration.

The third migration, mainly from the present Iranian Balochistan, took place by the turn of the fourteenth century. Among the migrants were Rind and Lashar peoples who subjugated the state of Kalat and moved onwards separately; the Rinds, following the northern Bolan route, founded the state of Sibi with its capital at Fatehpur, and the Lashar moving eastward established their state of Gandava. Here they fought the Rind-Lashar War for thirty years (c. 1490-1520) which sapped their energies, brought in the Arghuns from Kandahar, and dispersed the bulk of the Baloch communities into Sindh and Punjab.

The barren buff and black mountains arrayed in the Quetta-Kalat region, interspersed with inhospitable stone valleys, slope from the north into the lower ranges of Chagai-Kharan-Makran in the north-west and of Kirthar-Pub in the south-east. Contrast is provided by arid deserts extending

With the Scythian conquest of south-eastern Iran (100 BC), the first Baloch people appear to have migrated eastward into the present area of Balochistan and Sindh. The bulk of the present Brahui-speaking stocks and the Sindhi Siraiki-speaking Jats were the pioneers of this first big migration into Balochistan and adjoining provinces of Pakistan.

Realising the growing power of the Balochi, the last of the Sassanid rulers turned against them and, according to Firdausi, Nausherwan (531-578 AD) tried to exterminate them. During the seventh century AD, these Baloch were

through Chagai, Kharan and Makran; swamps of Lora and Mashkel adjacent to the Afghan-Iran borders; vast stretches of flat hard-crusted peat, plains formed by thick deposits of alluvium in the Sibi and Kachchi districts in the east; and saline plains stretching along the western coastline.

For most of the year, the climate is hot and dry. Scorching hot winds, dust storms and towering whirlwinds sweep the plains. The north-westerly *gorich* wind, bitterly cold in winter but very hot in summer, blows across the west, and to the west of Chagai the country is swept by the hot *simoon* and the "120-day wind" (*bad-i-sad-o-bist rot*) from Iran. Even in the shade the temperature can rise to 130°F in summer. In winter, snow falls on the central Quetta-Kalat region which is also exposed to the dry and cold Kandahari *hava* (wind) from the north.

After their chequered history culminating in encounters with mighty emperors, the people of the Balochistan region, in alliance with the forces of nature, have been able to survive in isolation, but at the cost of social development, because no *simoon* or *hava* could sweep away from them the feudalistic cobwebs which retarded their growth. The original role of the chiefs was to provide protection and guidance to their people but with time they became extortionary and

density population in Pakistan – the 1995 census estimated it as 6.5 million – has, until the recent advent of roads, changed slowly. The people of the vast rural areas have mainly been nomads, grazing their herds of sheep, goats or camels during the dry months on scanty grass, dwarf-palm, wild caper, tamarisk or acacia. During the light rains in July and August their fare is greener and more ample.

Most of the nomadic tribes of the central Sarawan-Jhalawan region leave their settlements in winter to escape its severity and migrate eastward to Sibi and Kachchi and to the Indus valley area in Sindh. This annual transhumance from the cold high plateau to the warm lowlands has been going on since time immemorial.

Water being a precious commodity in Balochistan, the early permanent settlements – many of them now developing into towns and villages – were founded where water was available. In the central region, from Quetta to Khuzdar, there are a few natural springs and the ingenious age-old *karez* tap and channel water underground to irrigate orchards and seasonal crops. The few rivers are no more than hill torrents, such as the Narri, Habb, Purali, Hingol, Shadikor and Dasht, and they sustain limited agriculture, largely grain and millet. The Dasht valley in Makran produces a fine variety of date palms.

Left *Rigid tribal practices and sanctions, engendered by life in such uncompromising terrain, are at last softening. Hereditary chieftains, or sardars, often look venerable. But many are alert to rising expectations*
Centre *Women in Balochi nomadic families cook, wash, tend animals and fetch water, frequently from considerable distances. Their brightly coloured clothes are hand-woven and embroidered and even the poorest among them will wear elaborate jewellery*
Right *A Balochi fisherman examines his nets for tears. Fishing has always been the mainstay of the economy for the Balochis on the Makran coast*

feudal *sardars*, living in a large area which came to be called Balochistan for the first time in the fifteenth century. In the nineteenth century, the British, who were more concerned with the maintenance of their authority than with social progress, confirmed the powers and privileges of the tribal *sardars*.

Most of these tribes lived in what the fifteenth century poet Revragh called the "mountain fortress". A later poet, Baloch, spelt out the terms of the alliance between the indefatigable people of the area and nature, when he affirmed that, "mountains were the forts of the Baloch, high peaks their comrades, hills their army, trackless furrows their friends, spring water their drink, leaves of the dwarf-palm their cup, thorny bushes their bed, and stony ground their pillow."

Traditionally, life in this province, with the lowest

The scanty monsoon rains, averaging five inches in the plains, provide water for lean crops. Only the southern Nasirabad district adjoining Sindh, which is served by a perennial canal from the Guddu Barrage, completed in 1963, has a permanently settled population. It consists mainly of farmers who are used to regulated irrigation which canals provide for their crops.

The 471-mile-long coastline is dotted with settlements of fishermen, a mixed ethnic stock of the ancient Medes, and the early settlers in this region who still net their fish: the *mangra*, their colloquial word for sharks and skate, the *mahi*, which are sole, sardine and pomfret, and also prawns and shrimps. With the development of technology, the fishermen, with State help, are modernising their equipment.

The herdsmen of Balochistan are among the best breeders of sheep, goats, cattle, horses and camels in Pakistan.

THE LAND AND PEOPLE

Above *Babies, like this Pathan infant from near Ziarat, are usually swaddled until they are six months old*
Left *A mother and child from Sibi, where, in the summer, recorded temperatures are the highest in the subcontinent*

The *Hirzai* horse of Sarawan, the horses of Sibi, the *Bhagnarri* cattle of Narri and the sheep of the Marri-Bugti area, are the best of their kind.

Though traditional nomadism, ruralism, herding and coastal fishing are still the principal way of life for much of the province, Balochistan is changing as the infrastructure of socio-economic development expands, offering greater employment opportunities, better mobility due to networks of roads and new transport facilities, new industries, increased coal-mining activity, more extensive exploitation of mineral resources and expanding agriculture and fruit cultivation. The process of development has gained momentum since 1973 and water and power resources have been given high priority. During these years this infrastructure has been created by the local population aided by army engineers. The rural population is being provided with more schools, medical centres and deep tubewells: and these amenities are encouraging people to live more settled lives.

Economic development was considered by some *sardars* to be a threat because better communications meant the end of tribal insularity. Some of them took up arms against the road builders, but their insurgency was short-lived, and only delayed the implementation of the development schemes. The *sardari* system was formally abolished in April 1976, and civil administration established in the former *sardari* regions.

An insight into fifteenth and sixteenth century communities in Balochistan is provided by the Balochi and Brahui folk literature. Some of it is sung by professional minstrels and listened to fondly by both young and old. Lyrical love poetry found its earliest expression in the verse of Sheh Murid, who was in love with the beautiful Hani. Jam Durrak, the eighteenth century court poet of Nasir Khan the Great, gave the Balochi verse the imagery and flavour of Persian ghazal. Both the great epic poetry and the abundant tradition of folk song have shaped the songs and music of Balochistan.

Though Balochi is spoken over extensive areas in Balochistan, the province is multilingual. In many regions, Brahui, Pushtu, Siraiki and dialects such as Dehwari, Khetnari and Mokaki of the Loris, are also spoken in the

Top right Quetta, the provincial capital, is surrounded by abundant orchards
Above right and right The ancient karez *underground irrigation system, tapping the water table, is still efficient*
Top left A Hazara child works an intricate cushion cover in mirror embroidery
Above left Two little girls, seated at their looms, call out the patterns of a rug

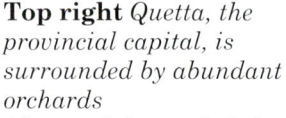

Top left Fruit of many varieties abound at Quetta, at 5,500 feet
Top right Much ingenuity is devoted to the decoration of lorries: drivers vie for individuality
Above The coastal Makranis are fishermen and small traders, linked by race to north-east Africa
Right Quetta carpets of high quality are a growing export. This design comes from Central Asia

province. The bulk of the present Baloch population is bilingual, and sometimes trilingual. Balochi and Brahui remain their mother tongues in the interior, while Sindhi and Siraiki have been adopted by the majority of the Baloch population living in the neighbouring provinces of Sindh and Punjab.

Tent-camps are an essential feature of nomadism which is gradually being affected by the inexorable process of urbanisation and socio-economic progress which is now a pervasive element in the life of modern Balochis. The camps are usually small, ranging from a single to about a dozen households, Each family owns a black tent of goat hair or sheep wool called *gidan*, or of dwarf-palm called *hirri* or *kul*. The traditional name for the camp, in eastern Balochi is *halk*, or community. Normal camp life is attuned mainly to the needs of the flock: herding, milking, tending young and sick animals, protecting the herd from jackals and wolves, shearing, and searching for water and grazing. Women fetch wood and water, gather wild fruits, mushrooms, wild onions, other edible roots and plants, collect fresh dwarf-palm fronds to make mats, ropes and sandals, cook and knit. The staple food of most of the rural people of Balochistan consists of unleavened bread, milk, butter and curds. *Sajji* meat roasted on a wood fire is the most relished dish.

The Balochi men usually wear thick long beards and both men and women wear long plaits. Balochi dress is enormous, with a big turban tied in different community styles, a long, loose shirt, and bulky trousers. The women wear a long dress, with long sleeves called *pashk*. The *pashk* is beautifully embroidered and the quality and extent of it usually indicates the social status of its wearer.

The beard and the turban are symbols of honour; and the elders often swear "by my beard" and "by my turban". Tweaking the beard or displacing the turban are regarded as great insults and the dishonour done is invariably resented and avenged. Close friendship and a relationship of complete trust and confidence between two men is symbolised by a ceremony of exchanging turbans. Herding, milking, embroidery, mat-making, rug-weaving and saddlery are the traditional arts of the communities in Balochistan. The tribal women are expert in needlework and their embroidery is some of the best in the world. Each community has its distinctive style of stitch and colour combination.

Wrestling, horse racing, religious feasts, *melas* (fairs) and marriage feasts are the main recreational and ceremonial functions in Balochistan, In the Makran region, the seasonal harvest of the date palms called *hamen* is an occasion for rejoicing and reunion of friends and relatives who return home for the harvest.

N.A.B.

chieftains more or less in check. At the height of the Great Game with the Russian Czar, Lord Lytton, Viceroy of India (1876-80), persuaded the Khan of Kalat to cede Quetta to the Crown in view of its strategic location. The rugged frontier town was soon developed into a military cantonment and its army staff college became well known for the excellence of its instruction. Expanded and modernised, the college continues to train senior army officers from different parts of the world. The railway line linking Quetta to the rest of British India was a major engineering feat, tunnelling through rocky mountains and traversing deep gorges.

The character of Quetta changed considerably since the Afghan war began in the late Seventies. Tens of thousands of refugees established camps on the outskirts of the city, and gun-running and drug smuggling became widespread. International relief agencies set up their offices, and very soon, money began pouring into the sleepy garrison town. As a result, barren land was transformed into housing colonies where ornate structures suddenly sprang up. Simultaneously, the roads became crowded with luxury

Quetta: skills of the cobbler's craft are passed from father to son

Quetta

Situated in a valley among the moonscape of the Chiltan and Murad mountains, the earliest reference to Quetta appears in Herodotus' account of his travels. Practically razed to the ground in the great earthquake of 1935, the city limped back to life, and is today the bustling capital of Balochistan with a population of over a million. But since Independence, its character has undergone a vast transformation: today, traders from Sindh rub shoulders with refugees from Afghanistan, and the shops are overflowing with local dried fruit, crockery from Iran, carpets from Central Asia and electronic goods from Japan and South Korea.

Although Balochistan was not formally annexed to the British Crown, a series of treaties kept the various tribal

four-wheel drive vehicles of every description, and Quetta acquired the appearance of a boom town.

Fortunately, the nearby orchards remain unspoiled, and although water remains a scarce resource in Quetta, the icy streams in the surrounding mountains have created unexpected and delightful pockets of greenery where picnickers go to cool off during the hot, dry summer months. But within the city, tall, graceful trees have been felled to make way for wider roads and taller buildings. Lytton Road, once cool and shaded even during the hottest summer day, has been largely stripped of its lovely *chenar* trees. Quetta may have grown a lot over the past half century, but it has lost much of its easygoing charm.

I.H.

4. The Economy

Above *Controlling the Indus: power house of the Mangla Dam*
Below *Steel Mill Complex, Karachi: the nation's largest single public sector industrial unit*

Pakistan's potential as an emerging Asian economy was first recognised during the sixties when it was introduced by the economist Gustav Papanek as a model of economic growth in the developing world. Much water has flowed under the bridge since then. After going through almost all the motions of progress and reversal experienced by many Third World countries during the same period, Pakistan finds itself again as an emerging Asian economy, albeit vulnerable and beset by challenges.

In 1947, fledgling Pakistan inherited a largely agrarian economy, poor infrastructure, a narrow industrial base, and a weak institutional framework. The first ten years were largely concentrated on the development of the government machinery in the two wings of the country, rehabilitation of refugees, and gearing up of the infrastructure.

Government laid the foundation for a *laissez-faire*, private sector-led economy. One consequence of this policy was illustrated by the census of 1957, which showed that 51 per cent of total output in large scale manufacturing was controlled by only 6 per cent of the business houses in the country. The domestic market was protected by strict quantitative and exchange restrictions providing scope for cartels or monopolies in market structure, which manipulated production levels and prices and inhibited expansion of the manufacturing base. The axis between a powerful bureaucracy and a patronised business class led for the first time to the development of the concept of "rent-seeking", or backhand payments to individuals, which has pervaded not to say plagued government activities in varying degrees from then on.

In 1955-56, raw jute constituted almost 49 per cent of total exports. By 1963-64, jute exports accounted for 33 percent of total exports, jute manufactures 15 per cent, cotton 19 per cent and cotton manufactures 5 per cent. The ratio of manufactured exports had grown considerably and domestic industry had diversified to light engineering goods, paper, fertilisers, leather manufactures, beverages, agro-based preserves and consumer products.

An important feature of economic development in this phase was the unequal rate of growth between the two wings of the country. In 1957, only one fifth of large-scale manufacturing was located in East Pakistan, and combined public and private investment during the First Plan period in West Pakistan was twice that of East Pakistan. Regional disparity was aggravated by the government's programme of directly participating in the setting up of industries in areas where the private sector was found to be inactive. The bias of government allocations through such organisations as the Pakistan Industrial Development Corporation, the Industrial Credit and Investment Corporation, and both the Industrial and Agricultural Development Banks was strongly in favour of entrepreneurs of West Pakistan.

Nevertheless, high growth rates measured during the 1960s despite low domestic savings, and the economy showed visible structural change. The Green Revolution had improved the performance of the agricultural sector, especially in the bigger landholdings of West Pakistan. The share of industrial output and of manufactured exports in the late sixties was higher in Pakistan than in countries like Korea, Thailand and Malaysia. In the preface to the Third Plan, (1965-70) President Ayub Khan noted that incomes had risen by 66 per cent in the previous plans. This famous Third Plan envisaged a more equitable distribution of wealth in the future on the basis of the trickle-down effect of industrial growth. But he was out before it could be implemented.

Ironically, the Decade of Development ended on a high crescendo of popular unrest in both wings of the country. While in West Pakistan, the inequitable income distribution and concentration of wealth in the hands of a few led to the removal of the government, in East Pakistan civil war broke out which by the end rent the country asunder and gave birth to Bangladesh in December 1971.

This period of unrest in Pakistan reflected a global debate in the late sixties which questioned the premise of economic growth vis-à-vis a new concept of balanced socio-economic development. The elections of 1970 focused on this issue and when Z.A. Bhutto assumed power in December 1971, he set about bringing fundamental changes in the economy.

Under the Economic Reform Order of 1972, the government nationalised 32 private units in ten basic categories: iron and steel, basic metals, heavy engineering, heavy electrical machinery, assembly and manufacture of motor vehicles and tractors, chemicals, petrochemicals, cement and public utilities. In September 1973, the government took control of vegetable oil industries, life insurance, shipping, cotton and rice export marketing excluding textile production. By January 1974, banks had also been nationalised. In 1976, an Act was passed in the parliament to safeguard the interests of multinationals and foreign investment in the country.

During this period, a much needed devaluation was allowed, and exports recorded a growth of 38 per cent in 1972-73. The next year, the $1 billion mark was crossed. The government introduced the Export Finance Scheme in 1973 to facilitate non-traditional and emerging exports. In subsequent years, increased production of cotton manufactures, fabric, made-ups, knitwear and hosiery further improved the export profile.

The shift in emphasis slowed down the rate of growth considerably, but infrastructural expansion laid the foundations for future large-scale industrialisation. This period saw the establishment of the largest state-owned steel mill plant in Pakistan, the Heavy Mechanical Engineering complex at Taxila, Pakistan Machine Tools, the Karakoram Highway, mining, oil and gas exploration and new airports in the country.

Mass nationalisation of big business broke the confidence and crippled the performance of the private sector in the country. While the public sector enterprises created a strong base, they could not be run economically by the government and suffered heavy losses. The overall economic policy was characterised by regulation, subsidies and mismanagement.

Even after change of government in 1977, no basic improvement was visible in the economic system throughout the next decade. In 1978, despite a smaller overall share in economic activity, a considerable portion of the investable resources were pre-empted by the public sector, which stood at 52.8 per cent of gross domestic investment. Attempts were made in 1978 and 1985 to disinvest public funds, but these met with very little success.

In the meantime, in 1979, Soviet intervention in Afghanistan aligned the military regime of General Zia with western interests, and Pakistan became a front-line state in the war, receiving military and economic aid from the US on a large scale. There was a large influx of Afghan refugees, and funds from international agencies and donor countries started to pour in. The country's foreign debt grew to new levels. At this time also, the so-called Islamisation process was initiated, with the introduction of the Zakat tax and Ushr, the agricultural tithe, and an interest-free banking system. The position of women was adversely affected, and the education system collapsed. The unstable political system, scheduled power cuts, inflation and stagnation compounded the problems of the economy.

It was Mohammad Khan Junejo's elected government that initiated the Hubco Power Project in 1986. This was the first and largest power project in the private sector in Pakistan, designed to produce 1200MW of electricity in a joint venture with National Power of Britain. The Hubco agreement laid down the framework for the country's future investment policy formulation.

The first government of Benazir Bhutto was faced with problems that proved insuperable. The emergence of new developing economies attracting global investment had brought about a closer integration of the international financial market. An agreement was signed with the IMF in 1989 to bring about structural changes in the fiscal and monetary management of the country. As a result of higher taxes and increased government borrowings, the cost of capital grew, and despite efforts towards privatisation in 1989 and institutional reforms, industry as a whole could not gather momentum. The public sector enterprises continued to drain government revenues and a holistic approach towards deregulation was not evolved.

In 1990, the election of Nawaz Sharif as Prime Minister stimulated the revival of economic activity in the country. Himself a businessman, he immediately embarked upon a programme of improving the investment climate and liberalising the financial sector within a broader framework of economic deregulation. A comprehensive Investment Policy was introduced; an Investment Promotion Board was set up; Protection of Foreign Investment (1976) Act was amended to re-assure investors; tariffs were lowered, foreign exchange restrictions were removed, 100 per cent foreign equity in industries was allowed, and the system of permissions, licences and clearances from government departments was abolished. A mineral development policy was drafted, and fifteen agreements were signed with foreign companies for exploration of hydrocarbons in the country.

A high-powered Privatisation Commission was set up reporting directly to the Cabinet. Within a span of six months, the government announced the sale of 108 public sector enterprises in the production sector – automobiles, cement, chemicals, engineering, fertiliser, vegetable oil, bakeries, and rice milling – and by October 1991, 66 units had been sold through direct bids and auctions. Enterprises covering physical infrastructure such as power generation, transmission, gas distribution, shipping, port operations and telecommunications were also opened up for privatisation, but at a slower pace, in order to develop institutional and regulatory frameworks where necessary.

However, during this period, expenditure grew to unprecedented levels, pushing the fiscal deficit to almost 7 per cent. As with so many Five Year Plans, implementation targets especially in the social sectors could not be met, in fact the allocations were reduced, drastically affecting the education and science programmes so important for sustained economic growth. The government was dismissed in 1993 and a caretaker administration installed under Moeen Qureshi. The caretaker Prime Minister was a senior World Bank official who set about to correct the fiscal distortions in the economy. One of the most important moves in this direction was to free the Central Bank from government control and make it autonomous.

Outside Pakistan as well, the world was changing rapidly: globalisation, integrated markets, information technology, and the dissolving of the ideological frontiers of the Soviet bloc had a direct impact on international economic relations. The World Trade Organisation replaced the old economic world order, hitherto been dominated by North-South confrontation and the restrictive regime of the General Agreement on Trade and Tariffs (GATT). Trade blocs were being formed and new regions were catching up rapidly with the developed world. The late Eighties and early Nineties saw new foreign investment pouring into developing countries, many of which were re-defined as emerging markets. The South Asian Association for Regional Cooperation (SAARC) and Economic Cooperation Organisation (ECO) had been formed, with Pakistan as a founding member of both organisations.

The 1993 Bhutto government adhered to the programme of deregulation and privatisation, and attracted large foreign direct investments into the country. The 1994 Private Power Policy was announced in view of the power shortages which were hampering growth. Demand for power had been rising annually at 12 per cent, nearly twice that of GDP, while supply was growing at 8 per cent only. Scheduled power cuts were estimated to cost $1 billion in productivity every year. The Policy offered attractive incentives in fixed purchase price, duty free imports of plant and machinery and income tax exemptions which amounted to a return on equity of 17 to 18 per cent in dollar terms.

International commitments to invest in Pakistan rose to an unprecedented $14 billion by the end of 1994, although much of this was in the shape of Memoranda of

Understanding. Investments were mainly in the power generation and transmission sector, oil and gas exploration and the setting up of a pure terephthalic acid (PTA) plant by ICI. Apart from traditional partners like USA, Britain and Japan, investments from South Korea and the UAE increased substantially in the manufacturing sector and portfolio investment.

Efforts were made by the government to streamline the bureaucracy and set up institutional frameworks to facilitate the volume of investments. The National Energy Regulation Authority was established to create a legal framework to regulate payments to and monitor prices of power generation projects. A Board of Investment directly responsible to the Prime Minister established up to facilitate foreign projects, and a comprehensive investment incentive package was drawn up, still considered to be the best in South Asia.

However, the Bhutto government could not implement the IMF's Structural Adjustment Programme successfully. An inefficient and top-heavy state apparatus, high military expenditure compounded by a faulty taxation system resulted in heavy government borrowings. To increase revenue earnings, indirect taxes were imposed which had a regressive effect on incomes and the already battered economy went into recession. The high cost of domestic capital squeezed the private sector out of much-needed resources, affecting production, export and growth targets.

A sound monetary policy could not be developed due to inherent weaknesses of the banking system and mismanagement of macro-economic policies. The autonomy of the Central Bank was curtailed by a government seeking to free itself from its IMF commitments. This distorted the reforms of the previous caretaker government. The government's evident lack of control over expenditure had a direct impact on the process of implosion within the bureaucracy which had been going on since 1990. Frequent withdrawal of administrative orders and lack of vigilance over the performance of government departments reflected an slackness of governance that divided the bureaucracy and increased the milking of the system by so-called rent-seeking. Within a span of 10 months in 1996, the government had to go back to the IMF twice for standby arrangements. Short-term foreign debt grew rapidly, the balance of payments dipped, and the government was sacked by Presidential decree in November 1996.

The government under Nawaz Sharif which won the February 1997 elections with a two-thirds majority in the parliament, was faced with the formidable challenge of bringing down the budget deficit to sustainable levels within the ambit of a sound fiscal policy on the one hand, and providing capital for the revival of the industry on the other.

Within a week of assuming power, the Prime Minister announced his intention of reviving the economy through a supply-side strategy, and reducing establishment costs and defence expenditure. A National Debt Retirement Scheme was initiated, offering high returns on fixed term deposits in local and foreign currency. A conference was organised in Islamabad for over 400 top businessmen to work out an effective and sustainable policy to revive the industrial and financial sectors.

An economic stimulus package was announced within a few weeks, which set about to reduce personal income and wealth tax, corporate tax and general sales tax. Tariffs were lowered to a maximum of 45 per cent, import duties on machinery and raw materials reduced to 10 per cent and regulatory duties withdrawn. This growth-oriented strategy was perceived to increase pressure on government borrowing

Left *Sayyed Engineers manufacture ballpoint pens to the highest international specifications*
Right *Cans of ghee (cooking oil) ready for distribution*

and affect the balance of payments adversely. The IMF, although refusing to fill the resource gap, endorsed the strategy, calling it "a risk worth taking", thereby reducing the perceived hazards of investing in the Pakistan market.

However, it seemed clear that the government and the private sector would have to collaborate closely for the success of this programme. As with most supply-side strategies, a relatively quick response from the business sector would be the only way to ensure its continuity in the long term. The policy prescriptions announced by the government would have to be sustained with additional measures of currency depreciation, and acceleration of the privatisation programme.

The government was set to embark upon a programme of reviving the neglected sector of human resource development. While overall production costs are considered low in Pakistan because of lower labour and building costs, overheads are high because labour has to be trained to achieve acceptable productivity levels. There is a need to invest in vocational centres, manpower training programmes and technological know-how to upgrade the level of skills available in the country. Similarly, women development and education, which are seen as critical factors in productivity costs, would have to paid much more attention than ever before.

In the export marketing area, vigorous efforts would need to be made by the private sector both for value-addition and product diversification to reach government targets dependent on export-led growth. The government would also have to curb bureaucratic arrogance and streamline the working coordination to facilitate foreign direct investment into the country.

The government also announced agricultural reforms to remove significant economic distortions in this sector. Support prices for wheat, canola, sunflower and *irri* rice were raised substantially, agricultural credit was enhanced, land was distributed to landless peasants and duties on reconditioned harvesters were lowered. The government also undertook to set up micro-credit institutions, improve water courses and irrigation networks, and provide additional funding for research in agriculture.

Agriculture is the mainstay of the country's economy, and although more than 50 per cent of the industry depends on the land, farming has suffered on account of depressed (controlled) prices and the low priority given to the development of agri-business by successive governments. The sector offers opportunities in farm management, livestock breeding, food processing, dairy products, horticulture, animal feed and oilseed processing plants. The new government faced the requirement of increasing opportunities for

also important exports.

In April 1997, the Aid to Pakistan Consortium met in Paris to negotiate an aid package on the government's request for $3.26 billion. The Consortium, re-named as Pakistan Development Forum, announced its support to the reforms and conditionally agreed to raise $2.08 billion for the government if the promised expenditure cuts and structural economic and taxation reforms were implemented in the budget.

The 1982 Structural Adjustment Programme agreement with the IMF had stalled and the Fund initiated a Staff Monitoring Programme to monitor structural fiscal and monetary reforms promised by Pakistan, and advise in the implementation of required economic measures in the budget. Although the IMF and other international opinion had accorded qualified approval of the growthbased economic strategy introduced by the incoming government of 1997, the macro-economic imbalances still awaited to be controlled by a committed overall reform programme.

R.S.

Left *Distinctive blue and white pottery is manufactured on a large scale in Multan, Punjab*
Right *Textiles are Pakistan's single biggest income earner, with over 240,000 sq. metres of cloth produced a year*

investment in this sector, providing appropriate incentives and establishing the necessary infrastructure to raise the level of agri-business activity.

Pakistan's cement sector has an installed capacity of about 8.5 million tonnes per annum with capacity utilisation of over 90 per cent. There are ten fertiliser plants with a capacity of 4.1 million tonnes per annum.

The engineering sector provides manufactures in light engineering, metal products, non-electrical and electrical machinery, electronic and transport equipment, agricultural and textile machinery, machine tools, cutlery, and surgical instruments.

The textile industry accounts for over 60 per cent of exports and provides employment to one third of the industrial labour force. Joint ventures and better technology have increased the efficiency of the industry, which manufactures under franchise for a number of famous brand names. Rice is a highly valued cash crop and has been a key export. Leather and leather products, footwear, carpets and rugs, sports goods, *guar* gum (for textiles), fish and fish preparations, pet products and fruits and vegetables are

Mining

The government has a general policy to privatise most economic activity currently in the public sector, including mining, to accelerate development. Major solid minerals being produced in Pakistan are coal, rock salt, limestone, marble, china clay, dolomite, gold and associated precious metals in the Northern Areas. The Pakistan Mineral Development Corporation, Balochistan Development Authority and PASMINCO are all involved in mining to varying degrees. The Saindak Copper and Gold Project in Chaghi, Balochistan, is the first large-scale metal mining project in Pakistan. The project is designed to produce 15,810 tonnes of blister copper annually with contained gold (1.47 tonnes) and silver (2.76) tonnes. When completed, the Lakhra Coal Development Company will supply 750,000 tonnes of coal per annum to WAPDA, the Water and Power Development Authority for its three 50 MW coal fired power plants in Sindh. The small scale industrial sector employs far less fixed capital. Yet it generates more employment opportunities, uses indigenous technology and raw material, and plays a key part in stemming the flow of people to the cities. Its contribution to GDP is around six per cent and it employs about eighty per cent of industrial labour. Its share in the manufacturing sector is put at 32.8 per cent.

B.A.

Agriculture

As the country enters its second half-century, we can assess the formidable advances made by Pakistan's agriculture, industry and service sectors.

With the expansion of the other sectors, agriculture's share of GDP has fallen, yet still contributes 25 per cent and employs almost half the labour force. Recently, agriculture has been given a boost through higher support prices of the major cash crops like wheat and cotton to bring them nearly at par with international rates and to increase investment in the sector. This politically tough decision cleared the way for Pakistan's agriculture sector to reach world yield levels as it entered the 21st century. The 1995-96 average per hectare yield of wheat was 2100 kg; rice 1823 kg; sugar cane 47 tonnes; and cotton 601 kg. The 1995-96 production of wheat stood at 17.57 million tonnes, rice 4 million tonnes, total food grains 24 million tonnes, sugar cane 45 million tonnes and cotton 10.55 million bales. Pakistan also produces 1.9 million tonnes of citrus fruit, 884,000 tonnes of mango, 533,000 tonnes of apple, 80,000 tonnes of banana, and 153,000 tonnes of apricot. The fact that only 49,000 tonnes of fruit were exported gives an indication of the export potential

Pakistan has one of the most developed canal irrigation systems in the world with water availability of 130.90 million acre feet irrigating the bulk of Pakistani farmland. The remainder depends on tubewells and rainfall. There are around five million farms in Pakistan covering 47.31 million acres.

Over the years, the use of fertiliser in the country has been increasing. A number of private firms market nitrogenous, phosphatic and potassic fertilisers. Prices are determined by the market.

The Federal Seed Certification Department evaluates the quality of seed being procured by public and private sector agencies, and carries out crop inspection to assess genetic purity. It also tests seeds to evaluate their quality. To control locusts and other pests, the Plant Protection Department carries out aerial sprays with a fleet of twenty-two aircraft. By the mid-Nineties, some 126,000 acres were being sprayed annually. Meanwhile, government has taken several measures to support modernisation. Emphasis has been on rapid mechanisation through provision of tractors at concessional rates and information on better farming techniques, management and operation practices.

Trade in agricultural and livestock items is freely allowed and is wholly in the hands of private enterprise, prices are determined by market forces. The government occasionally intervenes in the marketing of some essential items like food grains, sugar, meat, milk and eggs to ensure that they are available to consumers at reasonable prices.

The Rice Export Corporation of Pakistan (RECP) and the Cotton Export Corporation (CEC) were created in the Seventies to provide stable exports. The Pakistan Storage and Supply Corporation – PASSCO – has been established to deal with less perishable commodities in the country, as well as to construct and maintain silos and warehouses for produce. Market intelligence, vital to an efficient market was being provided by the Agricultural and Livestock Products Marketing and Gradation Department (ALPMG). A firm

Left *Some of Pakistan's vast population of buffaloes cool themselves in a pool under the mid-day sun*
Centre *Farm workers gather the straw, after the harvest*
Right *Billowing fields of wheat, Punjab: wheat is an increasingly important cash crop for Pakistan*

Far left *Camels bear the load in rural drylands*
Left *A young shepherd works alongside his elders, leading the flock to greener pastures*
Centre *Driving an oxcart along a country road: this ancient transport is still part of rural life today*

Above *Marine fishing provides the majority of Pakistan's catch, although inland fishing contributes substantially. The industry is currently being developed and strengthened*
Right *Bringing in the year's crop of oranges: agriculture employs almost half of Pakistan's entire labour force*

policy was established in the light of the limited resources of small farmers. Institutional credit is provided to them by the government at a concessionary interest rate. Production loans are provided on the basis of the actual crop requirements rather than a flat assessment on the basis of acreage.

Government annually reviews and fixes support prices of important crops on the recommendation of Agricultural Prices Commission while the Pakistan Agriculture Research Council assists, undertakes, promotes and coordinates research.

Pakistan's livestock population is estimated to be around 20.2 million buffaloes, 17.9 million cattle, 45.6 million goats, 29.8 million sheep, 345 million poultry, 1.1 million camels, 4.1 million donkeys and 0.1 million mules. In order to prevent depletion of these stocks, two meatless days are observed every week when the slaughter and sale of meat are prohibited. Pakistan's livestock produces around 20 million tonnes of milk, one million tonnes of beef, one million tonnes of mutton, and 321,000 tonnes of poultry, annually.

The total forest area of Pakistan is estimated at 4.20 million hectares or 4.8 per cent of the total geographical area of the country. This is below what is considered the desirable ratio of 20 to 30 per cent. Indeed, the last half-century has witnessed an inexorable deforestation as a growing population, especially in the Northern Areas, has deeply encroached on Pakistan's forests.

The *per capita* forest area has been reduced to 0.037 hectare which is far below the world average of around 1 hectare. The forest sector contributed only 0.2 per cent to the GDP during 1995-96. However, under a massive afforestation programme, 250 million saplings were being raised in the mid-Nineties by the provincial Forest Departments for

supply to public sector organisations and the private sector.

As of 1996, fishery was contributing about 1 per cent of GDP, around 4 per cent in agriculture sector production and 1.7 per cent in total exports. Fish and fishery products worth US$100 million were exported in 1995-96. However, the catch was being reduced by the activity of foreign trawlers in Pakistani waters.

Total marine and inland fish production is estimated at around at 558,000 metric tonnes annually, out of which over 418.580 metric tonnes was marine production and the remaining catch came from inland fisheries.

B. A.

Below *A Marri settler tends the fields*
Below right *Pakistan produces an abundance and variety of superb fruit. There is great potential for growth in exports*
Above right *Cotton is one of Pakistan's main cash crops, with almost 3 million hectares under cultivation*

The Physical Infrastructure

As the 21st century approaches, Pakistan's requirement for an updated communication infrastructure has never been greater. The need may be seen as two-fold: to harness more effectively the energies of the community that constitutes the nation, and to achieve a higher level of interaction with the global community. Elsewhere in the infrastructure, given the significance of agriculture in Pakistan's economy, water for irrigation has always been a key concern. So also is power for the industrial sector, which has assumed ever greater significance as Pakistan seeks to modernise and compete in a world where competition gets tougher by the day. Today's physical infrastructure in all these areas is still recognised as inadequate for the kind of growth required for achieving high and sustained economic growth.

From its very inception Pakistan has been an outward looking nation and its flag-carrier Pakistan International Airlines (PIA) has been a vibrant symbol of that orientation. In 1955, the year it was established, PIA started its first international service from Karachi to London. Only five years later it became the first Asian airline to operate jet aircraft. It was the first non-communist airline to fly to the People's Republic of China and to operate a service to Europe via Moscow. PIA flights to the Northern areas of Pakistan are some of the most spectacular routes among high mountain peaks, which test the skill and versatility of its pilots. Today PIA's network covers forty-nine international and thirty-four domestic stations. The airline is now looking for new destinations. Expansion in size has not, however, been at the cost of the quality of service. PIA achieves schedule punctuality of eighty per cent over a total of more than 46,000 flights operated, and it has been a tough task for the

Traversing the mountains and rivers of Pakistan:
Above *Army engineers build a temporary bridge high up in the Karakorum mountains*
Top *Aerial view of the Mughalpura railway goods manufacturing workshop in Lahore. Rail is of vital importance for long distance transportation in Pakistan*
Right *A bridge bestrides the mighty Indus in Kohistan*

national carrier to keep pace with the burgeoning demand for air travel. In line with its emphasis on liberalisation, the government has encouraged private airlines to start operations within the country. Already Aero-Asia, Shaheen Airlines and Bhoja Airlines have created niches for themselves in the rapidly expanding domestic air travel market, and are helping to ease the load on busy air corridors.

A major objective of successive governments has been to upgrade safety facilities – both off and on the ground. Earlier, some of Pakistan's airports had been designated Red ("land at your own risk") by the international pilots' organisation. Even Karachi airport which handled 95 per cent of international traffic and was used by more than two dozen international airlines was in bad shape. Happily, all this is now history. All airports in Pakistan now have a Green ("safe to land") designation. There has also been a major effort to expand Pakistan's network of international and domestic airports as well as to upgrade facilities for accommodating larger and more modern aircraft.

By the early Nineties, a new airport in Karachi – Pakistan's key urban centre and commercial metropolis – capable of handling a much increased volume of international traffic was already in place. Similar plans for a new airport in Lahore, capital of the country's most populous province, were being finalised in 1996. The aim was to expand the present capacity of 2.5 million passengers to six million annually while making available the most modern facilities. The new airport will serve to facilitate trade and tourism to what is sometimes affectionately referred to as the heart of Pakistan. The main seaport of the country is Karachi which serves not only Pakistan but also landlocked Afghanistan. Once conditions stabilise in Pakistan's troubled neighbour and that country begins the urgent and long-awaited task of reconstruction, Karachi will also

Below *A Boeing 737 makes a neat landing in tricky conditions: this is the 8,000 ft. runway of Skardu Airport, set high up in mountains*

Pakistan International Airlines flies some of the world's most spectacular mountain routes, calling for great skill and versatility on the part of its pilots. PIA has expanded in size and upgraded its services in response to the growing market for air transport. It is also being joined by new private airlines such as Aero Asia, Shaheen Airlines and Bhoja Airlines

become a key port for Central Asian trade with the rest of the world. Situated a few miles south east of Karachi, newly-constructed Port Qasim has already started sharing the increasing burden on the facilities at Karachi port which handled more than 23 million tons of cargo in 1994-95. To handle the ever-increasing tonnage, a phased programme is under way for the modernisation and expansion of facilities at Karachi port. The private sector is also being encouraged to participate in various related schemes such as the construction of integrated container terminals, building of a warehousing complex and contract dredging of the harbour. There are plans to develop the small port of Gwadar westwards along the Makran coast as well as Keti Bandar. The Pakistan National Shipping Corporation (PNSC) is modernising and expanding its fleet of sixteen vessels. The liner services of the Corporation operate from Pakistan to the rest of the world.

Relatively few Pakistanis travel by sea or air. For the bulk of the population road and rail provide the principal means of movement. Good roads are not new to the subcontinent. During the 16th century, Sher Shah Suri during his brief but brilliant rule of India built many wide and permanent roads to link distant parts of his empire. The present highway from Multan to Torkham virtually retraces the road built by Sher Shah on this route. Pakistan's national highways carry more than sixty per cent of the freight and passenger traffic of the country and cover nearly 4,000 miles. But this is only 3.5 per cent of the total road length in

Quaid-e-Azam International Airport, Karachi: Pakistan's airports are serving greater needs. Further capacity is planned

The National Shipping Corporation is expanding and modernising its fleet of container ships to handle more trade

Pakistan, the remainder varying in quality of surface and width from well-paved roads to mountainous dirt tracks. The most spectacular sector is the Karakoram Highway or the fabled Silk Route which cuts across the Karakoram mountains to link Pakistan with China. First opened by traders in the 7th and 8th centuries, this narrow route is now a well-built road – the result of a joint effort by Pakistani and Chinese workers and engineers and a testimonial to their skill and dedication as well as a symbol of the ties between the two countries. One of the most well-travelled sectors in the country is the Lahore-Islamabad highway where work on a new six-lane motorway over 335 kilometres was to be completed in 1997, promising greater traffic flow between these two important centres. Work was in progress on a new Karachi-Lahore-Peshawar-Torkham four-lane highway, as well as on the rehabilitation of the existing road. There was also a broad effort under way to improve the rest of the national highway system, provide dependable farm-to-market roads and construct bridges. In addition, the private sector was to be increasingly encouraged to invest in the toll-bearing "Build Operate and Transfer" model that has proved so successful abroad.

While roads carry a greater proportion of the traffic, travel by rail remains popular for travel over long distances. At Independence, Pakistan inherited one of the most efficient and elaborate railway networks in the developing world. For years, the steam locomotive chugging along was a familiar sight from Khyber in the north to Karachi in the south. Alas, over the years, diesel and electric engines have replaced many of these workhorses of the past. The need for a modern railway system is greater than ever as a more mobile population, characterised by an expanding middle class and enhanced production of industrial goods and agricultural produce, has put ever greater pressure on the roads. This load is likely to increase sharply once the potential for Central Asian trade via Pakistan is realised.

The Pakistan Railways network comprises 8,500 route kilometres and extensive assets in the shape of railway stations, rolling stock, factories and workshops. But most of the assets are over-age and in need of rehabilitation and modernisation. By 1997 a determination prevailed to overcome the effects of past neglect, and to upgrade and develop the railway system. More than Rs 3 billion was allocated for the development of Pakistan Railways during 1995-96. Concerned that the share of railways in domestic traffic has shrunk to a mere 15 per cent, the government was determined to restore its role as the main carrier of bulk freight over long distances. Revitalisation of the system was also to get a boost from private thermal power plants: bulk transportation of fuel oil from ports to these power plant sites is an activity particularly suited to the railways. Foreign investment was being sought in this sector.

While transport and communications were seen as crucial to the national enterprise, water for irrigation and energy for turning the wheels of industry have been central concerns for Pakistan from the time of its inception. Soon after Independence India diverted the rivers supplying its lower riparian neighbour. After extensive negotiations, the Indus Waters Treaty was signed in 1960 by the two countries under the auspices of the World Bank, dividing the Indus irrigation system between Pakistan and India. Pakistan received the three Western rivers – Indus, Jhelum and Chenab – while India received the three Eastern rivers – Ravi, Beas and Sutlej. The Indus Basin Project which included Mangla Dam, five barrages, one siphon and eight link canals, was completed in 1971. Next to be built was the Tarbela Dam, which started operation in the mid-Seventies. Two other major projects on the Indus are now on the anvil.

Work on the Ghazi-Barotha hydro power project was launched in 1996. The Kalabagh dam is scheduled to get under way as soon as inter-provincial consensus is reached and concerns of different provinces regarding possible negative environmental and other implications were resolved.

While dams – big and small – are needed for irrigation purposes, power generation has also been a major consideration in these projects. Even today, many villages in Pakistan are without electricity, and major urban centres suffer power breakdowns during peak hours in the dry season when the rivers are running low. For years industry has suffered losses worth billions of rupees in lost production due to an inadequate and irregular power supply. Currently, according to various estimates, Pakistan is over 2000 MW short of energy requirements. The dependable capacity of the system is approximately 11,000 MW while the demand is around 13,000 MW. This at a time when the *per capita* consumption of electricity in Pakistan is low – at around 300 kwh which is even below the global norm of 1 kwh *per capita* electricity consumption per $1 *per capita* GDP. The current annual growth in demand is about 9 per cent while the increase in supply lags behind at 7.7 per cent. Consequently, in addition to existing and proposed hydro-power projects in the public sector, the government has encouraged the private sector to enter the field. The vast Hubco power plant near Karachi started production in 1996 and was fully on stream by 1997. One of the world's largest private electricity generating plants, Hub has a gross capacity of 1300 MW and has by itself the capability of supplying nearly 13 per cent of Pakistan's current energy needs. Elsewhere, too, the private sector's response has been very positive, and foreign investors have expressed their interest in pumping in billions of dollars into the energy sector since early 1994 when the policy was first announced. Applications for setting up 25,000 MW have been received as against the requirement of about 5000 MW. While thermal power plants have been necessary to make up for the energy gap in the short and medium term, hydro power is the preferred option in the long term. For one, it is an environmentally safer method of generating electricity. Secondly, the very high initial investment required for hydro power is offset by a running cost advantage when compared to thermal plants.

Pakistan's large and growing demand for both local and international telecommunication requires a highly reliable network. The Pakistan Telecommunication Corporation (PTC) has modernised and expanded its system rapidly. Pakistan now has a large number of citizens working abroad in the Middle East, Europe and USA, and a reliable system linking Pakistan with the outside world has come as a great boon to millions of expatriate Pakistanis. Contact with loved ones back home is no longer a formidable enterprise. In addition to these personal considerations, economic liberalisation and encouragement of foreign investment has also made a highly efficient and reliable communication system imperative. The need for modernising the communication system has meant encouraging foreign participation in this sector. This has been done through the sale of the PTC shares in the international market. Sale of additional shares is envisaged as is the transfer of management to a "strategic investor" to ensure greater efficiency Meanwhile, the high performance of the PTC has made it one of the most profitable of all public sector enterprises. But in 1997, much still remained to be done to reduce the line fault rate as well as the unsuccessful call rate and to improve telephone density. A Pakistan Telecommunication Authority was envisaged to oversee the growth of parallel public and private systems and ensure healthy competition.

Ab. R.

Finance

Pakistan's financial sector has expanded dramatically since the late 1970s by opening up to the private sector. In the late Nineties the banking sector was in the process of reform and liberalisation. There are 25 domestic commercial banks with 8,326 branches and nineteen foreign banks with 74 branches in operation in the country. Total assets of the domestic scheduled banks amount to over Rs 1,760bn.

Other financial institutions include development finance institutions (known as DFIs), specialised banks, investment banks, cooperatives, *modarbas* (Islamic investment instruments – essentially closed-end mutual funds) and leasing companies. The nationalised banking sector still suffers from over-staffing, high operational costs, and poor quality services. There has been a turnaround in the quality and results of the banking industry since the privatisation drive began in 1990. Two banks have already been privatised. Privatisation of the state-owned United Bank Limited and Habib Bank Limited was on the government's immediate agenda. Of the DFIs, only Bankers Equity had been privatised.

Deposits held by the banks have risen to more than Rs700 billion. At the same time, the number of institutions holding deposits has been increased. By late 1994, the share of deposits held by five major banks had declined from 90 per cent to 83.95 per cent, with new private banks picking up 2.43 per cent of the deposit base, and the share of foreign banks rising from 10.11 per cent to 13.62 per cent in the same period. Total paid up capital and reserves of the scheduled banks was greatly expanding in the Nineties. Those of the scheduled banks topped Rs 50bn in 1995. The lending pattern has also reflected diversification away from inter-bank and government lending towards the productive sectors of the economy. Credit advances in 1995 stood at Rs400bn.

The State Bank of Pakistan is the central bank, working closely with the Ministry of Finance to formulate the monetary policy and monitor its implementation. It regulates the working of all banks, as well as controlling the issue of currency, providing banking services to the government, and banking system and foreign exchange control. The government in the mid-Nineties had started auctioning debt instruments in open markets in order to implement reform of domestic public debt management and to pursue monetary policy through open market operations.

Specialised credit institutions include Pakistan Industrial Credit and Investment Corporation (PICIC), Industrial Development Bank of Pakistan, Agricultural Development Bank of Pakistan, National Development Finance Corporation, Bankers Equity Limited, National Investment Trust, Investment Corporation of Pakistan, House Building Finance Corporation and the Small Business Finance Corporation.

The equity market in Pakistan has developed tremendously in the Nineties, as the trend for deregulation and privatisation gained pace. It grew not only in size, but was also moving towards more sophisticated financial instruments and research-based brokerage houses. The issue of shares in the primary market has risen sharply, as has liquidity in the secondary market. The country now has three stock exchanges – at Karachi, Lahore and Islamabad – each operating computerised trading. The Karachi Stock Exchange (KSE) in practice dwarfs the other two exchanges, although the equity of the listed companies is tradeable on each of the exchanges. Stock market performance was buoyant in the early Nineties due to the relaxing of curbs on foreign ownership of shares, and the introduction of incentives to attract both direct and portfolio investment from overseas. The KSE-100 index had slumped from 2,600 to 1,300 in 1996 due to a number of ephemeral factors, not least the high level of speculative activity and the unusually large proportion of shares held by family members, to reduce the risk of take-over and to avoid accountability by shareholders. In 1992, for example, the ownership of the stock market was broken down as 60-70 per cent by sponsors, families and associates, 20-30 per cent by institutions and only 5-10 per cent in "public floats", typically held by long-term investors such as the big insurance companies and *modarbas* . The low level of public ownership and institutions is a problem for new investors, as there are often not enough shares to go around.

The Islamabad and Lahore exchanges have typically accounted for only a small fraction of overall equity market liquidity. As individual savings, however, the regional exchanges are expected to play a greater role in mobilising capital, especially as Lahore is now a bustling industrial and commercial centre of five million people.

Habib Bank is Pakistan's largest bank and was nationalised by Zulfikar Ali Bhutto in 1972

The main regulatory bodies are the Corporate Law Authority under the Ministry of Finance, the State Bank of Pakistan and the Religious Board, which supervises the working of the *modarbas*.

The insurance market in Pakistan saw a ban on registration of new insurance companies for about two decades after 1970. Then this embargo was lifted and the number of companies entering this business soared to sixty, resulting in too many companies chasing too little business. The total premium generated in Pakistan by the private sector companies was Rs 6.8bn in 1995, with the largest company having 35 per cent of this business.

Pakistan Insurance Corporation (PIC) was established by the government under an Act of Parliament. Every insurance company in the country is required to cede it 20 per cent of sums assured on all policies except bond business. Moreover, under surplus reinsurance deregulation, PIC also has the right to take up 35 per cent share in all reinsurance treaties. PIC has been managing the Export Credit Guarantee Scheme since 1962, and from 1st January 1996 it has also assumed responsibility for management of the reinsurance pool.

B.A.

For shipping and communications industries see *Physical Infrastructure*.

The Media

In 1947, Pakistan inherited a press with a tradition of defiance. Several newspapers which commenced publication in the Forties played a historic role in mobilising support for the independence movement, in the face of persecution and repression. Among these newspapers were *Dawn*, *Jang*, the *Pakistan Times*, *Nawa-e-Waqt* and *Morning News*. In fact, Mohamed Ali Jinnah, the founder of Pakistan, took a personal interest in the publication of *Dawn*, making it an influential voice of the freedom movement.

Political instability, following the death of Jinnah, had serious consequences for the freedom of the press. Even before the imposition of martial law in 1958, the press had begun to be manipulated by powerful bureaucrats, and was persecuted by those in power. The first victim of the first martial law was Progressive Papers Ltd which was taken over by the military regime in 1959. Its publications included the liberal and outspoken *Pakistan Times*. The government strengthened its hold on the press with the promulgation of the Press and Publications Ordinance 1963, virtually ending the limited freedom the press enjoyed. In spite of continuous protests by journalists and publishers through the decades, it took until 1988 for the ordinance finally to be replaced by Repeal of the Press and Publications Ordinance (RPPO.)

In spite of a hostile environment prevailing during successive governments, the press continued to grow, both nationally and regionally. Newspapers in Pakistan are published in Urdu and English, as well as in Sindhi, Gujarati, and Pushto. The press exercises influence disproportionate to its circulation which remains limited due to low literacy levels. And while Urdu newspapers have far wider circulation, the English press is more influential because it is read by policy-makers.

Freedom of the press received a further setback with the imposition of martial law in 1977. The military regime clamped pre-censorship on the press, following the cancellation of the general elections scheduled for October. When newspaper editors began to leave blank spaces to indicate censored portions, this witty gesture of protest became a punishable offence under martial law. Several publications were banned, and four journalists were threatened with flogging for defying martial law regulations.

Newspaper publishers explored other means to secure readership. Technological innovation was to play its part. Urdu newspapers, which were calligraphed by hand, began to switch to computerised composing. Colour printing was introduced in the major newspapers and more attention began to be paid to the layout and appearance of a newspaper and graphic designers began to be employed. Today, the print media has caught up with worldwide developments in printing and communications, with computerisation, the use of electronic mail and the Internet and the latest in printing technology.

The lifting of martial law in 1985 brought some relief to a battered press. It became truly free after the elections of 1988. Although Benazir Bhutto's elected government proved to be fairly tolerant of a vigilant and far from muzzled press, the press itself demonstrated that having survived martial law it could not be intimidated by politicians. In a democratic system, the threat persisted from armed militants of political and religious groups, who could not bear criticism, attacking several newspaper offices and journalists. The growing trend towards investigative journalism has also led to several key figures in government filing (with varying justification) libel suits against journalists and newspapers – usually protracted or settled out of court.

The press's new-found resilience ensured that the process of development did not slow down. Several new publications began to compete for an overall readership that was hardly growing, specially for the English language press. The Urdu press in Karachi found a new niche in the afternoon newspaper segment and many newspapers were launched. *Awam*, a new paper was soon to surpass the circulation of Karachi's most popular newspaper, *Jang*. The Sindhi language press proved to be the most vibrant and several newspapers were launched in the late 1980s. However, even today, there are no reliable audits on circulation and readership of newspapers.

Pakistan Television (PTV) started transmission with two stations in 1964. By the Nineties it was broadcasting from five cities. With satellite transmission and rebroadcast stations, it covered about 85 per cent of the population. PTV's second channel, introduced by satellite transmission on Asiasat, covers thirty-eight countries in South Asia and the Middle East, and is aimed at Pakistan's substantial expatriate community, especially in the Persian Gulf. PTV has come a long way from a few hours of live broadcasts of programmes in the initial years to technically sophisticated productions and 24-hour transmission. Its programmes are not only in the national language, Urdu, but in English and in most regional languages.

In 1989, the government set up another network, Shalimar Television Network (STN) in Karachi, Lahore and Islamabad. For the first time, prime time on a television network was contracted out to a private company, Network Television Marketing which telecasts privately produced programmes on STN. The STN network now covers ten cities of Pakistan. The development of television in Pakistan also resulted in a mushroom growth of video production units in the private sector. Meanwhile, satellite dish antennae are breaking the boundaries of communication and of censorship, often to the government's dismay.

In terms of programming, a relatively liberal policy had evolved for entertainment programmes and talk shows. However, PTV news bulletins continue to be propagandistic in content and tone, focusing on the activities of government functionaries rather than on events evaluated for their news value.

At Independence, Radio Pakistan had only two transmitters, in Peshawar and Lahore. Within two decades, eight stations were on air. Radio's role in the early years as a medium of information, education and entertainment was truly significant, specially in the absence of television and the prevalence of large-scale illiteracy which affected the circulation of newspapers. The number of sets increased phenomenally with the introduction of transistor radios. Radio Pakistan was converted into the Pakistan Broadcasting Corporation (PBC) in 1972. In 1997 there were 27 radio stations, covering 97.5 per cent of the population. The introduction of FM stations in the private sector has been tremendously a popular development, with its call-in programme formats.

In quite different ways, the print and electronic media in Pakistan have made significant progress since Independence. Both have developed dramatically in terms of technology and in the choice they now offer their audiences. But while the electronic media's growth has been in terms of greater reach and coverage, the print media has emerged from the relatively short period of censorship to come into its own as an outspoken, and independent, voice.

Z. Y

The Social Infrastructure

Progress in education, health and family planning may seem painfully slow, but the fact remains that in terms of schools, colleges and universities built, hospital beds added and rural clinics opened, Pakistan has come a long way in its first half-century. Had population not grown at around three per cent per annum, the results of the investments made in the people of Pakistan would have been more evident. As it is, life expectancy has increased significantly, children have a far better chance of growing up, and mothers bear healthier babies than their mothers did. So, compared with the situation at Independence, there have been clear gains. However, when compared with the improvements in virtually all the social indicators in the international region, Pakistanis have not fared so well. One reason for this is that in the country's long periods of military rule, welfare was low on the priority list. Even civilian governments have been unable to allocate the funds required to meet the backlog of unmet needs due to competing demands from other sectors.

Pakistan thus figures low in most international tables of social progress. But the importance of investing in people has finally dawned on policy-makers. This realisation is largely due to the startling success of the Pacific Rim countries which, only a generation ago, were on a par with Pakistan in terms of economic development, but have sprinted far ahead not least because of their educated and healthy workforce. They have thus demonstrated that, moral considerations apart, investment in education and health has a direct and quantifiable return. The attitude of international donor countries and agencies reinforces this idea. Increasingly, grants and soft loans are now being diverted to the social sector under the umbrella of the Social Action Programme.

In response to the perennial neglect of education and health, private schools, colleges and universities mushroomed during the Nineties, as did hospitals and clinics. This phenomenon further marginalised those who were unable to pay for these services and therefore had to depend on the ramshackle public facilities. This trend widened the gap between the haves and have-nots, especially since all the best private schools instructed their pupils in English. This was giving rise to a two-track system in which those who received their education at public institutions were at an increasing disadvantage when competing for top jobs. And given the steady decline of higher education, parents who could afford to were sending their children to universities abroad. However, the Lahore University of Management Sciences and the Aga Khan Medical University provide instruction that is as good as anywhere in the world. In recognition of these realities, the government has agreed in principle to grant charters to more private universities.

Simultaneously, non-governmental organisations (NGOs) have become extremely active in education, health, family planning and environmental matters, specially in the cities. There is a growing realisation and concern that the government does not have the resources to meet the growing demand for a wide range of social services, and a large number of voluntary organisations across the country have sprung up to fill this void. Although most of these organisations are relatively small and run limited operations, many donor agencies prefer to channel their funds through them because they consider the government too unwieldy and inefficient, specially when dealing with social issues. This has

Top *Beaconhouse school is a private chain which educates 30,000 children throughout Pakistan's towns and cities*
Above and below *Traditional values mean that in many families boys are still given preference over girls in education, but this is slowly changing*
Bottom *Girls in urban schools are studying for longer than ever and many are now going on to take university degrees*

Above and Top *Agha Khan Medical University provides world-class teaching and care*
Below *Netball features at a girls' private school*

caused some friction between the NGO movement and various official agencies, and the government is considering legislation to regulate the activities of NGOs.

One of the oldest and largest NGOs in the country is the Family Planning Association of Pakistan (FPAP). Established in the early Fifties, FPAP has pioneered a number of important programmes and initiatives. Indeed, Pakistan's population explosion is perhaps the country's biggest single problem. Currently growing annually at 2.8 per cent, the population is estimated to be around 135 million in early 1997, and is projected to grow to 150 million by the turn of the century. Considering that there were only about 37 million Pakistanis in the Western Wing at Independence, this is a frightening growth rate, with little relief in sight.

A major problem in limiting this crippling annual increase has been the inconsistent approach of successive governments. Indeed, until the Sixties, population growth was not considered an issue. When Ayub Khan launched his "planned parenthood" movement he was countered by the

orthodox elements of society, who started rumours that government field staff were carrying out vasectomies by force. Fearing a nationwide backlash, Ayub Khan softened the programme. It was revived in the early Seventies, only to be shelved by Zia as being "anti-Islamic" – in spite of religious texts containing no injunction against birth control. Once more, the "small family norm" is being promoted officially and increasing funds being allocated to this key area.

The conservative mindset of the majority, especially the male of the species, has proved a huge stumbling block to family planning. Many surveys have indicated that women now want to limit the size of their families, but since they cannot go for advice to the nearest clinic (usually a long way away) without their husbands' consent, birth control techniques and information are thus beyond their reach. Moreover, two out of three Pakistanis are illiterate. The majority of women have no access to any kind of literature on family planning. Another cultural factor leading to Pakistan's large families is the social need for sons: mothers are under tremendous pressure to produce male babies, and far too often continue getting pregnant in order to bear a son and heir. Girls are usually neglected at home, and receive a scant education even if they are sent to school at all.

In many developing countries, there is now conclusive data available to prove a correlation between female literacy and population: the more educated women become, the smaller the size of their families. Despite this linkage, girls' enrolment at school remains persistently low, and their dropout rate exceedingly high. Indeed, the enrolment rate for girls is half that for boys, and this rate is far lower in the rural areas, particularly in the North-West Frontier Province and Balochistan. Out of the three million or so children entering the first grade, barely a million were making it to the fifth, by the later Nineties. Small wonder that the the adult literacy rate stood at only 35 per cent in 1997. Even so, around 40 million Pakistanis could read and write; this was more than the population of the entire country in 1947.

In the cities, at least, this dearth of educational facilities was being partly filled by the proliferation of private schools. These ranged from the very good to the mediocre, but middle-class urban parents felt they had little choice except to send their children to English-medium private schools, irrespective of the quality of instruction. The success of the Beaconhouse chain illustrated the role the private sector had come to play: with around sixty branches all over the country, this remarkable system imparts a good English-medium education to 30,000 children in virtually every large Pakistani city. At the other end of the spectrum, individuals and NGOs cater to the needs of underprivileged students in certain urban areas. With the guidance and motivation provided by the remarkably successful Orangi Pilot Project, for instance, housewives opened small schools in their homes where parents were charged as little as 30 rupees (or a little under a dollar) a month as fees. The result of this grassroots-level educational system has been to increase the literacy rate of this huge low-income settlement by 1996 to over 78 per cent as against 62 per cent for the rest of Karachi. Higher education, too, was reflecting the same dichotomy between a few excellent private institutions and generally mediocre public universities.

In the health sector, the growing population and limited resources have combined to reduce the effectiveness of the public system. The fact that only two-thirds of the population had access to clean drinking water added enormously to the widespread prevalence of communicable diseases. Government hospitals and clinics were overcrowded and poorly equipped, and few doctors volunteered to serve in the rural areas. In the cities, this vacuum has been partly filled by the mushroom growth of private facilities for those who can afford to pay. These ranged from the state-of-the-art hospital at the Aga Khan Medical University to traditional homeopaths purveying cures in the back-streets of all Pakistani cities and villages. Here, too, the NGO movement was striving to fill the breach. Karachi's Institute of Urology was providing an excellent example of this approach: under the highly professional team led by Dr Adeeb Rizvi, the Institute has been catering to thousands of kidney patients every year without charging a penny for treatment or medication. This impressive operation is made possible by donations from philanthropists together with limited government support.

These private initiatives have been largely restricted to cities, but this is gradually changing as many donor agencies adopt a more rural-based approach. FPAP has been operating in small communities since the 1970s, and Baanh Beli is running a successful health and educational programme in a number of villages in Tharparkar, a desert region of Sindh province. Other NGOs such as Oxfam were involved in social development projects in different parts of the country. Perhaps the most successful rural-based approach was taken by the Aga Khan Rural Support Programme (AKRSP)

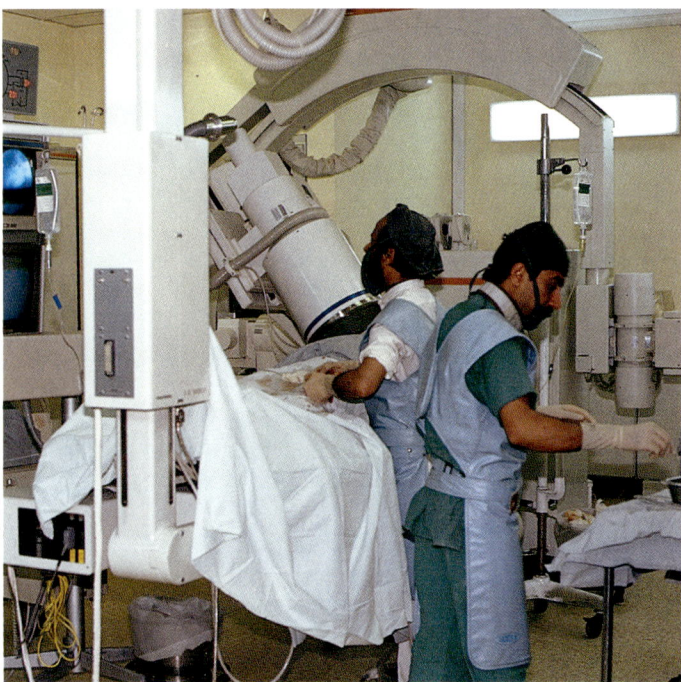

which has been operating in the Northern Areas since the Seventies and has built up an extended network of schools and clinics, as well as assisting villagers in remote areas to learn new skills and enhance their productivity.

The government — like many another — is faced with a perpetual struggle to produce a nation of healthy and educated citizens. But through key investments in the infrastructure, it could forge a creative partnership with the NGO movement and private entrepreneurs. Many school buildings in rural areas were standing empty in the later 1990s because of ill-paid teachers working elsewhere to make a living, and government clinics vacant due to lack of housing for doctors. Government had the option of handing over these facilities to NGOs or entrepreneurs to run, and to pay them a management fee. This, or some variant, may prove the way ahead in developing the social infrastructure. Whatever strategy prevails, if Pakistan is to progress and summon its human resources, it would have to reduce its population growth rate while providing effective education and health care.

I. H

Women

Pakistan's women reflect the contrasts and diversities prevailing in the country at all levels: social, cultural, geographical, rural, urban, and of class. There are women who are bound by tradition – voiceless and apparently dependent on the family role and traditional structures; then there are the women charting out new avenues, broadening their horizons – dynamic, creative and articulate. But, overall, the indicators show that women are less literate than men, less mobile, inadequately represented in administrative services, fewer in the labour force and with a persistently high maternal mortality rate (hovering between 5 and 6 per 1000).

Yet over the years the situation of women has improved in some areas. For instance, the ratio between male and female population has narrowed to 104 men to 100 women (from 110:100 in 1981); life expectancy of men and women has evened out at 62 years (previously women had a shorter life span); the proportion of women in paid jobs has increased to 13.32 per cent from the much contested figure of three per

cent of the 1981 census. The number of children borne by the average women has also declined in a decade and a half from 8 to 5.6 according to recent official statistics; and women's marriage age has risen from 15 to 22 years since the Fifties.

Female literacy is estimated to have increased in 1995-96 to 25.3 per cent (16 per cent in 1980-81). This reflects the strongly expressed demand for primary schools for girls, especially in rural areas. There is evidence that a substantial number of girls are in fact being educated in boys' schools. It was found (1993) that one-third of all primary school girls in Balochistan and one-fifth in NWFP attend boys' schools.

Underprivileged or not, women in Pakistan have repeatedly demonstrated their capacity to organise and lead, and be bold, astute and competent. Women were active in the struggle for political independence in 1947. In the post independence period, women's concern focused upon their rights and their militancy has frequently been witnessed. Repeatedly a handful of women have taken the lead to mobilise other women into action. As early as 1948, Begum Ra'ana Liaqat Ali Khan, wife of the Prime Minister, formed the Women's Voluntary Service to help in the rehabilitation of refugees and the displaced. Largely inexperienced women, many who had never stepped out of their homes, administered first aid, organised food distribution, dealt with health problems, epidemics and clothing, and provided moral and emotional support. The subcontinent's WVS became the precursor of the first women's organisation of Pakistan, i.e. the All Pakistan Women's Association (APWA) formed in 1949.

The moving spirit again was Begum Liaqat Ali Khan. Its objective was the welfare of Pakistan's women and its activities spanned the social sector: girls' schools and colleges, health centres and industrial homes to provide skills and income-generating opportunities. In 1955, APWA spearheaded the campaign against second marriage. This led to the setting up of a commission to review personal laws and ultimately the codification of family laws through the Family Laws Ordinance in 1961. Though not as protective of women as some desired, the law nevertheless was subsequently a major factor in providing for registration of marriages through a standard *nikahnama* (marriage contract), the delegated right of divorce for women and the right of maintenance and custody of children.

The two women members of Pakistan's first legislature, Jahanara Shahnawaz and Shaista Ikramullah, were strong champions of women's rights and responsible for the passage of the Muslim Personal Law of the Shariat (1948) whereby a woman's right to inherit property – including agricultural property – was recognised. They also raised the demand for a ten per cent quota of reserved seats for women in the assemblies.

Progressively women became more visible in political and public spheres. Fatima Jinnah, the Quaid's sister, challenged General Ayub Khan in the closely contested presidential election of 1966. Large scale mobilisation of women by Pakistan People's Party was seen during the 1970 elections. Over the years women demanded and received greater rights and space for their activities: the right to vote, to sit in assemblies, receive education, have relatively greater security in marriage, enter new fields and professions. However, they were jolted out of complacency when in 1979 General Zia ul Haq introduced measures that were harsh and discriminatory upon women, such as the Hudood ordinance (1979), the Law of Evidence (1984), restrictions on women's participation in sports, prescription of a dress code and putting an end to foreign diplomatic postings.

The most far-reaching, in terms of adverse effects, were the Hudood Ordinances (1979). They were presented as part of the Islamicisation of the country and its people. They cover adultery, rape, theft, drinking of alcohol, and bearing false testimony. Women have been subject to excessive victimisation under this law; their evidence is not admissible for maximum punishment and the same level of proof is required for both rape and adultery (four male eye witnesses of good repute).

In response to these measures women swiftly came together (mostly, urban professionals) to organise and resist. Women's Action Forum (WAF) was formed as an autonomous platform-cum-pressure group in 1981. The most significant impact of WAF was the recognition at the national level of the women's question. All political parties began to include women's issues in their manifestos and establish women's wings/sections, including the religious parties. In the same period (Zia's martial law) Sindhiani Tehri, the first rural women's organisation in Pakistan, was formed in Sindh. It forged links with WAF working in the

Opposite and this page *Women at work: women are entering the workplace in greater numbers and in new fields such as banking and architecture, but the pace of change is slow. Women's economic and political autonomy is still very much regarded as a threat to the* status quo

urban areas on issues of women's rights. The Eighties saw perhaps the greatest politicisation of women. it also saw the stormy return of Benazir Bhutto from exile and her election as Prime Minister in 1988 and then again in 1993, yet without an overall majority.

Despite a number of gains made by women, attitudes towards women and perceptions about their subservient role, position and limited ability persist. While change is evident — with girls flocking to schools in larger numbers, young women seeking professional skills, more bringing incomes to the households, entering new fields like architecture, nuclear physics, theatre and banking – concomitant change in attitudes is slow.

Commitments to safeguard women's rights and repeal discriminatory laws have been made repeatedly by recent governments, but "democratically" these can only be fulfilled if there is a consensus on these issues as represented in parliament. There remains, therefore, tension in society. Women's potential autonomy is perceived as a threat to the existing structures of authority both within the family and in the public and political arena. However, history provides testimony to women's determination to struggle for their rights, and the current trends indicate that women of Pakistan are poised for change.

K. M.

PAKISTAN

5. Culture

The yeast of the arts is among the ordinary people, along the length and breadth of the land. They grow up to recite their poets and compose anew, to sing and play musical instruments, to dance, to act, to pot, to weave, to paint, to work metals, to carve, to decorate, to build small things and great. Past treasures only are glass-cased – the manifold culture itself is alive in every community.

Above *Pigeons circle a saint's tomb in Multan, Punjab*

Architecture

The process of modernisation for many traditional societies in Asia, Africa and Latin America began with their subjugation by a European colonial power. In the Indian sub-continent, the cultural dualism resulting from a hundred years of British rule, was to characterise the dynamics of the societies of the inheritor states after independence in 1947. Thus in Pakistan, as no doubt elsewhere, the conflicting influences of modernity and tradition have emerged as a central issue in the contemporary cultural discourse. But the manner in which notions of modernity and tradition have been reflected in architecture has been modulated by the respective sensibilities of the architect, the builder and the client.

The sensibilities of the architect are moulded by his academic training. As in other disciplines, modernisation thrust aside most of the traditional attitudes of the architectural profession. The post-Independence generation of architects were alien to contemporary European concerns, such as form, function and the "pure" aesthetics of the Bauhaus, but not to the syntax and grammar of their own regional architectural heritage. Thus it was only in deference to a client's specific requirement that the architect could be persuaded to incorporate some traditional form or motif as a cultural metaphor or token reference into his otherwise modern designs.

The cultural dualism became evident. While the westernised urban elite were keen to promote an architecture which symbolised their modern, progressive, scientific views and tastes, the majority of clients, particularly in the public

CULTURE

Above *The striking Faisal Mosque, Islamabad, was designed by the Turkish architect Dalukai. Its light, airy interiors* **(right and below)** *reflect a modern sensibility*

sector, have been unequivocal in their demand for an architecture rooted in the region's own culture and history. Nowhere is this conflict between modernity and tradition better illustrated than in the capital city, Islamabad. In 1958, when Ayub Khan decided to shift the capital to a site near Rawalpindi and to name it Islamabad – the city of Islam – the chairman of the Capital Development Authority noted that : "Though a new country we, as a people, are an old nation, with a rich heritage, inspired by a historical past... (we are) eager to build a new city which, in addition to being an adequate and ideal seat of government, should also reflect our cultural identity and national aspirations."

The geometry of the grid-iron plan based on Doxiades' idea of "dynapolis" was considered to be in accord with Islam. But ironically, no mosque had been included among the buildings of national government and national culture in the focal "Red Area". Eventually, a site was earmarked for a grand national mosque at the foot of the Margalla Hills, beyond the northern periphery of the city. The international jury for the Shah Faisal Mosque, dominated by architects, rejected designs that did not "fit the contemporary planning and design ideals of the modern city of Islamabad." The criteria it adopted made no reference to history, heritage or tradition.

By contrast, when the Parliament building was first mooted in 1962, the Capital Development Authority (CDA)

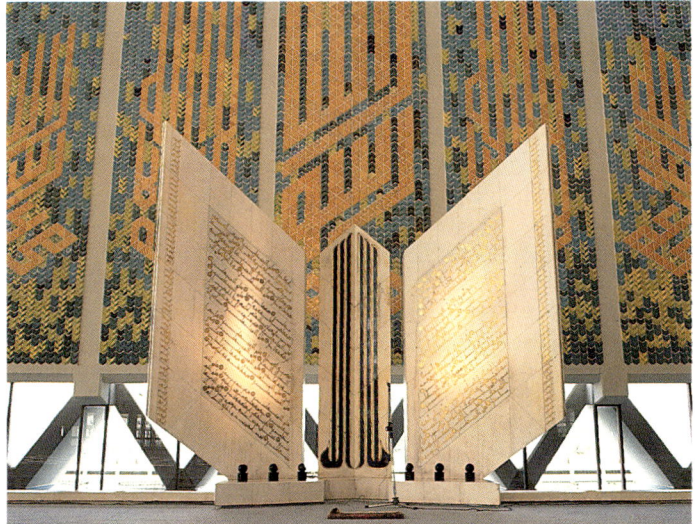

made it very clear that it would have to be carefully designed to "reflect our past culture...". Both Arne Jacobsen's and Louis Kahn's uncompromising modern proposals for the assembly were rejected for not being "national" and "Islamic", whereas Edward Stone was commended for his "love of the Mughal architecture" and was considered to be the only leading architect of world fame who has "imbibed the spirit of Mughal architecture and beauty". He was considered for the design of all the four buildings in the most prominent square of Islamabad, namely the Supreme Court the National Assembly, the Foreign Office and the President's House. The bureaucrats were keen to ensure the region's Islamic heritage of architecture was reflected in the public buildings of Islamabad, and reminded the architect that there was a "grave dissatisfaction" in Government and among our people regarding the architecture for the public buildings put up so far in Islamabad. The planners agreed that the internal arrangements of these buildings should be as modern and sophisticated as possible. But they wanted the buildings to look "native to the soil". In the event, the domes and arches proposed for the Presidency by Stone were eliminated and the verandas and overhanging canopies were reduced due to financial constraints. The National Assembly building was similarly trimmed down to its present austere façade.

The parallel processes of "Islamicisation" of modern architecture and "modernisation" of Islamic architecture, which had started with some of Pakistan's earliest public buildings, continued to gather momentum. The "modernisation of the Mughal garden" was a central theme in the landscaping of Gio Ponti's Secretariat Complex and Denis Brigden's Government Officers' Hostel. Ponti's elegant modern buildings, built in the Sixties, were among the first to be given the "Islamic" treatment with the application of discreet pointed arches on their lift shafts. The Supreme Court, designed in the early Nineties by Kenzo Tange as a theatrical "modern" extravaganza, has been made more ridiculous by the addition of cosmetic Islamisation on the insistence of the CDA. Now completed, it reflects the uncomfortable compromise forced upon the architect.

Beyond the capital, foreign architects seem to have fared better. Ecochard's Karachi University and his museum at Mohenjodaro, William Parry's American School and Institute of Business Administration in Karachi and Doxiades' new campus of Lahore's Punjab University are in the best traditions of modern architecture, in which form is dictated by the logic of function, material, structure and climate.

More than any other Pakistani architect of his generation,

Above *Islamabad's Saudi-Pak tower is built in a post-modernist style, combining clean lines with Islamic motifs*
Right *The Supreme Court building, by Kenzo Tange, has been Islamicised by adding motifs not in his original designs*

Mehdi Ali Mirza absorbed and understood the philosophy of the Modern Movement. But the unremarkable buildings he designed in his official capacity for the Public Works Department stand in sharp contrast to his private commissions. The influence of Frank Lloyd Wright in Mirza's work can be recognised in the floating horizontal planes, boldly cantilevered concrete slabs, the integration of the building with the site, the exploitation of the expressive potential of structural form, and the thoughtful detailing.

Like most of the handful of "legitimate" architects inherited by Pakistan at the time of partition, Mirza had studied at the Sir Jamsetji Jijibhoy School of Art in Bombay. After partition, and till the upgrading of the Mayo School of Arts in Lahore to the National College of Arts in 1958, the only course open to young aspirants in the field of architecture had been to travel abroad. Among the few who took that route included Habib Fida Ali, Kamil Khan Mumtaz and Yasmeen Lari. Habib, who is at his best in his offices for corporate clients such as Shell and IBM in Karachi, has remained consistently faithful to the modernist school. However, in the geometric configurations of the plan for the Lahore University of Management Sciences and in the decorative use of local brick on an office building in Lahore, he makes a definite gesture towards the city's rich architectural heritage and history.

Another architect who has remained constant in his "modernism" has been Anwar Saeed in Islamabad. His prolific output in both the public and private sectors has included community buildings such as neighbourhood mosques and a church, office façades, as well as private and public housing. His elementary geometric forms are often bold and provocative, but this formal vocabulary does not appear to be related to issues of available technologies, material structure, climate or indeed culture.

Kamil Khan Mumtaz and Yasmeen Lari have both distanced themselves from their earlier commitment to the Modern movement. In the process, as each has re-examined indigenous vocabularies of built forms, their documentation of the regional vernaculars and conservation efforts have contributed much to the recent revival of interest in the regional heritage among the younger professionals.

Yasmeen Lari has moved from the uncompromising, brutalist modernism of her houses of the sixties in Karachi, to a greater deference to regional inheritances as in the Angoori Bagh scheme in Lahore of the seventies. A slick commercialism characterises her Finance and Trade Centre and a hotel in Karachi built in the Eighties.

In his search for an alternative basis for architecture, Kamil Khan Mumtaz has been more consistent in exploring traditional design principles and building practices. The application of these principles to contemporary structures is best illustrated in his Dar ul Hikmat education centre in Lahore and the Chand Bagh School in Muridke. In addition to his practice, he has had a wide influence as an author and educator.

Academic institutions are be expected to play a leading

Above *Kamil Khan Mumtaz uses traditional building and design techniques to restore indigenous forms and style*
Below (left and right) *Habib Fida Ali uses a Modernist style to give his buildings clean lines and confidence*

role in documentation of the built heritage, critical analysis, research, publication and debate on contemporary issues. But the handful of local schools of architecture in Pakistan have usually been content to act as passive conduits for the transmission of ready-made imported solutions. In the absence of debate on the profounder role of architecture, issues like "tradition" or "modernity" are liable to be reduced to the level of style, fashion and individual fancy.

Lahore's National College of Arts has, however, acquired a penchant for skilful manipulation of visual form. Among the earliest graduates from this institution was Nayyar Ali Dada. The modernist styling of his earlier work, such as the Shakir Ali Auditorium, has been tempered in his more recent works, such as the Alhamra Arts Council and the Cultural Centre buildings in Lahore, with "traditional" materials and forms. His elegant archives building in Peshawar and a bank in Lahore are both successful responses to the colonial heritage of these cities, and demonstrate his sensitivity to regional and urban contexts.

Similar directions can be discerned in the work of Sohail and Pasha in Islamabad. This relatively new partnership has been successful in satisfying the often contradictory demands of private and public clients for a contemporary Pakistani architecture simultaneously modern and traditional. Retaining a level of professional integrity and standards in the face of such demands has been one of the challenges of architectural practice in Pakistan. For the government-owned consultancy PEPAC, catering almost exclusively to large projects in the public sector, this challenge must be all the more daunting. That it has been able to meet this challenge is largely due to this firm being able to attract some of the most talented young graduates from the handful of schools of architecture in Pakistan.

Today, the number of institutions offering regular courses in architecture has risen to five. In form and content these courses are modelled on Western prototypes, and have tended to follow the design theories and teaching methods defined by the modern movement in Europe and America.

The youngest of these institutions, Karachi's privately owned Indus Valley School of Art, boasts one of the best buildings in the spirit of the modern movement built in Karachi in recent decades.

In the 1980s the modernist paradigm was challenged in the industrially advanced societies as much as in the countries of the South, but for different reasons. In postcolonial societies the questions of national identity and culture had been closely related to national liberation movements. But regionalism and the quest for alternative strategies for development have emerged as global concerns with the growing awareness of the negative impact of irresponsible industrialisation, and the corrupting potential of materialist culture.

Most architects have responded to these changes only to the extent of switching clichés. The old international style of the previous generation has been replaced by the new international style. Naturally, the architects returning to Pakistan with foreign degrees have demonstrated the greatest facility in the post-modern idiom. Among them are Ijaz Ahad, the Abdullah brothers and Tariq Hassan in Karachi. Others such as Qamar Ali in Hyderabad, Qayyum and Willayat Khan in Peshawar, and Sajjad Kausar in Lahore, have turned to the regional vocabularies of form.

It is a rare architect who strives to do justice to the region and still make a modern building. One organisation that has tried to overcome these handicaps is the *Anjuman Mimaran*. Through a programme of field studies, seminars, exhibitions and publications it has done much to rediscover the traditional design principles and building practices, and to restore the link between the professional architect and the hereditary craftsmen who still have access – if only just – to the traditional vocabularies. The latter have remained in fairly constant demand from lay committees for the design and construction of local mosques, tombs, *madrasah* or religious schools and *daar-ul-uloom* seminaries. It is in buildings of this genre, such as the Bhong Mosque complex near Rahimyarkhan, that religion and the craft sensibilities appear on centre stage in the combined roles of principal actor, director and producer rolled into one. The dexterity and skill of these craftsmen in exploiting the potential of new materials is often admirable. But the tendency to incorporate forms perceived as symbols of modernity, is a tragic reminder of the limitations of a craft tradition deprived of nourishment from the mainstream and guidance from the professional architect in his rightful role of creative leader of the team.

K. K. M.

Other Religions

Religious minorities may only form three per cent of Pakistan's population, but in business, education, medicine and the arts their contribution is significant. All religions enjoy equal status under the Pakistani Constitution.

Christians are the biggest minority group in Pakistan; they are distributed throughout the subcontinent and represent a wide cross-section of ethnic and linguistic stocks. Churches of virtually every denomination embellish the architectural horizon of most Pakistani cities. Although Pakistani Christians have not restricted themselves to any one area of activity, they have traditionally made an outstanding contribution in health, education, railways and the police force. They are also playing a growing role in the civil and defence services.

The second biggest minority is the so-called scheduled castes; these are former "untouchables" from the Hindu caste system in pre-Partition days. In Pakistan this group is not legally or economically discriminated against – but old habits die hard and many are engaged in largely menial tasks. This group is diminishing as more and more of them become educated and make their way up the socio-economic ladder.

The Hindus of Pakistan are mostly found in Sindh where they concentrate on agriculture. In the larger cities (particularly in Karachi) Hindus are very active in commerce. Their holy days are celebrated with all their traditional colour.

The Ahmadis follow the preaching of Mirza Ghulam Ahmad at the end of the nineteenth century. The doctrine is very close to Islam on most points, but differs over the inviolable finality of Prophethood. Ahmadis are mainly of Punjabi origin and are represented in virtually every field of economic activity.

The Parsis (or Zoroastrians) are a very small minority concentrated in the larger cities and are almost exclusively engaged in business. Some of Pakistan's foremost hotel and shipping magnates are Parsis and the richer members of this community are well known for their philanthropic activities.

The Buddhists are numerically very few but the cultural impact of their ancestors has enriched the heritage of Pakistan. Ancient Buddhist temples, schools and cities dot the archaeological map of Pakistan.

There are many important Sikh temples and shrines in Pakistan, most notable is Nankana Sahib. Every year Sikhs from India make pilgrimages to these place, which are looked after by the Sikhs themselves.

S.M. et al

The main dome of the Samadhi of Ranjit Singh, Lahore. Pakistan's Sikh shrines have been reverently preserved

Large numbers of Sikh pilgrims gather every spring at the shrine of Punja Sahib, near Rawalpindi

Painting and Sculpture

Pakistan inherited a rich and ancient tradition of art. The human and animal figurines modelled and carved five thousand years ago reveal a lively appreciation of natural forms. Sculpture reached its zenith during the Gandhara period. Along with the idealised image of Buddha the demeanour of priests and devotees is objectively and sharply perceived. Today sculpture is largely confined to the art schools and there is little evidence of it in public life. In recent years, however, collectors have begun to show a livelier interest in the field. Small pieces of terracotta, fibreglass, bronze, ceramic reliefs, wood carvings and metallic fabrication can be seen adorning the tables and walls of many private homes. After the creation of Pakistan, sculptors focused on producing plaster busts of notables. Later some artists, influenced by abstract art, tried to form their work with cubistic simplicity. In the field of sculpture, Shahid Sajjad has laboured most consistently and prolifically. In his

The disintegration of the Mughal empire which began in the 18th century forced many painters to find patrons in the Punjab Hill States. Simultaneously painting continued to be patronised by the Sikh rulers of Punjab who were particularly fond of sitting for portraits. Punjab was annexed by the British in 1857 and painters tried to introduce a new direction in the visual arts. European influences had actually been introduced as early as the 16th century through engravings presented to the Emperor. These helped to create a greater sense of depth and volume. The British introduced examples of Victorian art to local artists, and these inspired many of them to paint romantic views, portraits of beggars and picture postcards of scenes and places considered typically local. Ustad Allah Baksh was the leading figure of the period, and he tried to integrate the ideals of Victorianism with his own knowledge of common life and popular lore.

Abdur Rehman Chughtai without doubt was the most celebrated artist of the early 20th century. Rather than concerning himself with English romanticism, Chughtai aspired to revive his own country's past. He succeeded in evolving a unique style comprised of delicate flowing lines and pastel hues achieved through successive water colour washes. His paintings either illustrate couplets from classical poets or celebrate national heroes and romantic legends.

Above *Anna Molka Ahmed was a major influence as an artist and teacher in the figurative tradition. She painted in soft colours but her work is bold and striking in concept and execution*

earlier work he was carving highly stylised but simple images in wood. He now works largely in bronze and has produced objects with delicate surface effects enveloped in a strange aura of extra-terrestrial reality. Kohari, a Pakistani artist now living in France, calls his ceramic reliefs "fire-paintings". These are composite creations in melted glass, wire netting and rich glazes, throbbing with colour and texture. There are now quite a few avant-garde artists like Jamal Shah working in sculpture using all kinds of material ranging from glass to *papier mâché* and grappling with contemporary issues. Durriya Kazi and her husband David Aynesworth have have been working in abstract metal forms.

Pakistan has an uninterrupted history of painting since Vedic times. Most ancient painting has been lost but there are references in ancient texts which speak highly of the painter's skill in capturing life and nature. The school of fresco painting of the Buddhist period in subsequent centuries followed similar ideals.

The Sultanate period (13th to 15th centuries AD) prepared the ground for the great school of Mughal miniature paintings which brought about a synthesis of Persian, Central Asian and indigenous traditions. Mughal painting is characteristically inquisitive about nature and life and depicts individuals with marvellous insight.

Other artists like Haji Muhammad Sharif were content to work in the traditional style without introducing any essential change. They thus became instrumental in keeping the techniques of Mughal and Pahari painting alive for later artists.

Many modern painters have discovered that traditional heritage can enrich their endeavours. Calligraphy, nuances of arabesque and images of imperial grandeur have been a ready source of inspiration. Haneef Ramay was the first of his generation who enriched calligraphic forms with vivid colours and textures, transforming them from simple words to visually pleasing paintings. Later Shakir Ali produced some vibrant murals based on calligraphy which greatly extended the scope and possibilities inherent in this art form. A number of other artists have also made valuable additions. Guljee, an artist of unusual innovative skill, demonstrates amazing dexterity in manipulating calligraphic forms to create striking abstract images adorned with glass-beads and gold-leaf.

The very first exhibition of abstract works was held by Zubeda Agha in 1949, after her return from Paris. Her early canvases were muddy in colour, eschewing sensuousness for cerebral content. Since then, she has evolved into a bold colourist who engages the viewer by her seemingly artless manner. In her paintings, natural elements coalesce with

Paani *(water)*: Unver Shafi Khan represents the new generation of artists. His handling of form and colour is fresh and imaginative

her feelings to create dream-like visions.

The impact of Western painting in the Fifties encouraged young artists to turn away from Chughtai, finding his paintings too aesthetically refined and placid. They wished to experience their own ethos rather than look back to a classical past. The influence of Impressionism and Post-Impressionism was soon followed by that of Cubism and Expressionism. Moyene Najmi, A.J. Shemza, S. Safdar, Ali Imam and Ahmed Pervez were the principal abstract artists of the period. Moyene Najmi's paintings are adorned with studied textural affects and architectural details. Shemza's works are based on linear and calligraphic patterns enriched with elements from life. Ahmed Pervez follows his intuitions and instinct without pausing even to reconsider a stroke, and his canvases are a riot of colour and a maze of writhing forms. Ali Imam's textured ivory surfaces reveal human forms who are obvious and yet intriguing. Safdar's paintings follow a rather elementary Cubism to assemble and dismantle his objects.

Shakir Ali's arrival from Europe – where he had studied at the Slade School before working with André L'Hôte in Paris – strengthened these and other younger artists' resolve to follow the procedures of abstract art more vigorously. His influence in developing the ideals of modernism has been vital. He lent solid structure and meaning to notions of abstraction circulating in Pakistan's artistic circles, and his canvases portray man's irrepressible spirit to be fully human and free. In his works man stands alone, declaring his intentions through images and symbols. Among later artists Jamil Naqsh demonstrates inventive skill in exploring an individual subject to its endless limits. His long love affair with pigeons and with the nude female form has produced an arresting and absorbing series of paintings.

In the late Sixties and Seventies, political and social changes in Pakistan and abroad motivated many painters to veer away from the pursuit of formalism to the events and ideas of the time. For Sadequain, the *raison d'être* of painting always lay not in pursuing aesthetic niceties, but in asserting his belief in man's inherent strength to conquer evil and harness nature. He visualised all his important undertakings on an epic scale and his paintings and murals opened new avenues for painting in Pakistan. Mansoor Rahi, following in Sadequain's footsteps, tries to express his personal fears and social concerns.

During this period Zahoor-ul-Akhlaque was introducing living images into his non-figurative works. The atomic mushroom cloud, and effects of nuclear fall-out subtly entered into his work along with the traditional arabesque. The ethos of the Seventies also strengthened Bashir Mirza's determination. From his earliest days he had attempted to express his vision in bold and arresting forms. His recent works reflect his concern with contemporary issues such as the environment, nuclear proliferation and women's rights. Saleema Hashmy creates muted collages in which she censures chauvinist attitudes towards women. Iqbal Jaffry who in the Sixties relied upon doodlings, scratchings and obscure symbols to create provocative aesthetic effects, has come later to lash out at individual hypocrisy and the Establishment. As a painter, A. R. Nagori is even louder and angrier. His paintings alert us to immediate issues in stark, unambiguous terms. Nahid Ali and Qudsia Nisar have in the past enjoyed considerable success for their abstractions. However, today while Nahid's compositions articulate social issues like the trials and tribulations of Pakistani women, Qudsia's thoughtful abstractions and colour washes condemn and highlight Karachi's random violence. In the last few years Mehr Afroze, once a professed aesthete who carefully nurtured surface effects, has also been roused by harsh, everyday events.

Many younger artists pursue their destinies, guided by their instincts and circumstances. Akram Dost paints the distress and dismay of men and women. Qudus Mirza simulates the doodlings of a child to contrive a world of contrasting beauty and ugliness. Imran Mir resists extravagance for post-painterly abstractions. Wahab Jafar, deeply influenced by Ahmed Pervez, has experimented with the palette, producing a body of rich and textured abstract paintings. Tasadaq Sohail creates a world of myth and fantasy illuminated with human and animal forms scratched upon layers of textured paint. Unver Shafi conceives his abstractions in bold colours and forms with a sense of aesthetic and intellectual purpose.

Pakistani painting is unique in one sense: while many artists in the Fifties and the Sixties were trying to come to terms with abstract painting, influenced first by Paris and then later by New York, a number of artists resisted this trend and insisted on working in the figurative tradition. Anna Molka Ahmed who had established the Department of Fine Arts of the Punjab University in the late Twenties, has proved herself a strong force in propelling painters in this direction.

The artist who has covered most ground in the pursuit of objective reality has been Khalid Iqbal. His style and work has influenced an entire generation of artists. His landscapes embrace the rural belt on the fringe of Lahore where he observes subtleties of tone and light and textures with a

Above *Allah Baksh's work brought rural scenes into private collections for the first time. Landscapes are much a part of Pakistan's art scene, with the work of such as Khalid Iqbal, Zulqarnain Haider, Ghulam Rasul and Shahid Jalal*

clear-eyed detachment. His work is relaxed and reposeful. Zulqarnain Haider works with similar ideals focusing on the familiar and carefully chosen scenes. In Ghulam Rasul's landscapes iridescent greens are drowned in deep shadows and contours traced with lemon to establish contrasts. The territory which Shahid Jalal prefers to claim is often arid, where barren earth spews out salts, sustaining tough plants and marshes which contrast with Kaleem Khan's pale mountains and verdant valleys around Quetta. Ghulam Mustafa also paints mountains and flatlands, but finds greater relish in wandering through the dark alleys of old Lahore. Colin David who originally enjoyed painting sharp-edged reality, now includes stylised passages in canvases mostly comprising of nudes. Iqbal Hussain paints the sadness and rejection of prostitutes in Lahore's red light district. In portraiture, Saeed Akhtar excels in idealising his model with the skill of his draughtsmanship, while Musarrat Hasan proceeds to interpret their personality with great sensitivity and insight.

In fifty years, painting in Pakistan has come of age. It has been investigative and experimental. It has been eclectic and plural. In Pakistani painting, everything goes. A conventional portrait can be seen next to an abstraction, a post-modernist endeavour flanking a landscape, an extravagant non-figuration rubbing shoulders with a quiet miniature. It borrows from its tradition and from near and far without prejudice. It has always spurned ethnic bias for human concerns and obscurity for truth. In painting, our half century of the territory's national existence has added a new chapter to a rich and diverse past.

I.U.H.

Left *Ahmad Pervez's use of vibrant colours and bold shapes displays a playful imagination*

Centre *Shakir Ali, a major influence on the Modernism of the Sixties, was a gentle teacher, loved by his students and circle*
Left *Sadeqain's powerful images, often distorted, challenge the onlooker*

Ijaz ul-Hasan's "Lilies at Dusk" is a far cry from his work as an "angry young man" in the Sixties. He is now a prominent landscape painter, critic and art historian

Miniature Painting

Miniature painting was a peacock in the aviary of Muslim arts. Exuberant, iridescent, it invariably overshadowed its more articulate companions in literature and calligraphy, needing the conceit of kings to guarantee its existence. Before the advent of the Mughals in the sixteenth century, miniature painting was already being practised in the subcontinent, in the main as illustrations to religious texts. The arrival with Emperor Humayun in 1558 of two Tabriz painters, Mir Sayyid Ali and Abd-as-Samad, and the subsequent development of an atelier under their supervision during the reign of Akbar, brought about a detachment of painting from the binding strictures of religious dictates. Secular, often romantic, ballads and legends, became subjects. A folio from the Lor and Chanda poem, prepared during this transitional phase, shows the author-poet Mulla Daud as the story-teller reciting from an alcove above the dramatic action.

The Emperor Akbar built sumptuous palaces at Fatehpur Sikri and Lahore, and had them decorated with paintings. He commissioned important works of literature to be translated and copied for his library the most ambitious of which was the *Dastan-i-Amir Hamza*, containing 1,400 illustrations painted on linen. His heir, Jehangir, inherited both trained artists and a trained eye. An avowed naturalism stemming from the new Emperor's own response permeated artistic work during his reign, continuing under his successor Shah Jehan, when the art of formal portraiture achieved an added dimension of expression. This euphuistic style in miniature painting continued into the reign of Aurangzeb, as an early portrait of him indicates. Most of Aurangzeb's later years were spent in subjugating the Deccan and paintings of this period in his life depict an aged monarch outside the walls of Golkunda.

The gradual decline of the Mughal Empire released provincial aspirations. Smaller courts at Murshidabad, Lucknow and the Deccan attracted minor artists who relied upon gaudy effect and technique. Some artists moved to Rajasthani courts, others were attracted to the secluded

Above *"Flute Player": Twentieth century master Chughtai remained true to ancient Eastern symbolism and techniques*

Rajput principalities in the Punjab Hills where many distinct substyles, the most famous of which were Basohli, Ghuler and Kargra, were to emerge with flamboyance throughout the eighteenth century. In Sindh, an interesting illustrated manuscript of the *Saiful Muluk* written and completed in Thatta in 1775 provides confirmation that by the late eighteenth century Muslim miniature painting had lost momentum. Relying as it did upon courtly patronage, it responded weakly to diminishing support. Revival by the British in the nineteenth century, first to suit their own taste, and later to reactivate an indigenous craft, resulted in the gaunt mannerist hybrids of the Bengal neo-classical school. The significant illustrative function of the miniature painter was no longer required; the decorative value of the peacock no longer essential.

F.S.A.

The art of miniature painting reached its zenith under the Mughal kings
Opposite *Painting of a woman reclining with a huqqa pipe, Deccan, eighteenth century*
Right *The construction of a palace is depicted in this Mughal miniature of the early eighteenth century*

PAKISTAN

Music

Pakistan has inherited musical traditions that go far back into history. The foundation of classical music was solidly laid by Amir Khusrau in the thirteenth century who introduced the *qawwali* tradition. Since then this art has almost exclusively been in the hands of Muslim musicians. In the past three centuries there have been legions of Muslim masters, and all the prominent *gharanas* or schools of classical music were founded by them; the few Hindu musicians of note received their training there. In the ancient civilisation of the land that now comprises Pakistan all the permutations and combinations of the twelve semi-tones, which form the universal basis of music, have been sifted, given individual names and identified with their appropriate times, seasons and emotions, hundreds of years before Palestrina showed the way to Western music.

Broadly, music in Pakistan can be classified as traditional or modern. Traditional music includes classical and semi-classical music, folk music and mystic music composed by the great saints of Pakistan. among them Shah Abdul Latif Bhitai, Sachal Sarmast, Khwaja Ghulam Farid, Shah Hussain, Bullhe Shah and many others. A poet-saint who was also a versatile musician (like Abdul Latif Bhitai or Shah Hussain) may use various classical *ragas* (melody modes or leitmotifs in his compositions, but the bulk of such music is in *bhairvi* and *kafi*. These two *ragas* have been preferred for their simplicity, tunefulness and their mass appeal. The compositions emanating from different regions of Pakistan are collectively known as *kafis* (from the *ragakafi*) with slight stylistic variations depending on their place of origin. Themes of *qawwali* are mystical and moral, based on a deep love of the Prophet Muhammad and the saints and a desire to be one with the Infinite. The rhythmic pattern of hypnotically persistent beats is successfully employed to create a climax of hysterical ecstasy. Recent years have witnessed a tremendous rise in the popularity of *qawwali* with Nusrat Fateh Ali Khan, a traditional *qawwal* with impeccable antecedents, becoming something of a cult figure. He has performed all over the world, winning some of the most prestigious awards and prizes.

By using the most technologically advanced electronic equipment he has supplemented his main melodic singing with orchestration so as to sound very contemporary. Coupled with the rich texture of rhythmic variation, the porous format of the *qawwali* accommodates experiments with a fair measure of success without losing the element of ecstasy and hysteria which its persistent beat is traditionally meant to evoke.

Folk Music too has become more popular in the urban areas of the country. Abida Parveen and Pathaney Hamid Ali Bela have excelled in the rendition of *kafi* while Ataullah Isakhelvi has devised a more modern variation of folk which relies as much on simple tunes as on the spoken idiom of the songs.

Classical music in the subcontinent has always stood in need of financial patronage for its survival because the audience who can appreciate its intricacies are too few to pay the performing musicians. In Pakistan, this patronage suddenly came to an end after the departure of the rajas and nawabs after Partition. The result was almost catastrophic. Great masters like Ustad Ashiq Ali Khan, Ustad Abdul Waheed Khan and Ustad Tawakkal Hussain Khan died within a decade and the most famous classical singer, Ustad Barey Ghulam Ali Khan, migrated to India. In the late Sixties classical music in Pakistan was at a low ebb. In 1972 the Pakistan National Council of the Arts was established to promote cultural activities and it was only then that the revival of classical music was made possible. A classical music research cell was established for research on and documenta-

Right The murli *is played by snake charmers in Sindh*
Below *The Kalash's* dhol **(right),** tumbrak *and* **(far right)** *the* tabla

Above *A folk musician plays the* shahnai *at the Awami Mela (People's Festival) in Lahore*
Right *The* dam dama *is a percussion instrument popular in the northern areas*

Right *Munir Sarhadi won fame as a* sarinda *player*
Below *The* santoor *is from Kashmir*

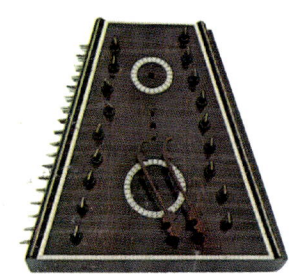

Above and right *The* rabab *is widely played in north-west Pakistan*

tion of classical music. Work began on an exhaustive collection of classical *ragas* on tape and long-playing records.

The accredited representatives of the recognized *gharanas* of classical music – Roshan Ara Begum (Kairana), Ustad Salamat Ali Khan (*sham chorasi*), Ustad Fateh Ali Khan (*Patiala*), Ustad Ramzan Khan (Delhi), Ustad Asad Ali Khan (*Agra*) – are all now preserved in these forms. Traditional light classical music includes *thumri*, *dadra* and *ghazal*. Of these, *thumri* and *dadra*, being products of the times of the nawabs of Oudh, no longer enjoy their former popularity in Pakistan. Farida Khanum and Iqbal Bane, two notable exponents of this art, are struggling to keep it alive. But the signs are that these two forms of music will finally merge with the modern *geet* or song, a medium that has become the vehicle of modern Pakistani music. Since Farida Khanum and Iqbal Bane excel also at *ghazal* singing, this form of musical composition has been brought to perfection. Ghulam Ali and Mehdi Hassan are two other *ghazal* singers whose styles have captivated listeners the world over. Currently Mehdi Hassan's style is being adopted throughout the subcontinent.

Sarangi is a stringed instrument perfectly adaptable to all the nuances of Eastern music. In Pakistan, the late Ustad Bundu Khan was a consummate exponent of both the theory and practice of *sarangi* playing. It is universally acknowledged that a *sarangi* player of his calibre has not appeared on the musical scene of the subcontinent for centuries. It now appears that the art of *sarangi* playing is slowly disappearing, a great loss to the instrumental classical heritage of Pakistan. In Ustad Sharif Khan of Poonch, Pakistan has an outstanding sitar player – he ranks among the finest sitar players of the subcontinent with Ravi Shankar and Vilayat Hussain. Outstanding among the folk instrumentalists of Pakistan are Munir Sarhadi (*sarinda*), Misri Khan Jamali and his disciple Khamisoo Khan (*alghoza*), Sain Allah Ditta Qadri (flute) and the late Sain Mama (*iktara*). They have all performed with distinction abroad. The folk music of Pakistan, together with *qawwali* and mystic music, represents the real culture of the masses, their loves and hates, their joys and sorrows, their colourful

Rhythm divine: Nusrat Fateh Ali Khan has won an international audience for his qawwali *singing, combining traditional forms with state-of-the-art electronic orchestration*

The single-string iktara, *introduced by Sain Marna*

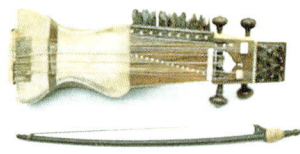

The sarangi *is a classical bowed instrument*

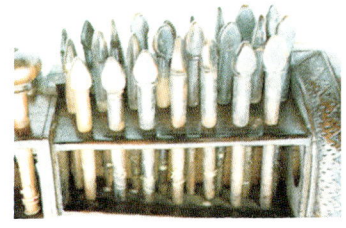

This close-up shows the sarangi's *multiple strings*

The sitar *was developed by Hazrat Amir Khusrau. Music is everywhere in Pakistan, and for every performer of folk music, vocal or instrumental, who has become famous there are a hundred more of similar talents and skills known locally and in the villages*

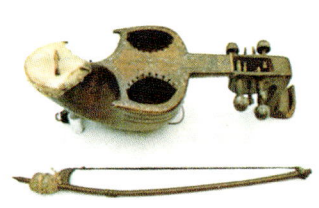

The suroze *is popular in Sindh and Balochistan*

ceremonies and festivities, and above all their spiritual entity. It includes all the songs and dances spontaneously originating among the common people of the different regions of the country. Like folk songs all over the world, these songs too are predominantly strophic in pattern – the same music is repeated for each stanza. This pattern is most suitable for simple lyrical pieces with regular metre and uniform stanzas. Pushtu, *tappa*, *sammi*, *mahiya*, *gidda*, *jugni* and *jamalo* are but a few of them.

Similarly, the epic love poems of Heer Ranjha, Mirza Sahiban, Sohni Meha Sorath and Rai Dach, Umer Marvi, Momal and Rano are sung in specific mode (*sur*) and have their own distinct style of presentation. In Sindh, this mode of presentation has given rise to "thematic" or *sur* music, perfected by Shah Abdul Latif Bhitai, affectionately called *Shah-Jo-Rago* (Shah's music) it is a synthesis of Sindhi classical and folk traditions.

Present folk artists like Alam Lohar, Sain Akhtar, Reshman, Munir Sarhadi, Khamisoo Khan, Faiz Muhammad Baluch and Misri Khan Jamali have performed all over the world. A national institute has been established in Islamabad for the promotion and preservation of folklore and folk music. Modern music in Pakistan is characterised by the use of Western instruments and is wholly confined to light music. There have been no modern trends in classical music. Lately, electronic instruments have also come into vogue. Because of the extemporaneous nature of classical music and the improvisation freely employed in the exposition of classical *ragas*, the need for a notation system was never felt by the masters. The teaching of music was oral. Recently, however, composers have acutely felt the need for notation. Instead of evolving an indigenous system. however, the Western notational system was introduced and is now being widely used, even though it has proved inadequate for classical music. Ustad Muhammad Sharif Khan has now evolved a system that could transcribe all the peculiarities and niceties of classical music, but this is still at an experimental stage.

K.A.

Crafts

Even among the developing countries where crafts are fast turning into mechanised cottage industries, Pakistan remains one of the last citadels of a hand-wrought heritage. More than architecture or painting, handicrafts are the easiest and closest source of a people's identification – their passion for tradition, their patience with intricate techniques and their pride in beautiful results, even when rewards are low.

Pakistan's early history is moulded in ceramics, welded in metals and woven in textiles. The bronze-caster of the famed dancing girl unveils a high level of artistic expression from Mohenjodaro, even when its script remains undeciphered. Gandharan jewellery and ivory carvings reveal cosmopolitan influences. The Hindu craftsman seems to have been a wizard in weaving, carving in the round and metal-moulding; to this land rich in grains, gold and gods, Muslims then contributed entirely different aesthetics. Craft historians of the

Top (left) *close-up of* mashrabiya *woodcarving* **(right)** *Balochi embroidery* **Above (left)** *A* namda, *or felt floor-spread, in close-up* **Above (right) and Left** *contrasting styles of embroidery*

West have recorded a unique ferment in the Muslim world, spilling over in phases into the subcontinent.

The pre-Mughal period witnessed not only the imperial centre but regional kingdoms as glittering nuclei of arts and crafts excelling in textiles and tiled ensembles. Graphically recorded renaissance in crafts begins with the Mughals, who perfected many crafts and introduced new highly developed ones. The royal *ateliers* gave designs to the workshops which were supervised by technical experts from abroad. After the sun set on the Mughal empire, the British could not sustain an ardent patronage of crafts, which found their last asylum in the wealth of the princely states. Since Independence, craftsmen have at last found a stable market reinforced by immigrant Muslim artisans from India.

Within the vast and diverse landscape of Pakistan, they have their characteristic provincial profiles. Sindh is the richest in colour and range of crafts, particularly in the folk tradition. Punjab, with Lahore as one of the three Mughal capitals, continues to carry the notes and strokes of a wider culture. The North-West Frontier maintains sturdiness of materials with eclectic echoes in folk carvings, ceramics and jewellery. Balochistan crafts draw on tribal talents for embroidery, leather accoutrements, decorated weaponry and rug weaving.

Carpets remain the *chef d'oeuvre* of Pakistan's heritage. During Akbar's reign the establishment of workshops in Lahore is recorded, but some existed much earlier during the Sultanate. This craft is a total transplant, proudly retaining its classical designs and hallmarks named after the celebrated production centres of Iran. Originally confined to court-looms, carpet weaving today has proliferated into nearly all the major cities and towns, with Karachi and Lahore as the leading emporia drawing on the mass production of the hinterland, selecting the choicest for export.

The North-West Frontier area, Sindh and Balochistan have their own local versions of folk rugs. Small goat hair rugs, *farasis*, are made all over Sindh of particularly fine quality; a mixture of sheep wool and camel hair is woven into striking patterns near Thatta, Tharparkar and Sanghar. Weaving centres are active in Thana Bula Khan, Mithi, Dadu, Naudero, Tajal Naro, Dipli, Salehpat. From Gilgit and Hunza come *sharmas*, goat hair rugs in natural colours. The Frontier *taghar* and *nakhai*, flamboyant rugs with twisted knots, are a speciality of Dera Ismail Khan, Mardan, Rannu and Kohat. The sturdiest mixtures of wool and hair rugs are woven by Badinzai women in Jhalawan, but weaving is widespread in Sarawan, Makran and Las Bela (Balochistan). *Namdas*, felt floor-spreads, are crewel-embroidered in chain-stitch by Kashmiris. Less ornate *namdas* are available in Ziarat, Zhob, Sibi, Peshawar, Kohat and the majority of the Frontier regions.

Metalcraft is a tradition encompassing centuries of hereditary expertise in casting, chasing, incising, repoussé, cut-work, filigree and inlay. Jewellery, the most ravishing form of feminine capitalism, is a legacy from the fabled past. Gem-inlaid *kundan* and *jarao* have always been the preference of the affluent, while solid gold ornaments are an investment of the middle class. Enamelled ornaments are in vogue again (the best made in Hyderabad and Lahore) and silver jewellery is fashionable now in the cities, but has long been the standby of the masses. Apart from folk motifs, almost any design in gold jewellery is copied in silver by city shops. Fine Kashmiri silverwork and parcel gilt (*gangajamni*) decoration pieces are of the highest quality in Rawalpindi and Karachi. Bidri-silver inlay on a black metal amalgam is an exquisite survival from the seventeenth century in all forms, decorative and functional, from *aftaaba* to paper knives and studs. Damascene, perhaps an Arab import and later known as *koftgari*, is gold or silver wire inlay on steel for arms, armour, astrolabes, mirror frames, jewel caskets and pencases. Sialkot and Lahore were the famous centres of damasceners, who switched over from weaponry to cutlery in the nineteenth century.

Copper and brass are fashionable again, supplying domestic demands for lamps, coffee tables, flowerpots and door knockers. Apart from Persian and Turkish traditions, Gandharan forms and motifs have recently added to the metal repertoire; chic combinations of these glowing metals are worked with wood, marble and ceramics. Peshawar leads in chased and engraved copper work with fine arabesques. Multan, Karachi and Lahore abound in unequalled talent in cut-work and repoussé.

Textiles can be categorised, since Vedic times, into brocading, embroidering, hand-painting and tie-dyeing. The medium was invariably cotton, the finest ever woven, as transparent as water. Several varieties of silk from wild, raw and Chinese yarn were reeled off by the nimble hands of the seasoned weaver.

Textiles reached their apex under the Sultanate; the imperial workshop of the Tughlaqs in Delhi with four thousand weavers, and those of provincial kingdoms such as Gujrat, Malwa and Bengal, had samples of fabrics imported from the textile centres of the Islamic world. Sophisticated patterns under Nakshabands, with mechanical contrivances for woven figurals are recorded during this period. Damasks, satins, mixed weaves like *himru* (Gulbadan and Shah Muhammad), *mashru*, *shirinbaf*, *tabrizi*, *shusteri*, *shinbaf*, *atlas*, *bairami*, *aksun*, *deogiri*, *bihari*, *gul-bakavali*, *harir*, *juzz* and *diba* were shuttled back and forth as court presents and diplomatic overtures. The contemporaries of the Mughals, the Ottomans and the Safavids, set a high standard for them to imitate. Mughal looms added figured silks and personage-velvets.

What we have today is a continuation of past tradition. Hyderabad, Khairpur, Karachi, Lahore and Multan produce costly and comely brocades, raw silks and a variety of floral and patterned silks under the generic name of *banarsi*. Sindh, which has been exporting handspun fabrics to the Roman and west Asian world since ancient times, continues to produce *soosi*, *mothra* and *gharbi*. Silk and cotton looms are active in Jacobabad, Thatta, Sukkur, Ranipur and Tand.

With gem-like brilliance the silken *khes* of Gambat and Nasserpur has to be touched to be believed. Mixtures of cottons with other yarns emerge in boldly conceived *khes* from Multan, Sahiwal, Pind Dadan, Jhelum, Mianwali and Dera Ghazi. The patterned hand-spun *khaddar* makes attractive upholstery. The *lachcha* and *lungi* of the Punjab and the *dastaar* from the Frontier add to the brightly-coloured variety from the handloom. Narrow strips of woolly *pattu* from Kaghan, Kashmir, Gilgit, Chitral, Dir and Hunza are tailored into *chuga* and overcoats. Coarse striped woollen shawls from Swat regain popularity every winter. Kashmiri shawls (of soft wool, from the underbelly of the Central Asian goat) originate from the enlightened reign of Zain-ul-Abedin, who is supposed to have brought the skills and twill-tapestry technique to Kashmir from Samarkand in the fifteenth century. The loom-woven pieces, called *tilli* shawls, are now collectors' acquisitions. Sometimes as many as 1,500 bits were woven – each with a separate design – and stitched together so remarkably well that the naked eye could not detect the joins. Loom-woven *pashimina* is still embroidered throughout Kashmir.

The history of ceramics leaves much to the imagination, despite innumerable archaeological finds. Glazed tilework, *kashigari* is recorded in thirteenth-century Multan in the pure Iranian tradition, leading to a long succession of tiled frescoes and mosaics in mosques and mausoleums until the nineteenth century. Three known centres of ceramics now, each with a distinctive colour-scheme and pattern, are Hala, Peshawar and Multan. The fertile alluvial soil of the lower Indus provides excellent clay for the glazed ware of Hala and Sehwan. Jugs, jars, vases, bowls, dinner sets, mugs, in all shades of chocolate and brown are enlivened with yellow and touches of green. Multan's distinctive colours are blue and white, like its enamels and architecture. These are reproduced mechanically in Gujranwala and Gujrat. Peshawar has maintained the most durable glaze in functional pottery in addition to the merely ornamental. Its refreshing colours – jade-green, lemon, rust, blue and black – add sparkle to any home. Paper-thin pottery, *kaghzi*, is the glory of Bahawalpur, whose potters turn out delicate amphoras, goblets, vases, candleholders and platters in natural terracotta colours. Unglazed folk pottery used in rural hinterlands is to be found in every village household.

The ancient carver made good use of rich timber reserves, but the finest reliefs, chiselled on temples, did not survive climate and vandalism. The Arabs brought with them the exquisite genre, *mashrabiya*, a kind of geometric wood-joinery avidly adopted by the North-Western regions and re-christened *pinjra*. These *pinjra* lattices inspired a new trend throughout Mughal, Rajput and later Sikh spheres of influence. The *tarkhan* of Punjab is not a mere carpenter but a real artist, shaping furniture and daily utilities in forms old and new, with both classical and folk motifs in almost every wood from *shisham* to teak. Shahpur, Bhera and Sialkot have become legends, but Lahore, Multan and Karachi are living centres, with Chiniot leading in brass-inlay on wood. Tea trolleys, teapots, cigar boxes, egg-cups, salad bowls – almost anything is wire-inlaid. Peshawar and Rawalpindi specialise in finely carved and inlaid furniture, as the best Kashmiri carvers have gravitated there, creating marvels of cut-work and reliefs mainly in walnut. Ivory-inlay in geometric and semi-floral layout, historically linked with the Muslim period, comes naturally to Pakistani craftsmen.

Dyeing is as old as the first civilisation, but block-printing

The illustrations above give a sample of the variety and vigour of decorative jewellery and other crafts throughout Pakistan.
Top row (left and centre) *Gypsy women of the Od tribes wear these silver necklaces in Sindh* **(right)** *a Balochi hair clip*
Second row (left) *A Sindhi hair clip* **(centre)** *A silver necklace from Tharparkar in Sindh*
Third row (left) *Decorative silver hair ornaments* **(centre left)** *One of a pair of gold, enamelled ear ornaments, set with pearls, turquoise and jargoons. Delhi, eighteenth century.* **(centre right)** *A* moodi *adorns these Baloch hair clips.* **(right)** Peerah *is a common style of chair made in Dera Ismail Khan and Punjab*
Bottom row (left and centre) *A* khusa *or man's shoe worn on festive occasions by Gujjar tribes in the north* **(right)** *A* sindhani *is embroidered and worn by Sindhi women*

too was exported to China a little before the Christian era and later to Egypt. The earliest samples extant, however, are from fifteenth century Fustat (old Cairo) of low grade cotton with indigo prints. The centuries under the Mughals marked the glowing peak of printed and painted fabrics, a specialised genre of which *qalamkari* was initiated by the Persianised dynasty of Golkunda. The designs to this day seen all over India and Pakistan are of the same inspiration – cypresses, paisleys, carpet-cartouches, arches, niches, floral creepers and all the vernal variety romanticised by Persian literature. Block-printing, however, in folk tradition is almost universal. Tie-dyeing is one of the oldest skills on record in the desert regions of Sindh.

The renowned *ajraks* of Sindh (favourite combination being indigo and maroon) are best done in Muttiari and Hyderabad. Cotton bed and table covers along with wraps are mass-blocked in all the leading towns of the Punjab. Those outstanding are *karore-panna* printers of Multan and *chappey-walas* of Lahore, secretive masters of their trade in

    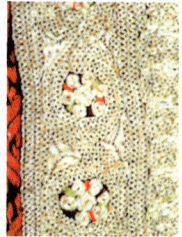 

floor coverings, table-linen, curtains, canopy-liners, and the latest sartorial trends. The finest block-printing is now being done on silk kaftans and saris in Karachi, where the effect is enhanced by embroidered trimmings of gold and silver.

Lacquer-work is potentially a thriving industry in Pakistan. Once the wooden objects have been lathe-turned and rounded, they are lac-layered in fast rotation and patterned by etching out one colour from beneath another. Lacquer-work is now used in furniture, swinging cots, beds and divans, not to mention old butter churns and spinning wheels in Sindh where the *jhundi-wara* of Kashmir, Khairpur and Hala cater to all tastes. Coloured lacquer ware is produced in Sillanwali, Muzaffargarh, Dera Ghazi Khan, Jhang, Multan and Pakpatten. The *kharadi* of Lahore employ contrasting colours, like black and white. Mirror frames and tea-trolleys, hat hangers, caskets and standard lamps are made in striking colour combinations. A style perfected by Dera Ismail Khan is *abri* (mottled) though coupled with *atishi* (from fiery tinsel paste), it is as endemic to Sindh as to Punjab.

There are two distinct divisions of embroidery; metropolitan and folk. The former, previously a favourite with harems and the nobility, is only patronised by the rich to day. *Zardozi, kaar-chob, jali, salma-sitara, kalabatoon, baadla* or *kaamdani, gotakinari,* and *dori* cover the entire range of stitchery. The finest masters of the craft are now employed by the leading shops of Lahore and Karachi which are back-logged with orders both local and foreign. *Chikanari* – an echo from the nawabs of Murshidabad, Dacca and Lucknow – is made by Muslim immigrant embroiderers on transparent muslin shirts, saris and table cloths. It involves shadow-work, running-stitch (*tepchi*) for outlines, knotted-stitches (*murri* and *phanda*) and network. Though the multi-hued *rilli*, patchwork, one of the salvage crafts made from bits and pieces, is a speciality of Sindh, its broader conception in appliqué is displayed by tent makers of Multan, Bahawalpur and Lahore. The most sparkling is the mirror embroidery of Sindh and Balochistan. Thick-set with chain, buttonhole and stem stitches, *gajj*, of Lohana tribes and gypsy-women from the Tharparkar and Rajputana deserts, is a family heirloom. The Balochi *pashk*, a woman's garment, with delicate cross and chain-stitch and Balochi *lohri* with rows of chain-stitch roundels on silk or satin, are beautiful. In the north, particularly Kaghan, the long *pugree* in satin-stitch (magenta or maroon on black ground) is coveted, as is the Swati *kurta*, table and cushion covers. *Phulkari* – rust home-spun cotton lozenges or rosettes worked in freehand from the reverse in darning stitch, mainly of white silken floss – is a lost craft. Its diluted versions hang in bazaars but the classic Hazara *bagh* and *kakri* are only mementoes in a family chest.

Leather craftsmen were regarded as lowly untouchables in Hindu society, until the advent of Islam in the subcontinent gave them new status. Marco Polo in the thirteenth century gives details of Moorish mats portraying birds and beasts in silver and gold threads. After seven centuries Sindh still exhibits *nats* of *sambar* leather with a central medallion, borders and corners appliqued with different

Above (left) *Such coats are made and embroidered in Dera Ismail Khan, the intricacy of this work is shown here in detail*
Above *An embroidered* kurta *from Punjab, worn at weddings and other celebrations.*

Top (left) *An enamelled* huqqa *bowl from Lucknow, eighteenth century*
(Right) Huqqa *bowl from Bidri, eighteenth century*
Above (left) *A brass box and cover, gadrooned with floral ornamental vertical bands and* lac *inlay*
(Right) *A leaf brooch in* koftgari, *of gold inlay on steel, from Punjab, nineteenth century*

Top (left) *An enamelled dish from Kashmir, nineteenth century*
(Right) *A glass rosewater sprinkler, Mughal period, eighteenth century*
Above (left) *An enamel box and lid, also of Mughal origin, probably early nineteenth century*
(Right) *A dark green mirror-back of nephrite and gold set with rubies*

leather or embroidered in multi-hued silk, silver or gold threads. Handsome leather saddlery jackets, purses and shoes, embellished with colourful stitches, can be bought in Quetta, Kalat, Hyderabad and Thatta. The horse and camel gear with its accessories, pouches, pommels, belts and bags are embroidered in Lehri, Makran, Las Bela and Kutch areas. Gold-worked shoes and sandals (the *zari khussa* and *chapli*) along with waistcoats are sold in all the leading towns of the Frontier and Punjab. Multan manufactures lamps of camel skin with transparent designs and colours reminiscent of glass mosque lamps from the Mamluk period of Syria and Egypt.

A few minor crafts like basketry, papier-mâché, doll-making, glass bangles, *moradabadi* inlay and lapidary skills also flourish in Pakistan. After agriculture and industry, handicrafts provide employment for a large proportion of the working population, hence its preservation is as much a commercial as a cultural imperative.

Ak.R.

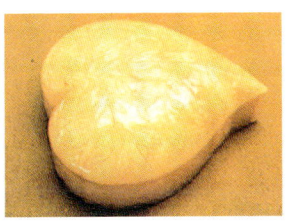  

Top row (left and middle) *Embroidered* kurta *from Balochistan* **(right)** *The famous Multan blue pottery*
Second row (left) *A Mughal mango-shaped box and lid in* nephrite **(centre)** *Mughal* huqqa *bowl, with gadrooned body inlaid with silver wire and sheet metal* **(Right)** *Mughal clear-green glass and gilded* huqqa *bowl from Bidri*
Right (above and below) *Mughal floral patterns are exquisitely woven in modern rugs made by hand in Karachi*

Above *This pre-Islamic carving, which embellishes a tomb at Chaukundi, depicting anklets and bracelets, denotess the resting place of a lady*

Museums

Stone implements and earthenware vessels at the museum at Mohenjodaro, Sindh: the site of Mohenjodaro is the most impressive evidence of the Indus Valley Civilisation which reigned between 2600-1900 BC. The first excavations were in 1922, under the India Archaeological Survey, directed by Sir John Marshall. Further excavations have revealed remains of a thriving, and well-organised city, about three miles in circumference

Museums present a useful summary of the evolution of civilisations, and Pakistan's past encompasses six millennia of civilisations which rose and fell along the banks of the Indus. Invaders came and left their imprints on the cultural matrix of various societies. Accordingly, the land is fertile in historic sites and relics which present a composite picture of how Pakistan's ancestor's lived and died.

Pakistan's wealth of the residue from the past is housed in a number of museums spread around the country. Lahore Museum is probably the richest of them, being especially well-endowed with a fine collection of miniatures which are displayed in a hall the ceiling of which has been painted by Sadequain, one of Pakistan's best-known artists. There is also a unique collection of Gandhara art, including the famous "Fasting Siddhartha".

The National Museum at Karachi, built in 1851, is now housed in a modern building equiped with the latest aids for re-creating the past through lectures and slides. The old site, a magnificent Victorian building, is being renovated to house a library.

The other major museums are located in Peshawar and Hyderabad. Apart from these, there are museums located at excavation sites at Mohenjodaro, Harappa, Taxila, Bhambore and Saidu Sharif in Swat. Each of these helps to give visitors a better idea of the pattern and flow of life at these sites when they were vibrant centres of civilisation.

The Lahore Fort museum includes a Mughal section for miniatures, manuscripts and coins of the period. Apart from a special Sikh collection, it also exhibits types of weaponry used at various periods in the subcontinent.

A small but nonetheless famous museum is the one at Umarkot fort, near Emperor Akbar's birthplace. There are also many small, specialised museums attached to various universities and institutions. Probably the most famous private museum is at the Faqir Khana at Bhati gate in the walled city of Lahore. It contains objects from the late Sikh period, as well as unique curios such as a miniature of Emperor Akbar's Spanish wife and the prayer rug used by Empreror Aurangzeb to say the first prayers held in Badshahi Mosque.

Recognising the need to preserve and encourage traditional art, the Government has established a small folk art museum in Islamabad. Shakir Ali, the famous artist, spent eight years designing and building his house in Lahore. After his death, the Government acquired this original and beautiful house and converted it into a museum for his paintings, as well as for those of other leading modern artists.

B.A.K. and F.S.H.

Top (far left) *Lahore Museum, established in 1864, the oldest museum in Pakistan. Its eight galleries include Gandharan, Mughal and Chinese art*
Top (left) and Right *The museums at Peshawar and Karachi also house extensive collections of national treasures*
Bottom (left) *At Harappa and Taxila small museums present a picture of life in ancient civilisations*

The Literary Heritage

The cultural heritage of Pakistan in its non-literary manifestations can be traced back to the great Indus civilization of the fifth millennium BC. But its literary traditions originate from the Muslim period commencing with the advent of the Arabs in this region early in the eighth century AD. The Arabs ruled over Sindh and a part of lower Punjab with two separate seats of government; one in Mansura in Sindh and the other in Multan in Punjab. During this period, Arabic was the language of government, learning and culture in the areas under Arab dominance. The spoken language of the native population in Sindh was termed Sindhi by the Arabs. Lower Punjab spoke a compound of Punjabi and Hindvi. During the early decades of the eleventh century, Northern Punjab and some adjoining areas were overrun by the Turko-Afghan armies of Sultan Mahmud of Ghazni, and a new Muslim kingdom was established with its capital at Lahore. Sultan Mahmud had gathered in his court some of the greatest Persian poets of his age. Thus Persian was introduced to this land and it held sway over a major part of the subcontinent for many succeeding centuries. The admixture of Persian and local dialects of the northern areas of the subcontinent gave birth to the national language of Pakistan, namely, Urdu.

The literary heritage of Pakistan, therefore, has been trebly enriched by three classical languages: Arabic, Persian and Urdu. Parallel with these three literatures, there is the wealth of folk classics in various regional languages, Sindhi, Punjabi, Pushtu, Balochi, Brahui, Kashmiri and the more localised dialects.

The educational system during the Arab period, and later almost down to the British days, centred primarily round religious studies called *Manqulat*. Some secular subjects were added to the curriculum during the reigns of the Delhi Sultan Sikander Lodhi (1489-1516) and the Mughal Emperor Akbar (1556-1605). Even to this day in all the religious seminaries in Pakistan, Arabic writings of earlier epochs are still being studied and, therefore, continue to be part of a living tradition.

Understandably the bulk of this literature in Arabic is mainly religious and theological, i.e. commentaries, expositions and exegeses of sacred texts or jurisprudence, and dialectics and discursive or exhortative pamphlets based on religious themes. Nevertheless, a number of important works were also produced on historical, biographical, geographical, philosophical or sociological subjects. Mention might be made, for instance, of Najih-bin-Abdur Rehman al-Sindhi (d. 787) whose *Kitab al-Maghazi* was used as a source book by the well-known Arab historians Waqidi and Ibn Saad, and the great Abu Raihan al-Biruni (d. 1048), historian, mathematician and jurist. His *Kitab ul-Hind* is still regarded as the most authentic source book on the history, religion, philosophy, geography, social life and anthropology of mediaeval India. Then there were lexicographers like Sanaani (d. 1252) and jurists like Badr bin Taj of Lahore, who are famous in the world of Muslim scholarship. In religious literature, the works of exegeses by scholars like Ali bin Ahmad Mahaini (d. 1341), particularly his *Tayassar al-Mannan fi Tafsir al-Quran* and writings on the life and sayings of the Holy Prophet by Sheikh Abdul Haq Muhaddis of Delhi, like his *Madari-al-Nabuvvat* or historical treatises like *Tarikh-i-Haqqi*, were also compulsory reading in Muslim religious schools for centuries.

Shah Waliullah of Delhi (d. 1752) is perhaps the greatest name in this line. As a political thinker, social reformer and religious ideologue, his writings, particularly his definitive work, *Hujjatullah al-Balighah*, influenced both popular and scholarly thinking in many Muslim lands. His eldest son, Shah Abdul Aziz, was an equally gifted scholar. His expositions of the traditions of the Prophet of Islam and his compendium of Muslim case law are also internationally known. This tradition of religious scholarship has continued unbroken to the present day. Notable among contemporary writers is Maulvi Abdul Haye of Lucknow (d. 1923) whose monumental work *Nuzhat-ul-Khawatir* is a many-volumed biography of famous Arabic scholars and Muslim divines of the subcontinent. Later scholars wrote mostly in Persian or Urdu.

Unlike Arabic literature of various periods which is mainly religious or theological, the literary legacy in the Persian language is far richer and more varied. It encompasses most forms of literary and scholastic expression: poetry, history, biography and autobiography, epistles, fiction, reminiscences, dictionaries, commentaries on juristic and religious classics, and *belles-lettres*. Perhaps the only exception is drama of which there was no tradition in Arabic or Persian literature.

The pride of place in this vast store-house belongs to poetry which has been the daily food of innumerable generations over the centuries. After the consolidation of the Delhi Sultanate in the thirteenth century, all through the Muslim period of Indo-Pakistan history, this literature was being constantly enriched both by the many gifted writers indigenously born and bred and by a stream of talent from Iran and other Persian-speaking lands. This resulted in the evolution of a new and distinctive school of Persian poetry, which the Iranians called *Sabke Hindi* (the Indian School). Very different from the products of classical Persian, it introduced to Persian poetry new nuances of feeling and expression, deeper and more delicate explorations of subjective experience and subtler modes of social and political comment.

The main forms of poetry in Persian are *qasaid* (panegyrics with a semi-philosophical exordium or historical narrative) *mathnavis* (narrative poems on romantic, historical, mystical, philosophical or metaphysical themes) *rubaiyat* (epigrammatic quatrains) and *ghazals* (short lyrical poems of a limited number of couplets, each more or less self-sufficient in meaning). It is this last highly complex and symbolical form which was later adapted and perfected by Urdu poets and attained the greatest popularity.

The earliest poets in Persian, i.e. Abul Faraj Rumi (d. 1114) and Masud Saad Salman of Lahore (d. 1121) may not be read very much today, but the *ghazals* of their illustrious successor, Ibnul Hasan Amir Khusrau (d. 1325) historian, thinker, musicologist, linguist, and political theoretician, are still popular and are permanently included in the musical repertoire of *qawwali* singers (chorus singers of mystical or devotional songs).

There are other celebrated names in this great tradition. Outstanding among these are Urfi (d. 1591), Faizi (d. 1595), Naziri (d. 1614), Ghani Kashmiri (d. 1668), Abdul Qadir Bedil (d. 1720), Asadullah Khan Ghalib (d. 1869), and the poet Muhammad Iqbal (d. 1938) of contemporary times. Of these Urfi with his poignant lyrics and almost modernistic diction, Faizi with his versatile mastery of narrative and descriptive verse, Naziri's delicate handling of social and philosophical problems and Bedil's deeply intellectual approach to metaphysical themes, have all left their stamp on the heritage bequeathed by them to their successors.

Towards the middle of the eighteenth century, the rise of

Urdu and its growing popularity displaced Persian as the favourite language of princely courts and their retinue of talented poets. Although Persian retained its place as the official language and the vehicle of scholarly discourse or correspondence, a succession of Urdu classics opened a more accessible avenue of poetic expression. The glory of Persian was revived once again, however, by two great masters, Ghalib and Iqbal, who wrote with equal facility in both Urdu and Persian. Ghalib articulated with great insight and passion the intellectual ferment, soul-searching and heartbreak of the generations which witnessed the final decline and fall of the Mughal empire and the vanishing of their glory. Iqbal did the same for the bewildered Muslim intelligentsia which grew up during the turbulence of the three or four decades of the present century. Their fame has travelled far beyond the borders of the subcontinent.

In Persian prose, generally cadenced and highly ornate as a rule, there is a voluminous literature, particularly in historiography and related fields. Gifted chroniclers were commanded by almost every ruling dynasty to record contemporary life. *Tarikh-e-Firoze Shahi* and *Fatawa-e-Jahandari* of Zia-ud-Din Barni (d. 1357), *Akbar Nama* and *Ain-e-Akbari* of Abul Fatal (d. 1602) *Muntakhebut-Tawarikh* of Mulla Abdul Qadir Badayuni (d. 1615), *Gulshan-e-lbrahimi* or *Tarikh-e-Farishta* of Muhammad Qasim Farishta (d. 1623), *Badshah Nama* of Abdul Hameed Lahori (d. 1647), *Maasr-e-Alamgiri* of Nemat Khan Aali (d. 1710) and *Siyar-al-Mutahhirin* of Ghulam Hassan Tabatebai (d. 1781) are some of the most valuable works. Each contains a first-hand account of historical events, doings at court, racial and cultural affairs and sometimes a perceptive analysis of statecraft and court politics.

In the field of biography and autobiography perhaps the most interesting documents are the writings of kings and princes themselves; for instance, *Babur Nama*, the autobiography of the founder of the Mughal Empire, Zaheeruddin Babur (d. 1530) *Humayun Nama*, an account of the life of the second Emperor (d. 1556) by his sister, Gulbadan Begum, and *Tuzk-e-Jahangiri* – an autobiography of the fourth Mughal Emperor, Jehangir (d. 1627). There is also a whole body of literature on the lives of saints, scholars, poets and notables.

There are a number of important religious studies. Works on mysticism and related subjects have influenced not only the religious, but also the social and political thought of many generations. Outstanding among these are *Kashf-ul-Mahjub*, of Syed Ali Hujweri, known as Data Ganj Bakhsh of Lahore, perhaps the first extant work of Sufi doctrines, discipline and practice in the Persian language, the *Fazail-ul-Fawayid* – a collection of the teachings of Nizamuddin Aulia of Delhi compiled by his poet-disciple Hassan Sijzi, and *Maktubat-e-Mujjadid Alf-i-Sani* – the credo of the militant religious divine and reformer, Sheikh Ahmad of Sirhind (d. 1625). Both in the original Persian and in Urdu translations these are still standard reading. The origins of the Urdu language can be traced to the eleventh-twelfth century when the first Muslim kingdom was established in Lahore and Persian-speaking settlers learnt to communicate in the local language which they named Hindvi. Masud Saad Salman (d. 1121) one of the Ghaznavid court poets composed a *divan* (collection of poems) in this language. The songs, riddles, doggerels and musical compositions of the great thirteenth century poet, Amir Khusrau, first brought respectability to the Hindvi and Punjabi languages.

Strangely enough it was not in the north of the subcontinent, where it was born, but in the south that the new language, which later came to be known as *rekhta* or Urdu,

matured and developed. This is because, towards the middle of the fourteenth century, the principalities of upper Deccan broke away, not only from the imperial court in Delhi, but also from its court language, Persian. The rulers of these small kingdoms of Golkunda (1518) and Bijapur (1489) actively patronised literary endeavour in the spoken language. Poets and writers of eminence emerged in the Deccani or Urdu language – an admixture of Persian, Turkish, Deccani, Hindvi and Punjabi dialects. The first long narrative poem in Deccani-Urdu, *Saiful Muluk-wa-Badi-ul-Jamal*, was composed by Gavasi (1618) and the first major book of prose *Sab Ras* by Mulla Vajhi (1637).

It was, however, towards the middle of the eighteenth century, when both the Mughal court and the court language, Persian, were already on the decline, that Urdu came into its own in its own homeland – the northern areas of the subcontinent.

In the early eighteenth century, a gifted poet from Upper Deccan, Wali Deccani, migrated to Delhi and his Urdu *ghazals* and lyrical poems found immediate and widespread response in the literary circles of Delhi. He may,

Asadullah Khan Ghalib (d. 1869), the great nineteenth century Urdu poet, breathed new life into the ghazal *poetic form and chronicled the passing of the Mughal age*

therefore, be truly regarded as the Chaucer of Urdu poetry. He was followed almost immediately by a whole line of distinguished poets, Mir Taqi Mir (d. 1810), Muhammad Rafi Sauda (d. 1782), Mir Dard (d. 1784), Mir Hassan (d. 1786), Nazir Akbarabadi (d. 1830), Hakim Momin (d. 1851) and Mir Anis (d. 1874).

Mir is known for his tender and nostalgic lyrics in the ghazal form which continue to be sung and recited. Sauda introduced incisive social and political satire into Urdu poetry. Mir Dard was almost the only mystical poet of the classical period, while Mir Hassan composed the most celebrated fairy tales in the form of *mathnavi*. Nazir Akbarabadi stands in a class by himself because he sang not for court circles but for the common man in the common idiom and not on romantic themes. Hakim Momin's distinction lies in his qualities of condensation, allusiveness and wit, strikingly resembling those of the metaphysical school of English poetry. Pulir Anis popularised a completely new school, that of the *marsiya*. The *marsiyas* are a cycle of poems devoted to the martyrdom of Hussain, the grandson of the Prophet of Islam.

The most eminent name in this hierarchy of poets is Asadullah Khan Ghalib. His slender volume of Urdu *ghazals* has had a profound influence on the entire stream of Urdu poetry. He liberated this poetry from clichés fostered by conventional imagery, diction and symbolism. The tragic experience of his age is distilled in his poetry, as he witnessed the collapse of the old order and the subsequent ascendancy of alien influences. He articulates the philosophical questionings that this experience impelled in the sensitive minds of his times and the new rational modes of thought and expression introduced by Western rule.

The end of the nineteenth century saw the birth of what may be called the modern movement in Urdu poetry actively directed and sponsored by the British *élite*. It was based on the critical dicta of Matthew Arnold and other Victorians. The main exponents of this school were Muhammad Hussain Azad (d. 1910) and Altaf Husain Hali (d. 1914), whose contributions to Urdu prose in the form of literary criticism, history and biography are of equal importance. With the passage of time and the closer acquaintance of Urdu writers with modern Western literature, this movement proliferated into a number of different schools. The towering figure among the moderns was Muhammad Iqbal, who is the subject of a separate study in this volume.

Before 1790, Urdu prose generally followed the ornate and florid style of Persian writings. Two gifted religious scholars, Shah Rafiuddin and Shah Abdul Qadir (sons of Shah Waliullah), brought out their translations of the Quran in simple Urdu.

With the consolidation of British power, some British scholars gathered round themselves talented Urdu writers to translate well-known Arabic and Persian classics into Urdu and to produce educational, instructive and scientific literature on Western lines. The first such centre of learning was set up by Dr John Gilchrist in Fort William College, Calcutta, to be followed by establishments in Delhi and Lahore. The Calcutta School developed a simple prose style which served as a model for the writers of Delhi and Lahore. Of these, Sher Ali Afsos and his translation of *Gulistan-e-Saadi* called *Bagh-e-Urdu*, Hafizuddin Ahmad and his excellent rendering of Abdul Fatal's *Bahar Danish*, renamed *Khirad Afroz*, Mazhar Ali Khan Vila and his translation of *Baital Pachisi* from Sanskrit were outstanding. In the evolution of this new prose style, a special place belongs to the collection of letters of the poet Ghalib, intimate and colloquial in tone, sparkling and witty in content.

Near the end of the nineteenth century, the school of Syed Ahmad Khan (d. 1898), scholar, educationalist, historian and social reformer, wrote prolifically on social, political, scientific and educational themes. A parallel school of religious learning was led by Shibli Nomani (d. 1917). His monumental work on Muhammad, *Seerat un-Nabi*, and his history of Persian literature, *Sher-ul-Ajam*, are regarded as standard works.

In fiction, a *dastan* (a long fantasy of love and adventure) was penned by the Emperor Shah Alam under the name of *Ajaib-ul-Qasais*. This tale served as a forerunner of a string of other tales produced by the Gilchrist School. Most famous is the *Dastane-e-Amir Hamza*.

This rambling and somewhat escapist literature later gave way to the Urdu novel proper. The first of these is a gigantic picaresque romance written by Rattan Nath Sarshar (d. 1803) entitled *Fasana-e-Azad*. The idea of this book was probably suggested by *Don Quixote*. Abdul Halim Sharar (d. 1926) wrote historical romances of Muslim heroes and realistic novels of contemporary social life. Maulvi Nazir Ahmad (d. 1912) wrote a number of domestic tales of ordinary men and women with a strong moral message. Both are current reading.

In the present century when a number of literary magazines came into vogue, the popularity of the novel was eclipsed by the short story. The influence of Maupassant, O. Henry, Maugham, Chekhov, Gorky and others was noticeable. A number of plays were also written for the short-lived professional theatre, by playwrights led by Agha Hashr Kashmiri who gained fame for his eloquent adaptations of Shakespeare.

F.A.F., F.M. and M.Y.B.

Muhammad Iqbal

"No man was ever yet a great poet", wrote that very discerning critic Coleridge, "without being at the same time a great philosopher." A succession of great names bears it testimony – Jalaluddin Rumi (1207-1273), Muslehuddin Saadi (d. 1313), Shamsuddin Hafiz (d. 1389), Ibnul Hassan Amir Khusrau (1253-1325), Asadullah Khan Ghalib (1797-1869). It is to the same distinguished line that the poet, Sir Shaikh Muhammad Iqbal (1877-1938), or "Allama" (Great Scholar) as he is reverentially called, unquestionably belongs. With this difference, that, unlike some of his mediaeval predecessors, he was not only equipped with education in various philosophical schools, both ancient and contemporary, but also commanded sufficient prose in more than one language to articulate his own answers to the problems of reality with logic and precision.

"Like all great "poets of affirmation", Dante, Milton and Goethe, Iqbal was no abstract thinker," stated V. G. Kiernan in his *Introduction to Poems by Iqbal*. Like them he was closely involved with the affairs of the world around him and, for the Muslims of the subcontinent, he has been not the unacknowledged, but the acknowledged law-giver of their social, religious and political thinking.

For the Muslim community of undivided India, the closing decades of the nineteenth century and the early decades of the twentieth, were a period of acute mental confusion and emotional distress. The downfall of the Muslim Mughal Empire, the bloody reprisals that followed the uprisings against British authority in 1857, the extinction of the privileges, values and usages of the old feudal order, the ascendancy of their non-Muslim compatriots to most available positions of power and wealth sorely lacerated the collective mind. Adversity had also made them kin to other Muslim peoples beyond their borders who were similarly afflicted, the Ottoman Turks, Arabs of the Middle East, Libyans, Moroccans and Tunisians, They awaited a consoling and uplifting voice to lead them out of their wilderness of despond. Leading voices of an earlier era, the timid voice of liberal reformists urging them to come to terms with the alien ways of their British rulers and the strident voice of religious divines exerting them to reject the blandishments of the infidel and return to the fold of ancestral tradition, no longer appealed to the new intelligentsia. Iqbal, the poet, was best attuned to the sources of their discontent and Iqbal, the thinker, best aware of the nature of their intellectual and spiritual malaise – of the giants of modernism and tradition pulling at their wrists. He loved them both wisely and too well. Over the years, he chiselled out his answers to contemporary problems of Indian Muslims, the Muslim peoples in general, and of the abstract trinity of God, Man and Nature.

While Iqbal sympathised with and assimilated many elements from Western philosophic and scientific thought, for example Hegel's concept of man and history being "Man's own work", Kant's critique of pure reason, Marx's denunciation of capitalism and class exploitation, Nietzsche's rejection of liberal bourgeois morality and glorification of the will to power, Bergson's defence of the validity of intuitive knowledge, Einstein's four dimensional time-space continuum, and others, he considered that both idealist and materialist philosophies of the West were largely irrelevant to the social and ideological predicaments of his own people. He devoutly believed that it was only the authority of their own religion – Islam – and the sanction of their own sanctified traditions – the life and sayings of the prophet of Islam that could truly validate the message he carried.

On these he focused the searchlight of his vision. Concurrently the Muslim mind had to be liberated from

Muhammad Iqbal was a great poet, statesman and philosopher. A master of the Urdu language, he wrestled to make sense of the relationship between man, nature and God

the sterility of nearly five hundred years of social and intellectual torpor and the tyranny of backward-looking, anti-intellectual orthodoxy. As a first step, therefore, like the prophets of old, he sought to cleanse the House of God of all false idols, of scribes and Pharisees, the obscurantist mullah, the withdrawn mystic, the charlatan and the demagogue.

"Why these curtains draped between the Creator and his creatures?
Drive out of my Church, these elders of the Church.
I am weary and displeased with these slabs of precious marble
Build me another sanctuary of humble mud."
 (God addressing the angels in *Bal-e-Jibreel* – The Wing of Gabriel)

Only thus could this House be made deserving of the "vice-regent of God" on earth, Man.

Iqbal is a humanist not only in the formal but in the literal sense of the word: for him "no form of reality is so powerful, so inspiring and so beautiful as the spirit of man." The fall of Adam was not a falling from grace but the opposite – his elevation to the position of a "Co-worker with God" (*Reconstruction of Religious Thought in Islam*, by Iqbal), in the process of creation – a process which is still continuing. For "our universe is not a complete factor. It is still in the course of formation and man has to take his share in it as much as he helps to bring order into a portion of this chaos." The terrestrial world is as much man-made as God-made, with the difference that while the creation of God-Nature or Matter is relatively static and immobile, the creative energies of man are geared to the dynamics of an evolutionary process which is both timeless and measureless."

"There are other worlds beyond the stars
Other testing grounds for the passion of love
Don't stay enmeshed in your (earthly) nights and days
There are other measures of time for you in other spaces
 (yonder)" (*Bal-e-Jibreel*)

"You created the night and I the lamp
You created clay, I fashioned from it the wine-cup
You created deserts, mountains, wastelands
I made them into orchards, gardens, flower-beds"

(Dialogue between "Man and God" in *Pyam-e-Mashriq*
– Message of the East)

As a corollary to this, Iqbal applies the Muslim concept of *tauheed* – the unity or oneness of God to the unity of the terrestrial and the celestial worlds, thus replacing the concept of transcendence of God by His Immanence (*Modern Islam in India and Pakistan*, by W. Cantwell Smith), and obliterating the quality of sacred and secular, spiritual and material. "The spirit finds its opportunities in the natural, the material, the secular. All that is secular, therefore, is sacred in the roots of its being."

Further, since the process of human evolution through a progressive mastery over material forces is continuous and unending, it follows that the only abiding element in the cosmic scheme is transition and change.

"In this world, only change has permanence."
 (Call of the Caravan Bell – *Bang-e-Dara*)

And this applies as much to subjective and ideological as to social and material factors – even to the edicts of religion. "Eternal principles when they are understood to exclude all possibilities of change, which according to the Quran is one of the greatest signs of God, tend to immobilise what is essentially mobile in its nature" (*Reconstruction of Religious Thought in Islam*). Having already parted company with the traditional mystic who dismisses the physical world as an illusion and human physical endeavour as mere vanity, Iqbal discards equally emphatically the dogmatic theologian and his static orthodoxy.

Finally, the principal agent in this creative process is the human Ego, or Personality or Self – *khudi*, as Iqbal calls it. To meet the challenge of creation, the human self has to be fortified `both by perceptual knowledge of the physical world and intuitive passion (or love, *ishq*, in Iqbal's terminology) for the realisation of higher values and ideals. It logically follows that "the idea of personality gives us a standard of value – that which fortifies personality is good; that which weakens it is bad. Art, religion and ethics must be judged from the standpoint of personality" (from the introduction of *Secrets of the Self* by Iqbal, translated by Professor Nicholson. But this personality or self cannot develop or fortify itself in isolation. It can do so only in the context of the totality of social relationships. And here Iqbal's Perfect Man, *Mard-e-Kamil*, disengages himself from Nietzsche's superman, for Iqbal's categorical imperatives rule out all forms of nationalist chauvinism, imperialist domination, racial discrimination, social exploitation and personal aggrandisement, since all of them make for the debasement and perversion of human personality.

Understandably, the bulk of critical literature on Iqbal is devoted to the study and analysis of his message and thought content rather than to an appreciation and evaluation of his poetry. And yet it is his vibrant and impassioned verse, and the persuasive appeal it carries, which accounts for much of his influence. In his poetic works, form and content, theme and style move along well-defined lines and their evolution over a long span of continuous creation makes an interesting study. In the first phase, lasting up to 1905, most of the poems relate to the wonder and questionings inspired by isolated phenomena of nature; mornings and sunsets, mountains and rivers, the moon, the stars and the causeless nostalgia of youth. This lyrical period of short pieces is followed by a series of long poems, passionate and rhetorical, mostly devoted to political themes – nationalist or pan-Islamic. All this work is in Urdu. In 1915, Iqbal brought out his first long philosophical poem in Persian *Asrar-e-Khundi*, "Secrets of the Self", which initiated the next phase of philosophic speculations mostly in Persian. And lastly, the early Thirties saw the final perfection of his teaching and poetic art, in the form of three volumes in Urdu, *Bal-e-Jibreel* (The Wing of Gabriel), *Zarb-e-Kaleem* (The Rod of Moses), and the posthumous *Armaghan-e-Hijaz* (The Gift of Hijaz) By this time his restless quest had moved from bits and pieces of subjective experience, the wonders of nature, the travail of Indian Muslims and the Muslim world to a calm contemplation of the ultimates of reality – God, Nature and Man.

With this progressive expansion in the field of his poetic vision, there is a corresponding reduction in his poetic themes, from profusion to orderliness, from dispersal to integration, terminating in the monolithic thought of his last years. There is a similar transformation in style from prolixity to precision, from ornate and involved phraseology to lucid direct statement, from flamboyant rhetoric to unadorned poetry. The long poem, philosophical or political in the *mathnavi* (rhymed couplets), or *musadas* (six-line stanza) form gives way to epigrammatic verse in the form of *ghazal*, *qita* or *rubaiy*. The emotional climate also undergoes a change from sentiment, *muhabbat*, to passion (*ishq*) or love. In this mature body of verse, Iqbal after discarding the normal conventional embellishments of oriental poetry employed a number of devices of his own to relieve the austerity of his verse and to maintain its heightened tenor. The first among these is the musicality of sound patterns and a number of prosodic innovations which are utterly lost in translation. Secondly, the introduction of highly evocative proper names, hardly known to Urdu poetry before him – the sands around Kazima, the snows of Mount Damavand, the deserts of Iraq and Hijaz, the blood of Hussain, the majesty of Rome, the beauty of Cordova, the glories of Isphahan and Samarkand. Thirdly, he gave currency to unfamiliar words which are antique without being archaic, unusual without being obscure. And he counter-matched them with rhythms and metres which had rarely been used in Urdu poetry.

At this stage, after much piecemeal thinking and intense subjective exploration he at last arrived at a theme big enough to fill the whole of his vision, the twin theme of Man's grandeur and his loneliness. The theme of human loneliness, centred round the immensity of the odds arrayed against Man: oppression, exploitation and various meannesses within; hostile and heartless Nature without. The grandeur of Man – the tragic hero – lies in his acceptance of this challenge, his destiny of unending struggle of perpetual frustration and fulfilment, to attain the wholeness of God. He sang of this glory and this pain, the hopes and the anxieties of the world of man with great tenderness and compassion, at times with great wrath and indignation. And he did so with a conviction and a sincerity, with a sweep and amplitude of expression unequalled in his age.

Iqbal was born on 9th November 1877 to Shaikh Noor Muhammad, a small trader of little learning and modest means, in the ancient Punjab town of Sialkol. The humble house in the lane of Koocha Churigaran, "the bangle-makers" where he was born has since been rebuilt. He was sent to the local mosque, as popular custom ordained, to learn his alphabet from a great scholar of his times, Maulvi Syed Mir Hassan, who also taught him Arabic during his later schooling. He attended the local school and college run by Scottish missionaries, the Scotch Mission High School, and Scotch Mission College (the latter is now known as Murray College).

In 1895, having finished his higher secondary education, he moved to Lahore and obtained his Master's Degree in Philosophy from Government College, Lahore, in 1899. His academic career was studded with a number of distinctions in his favourite studies which were Philosophy and Arabic. Fame came to him early when in 1899 he recited his first long poem *Nala-e-Yatim* (The Cry of the Orphan) at the annual meeting of the local Muslim educational and charitable organisation Anjuman-e-Himayat-e-Islam; his place in the front rank of younger poets of his generation was assured. Between 1899 and 1903, when he went abroad for higher

Iqbal's tomb of white marble, outside the main gates of the Badshahi mosque in Lahore, is a place of pilgrimage

studies, he taught Arabic, philosophy and English literature in two premier institutions in Lahore – Government College and Oriental College – contributed to the best known literary magazines, and was accepted as a leading figure among the social and literary *élite* of the town. In 1903 he proceeded to Trinity College, Cambridge, and obtained a degree. The subject of his dissertation was the Development of Metaphysics in Persia. Two years later he obtained a doctorate in philosophy on the same thesis from the University of Munich. In 1907, he returned to London, lectured in Arabic at London University, and was also called to the Bar from Lincoln's Inn in 1908. Towards the end of the same year, he returned home to Lahore and enrolled at the High Court as a barrister. He also served briefly as a professor of philosophy at Government College. From then onwards, until the end of his days, apart from a short interlude when he was actively associated with public affairs, between 1926 and 1933, he wrote a series of outstanding poetic works which first appeared in the form of small pamphlets or even leaflets. Later, after 1915, when his first long philosophical poem *Asrar-e-Khudi* was published, they took shape as an impressive cavalcade of works of great power and intensity. In 1918, came another long poem. *Ramuz-e-Bekhudi* (Aspects of Selflessness), *Pyam-e-Mashriq* (Message of the East), a collection of miscellaneous poems in Persian appeared in 1923, *Bang-e-Dara* (Call of the Caravan Bell), his first collection of Urdu verse; also in 1923, *Zahoor-e-Ajam* (Persian Psalms), another collection of Persian lyrics in 1927; *Javed Nama* (Testament of Eternity), a long philosophical poem in Persian in 1932; *Bal-e-Jibreel* (The Wing of Gabriel), a collection of short Urdu poems in 1935; *Musafir* (The Wanderer), and *Pas Che Bayad Kard Ai Aqwam-e-Sharq* (So What is to be done, 0 People of the East), two long Persian meditative poems in 1936; *Zarb-e-Kaleem* (The Rod of Moses), mostly epigrammatic poems in Urdu, also in the same year, and, finally, *Armaghan-e-Hijaz* (The Gift of Hijaz), a collection of short Urdu and Persian pieces, was published posthumously in 1938. He also wrote some text-books for schools on history, economics and literature which are now collectors' items. In 1930, he published in book form the lectures he had delivered in 1928 in Madras, Aligarh and Hyderabad (Deccan), under the title *Reconstruction of Religious Thought in Islam*, a closely reasoned and scholarly exposition of his own views on religion and philosophy, and a forceful criticism of prevalent Muslim ideological schools. He was also accepted as the leading thinker and ideologue of his community, and was elected to the Punjab Legislative Assembly in 1926, and later became President of the All-India Muslim League session at Allahabad in 1930, at which he said in his famous address, "I therefore demand the formation of a consolidated Muslim State in the best interest of India and Islam," marshalling arguments which were the origin of the whole movement for the creation of Pakistan. He was nominated by the British Government in 1931 (he had already been knighted in 1922), as one of the representatives of Indian Muslims at the Round Table talks in London on constitutional reforms for India, and again in 1932. This gave him an opportunity to travel abroad once again and visit some of the places he loved – Spain, Paris, Rome and Palestine. His later visit to Afghanistan, like the travels to Cordova and Palestine, is commemorated in a long poem.

On April 21st, 1938, after a prolonged illness, his long life ended. Followed by a vast concourse of mourners, he was laid to rest at the foot of the Badshahi Mosque in Lahore, built by Emperor Aurangzeb. His mausoleum of sandstone and lapis lazuli is now a place of pilgrimage in the city.

F.A.F.

Regional Literatures

Pakistan can boast a rich literary heritage in at least eight languages. From the beginning of Muslim rule over Sindh (711) and Multan, Arabic was used as the normal theological idiom. After 1,000 AD, Persian became the literary and official language and the medium of education in noble families. Turkish was spoken and understood at least during the sixteenth century at the courts of the Arghuns and Tarkhans in Sindh, and eventually Urdu became the general medium for literary expression in most parts of the subcontinent. There are also literatures in regional languages Pushtu, Balochi, Punjabi, and Sindhi.

The two languages of Iranian origin spoken in Pakistan are Pushtu and Balochi; and there are a number of nearly extinct Dardic idioms in the mountainous regions of northwestern Pakistan in the Pushtu-speaking areas and also a pocket of the Dravidian Brahui in Balochistan in Kalat. In all cases, only small fragments of popular poetry and narrative survive. In Balochi there are a number of popular ballads that deal with the heroic deeds of the members of tribes. Other ballads tell of the adventures of Islamic heroes, and popular songs display a remarkable tenderness of feeling, and an acute observation of nature. Balochi became a written language only recently, so that the treasures of its folk tradition (first collected by Darmesteter) have become better known and appreciated; a modern literature is emerging.

Pushtu has a longer history as a literary language; the first poem is believed to have been written by Amir Karore (d. 756). It is impossible to discover the beginnings of Pushtu oral literature. It is known from Amir Khusrau that it was spoken in the second half of the thirteenth century, and isolated sentences in the chronicles of the Pathan rulers in northern India trace its developments. Still extant are the first prose work, *Tazkiratul-Awliyya* by Suleiman Maka (d. 1215), the first historical narrative *Tarikh-e-Suri* by Muhammad Ali Abasti (c. 1349) and the first long poem in *mathnavi* form by Akbar Zamindari (d. 1369).

The first well known author in this language is Bayazid Ansari Pir-i-Raushan (d. 1585), whose mystical sect was soon condemned as heretic by orthodox Muslims. His work *Khair ul-Rayan* in rhymed prose, combines Arabic, Persian and Hindi. The mystics used the spoken idiom to preach their doctrines to the masses who did not understand Arabic or Persian. Pir-i Raushan's work was refuted, in Pushtu, by Akhund Darwaza (d. 1638). From that time onward, the language grew steadily as a literary medium, for, when its greatest master, the "father of Pushtu", Khushhal Khan Khatak (d. 1689), appeared on the scene, he found an expressive idiom for his purposes.

The zenith of Pushtu poetry occurred at the turn of the seventeenth and eighteenth centuries. This period, which marks the decay of the powerful Mughal Empire, and the beginnings of Urdu in the Delhi and north-western regions, was also the time when other regional languages flourished. The greatest masterpieces in Punjabi and Sindhi were produced at this time, and both languages, connected by Siraiki, share many tales and legends. Their imagery is largely rural, and the poems of the mystics overflow with love and a feeling of all-embracing unity; a feeling only rarely found in Pushtu poetry. Both languages praise Mansur Hallaj's ecstatic confession, *An-al-haqq*, "I am the Truth".

Punjabi has had a spoken tradition since the Middle Ages; its first written traces are found in some hagiographic works of the thirteenth century, and some *dohas*, or epigrammatic verses of Baba Farid Shakar Ganj (d. 1265) which survive to this day. By the sixteenth century notable classics were being written by poets like Peeloo, author of the metrical romance Mirza Sahiban. The first known literary figure is Madhu Lal Hussain of Lahore (d. 1593), mentioned by Dara Shikoh as an admirer of beauty, who sang of his love for it, using the symbolism of native folk tales, as did most later poets. His contemporary, Damodar, was the first major poet to versify the celebrated tragedy of *Heer Ranjha*.

One century later, Sultan Bahuu (d. 1691), wrote Siharfi or the "Golden Alphabet", one of the masterpieces of mystical folk poetry. The genre of siharfi was common to the languages of Pakistan, as was the baramasah, poems about the twelve months of the year, as seen through the eyes of a loving woman, a form derived from Sanskrit. Sultan Bahuu gave this form an imagery typical of the fertile soil of Punjab. His younger contemporary, the Qadiri mystic, Bullhe Shah (d. 1758), is considered to be the greatest Punjabi poet; his verses show the same enthusiastic rapture as that of the great Sufis of Turkey and Iran. He, like his predecessors, used the tale of Heer Ranjha, as a symbol of man's love of God and the difficulties of His Way; but the classical form of Heer Ranjha – a tale which was the subject of more than a hundred *mathna* in various languages – was developed by Waris Shah Maqbil and Ahmad Yar towards the end of the eighteenth century; ever since, it has remained the favourite of the Punjabi-speaking population.

In spite of various other mystical folk poets (Al-Haidar of Multan, or Ghulam Farid who wrote in Siraiki), Punjabi never became a literary language in the strict sense for the Muslim population; rather it was the sacred language for the Sikhs – Guru Nanak's poetry set the norm for them – and they write it in Gurmukhi characters. The medium of higher literature among the Punjabi Muslims was Persian, and later Urdu. There exist a considerable number of printed books, many of them on mystical themes, verse translations of Persian Sufi works, *marthias*, translations from English. However Punjabi did not become part of the mainstream of contemporary literature unlike Urdu and Sindhi.

Contrary to Punjabi, Sindhi did indeed become a literary language in the nineteenth century and developed remarkably swiftly. The rudimentary beginnings of Sindhi literature are documented in the fourteenth century, and ballads from that period, verses of divines like Pir Nuruddin, Pir Shamsuddin and Pir Sadaruddin (circa 1358) are still extant. Some mystical verses from the sixteenth century are the first written evidence. Here, as in Punjab, the mystics used the folk tales of *Sassi Punnu*, *Yusuf Zulaikha*, *Sohn i Mahinwal*, *Saiful Muluk* and *Omar Marui* as a starting point for their mystical songs, as much as they relied upon the indigenous imagery of gardens, fields and desert-life. The soul is represented in all these poems as a loving woman, true to the Indian tradition, and her trials and tribulations on her way towards God, her lost beloved, are dramatically described.

The poetry of Qadi Qadan of Sehwan (d. 1556) and of Shah Inat, as much as that of Shah Abdul Karim of Bullri show the same richness of language (which boasts an extremely refined grammar) as is characteristic of the poetry of the greatest Sindhi mystical poet, and contemporary of Bullhe Shah, Shah Abdul Latif Bhitai. *Shah jo Risalo* has been almost a sacred book for both Muslims and Hindus. Old Sindhi tales blend in the *Risalo* with Shah Abdul Latif's experiences on his wanderings with the Yogis; unsurpassed descriptions of long expected rain lead to praise of the Prophet, and images taken from daily life are fresh and poignant, as are his allusions to the works of early Muslim mystics, particularly Jalaluddin Rumi. More outspoken than Shah Abdul Latif, was Sachal Sarmast (d. 1826), whose lyrics in Sindhi and Siraiki belong to the most ecstatic verses ever written in any Islamic country. Sachal is one in a long line of poets – many of them from the Balochi clan of the Leghari – who used Siraiki besides Sindhi, and whose poems even today repeat the traditional adoration of beauty as well as the acceptance of suffering typical of Sufism.

However, it would be wrong to dwell only upon the hymnodists of Divine Love. Shortly before Shah Abdul Latif sang his verse, the Naqshbandi theologians of Thatta had begun to offer religious instruction in their native language; Makhdum Muhammad Hashim (d. 1761) heads the list of these writers and commentators. This trend continued, although it did not create a true prose literature; that came into existence only after 1852, when the modified Arabic alphabet was introduced by Sir Bartle Frere as a medium of communication, and printing presses were set up.

From that time onward, Hindus and Muslims competed in enriching their mother tongue – partly with translations of European and Indian prose and partly with their own writings. The leading figure among those writers who contributed to the development of Sindhi into a modern language, was Mirza Qalich Beg (d. 1929) of Hyderabad, whose profession as a British civil servant left him enough time to translate and compose more than three hundred works, among them a wide range of adaptations, from Shakespeare to Sherlock Holmes. He is the author of the first Sindhi novel on female education, *Zinat* (1890), which is remarkably enlightened. Mirza Qalich Beg also composed a book containing models of Sindhi poetry in all the Persian metres, for, from the early nineteenth century onward, some poets, particularly those living in the cities, had given up traditional folk poetry in favour of Persianising *ghazals*. Abdul Husa Sangi (d, 1924), the descendant of the Talpur rulers, was one of the main representatives of this style.

After World War I, the Sindhi press grew more active, and a fine journalistic style developed. Scholarly works in all branches of knowledge were published and a pliable prose emerged. Since Independence, there have been publications containing classical poetry and prose and large collections of folklore material. Modern poetry often experiments with lyrical forms, from the traditional *kafi*, to *ghazal* and *haiku*; among contemporary poets, Sheikh Ayaz is the most powerful figure, skilfully adapting old forms of language to modern themes. Short story writing has also become popular, and is now an established and successful literary form.

The efforts being made by a number of talented writers and scholars to bring these regional languages into line with the more developed classical and modern ones by creative writing, critical studies and historical research have a definite contribution to make to Pakistan's literary future. Their work does not weaken the national language, but rather enlarges those local and varied reservoirs of sensibility and expression from which Urdu has drawn its replenishment and vitality throughout its development.

A.S.

Literature since 1947

The contemporary literature of Pakistan is best described as a mosaic of various languages and traditions, bearing strong links with each other but each at its distinct stage of development. Fuelled by rivalries between various ethnic groups, the languages co-exist with friction and fusion, inadvertently but inevitably enriching each other. Certain patterns are common to all of the literary traditions in Pakistan today. The influence of modern Western writing is counterbalanced with that of traditional forms. The short story is generally better evolved than the novel, which is largely underdeveloped, while theatre is generally deficient.

Classical Urdu poetry was dominated by the *ghazal*, a powerful and sophisticated vehicle of the conventions and symbolism of Indo-Iranian eroto-mysticism, the last major exponent of which was Mirza Asadullah Khan Ghalib. The modern genre was consciously introduced by Altaf Hussain Hali and Muhammad Hussain Azad in the 1860s with a deliberate turning away from Persian to English models. Iqbal subsumed the anti-imperialist trends becoming popular in the first decades of the century and later turned to a philosophic polemicism confronting the West and advocating an Islamic resurgence. The *ghazal* successfully adapted itself to the changing world and continues to be the dominant form to this day.

Following closely on the heels of Muhammad Iqbal were Josh Malihabadi, Hafeez Jallindhari and Ehsan Danish. Josh came to be associated with the Progressive Movement. Two distinct trends are sometimes described in the poetry of that period as separate schools of thought: the Progressive Movement of the 1930s concerned with literature as an expression of social commitment, and the *Halqa-e-Arbab-e-Zauq* taking a more formalistic stance. Yet it is a mistake to divide the poetry of that rather fluid period into airtight compartments. The voices of Faiz Ahmed Faiz, N.M. Rashid and Miraji are distinct and regarded as major influences. Rashid and Miraji, together with Tassaduq Hussain Khalid, were the protagonists of the *azad nazm* or *vers libre*, a significant development in modern Urdu poetry.

In the early days of the newly independent country, the left-oriented and organised Progressive Movement was subjected to state repression as magazines were banned and writers like Faiz Ahmed Faiz and Nadeem Qasmi were jailed. Faiz wrote in a highly polished neo-classical style and spoke against tyranny with a consummate artistry. Widely loved, Faiz came to be regarded as the spokesman of all oppressed people. Translated into English and other languages, Faiz won the Lenin prize besides other honours. He continues to be Pakistan's best-known and best-loved poet long after his death. The role of the poet as the conscience of the people describes the position of Qasmi. While Miraji died in India at a relatively young age, Rashid went on to Iran and wrote about the subjugation of an Eastern nation. He developed into a highly skilled craftsman whose complex and rich vision of man as an undiscovered entity in a bewildering universe was initially called ambiguous and is now slowly being recognised as having given some of the most rewarding Urdu poetry of the age.

The most poignant post-Independence voice was the "new *ghazal*" of Nasir Kazmi who went back to classical roots to give lyrical expression to the tribulations of an uncertain era. The *ghazal* draws almost all poets to itself and showed its resilience when anti-romantic themes and a mock-serious tone deliberately inverting the old conventions were introduced by modern poets. Among those whose work is mainly in this form are Mehshar Badayooni, Shahzad Ahmed, Ahmed Faraz, John Elia, Athar Nafees, Obaidullah Aleem and Anwer Shaoor. Habib Jalib was a vastly popular poet who recited his anti-dictatorship poems to an adoring public. In the 1960s, the modern *nazm* established itself not as a separate movement but a distinct phase, and is exemplified by the work of Saqi Farooqi, Kishwar Naheed, Fahmida Riaz and Sarmad Sehbai. The "tradition of the modern" continues in the works of poets like Iftikhar Arif, Amjad Islam Amjad, Khalid Ahmed and others.

The first generation of poets born in Pakistan took the *ghazal* further, drawing upon images going back to the epic *dastaans* and the heyday of Islam. With them belongs the work of Parveen Shakir whose early death cut short a remarkable career. A new trend emerging from Ada Jaferey onwards is the increasing number of women poets who have formulated sharply-defined feminist perspectives.

In the late Seventies and early Eighties, yet another definable breakthrough was the establishment of the prose poem which, despite early controversy, was to become increasingly important in the Nineties and draws upon the work of post-modernist poets. The mundane activities in life's routine, an ironic view of history from the underdog's point of view and a cosmopolitan spirit characterise the new voice in contemporary Urdu poetry.

Introduced as a literary form around the turn of the century, the Urdu short story touched a kind of zenith with *Angarey* in 1936. This group collection was subsequently banned by the vice-regal government but exerted a strong influence by introducing bold iconoclastic themes and experimenting with form and technique. The short story became a powerful and influential vehicle for the voice of a new generation which included Ismat Chughtai, Krishen Chander, Saadat Hassan Manto and Rajinder Singh Bedi. Realistic portrayals and psychological insights were the hallmarks of this new genre which continued to dominate the scene in the years after Independence. Manto, who died in 1955, was a major voice in the nascent nation and his unflinching attitude brought about a brush with the authorities and resulted in short stories which remain one of the strongest features of Pakistan's literature.

The left-oriented Progressive movement championed the cause of fiction with a social purpose. It was exemplified by Ahmed Nadeem Qasmi, Khadija Mastoor and Hajra Masroor among others. The burden of history gave form to the work of Qurratulain Hyder, whose *Aag Ka Dariya* has the sweep of an epic. Not surprisingly, the trauma of Partition became a major subject for fiction. Displacement leading to the search for roots was the theme in the earlier fiction of Intizar Hussain who soon broke away from the overtly realistic mode dominant at that time; shadows of Kafka and the Buddha fell across his work. Four novels and several collections of stories as well as plays and essays make up Hussain's *oeuvre* as a major writer of fiction in Pakistan.

A new style in fiction emerged in the Sixties, alternatively called the symbolic or abstract short story. Some critics regard this to be a consequence of censorship during Martial Law, but it also represents a reaction to the dominance of social realism. The leading exponent of this style is Enver Sajjad. The symbolism of Khalida Hussain is indicative of realities on a deeper plane which cannot otherwise be grasped. This mode of expression provided a fitting form for Masood Ashar who wrote of the dismemberment of the country in 1971. Recently there are signs of a synthesis as critics are calling for a return to the narrative element. This may well prove the beginning of a phase of critical realism.

While the short story remained popular with readers as well as writers, good novels were rare, not only in Urdu but in the regional languages as well. Sordid realities grafted to an idealistic vision were the theme of Shaukat Siddiqui's *Khuda Ki Basti*. The changes in the lives of a family affected by the Independence movement were captured by Khadija Mastoor in her *Anagan*. Altaf Fatima, Bano Qudsia and Jamila Hashmi, three otherwise contrasting writers who exemplify the feminine sensibility, are equally at home in both the novel as well as the short story.

From the inter-war times of Maulana Hali, who must be regarded as the father of literary criticism in Urdu, the exploration of Western influences with a view to local application and the testing of literary works for social relevance remained the main concerns of critics. The critic and short story writer Dr Akhtar Husain Raipuri, who was of the founders of the Progressive Movement, in his later years wrote his well-received memoirs, *Gard-e-Rah*. Dr Jameel Jalibi has produced major studies of Pakistani culture and the history of Urdu literature.

Despite there being no shortage of targets for humour and satire, the genre is still in its infancy. The Urdu humour of Shafiq ur Rehman and Colonel Muhammed Khan is mainly situational while the satire of Ibne Insha is stylised. In Mushtaq Ahmed Yusufi, however, verbal fireworks reveal a wizard of a writer who must be ranked with the greatest stylists of the language.

The development of Punjabi literature should be seen within the context of the struggle to see the language gain recognition. The native genius of the Punjab has enriched Urdu literature throughout the century while the call for the greater use of Punjabi for literary expression is growing louder. Punjabi literature continues to thrive across the border in India but the link between the two offshoots of the language has been weakened by the use of the Gormukhi script in India and the Persian script in Pakistan. The influence of folk poetry, the mysticism of Sufi poets, a close kinship with Urdu and a conscious effort to imbibe global influences while striving to further develop the language are the main features that have shaped Punjabi poetry in Pakistan. The verse of Ustad Daman had a folk wisdom going back to the oral tradition. Going back to the roots in the folk culture, Najam Hussain Syed used traditional forms to express a thoroughly modern sensibility. The tradition of the *ghazal* continues to thrive. However, the short story occupied a back-seat in post-Partition Punjabi literature.

Contemporary Sindhi poetry is dominated by the giant figure of Shaikh Ayaz, whose distinct voice came into his own in the post-Independence days. In a graceful and polished style and powerful diction, Ayaz wrote of Sindh's aspirations and predilections and soon emerged as the poetic conscience of his land. Ayaz is well-versed in Western literature and equally at home in the Indo-Iranian ethos, prolific in output and with a variety of forms and themes at his command. The long night of Sindhi literature began with the imposition in 1956 of One Unit, abolishing the provincial entity of Sindh. Writers including Ayaz were persecuted and publications were banned. In defiance, a Sindhi nationalism has flared which persists as feature of Sindhi literature, despite the reinstatement of political structures in 1969. A graceful style and a developed political consciousness characterise the poetry of Imdad Hussaini who came to the forefront in the 1970s, as did Anwer Pirzado who fused political activism with a modern consciousness in the prose-poem. Creativity and diversity characterise the poetry scene today.

The Sindhi short story had entered a new phase of development in the Forties but, its Punjabi counterpart suffered a setback with Partition, as many writers migrated to India. A fiery new generation emerged in the Sixties taking the short story to a new and powerful phase of development with writers like Amar Jalil whose ironic view on the social scene give such effect to his work. Women writers such as Sameera Zarin and Mehtab Mehboob opened a new area of experience.

In Pushtu poetry, Amir Hamza Shinwari revitalised the *ghazal* in post-Indepence Pakistan, drawing upon the tradition of mysticism. Ghani Khan's actual output is slender but he wielded considerable influence. The poet-politician Ajmal Khattak was strongly influenced by progressive ideals and wrote plays as well as short stories. Poet and short story writer, Qalandar Momind is recognised as a major influence on later poets.

The realistic mode focusing on social problems continues to dominate the short story in Pushtu. While Zaitoon Bano has brought a woman's sensibility to social themes, Gul Afzal, Tahir Afridi, Abdul Kafi Adeeb, Hassan Khan Soz and Murad Shinwari are among the writers who have successfully depicted various aspects of the Pushtoon society. While the novel remains relatively underdeveloped, non-fiction has gained much ground in modern Pushtu literature.

From the oral tradition of epics and folk romances, Balochi literature entered a new phase with the adoption of a script for the language. Mohammad Hussain Anka (1907-1977) worked as a journalist for several nationalist Urdu newspapers and wrote many poems, collected after his death. The first monthly magazine in Balochi, *Oman* started publication in 1954 from Karachi and later on the *Balochi*, under the editorship of Azad Jamaldini, were conducive to the development of modern prose, specially the short story. Inspired by nationalistic ideals, the poet Mir Gul Khan Nasir (1914-1983) turned to Balochi poetry. His first collection appeared in 1952 and is often regarded as the starting point for a Balochi literary movement. A strong nationalistic trend and ethnic identity infused with a patriotic fervour have been identified by critics as important themes in Balochi literature. A sense of pride linked with a sense of deprivation is the shaping spirit in poetry. The concerns of the Balochi short story in its early phase were the tribal society, its strength and its oppressive influence, the hard lot of the poor and relentless exploitation of the land and its people. The publication of a Balochi dictionary in the mid-Fifties was an important event in the development of contemporary Balochi literature.

English is a language commonly used, but not for widespread literary expression. The body of work is patchy with a very few good books. Prominent among English language writers was Ahmed Ali who had already made a name for himself with *Twilight in Delhi* (1940) but devoted the major part of his literary activities to a series of remarkable translations from classical Urdu poetry and later the Holy Quran. The best-known writer today is Bapsi Sidhwa, whose four internationally praised novels in English are written from the vantage point of her Parsi community and combine humour with acute social observation. The London-based Aamer Hussain wrote poignant short stories of displacement and disorientation, loneliness and fragile relationships. In poetry, the sophisticated and urbane Taufiq Rafat is a major poet, while Daud Kamal, Maki Kureshi, Kaleem Umar, Salman Tarik Kureshi, Alamagir Hashmi and Waqas Ahmed Khawaja are the other important poets in English. Taufiq Rafat has translated classical Punjabi poetry while Daud Kamal has produced translations of Faiz. A recent trend is the growing number of translations from Urdu and other languages into English.

A. F.

Performing Arts

Theatre has prospered more than either film or dance in Pakistan's half-century since Independence. Folk theatre and the Parsi commercial theatre provided a firm foundation to build upon when the country came into being, though the limited but persistent effort by college plays to bring more meaning to the stage also played a significant role. As theatre picked up gradually after Partition, serious and contemporary plays were staged at the colleges and the Arts Councils (autonomous organisations funded by the government for the promotion of cultural activity), to small but discerning audiences. The most popular were adaptations of European or American plays but with the passage of time and growing popularity, these adaptations became freer, adding plenty of local colour. Gradually this trend came to be considered as the formula for box office success.

Khawaja Mueenuddin in Karachi established the first repertory company and staged his own original plays as satirical comment on the social changes taking place so rapidly, not all of them for the best. In Lahore, Safdar Mir, Farrukh Nigar Aziz, Imtiaz Ali Taj and Ali Ahmed inspired many talented young men and women to join them in promoting amateur theatre.

Theatre was given a further boost at the box office with the opening of the Alhamra halls in Lahore in the early Eighties. These were Pakistan's first true, custom-built theatres in the real sense of the term, and facilities like lights, sets, and a proper stage improved the performing quality of the plays which previously had to manage in small halls or makeshift arenas. But due to rigid censorship, plays tended to lack substance. Actors often resorted to ad libbing and indulging in an extempore exchange of repartee with fellow actors and occasionally even with the audience. The script was often deliberately left lifeless to get the blessings of the censor but on stage the actors took charge to create their own theatre. Neither the director nor the writer were in control, and many a brilliant performance was done spontaneously.

With the proliferation of commercial theatre, a more socially relevant theatre somehow came into being. Typically anti-establishment, this genre was not allowed to stage its plays in the government-controlled halls so it had to settle for back lawns of private houses, the premises of foreign missions and makeshift venues both in the urban and rural areas. Aslam Azhar's Dastak in Karachi and Madeeha Gauhar's Ajoka in Lahore led the way and soon they were joined by other groups (Lok Rehas, Tehreek-e-Niswan, Gripps), which played to small audiences whenever they could, on meagre budgets, attracting the intelligentsia and the educated middle class who shared the views being disseminated. The sets were kept to the bare essentials and the lights were barely adequate as the performers relied heavily on mime and exaggerated speech and gestures to communicate complex ideas.

After the restoration of democracy in 1988, most of these groups lost their relevance, but Ajoka continued to do socially incisive plays, concerned with important problems facing Pakistan like the deteriorating environment, the population explosion, women's issues and mass illiteracy. Mostly, the formal structure of these plays was inspired by popular indigenous folk forms, consciously chosen to preserve links with the ancient theatrical forms. The Alhamra Cultural Centre in Lahore too embarked on a programme to promote good theatre by sponsoring plays which were considered classics, albeit not overly political or "contemporary". Commercial theatre, was since to become so popular that three private theatres in Lahore alone have been commissioned since 1991.

Cinema did not fare as well. After the initial problems caused by a lack of technicians and studios destroyed during the riots at Partition, films started to be churned out to provide the cheapest form of popular entertainment. Deviating little from the song-and-dance format established as the prototype subcontinental film, some good musicals with memorable scores were made. But next to nothing was done to produce a serious, socially relevant cinema.

Until the Seventies, movies did good business but in the Eighties, strict censorship policies, expensive raw material and the cheap availability of videos were blows the film industry has still not recovered from. Despite the government's lack of support, the film business has started to limp back to solvency with a few hugely successful productions. The debate about vulgarity has been continuously fuelled by films made in Pushto, Punjabi and Urdu that grossly violate standards of good taste.

The National Film Development Corporation, a state-funded body which was formed in the mid-Seventies to promote film production achieved very little. Initially active in production and running a few cinema theatres and a film club, it gradually became yet another government department with no perceptible function save that of burdening the public exchequer.

Dance has never played a central role in Pakistan. From among the Hindu classical forms, Kathak was sometimes practised in Pakistan in its earlier, more liberal days while a whole spectrum of Pakistan folk dances remained popular. During the Zia era, Hindu classical dance was discouraged and only folk dances were performed in public. Luddi, Jhoomar and Bhangra in Punjab, Kathak in the North-West Frontier Province and Hai Jamalo in Sindh flourished because of the vibrancy of their tradition.

One of the most gifted exponents of the Kathak tradition, Naheed Siddique, has chieved international recognition. In Pakistan she has been busy resurrecting the classic dance scene. Her workshops, classes and occasional public performances attest to her passion for Kathak and her enormous talent. Some of her students show great promise, leading her devotees to hope that they will continue to develop, thus keeping this wonderful art form alive in Pakistan.

S. A.

Kathak is a classical folk dance of the Mughals of which the name speaks of story-telling. It is a balletic interpretation of human drama. Naheed Siddique is the finest performer of Kathak in Pakistan

The Sufic Tradition

The many Pakistani shrines of Sufis include that of Hazrat Data Ganj Bakhsh, author of Kashf-ul-Muhjub, *the treatise on Islamic mysticism*

The first account of Sufi activities in the subcontinent is the visit which Mansur Hallaj paid to Gujrat, Sindh and Multan in 905. The famous "martyr of mystical love", whose utterance *An-al-haqq*, "I am the creative Truth", was repeated by thousands of mystical poets, visited this area to call people to God and his name is still alive even in remote villages of Sindh.

More than one and a half centuries later, a disciple of the mystical masters of Eastern Iran came to settle in Lahore. He was Syed Ali Hujweri, called Data Ganj Bakhsh (d. 1071), whose tomb is as much venerated by the pious as his book *Kashf-ul-mahjub*, "The Unveiling of the Hidden", which is admired by scholars as the first comprehensive survey of mystical doctrine written in the Persian language.

The peak of mysticism in the subcontinent, however, was the thirteenth century, the age of the greatest masters of Sufism from Spain to Bengal. Mueenuddin Chishti (d. 1236) came from his native Sistan to Ajmer, which had become part of Bengal and ruled by Delhi, where his friend Qutbuddin Bakhtiyar Kaki (d. 1235) lived. Mueenuddin's preaching of the love of God for man attracted the masses, and soon the Chishti order spread over the whole of India.

Other outstanding representatives of this movement were the ascetic Fariduddin Shakar Ganj of Pakpattan, and Nizamuddin Awliyya of Delhi. The Chishtiya avoided contact with the ruling classes, but their influence permeated the lives of Indian Muslims. Their love of poetry and music (given lasting expression by Amir Khusrau and Hasan Dehlavi) added a new dimension to Muslim culture in the subcontinent. The sayings of the early Chishti saints (*malfuzat*) yield an insight into the social and cultural life of mediaeval India. An outstanding member of the early Chishtiya is Muhammad Gaisudaraz (d. 1422 in Gulbarga in the Deccan), famous as a prolific writer in Arabic, in Persian for his intense devotional poems and letters, and one of the first authors of a mystical work in Dakhni Urdu, *maarif al-ashiqui*. He wrote an appreciation of the teachings of the "greatest master" Ibn Arabi, who later deeply influenced Indian Sufism and led it towards existentialism. The Chishtiya became connected with the Mughal court – when Akbar's son Salim was born, the birth was ascribed to the prayer of a Chishti saint, in whose honour Fatehpur Sikri was erected.

Other saints reached the subcontinent at the same time. The fame of Bahauddin Suhrawardi (d. 1262) was such that Multan became a centre of spiritual life, and the Persian poet Iraqi spent 25 years there. From Multan and Uch, the Suhrawardiya, more closely in touch with the aristocracy than the Chishtiya, spread soon to Bengal where its cultural influence has never ceased. A unique figure in thirteenth century Sufism was Lal Shahbaz Qalandar, whose tomb in Sehwan is still a much frequented shrine.

In 1371 Syed Ali Hamadhani introduced the Kubrawiya in Kashmir. This order with its fine psychological insights seems to have influenced northern India more than can be proved at present. The Qadiriya, probably the most influential order in the Islamic world, reached India in the fifteenth century. Its most prominent representative was Mian Mir of Lahore (d. 1635), who inspired Prince Dara Shikoh in his vision of uniting "the two oceans" of Islam and Hinduism, and whose lovely tomb is in Lahore.

The influence of the Qadiriya can be measured best by the innumerable songs in regional languages that are dedicated to Abdul Qadir Jilani. An order whose influence extended over the borders of India is the Shattariya.

Its best known master was Muhammad Ghaus Gwaliari (d. 1562), the author of a complex mystical work, *Al-Jawahir al-Khamsa*, "The Five Jewels". His tomb in Gwalior, built by Akbar, is a superb example of Indo-Muslim architecture.

The Naqshbandiya order, originating from Bukhara and later politically influential at the Timurid court of Herat and in Turkestan, was introduced to India in about 1600. Its foremost representative, Ahmad Sirhindi (d. 1624) relentlessly fought against the strong tendency towards existentialism, mainly expressed in mystical poetry, which blurred the differences between Islam and Hinduism.

The claim of Ahmad Sirhindi to be the *qayyum*, the spiritual ruler of this world, and the title given him by his followers *Mujaddi-i-alf-i-Sani*, the leader of revival of Islam in the second millennium, is interesting for psychological and political reasons. The Naqshbandiya were largely responsible for the restoration of truly spiritual life in eighteenth century Delhi; Shah Waliullah (d. 1762), Mazhar Janjanan (d. 1781) and Khwaja Mir Dard, the "sincere Muhammadan" (*muhammadi-ya khalis*) (d. 1785) represent the attempt of Naqshbandi-oriented mystics to respond to the challenge posed by the decay of Muslim power in the subcontinent. The fervour of their commitment was an example to the freedom fighters of Sayyid Ahmad Barelvi, to the Deoband school, and to Sir Syed Ahmad Khan of Aligarh. The Naqshbandis in Sindh were the first to introduce religious educational literature in the Sindhi language.

The mystical orders, using the regional languages and infusing them with the literary idiom, have done much to acquaint the masses with a love of God and of the Prophet.

The mystics travelled widely and thus spread the message of Islam as far east as the Malayan Archipelago. The veneration shown to living and dead saints by the masses tended to dilute the purity of Islam. Likewise, the activities of the mystical leaders, the pirs, were not always restricted to the spiritual sphere and their power over their followers grew disproportionately. This caused the reformers' aversion to "pirism", which is a recurrent theme in Iqbal's philosophy. Iqbal himself went back to the classical, pure Sufism, drawing largely on the dynamic concept of love as preached in the Middle Ages by Jalaluddin Rumi (d. 1273), whose Persian poetry was widely read and commented upon in all Muslim languages of the subcontinent. Iqbal also resuscitated the essence of Sufism exemplified in the mystical doctrine and vision of *Al-Hallaj*.

A.S.

Sport

In Pakistan there is a wide range of sporting activities including indigenous sports and those sports introduced to the subcontinent by the West. In rural areas, traditional sports such as wrestling, horse racing, *kabbadi*, top (*lattoo*) and kite-flying predominate and contests are held in and between villages. Attendance is large, competition intense and a festive spirit prevails with dancing and music. Feats of champions are chronicled by village bards and become part of local legend.

In the urban areas sports such as cricket, hockey, squash, polo, tennis and football are popular and tournaments are organised in schools, colleges and at provincial and national level. At Independence there were few organised tournaments and very little training available. This was the background against which the first National Games were held in Karachi. Mr Jinnah specially flew from Peshawar to attend the games against the advice of his doctors.

Sport has played a key role in forging national identity and pride. In spite of the scarcity of funds and lack of facilities, Pakistani sportsmen registered unlikely victories at the international level in the decade after Independence through sheer talent and determination. The exploits of Fazal Mahmood (cricket), Hanif Mohammad (cricket), Naseer Bunda (wrestling) and Hashim Khan (squash) laid the foundation for a tradition of excellence which spurred later generations of sportsmen and in the early nineties Pakistan won world championships in sports as diverse as cricket, hockey, squash and snooker.

This success did not come easily. For example when British India was partitioned, India became heir to International Cricket Conference membership and Pakistan was left to prove its credentials. Membership of the ICC was granted four years later in 1952, after Pakistan had beaten a visiting MCC team in an unofficial series, a feat beyond the combined Indian team in numerous encounters before Independence. Less than two years later, an underrated Pakistan team led by A.H. Kardar beat the might of England at the Oval, thus levelling the first Test series, between the countries.

In Pakistan this historic victory provoked spontaneous

Above *A glorious moment as the Pakistani cricket team, captained by Imran Khan, wins the World Cup, 1992*
Below *Grass-roots cricket is learned on waste-ground*

celebrations and a national holiday was declared. Since then cricket has gone on to become the premier sport and the by-lanes and *maidans* of towns and cities pulsate with innumerable games of cricket. Some of the Pakistan's greatest cricketers such as Javed Miandad and Abdul Qadir honed their skills on the city streets, while others such as Imran Khan were fostered in the more luxurious surroundings of elite public schools.

In the late Seventies and Eighties Pakistan were the only team to defy the all-conquering West Indian side, drawing three fiercely contested Test series at home and away. It was in one of these encounters that Pakistan showed the way by inviting third nation umpires to officiate for the first time in a Test match. Cricket fever gripped the country in 1988 and 1996 when Pakistan co-hosted the World Cup, the latter as holders, having won the World Cup in 1992 in Australia, fulfilling the most cherished dream of a cricket-crazy country. More recently, a strong Pakistani team defeated England comprehensively in the 1996 season.

Pakistan's remarkable success in squash had the most unlikely of beginnings. At Independence there were only ten squash courts in the country. Hashim Khan learnt the game from his father, the chief steward of Peshawar Club. His father's death when Hashim was only ten left him the oldest male member of the family. He polished his skills and in time was able to support his family through coaching. In 1951 he was funded by the government to go to the UK to play in the British Open. In his maiden appearance at the age of thirty-five, the balding Pakistani shocked the squash world by defeating five-time winner Mahmoud Al Karim of Egypt in the final. Amazingly, he went on to win seven British Open titles, the last in 1958 at the age of forty two. He was the founder of the legendary Khan squash dynasty which has won thirteen out of nineteen World Open championships since the tournament began in 1975, and twenty-eight out of forty-five British Opens since Hashim Khan's first victory in 1951. Following in Hashim's footsteps Jehangir Khan, and then Jansher Khan have dominated international squash since 1980. Indeed, this complete dominance has no parallel in world sport.

One of the best-organised games at Independence was hockey. Half of Pakistan's first contingent to the Olympic Games comprised hockey players but an ageing team finished out of the medals. However at the next Olympics in 1956, Pakistan were silver medallists and in 1960 claimed the gold. The Pakistan team has remained in the forefront of world hockey and has won three Olympic golds and four World Cups. It has also been a favourite with spectators because of the artistry and speed of the forwards. The Pakistani forward line of the early Seventies was breathtaking to watch, comparable in its skills and creativity to the great Brazilian football team of the same era. In recent times Shahbaz Ahmed has been the most feared forward in the world.

While Pakistan has been a force in cricket, hockey and squash since the Fifties, more recently it has made a mark in games with strong minority following. One such is bridge, where since the early Eighties Zia Mahmood has emerged as the most charismatic and popular of the game. His involvement in the game was by chance. A girl Zia wanted to meet was fond of bridge and consented to meet him at a bridge party, unaware that he knew little about the game. To avoid embarrassment he quickly learnt as much as possible and in the process became "hooked". Utterly dedicated and with a natural flair for bridge, he developed rapidly, making a partnership with Masood Salim, a leading player, which carried of the Asia and Middle East Zonal Championships and qualified Pakistan for the 1981 Bermuda Bowl in which only zonal winners worldwide are represented. The unknown and unfancied Pakistan squad shocked the bridge world by reaching the final in which they lost to the US. In 1986, at the Bridge Olympiad in Miami, Pakistan were the only non-US team to reach the semi-finals. The entire bridge community present barring the Americans were behind Pakistan and T-Shirts emblazoned Paki Power" were being snapped up by spectators. Again Pakistan reached the final only to be beaten by the US.

Equally astonishing is the success of Pakistani competitors in snooker and yachting. Until quite recently snooker was an elite game played at clubs and *gymkhanas*. In the Nineties, snooker parlours became popular in the big cities and a number of promising youngsters were making their presence felt. The game received considerable impetus from Mohammad Yousuf's unexpected victory in the Amateur World Championship in 1994. Yousuf, a young immigrant from Bombay, earned his living hawking newspapers outside a snooker parlour. Fascinated, he spent some of his meagre earnings learning the game. Despite few means and little education, through perseverance and hard work he became National Champion and eventually World Champion.

By stark contrast, Pakistan's initial success in yachting

Shahbaz Ahmed thunders down the pitch, a force to be reckoned with in world hockey. Pakistan's team is known for its outstanding skill and artistry and its compellingly watchable style of playing

was based on the availability of personal resources. Confined to a few competitions in Karachi, yachting was largely an unknown sport. Encouraged by their success against India and Sri Lanka at a competition held in Karachi in 1977, Byram Avari, a hotel magnate and Lieutenant Munir Sadiq, a naval officer, decided to compete in the Asian games. Funded largely by Avari, the pair purchased equipment, trained extensively and paid their own way to Bangkok in 1978 where they won the gold medal in the Enterprise class of the yachting competition. Since their success, competitive yachting activity has grown steadily. Of the nine gold medals won at the Asian Games since 1978, Pakistani yachtsmen have won four.

Pakistan inherited a rich wrestling tradition and the legendary Gama remained unbeaten for nearly three decades in the subcontinental style. Initially Pakistani wrestlers were reasonably successful at the classical style and in 1962 won twelve medals at the Asian Games, including three gold medals. In 1960 Bashir won a bronze medal at the Olympic Games. Since then their performance has been disappointing due to a lack of training facilities.

Pakistan participated in boxing for the first time at the Asian level in 1958 and have since won fifty medals at the Asian Games as well as Hussain Shah's Olympic Bronze in 1988. This is in spite of limited opportunities and scant resources. In athletics, on the other hand, the record at the Asian level has been extremely poor since the early Sixties and much needs to be done before Pakistani athletes can compete at the international level.

Volleyball is a popular sport even in the rural areas. Golf and polo, on the other hand, are played largely by the urban elite. Several good golf courses exist in the major cities and the game has a growing number of adherents. The most popular sport in the villages is *kabaddi*, an indigenous team game requiring speed and strength in which a player has to cross into opposition territory, touch an opponent within twenty seconds and make it back over the line to home ground within twenty-five seconds after contact. The "touched" player has to stop him from making it back in time. *Kabaddi* is now a recognised sport at the Asian Games.

A. K.

6. Pakistan's Place in the World

Pakistan, it may be said, has three places in the world. By virtue of itself, as a land and people. By virtue of its Islamic *raison d'être*, in the midst of Southern Asia. And by virtue of its stance in world affairs. Where China, India and mid-Eastern Islam converge, there stands Pakistan – powerful, populous, determined and vigilant.

The Kilit Pass, where China, Pakistan and Afghanistan meet. Pakistani governments view their country as a cultural and economic bridge between East and West

External Affairs

Pakistan's fifty years have been years of upheaval and crisis, civil strife and secession, of Martial Law or emergency rule, of leaders assassinated or executed, constitutions overthrown, suspended or subverted. Even as the anniversary year opened, Pakistan was going through yet another constitutional and political crisis. Its recovery, however, was swift after the February 1997 General Election, and the emergence of a moderate government with a strong parliamentary majority and determined programme.

Looking back, one is struck by two facts. First, that through all the changes of government and regime, crises at home and upheavals abroad, the nation's aims, objectives and policies have remained broadly constant. This is especially so in the field of foreign policy which has never strayed too far from the direction set in the beginning and has retained its substance. Notwithstanding all the polemics between the government of the day and the opposition parties, there are no real substantive differences between them on the major foreign policy issues – relations with India, Kashmir, nuclear policy, pan-Islamicist aspirations and pro-Western orientation.

The other notable fact is that most of the foreign policy problems that existed at the beginning – Kashmir, the military imbalance with India, the trouble with Afghanistan – are still there and have, if anything, become more complex with the years. Some new problems, notably the difference with the United States over the nuclear question, have been added to the list.

Napoleon declared that a country's foreign policy is dictated by its geography. When President Ayub Khan quoted this dictum during a state visit to Paris, another Frenchman, Charles de Gaulle, responded that a nation's policy is also inspired by its ideals. Both elements have played an important role in defining Pakistan's foreign and security policy goals.

The ideals and inspirations of the Pakistan movement, even before the country came into being, were pan-Islamic – the dream to see the Islamic world revitalised and united as a prosperous and progressive community. The poet Muhammad Iqbal gave expression to the sentiment in his poetry and his lectures on Islamic thought. In the field of foreign policy, the aspiration was given an edge by Pakistan's search for an identity distinct from its erstwhile Indian identity. The re-emergence of the Muslim nations of Central Asia as independent countries has given a new impetus and direction to Pakistan's pan-Islamic impulse, for in these countries lie some of the roots of Pakistani nationalism. But the task of building up economic and material links among Muslim countries has proved slow and difficult and today the Islamic world and Islam itself are seen as a threat by some in the West. In Pakistan itself, the "Islamisation" introduced by Zia al Haq gave rise to controversy. Today, however, Pakistan with its pragmatic and modernising approach to the issue is well placed to give substance to the Muslim urge for unity and revival and to act as a bridge to other cultures and civilisations

Pakistan came into existence by an agreement between the sub-continent's two major communities, brokered by the departing British. Nevertheless the Hindu majority felt that it had been cheated out of its inheritance and it has been left with a lasting sense of grievance. This sense of grievance remains and it colours the Indian attitude to Pakistan. Pakistan sees the Indian attitude as a threat to its existence – sometimes specific, sometimes general but imminent and always there. What was accepted on paper as a settlement of the Hindu-Muslim issue thus became an India-Pakistan conflict on the world stage. It received specific shape when, unlike the rest of the subcontinent, the fate of Kashmir was decided without consulting its people and by force of arms, leaving it as a bone of contention between the two countries.

Geopolitics has not favoured Pakistan. The country's elongated shape, stretching almost 2000 km from the sea to the mountains, gives it long borders to defend and little strategic depth from which to fight back an attack. Thus the search for security was the primordial concern of Pakistan's foreign policy: security not only against a possible armed attack by India but also against India's hegemony – a somewhat vague expression which in practical terms means that, despite the all too evident disparities, Pakistan will try to keep up in the military field and seeks an approximately equal status with India on the world stage.

The search for security led Pakistan into a relationship with the USA. The initial step was taken when Pakistan's first Prime Minister, cancelling a scheduled visit to Moscow, went instead to the United States. Later Pakistan signed on as a member of the Baghdad Pact and of SEATO and became a fully-fledged US ally. Would Pakistan have been better off choosing non-alignment? The question is sometimes still debated in Pakistan but there is no clear-cut answer. At the time the need of the hour was for arms to defend the country's borders against a threat from India and to gain diplomatic leverage in seeking a settlement of the Kashmir dispute. In fact the American alliance did not help in either respect though it provided the arms and equipment to build up the Pakistan military into a reasonably credible force. Furthermore, from time to time Pakistan saw its American aid abruptly cut off for one transgression or another.

The alliance therefore, is not popular in the country and is overlaid by feelings of let-down and resentment. In fairness, it should be recognised that the United States never undertook to help Pakistan in achieving its own national objectives. For the United States, the alliance had relevance only in the context of the cold war. Pakistan was of course anti-communist but the United States cannot have failed to notice that Pakistan's fears and concerns were centred above all, if not wholly, on India. The terms of the 1959 bilateral agreement between the two countries may suggest that the US would help Pakistan also in case of an aggression from India. But then who would define aggression and what would be the nature of American help? The truth is that from the beginning the Pakistan-American relationship was based on a reciprocal and almost wilful self-deception.

But appearances could no longer be kept up when India and China came to blows in 1962 and the West, headed by the USA, rushed in with arms aid for India. Pakistan had seen the Sino-Indian conflict as providing the occasion for inducing or pressurising India to settle the Kashmir dispute. The United States and Britain did in fact prevail upon India to enter into bilateral talks with Pakistan on the subject but declined to put any pressure on India and nothing came of the negotiations. What the United States really desired was set out in a letter President Kennedy wrote to Ayub Khan urging that Pakistan put aside its concern with Kashmir and join India in confronting China from whom, in the American view, came the "real" danger to the subcontinent. Pakistan did the exact opposite, of course, and began to develop a close relationship with China.

In truth this was not the radical reversal of alliances that it seemed to be at the time, for it soon became apparent that China had no long-term designs on India or Pakistan or any one else in South Asia. In the course of a few years it also came to be realised that China was not the threat to Western interests and way of life that it was imagined to be. On the contrary it was going to prove a most valuable card in curbing Soviet trouble-making and would in due course become (thanks partly, to Pakistan's good offices) a virtual ally of the West against its erstwhile ideological comrade.

These events led to one of the high points of Pakistani diplomacy when, under Ayub Khan and Bhutto, Pakistan managed to be on good terms with all three contending great powers – the United States, the USSR and China – receiving economic aid and diplomatic support and even military equipment from all three. But this halcyon period was shortly afterwards overtaken by the worst period in Pakistan's turbulent history, when the country faced diplomatic isolation, suffered a military defeat and saw its eastern wing break away to become Bangladesh. The turn-around was brought about by fundamental contradictions in the country's body-politic and indeed in its very make-up and structure. No amount of diplomacy or stockpiles of weapons could have made a difference to the outcome, but misconceptions regarding Pakistan's diplomatic and strategic situation played a role in the mistakes and errors that led to the crisis. A clearer understanding of the forces at work in the country, in the region and the world at large might have brought about a Bangladesh settlement without bloodshed and dishonour.

There were other ups and downs in Pakistan's diplomatic history. Zulfikar Bhutto, assuming power after the trauma of secession and defeat in 1971, succeeded so well in putting back the pieces that the world press marvelled at Pakistan's ability to rise time and again phoenix-like from its ashes. There was reconciliation with Bangladesh and the country was once again on good terms with all three great powers. On the world stage Pakistan attained a prominence once enjoyed by rival India, playing a leading role in the United Nations.

Then everything seemed to come unstuck, Bhutto was overthrown and hanged and Pakistan found itself under military rule again. The apparent cause of the upheaval was the alleged rigging of the elections called by Bhutto in 1976. But many people believe that the United States' anxiety to put a stop to Pakistan's nuclear programme had much to do with these events and developments.

When India carried out a nuclear test in 1974, geopolitical arithmetic made it inevitable that Pakistan would try to follow suit. In time, despite American opposition and sanctions and various other hurdles, Pakistan did succeed in developing a nuclear capability to counter, if not match, India's. Now India has developed a missile delivery system and again Pakistan is faced with a challenge to its security. India's great power ambitions, Pakistan's security concerns and rivalry with India and the discriminatory non-proliferation policy of the United States have all played, in varying degrees, a part in bringing about this state of affairs. Will it all end in a nuclear holocaust? Or could a nuclear balance make South Asia's crypto-nuclear powers as careful about going to war as the recognised nuclear powers have been?

It seems incongruous that while the world is beginning to move away from nuclear weapons, a regional "balance of terror" should be taking form between Pakistan and India. But, sadly, that is the reality. A two-fold approach may help to stabilise the situation and avert the worst. In the first place, the two countries ought to consider reaching agreements and with the help of the more advanced nuclear powers, take appropriate technical measures to reduce the mutual vulnerability of their nuclear capabilities. A precedent exists in the 1989 agreement between them on the exchange of information about nuclear targets.

Secondly, setting aside pre-partition polemics, and instead of merely going through the motions, the two countries should start a sustained process of negotiation, on the model of the Conference on European Security and Co-operation to deal with the whole gamut of their relations and to remove the causes of conflict and tension. This will mean tackling the Kashmir issue, the substance of which has been dealt with elsewhere in this volume.

Given Pakistan's proximity and historical affinity with Afghanistan, it was inevitable that it should have been sucked into that conflict. But on the heels of the withdrawal of Soviet forces and with the collapse of Russia's Central Asian empire, came the emergence of newly independent Central Asian Republics, all Islamic and several well endowed with resources – a situation that offers great opportunities of trade and economic cooperation. Pakistan was swift to establish its presence in the capitals of nations – Tajik, Uzbek, Kirghiz, Kazakh and Turkmen, with whom its own peoples have had historical links. Friendly relations were already forged as the century moved to a close. Trade seemed sure to follow once the civil war in Afghanistan came to an end. The Taliban may bring about this result by imposing their control over the whole country and for this reason Pakistan is suspected of supporting this group. However, ideologically, the Taliban are poles apart from the moderate Islam prevailing in Pakistan and Pakistan's own long-term interests would be best served by a political settlement that could reconcile the warring brethren in Afghanistan and replace the deadly traffic in guns and heroin with trade in goods and services.

The schisms in the Muslim world have often made it difficult for Pakistan to play its preferred non-partisan and reconciling role. In the 1979-88 Iraq-Iran war two countries friendly to Islamabad bled each other white for years, testing Pakistani diplomacy to the extreme. The Gulf War created a comparable strain, as Pakistan joined the vast coalition led by the United States against Iraq, a decision that was not popular at home. Elsewhere, Pakistani governments have striven to stand aside from inter-Islamic conflicts.

Pakistan's geopolitical situation and its historical and cultural background could make it the linchpin in a new region of economic cooperation and development, stretching from India to Iran and the Gulf and northwards, to the landlocked republics of Central Asia. This vast area, surpassing the European Union in size, population and resources, when linked by oil and gas pipelines, motorways and telecommunications, trade and complementary industry, could bring undreamed of prosperity to its peoples and act as a powerful engine of growth for the world economy.

The key to this future lies in an understanding between India and Pakistan. The conventional wisdom is that India and Pakistan are locked in a rivalry that is age-old and nothing can be done about it. But the prospect is not necessarily so bleak. A stable relationship between Pakistan and India, free of rivalry and tension, is not unattainable. Consider the emergence of commonsense and justice in South Africa. It is not unthinkable that such a miracle could occur also in the subcontinent. The real and immediate problems of both countries lie not in the field of foreign affairs but at home – mass poverty, a galloping population growth, social backwardness and internal political tensions. The future lies not in two powerful nuclear-capable entities facing each other and moving against the tide of events but of two democratic federations co operating in all fields and at various levels.

I. A.

Pakistan and Afghanistan

The area that constitutes Pakistan has been linked with Afghanistan and Central Asia long before the Christian and Islamic eras. Over five thousand years ago, the first Aryan invaders from Central Asia reached the Indian subcontinent through Afghanistan and the mountain passes in today's North-West Frontier Province. Buddhist monks travelled to Central Asia and China, taking Buddhism to the Far East. Trade between Asia and Europe flourished along the fabulous Silk Route, parts of which ran through northern Afghanistan. The Mughals, once a ruling dynasty in Samarkand, conquered Afghanistan and India, and Emperor Babur, first of the great Mughals, is buried in Kabul.

The conquest of Central Asia by the Tsars in the nineteenth century bought Imperial Russia up against the British empire in India, triggering off the "Great Game" with both sides trying to restrict the movement of people and trade between Central Asia and the Indian Subcontinent, thus turning Afghanistan into a buffer state. The delinking of these natural neighbours was formalised by Stalin after the 1917 Russian Revolution. For more than seventy years Central Asia was cut off from Afghanistan and Pakistan.

Those linkages were only re-established after horrendous bloodletting. When Afghan army tanks rolled up outside the palace of President Mohammed Daud on 27th April 1978 and began an intense bombardment, a chain of events was unleashed that claimed more than a million Afghan lives in a bitter civil war that has lasted for nearly two decades. The coup by a small group of Afghan communists and the subsequent invasion of Afghanistan by Soviet troops in December 1979 seriously threatened Pakistan's security and national integrity. It placed Pakistan at the very centre of the Cold War between the US and the Soviet Union and led to the drugs and weapons culture in Pakistan.

When Soviet troops finally withdrew from Afghanistan in 1990 and Kabul fell to the Afghan Mujaheddin two years later, just a few months after the collapse of the Soviet Union, there was renewed hope and visible excitement amongst Pakistanis that stability in Afghanistan would open up new vistas of trade and investment between Pakistan and the five newly independent Central Asia Republics (CARs). Pakistan could provide the quickest and shortest route to the sea for their landlocked Muslim neighbours, and hoped to play a leading role in the reconstruction of Afghanistan.

Despite sustained diplomatic efforts by Islamabad to bring about stability and a workable power-sharing arrangement between the various Afghan Mujaheddin factions, a new and even bloodier civil war between the Afghan warlords erupted. Since 1992, the battle for Kabul has destroyed the city, claiming more than 75,000 lives and virtually partitioning the country into four separate fiefdoms, increasing fears about the possible fragmentation of Afghanistan.

Afghanistan has always been a fragile state. Its strategic location has consistently engaged the attention of empire builders from Alexander the Great to Lenin, from the Persian shahs to the British raj. Gradually, a process of state-building began some three hundred years ago when the Pathans, the largest ethnic group, united the country and established a monarchy. However, the partition of the Indian subcontinent in 1947 divided the Pathans between Pakistan and Afghanistan, creating a new source of tension between the two countries. In the Fifties both the USA and the Soviet

Union vied with each other to provide economic and military aid to Afghanistan.

The Iranian Islamic revolution, followed quickly by the communist coup in Kabul, dramatically altered the strategic balance in the region. Fearing the spread of Islamic fundamentalism northwards into the strategic underbelly of Soviet Central Asia and desperate to back an increasingly beleaguered hardline communist government in Kabul that had alienated the majority of the population, the Soviet Union made the risky decision to invade the country. In retaliation, Western and Islamic countries poured in billions of dollars in economic and military aid to the dozens of resistance factions that sprang up overnight. More than 50,000 Soviet troops and one million Afghans were to die before Moscow withdrew its troops.

However, the war had not only devastated Afghan society and the economy, but dramatically altered the ethnic balance in the country, thus giving rise to new centres of

Relic of the "Great Game": Winston Churchill served at the Malakand Agency in 1895. This outpost was a base for controlling the North-West Frontier

political and military power. The Pathans, who comprise forty per cent of Afghanistan's estimated fifteen million people, were no longer the country's undisputed rulers as the Tajiks (25 per cent of the population), the Uzbeks (ten per cent) and smaller ethnic groups such as the Hazaras raised their own largely ethnic armies and vied for control of Kabul. Moreover, neighbouring states – Iran, Pakistan, Saudi Arabia and later Uzbekistan and Turkmenistan – all backed different warlords and a bloody new civil war erupted.

Throughout the Eighties Pakistan had played a major role in supporting the Afghan Mujaheddin, channelling US aid to them and maintaining some three million Afghan refugees on its soil while another two million fled to Iran. Hundreds of Pakistanis living along the Pakistan-Afghan border were killed in cross-border bombing raids and terrorist bomb blasts carried out by Kabul's communist regime. But throughout the war, Pakistan had tended to favour the Pathan-based resistance. When the Tajiks under Burhanuddin Rabbani and his military strongman Ahmed Shah Masud gained control of Kabul in 1992, Pakistan's ability and political clout to negotiate a peace settlement between the warlords declined.

At the same time, the emergence of Central Asian states free from Soviet control opened up enormous new strategic and economic possibilities for Islamabad. The five new Muslim Republics were viewed by Pakistani strategists as offering new allies and greater strategic depth in the region against India. Pakistani traders and industrialists hoped for the reopening of the old Silk Route that would galvanise Pakistani business and expand their markets, while border cities such as Peshawar and Quetta could develop as major centres for trade with Central Asia. Meanwhile, intellectuals saw a new cultural renaissance fuelled by the chance to resume historical links with a region that had provided Pakistan with so much of its Muslim heritage.

At the heart of the issue was the question of routes. Pakistan needed stability in Afghanistan so that trucks from Peshawar could travel freely to Tashkent via Kabul, and traffic from Quetta to Herat could open up trade with Turkmenistan. Moreover, Karachi port could provide the closest access to the sea for the landlocked Republics desperate to expand their exports without the use of Russian ports.

So far the dream of accessing Central Asia directly by road has been blocked by the Afghan civil war, but Pakistan has tentatively explored other options. Islamabad is broadening and improving the strategic Karakorum Highway that links Islamabad to the Xinjiang province of China. This route is being extended to Kazakhstan and Kyrgyzstan. Despite the war, Pakistan is also hoping to open up a trade route between Quetta-Kandahar-Herat and Ashkabad in Turkmenistan, as there is relative peace in southern Afghanistan.

A new dimension of the many sided civil war inside the country arose with the growth of the Taliban movement in the winter of 1994. The Taliban are radical fundamentalist Islamic students, many of who had fought in the war and then retreated to *madrasahs* in Pakistan to study Islam. Fed up with the bickering warlords, the worsening law and order situation and keen to open roads to traffic so that refugees could return, they captured the southern city of Kandahar at the end of 1994.

From Kandahar they challenged all the other factions to either surrender their weapons or face military defeat. Their public appeal for peace won widespread converts, especially amongst the southern Pashtun. The Taliban captured the western city of Herat and then in a lightning offensive at the end of September 1996, they captured Kabul. Their imposition of a strict Islamic regime, which strongly discriminates against women, led to considerable international criticism.

The Taliban are now trying to conquer the entire country, putting military pressure on the largely Tajik forces of Ahmed Shah Masud who have retreated to the northeast of Afghanistan and the Uzbek warlord General Rashid Dostum, who still holds five provinces in the north. However the Taliban victories have increased the ethnic divide in the country, with all the non-Pashtuns now grouped against the largely Pashtun Taliban. Moreover their ability to rule the country is still in doubt, because of an acute shortage of trained personnel and the fact that the entire remaining urban middle class has now fled the country into exile.

However, the Afghan conflict remains a major factor of instability in the entire region. The civil war in Tajikistan has been partly fuelled by the Afghan warlords, while the plethora of weapons and sanctuary available in Afghanistan has encouraged international terrorism and Islamic extremism. Afghanistan is also now the second largest producer of heroin in the world, as the warlords fuel their war effort with exports of drugs via Pakistan, Iran and Central Asia. Not just Pakistan, but the entire development of Central Asia is being held hostage by the continuing fighting in Afghanistan. A peace agreement in Kabul could create the conditions for regional stability and the chance for all the neighbouring countries including Afghanistan finally to reap the benefits of the end of the Cold War.

A. R.

Defence

Most Pakistanis believe their country has continued to bear the undiminished hostility of India from its very birth. First, it was Lord Mountbatten's hurried – and in their eyes dishonest – demarcation of the boundary between the two countries. that created the debilitating and totally unnecessary dispute over Kashmir, a clearly Muslim-majority state that should have come to Pakistan in accordance with the rules of Partition applied everywhere else. Then, following the stalemated and costly wars of 1948 and 1965 between India and Pakistan over Kashmir came India's use of military force to help bring about the secession of East Pakistan in 1971. After spending fifty years as India's neighbour, the widely held perception in Pakistan is that the country has been fated to waste a substantial part of its resources to ensure its security in the face of continuing threats and crises.

At Partition in 1947, the inequitable division of financial and military assets between the two states appeared to be calculated to cause an early internal collapse of Pakistan and its inevitable re-absorption into India. As if to speed that inevitability, India reneged on the full transfer of assets. The well. Then came the arbitrary US weapons embargoes of 1965 and 1971. These brought home the realities of the one-directional defence envisaged by the CENTO and SEATO alliances. By 1979 Pakistan had quit both the regional security pacts, having gained from their membership only a limited measure of security for about fifteen years. The price it paid was the implacable hostility of the Soviet Union. Moscow's 1979 intervention in Afghanistan brought a more realistic US-Pakistan strategic relationship in which India's aggressive designs on the subcontinent came to be recognised by Washington. Consequently, a modest modernisation of Pakistan's armed forces was made possible against cash purchases from America and elsewhere.

A large number of the United Nations member states applauded Pakistan's courageous role in the Afghan war. For over a decade they funded assistance programmes to sustain the three million Afghan refugees who poured into Pakistan; contributing enormous amounts of food, clothing and other aid to the refugees. But the care and maintenance of this huge number of displaced and destitute persons caused intense socio-economic and infrastructural problems for Pakistan. All major road arteries from Karachi to the Afghan border were severely damaged, the western borderlands lay in ruin from over-grazing; what had been a trickle of drug traffic now turned into a flood and spread to all parts of

collapse did not occur, the armed forces of Pakistan learned early to operate under adverse conditions. Defence culture is deeply rooted in the wars Pakistan has fought outnumbered and outgunned.

Pakistan has a 4,000-kilometre border with India. East to west the country spans a mere quarter of this distance, and much of its communication network and major urban and industrial concentrations (such as Lahore) are barely fifty kilometres from the Indian border. Consequently its army must rely on forward defence and pre-positioned troops. Its 1,000-kilometre coastline has only one major port through which 95 per cent of its trade is conducted. The pivotal importance of air support to land and naval forces over this 5,000-kilometre line of exposure makes the country's air force a specially critical element of national defence strategy.

The Cold War brought with it both hope and frustration for Pakistan's security. Washington's policy of containment made Pakistan an active South Asian barricade against communism from 1954, and thus eligible for military assistance. This indeed helped to shore up its defence against India as Pakistan; and urban crime and violence erupted across the country, thanks to the free availability of modern arms originally meant for the Afghan resistance fighters.

With the end of the Cold War, Pakistan's security problems emerged vastly transformed. The strong anti-Soviet alliance with the US evaporated overnight and Washington's reawakened nuclear counter-proliferation agenda in South Asia was applied selectively with full punitive force against Pakistan. Pakistan's role as a key ally in the defeat of the Soviet empire was swiftly forgotten.

China has been a reliable ally to Pakistan throughout most of the last half century, and at the new millennium's approach remains steadfastly supportive of Pakistan's security concerns in the changing world order. However, its recent rapid and explosive economic growth has dictated some major policy reorientation. After being engaged for three decades in a costly border confrontation with the Soviet Union, Beijing appeared to be primarily occupied with the fruits of modern technology and prosperity. It quickly shed most of the bloc-system patterns of past confrontations.

China remains wary of Indian ambitions in Asia. Meanwhile, the risks of a nuclear war inherent in a possible Pakistan-India conflict has made China more circumspect in South Asian politics.

In contrast, the end of the Cold War and of Beijing-Moscow hostility has substantially improved India's security environment. New Delhi no longer needs to echo Moscow's rhetoric against the West. Yet India's relations with Russia, its major source of concessional arms purchases, remains as with the Soviet regime, and Delhi has even succeeded in pressurising Russia to deny Pakistan the option of purchasing Russian warplanes. The India-China tensions across the Himalayan border have been considerably reduced. Both countries have made it clear that their disputes and disagreements would not stand in the way of opening new, mutually beneficial markets. In Washington, India's former status as a Soviet ally has given way to a new, expanding relationship, including collaboration in defence production projects.

The emerging post-Cold War period has thus posed greater challenges for Pakistan's security. The government has been unable to maintain the defence budget at the former levels in real terms due to competing demands of social development. Adverse exchange rates have significantly eroded defence imports from year to year. The only noteworthy new acquisitions have been three Agosta submarines from France and six ex-Royal Navy frigates from Britain. The army has not had capability upgrades for several years. The air force, considered to be the decisive element in the country's defence, has been specially hard hit. The US government's refusal to deliver the thirty-eight F-16s (on the grounds of Pakistan's suspected possession of the nuclear deterrent), while continuing to receive payments from Pakistan for over three years, defied all norms of honourable dealing. A replacement for the denied F-16s had not yet been supplied by 1997.

Both Pakistan and India reportedly possess a small number of deliverable nuclear weapons. However unlikely their actual use in war, the very presumption of Pakistan's capability has surely acted to discourage aggressive or opportunistic impulses in India.

In spite of their relative numerical disadvantage, Pakistan's conventional forces are well-trained and motivated. Independent studies suggest that Indian forces could suffer unacceptable losses in attempting deep penetrations and large tank movements across Pakistani territory. This probability, and the uncertainty about the employment of nuclear weapons in a "last resort" defence, both lend credibility to Pakistan's military strategy. A number of defence commentators from both Pakistan and India acknowledge that the *de facto* nuclear stand-off between the two countries serves as a powerful mutual deterrent in the near term.

For the longer term, and in the spirit of the global post-Cold War emphasis on economic growth, Pakistan has sought to persuade India to reduce tensions on the subcontinent. Both need to reappraise the large defence investments they presently make every year, some $11 billion and five per cent of GDP between them. This massive outlay is seriously retarding urgently needed progress in their cash-starved social sectors. Several Pakistani proposals – including the declaration of a South Asia nuclear-free zone – have been rejected by Delhi. India also refuses adamantly to honour its commitments to permit a resolution of the Kashmir dispute through a UN-supervised plebiscite. An open rebellion in Indian-administered Kashmir since 1989 has obliged Delhi to deploy nearly 600,000 troops and uniformed personnel to force Kashmiris into submission. Yet condemnation of human rights abuses in Indian-occupied Kashmir is widespread. New Delhi remains obdurate in its refusal to settle the dispute peacefully in the light of existing UN Security

Opposite *A Pakistani Air Force fighter pilot climbs into the F16 Fighting Falcon. The nation's forces are well trained and motivated*
Centre *A Pakistani Army tank in practice manoeuvres*
Above *Northern Light Infantry carry out exercises at the 17,000 ft. theatre of the Siachen Glacier in the Northern Areas*

Council resolutions.

Such a security environment provides little promise of stability in South Asia. The failure of the international community to persuade India to resolve the Kashmir crisis leaves open a significant threat to peace. Concurrently, India's regional ambitions and its interventionist conduct towards its neighbours seem to endorse its declared quest for dominance over the South Asian land mass and the further reaches of the Indian Ocean. Unless kept in check by deterrent forces and international dissuasion, such ambitions will continue to threaten regional peace as the new century opens.

Z. A. K.

Bibliography

This bibliography offers a selection of wider reading on Pakistan for the general reader.

Historical Background

Bolitho, Hector *Jinnah: Creator of Pakistan*, John Murray, London, 1954
Durand, A.G.R. *The Making of a Frontier,* London, 1900
Hodson, H.V. *The Great Divide: Britain –India – Pakistan*, Hutchinson, London, 1969
Jinnah, M.A. *Some Recent Speeches and Writings of Mr. Jinnah,* Sh. Muhammad Ashraf, Lahore, 1942, 2 vols. (Compiled by Jamiluddin Ahmad)
Jinnah, M.A. *Selected Speeches and Statements of the Quaid-i-Azam Mohamed Ali Jinnah, 1911-34 and 1947-48,* Research Society of Pakistan, Lahore, April 1966 (Collected by M. Rafique Afzal)
Philips, C.H. and Wainwright, M.D. (eds.) *The Partition of India: Policies and Perspectives, 1935-1947*, George Allen and Unwin, London, 1970
Symonds, Richard *The Making of Pakistan*, Faber & Faber, London 1950
Wolpert, Stanley *Jinnah of Pakistan,* Oxford, 1984
Wolpert, Stanley *Zulfiqar Bhutto of Pakistan,* Oxford, 1993
Zaidi, Professor Z.H. *Jinnah Papers, Prelude to Partition,* National Archive of Pakistan, 1993

Land and Country

Feldman, Herbert *The Land and People of Pakistan*, Adam and Charles Black, London 1958
Shaw, Isobel *Pakistan: Collins Illustrated Guide,* Collins, London, 1985
Stephens, Ian *Horned Moon: An Account of a Journey through Pakistan, Kashmir and Afghanistan*, Chatto and Windus, London, 1953
Stephens, Ian *Pakistan,* Ernest Benn, London, 1963
Williams, L.F. Rushbrook *Pakistan under Challenge*, Stacey International, London 1975

Regional Studies

Balochistan

Khan, Ahmed Yar *Inside Baluchistan: A Political Autobiography of His Highness Baiglar Baigi, Khan-e-Azam XIII Mir Ahmed Yar Khan Baluch, Ex-Ruler of Kalat State,* Royal Book Co., Karachi, 1975

Northern Areas and NWFP

Caroe, Olaf *The Pathans, 500 HC-AD 1957,* Macmillan, London, 1958
Chenevix-Trench, Charles *The Frontier Scouts,* London, 1985
Mayne, Peter *The Narrow Smile: A Journey back to the North-West Frontier,* John Murray, London 1955
Schofield, Victoria, *Every Rock, Every Hill*, Pimlico, 1987
Spain, James W. *The Way of the Pathans,* Robert Hale, London, 1962
Spain, James W. *The Pathan Borderland,* Mouton, the Hague, 1963
Latif, Syed Muhammed *History of the Panjab from the Remotest Antiquity to the Present Time,* Eurasia Publishing House, New Delhi, 1964 (First published 1889)
Latif, Syed Muhammed *Lahore: Its History, Architectural Remains and Antiquities, with an Account of its Modern Institutions, Inhabitants, their Trade Customs, etc.,* Syed Muhammad Minhaj-ud-Din, Lahore, 1957 (First published 1892)

Society and Culture

Brohi, A.K. *Islam in the Modern World,* Publishers United, Lahore, 2nd ed. 1975
Chaghatai, M.A. *The Badshahi Masjid: History and Architecture,* Kitab Khana-i-Naurus, Lahore, 1972
Dar, B.A. *A Study in Iqbal's Philosophy,* Sh. Ghulam Ali, Lahore, 1971
Faiz, Faiz Ahmad (tr. Kiernan, V.G.) *Poems by Faiz,* George Allen and Unwin, London, 1971
Iqbal, Muhammad *Six Lectures on the Reconstruction of Religious Thought in Islam,* n.p., Lahore, 1930
Iqbal, Muhammad (tr. Kiernan, V.G.) *Poems from Iqbal,* Kutub Publishers, Bombay, December 1947
Khattak, Khushhal Khan (tr. Mackenzie, D.N.) *Poems from the Divan of Khushal Khan Khattak,* Allen and Unwin, London 1965
Mahmud, S.F. Ghalib *A Critical Introduction,* University of the Punjab, Lahore

Economy and Development

Burki, Shahid Javed *Pakistan: A Nation in the Making*, Westview Press, London,1986
Noman, Omar *Pakistan, Political & Economic History Since 1947,* Keegan Paul International, 1990

Government and Politics

Ali, Tariq *Can Pakistan Survive? The Death of a State* Penguin, London 1983
Bhutto, Z.A. *The Great Tragedy, Pakistan People's Party*, Karachi, 1971
Bhutto, Benazir *Daughter of the East: an autobiography* Hamish Hamilton, London 1988
Burke, Samuel M. *Mainsprings of Indian and Pakistani Foreign Policies,* Minneapolis, 1974
Gauhar, Altaf, *Ayub Khan, Pakistan's First Military ruler,* Lahore, 1993
Duncan, Emma *Breaking the Curfew: a political journey through Pakistan*, Michael Joseph, London, 1989
Jalal, Ayesha *The Sole Spokesman,* Cambridge, 1985
Jalal, Ayesha *The State of Martial Rule,* Cambridge 1990
James, Sir Morrice *Pakistan Chronicle,* London, 1993
Lamb, Christina *Waiting for Allah, Pakistan's Struggle for Democracy,* Hamilton, London, 1991
Symonds, R. *The Making of Pakistan. A Short Political guide,* London, 1950

Foreign Relations

Akbar Khan, Ex-Major-General *Raiders in Kashmir. Story of the Kashmir War (1947-48)* Karachi, 1970
Asghar Khan, M. *The First Round: Indo-Pakistan War 1965,* London 1979
Bhutto, Z.A. *The Myth of Independence,* O.U.P., Karachi, 1969
Birdwood, Lord *Two Nations and Kashmir,* London, 1956
Burke, S.M. *Pakistan's Foreign Policy: An Historical Analysis,* O.U.P., London, 1973
Burke, S.M. *Mainsprings of Indian and Pakistani Foreign Policies,* O.U.P., Karachi and Lahore, 1975 (First published 1974)
Chopra, Pran *India, Pakistan and the Kashmir Tangle,* New Delhi, 1994
Knight, E.F. *Where Three Empires Meet* London, 1893
Korbel, Josef *Danger in Kashmir,* Princeton University Press, Princeton, rev. ed. 1966
Lamb, Alastair *Crisis in Kashmir, 1947 to 1966*, Routledge Kegan Paul, London, 1966
Lamb, Alastair *Kashmir: A Disputed Legacy 1846-1990*, Herts, 1991
Lamb, Alastair *Birth of the Tragedy,* Herts, 1994
Yasin, M. *British Paramountcy in Kashmir 1876-1894*, New Delhi, n.d.

Index

Page numbers in **bold** type indicate additional illustrations. The following abbreviations have been used: BB for Benazir Bhutto; GG for Governor General; J for Mohamed Ali Jinnah; PM for Prime Minister.

Abbasid rulers 43, 44, 45, 47
Afghanistan
  British wars with 59, 61
  civil war in 25, 134, 153, 200-1
  foreign rulers in 38, 45
  invaders from 47, 49, 56, 145
  Islam arrived in 44
  refugees from 112, 141, 151, 201, 202
  relations with 136, 202
Aga Khan Medical University **165**, 166
Aga Khan Rural Support Programme 166
Agha, Zubeda, artist 173
agriculture 20, 148, 152-3, 155-6
  crops 99, 128, 155
  fields in **116-7**, **137**
  fruit growing 103, 148, 149
  of Indus Valley civilisation 30, 31, 33, 34
  and water 94, 102, 103
agriculture *see also* livestock
Ahmad Khan, Sir Syed 62, 66, 70, 187, 195
Ahmadis, in modern Pakistan 172
Ahmed, Anna Molka, artist **173**, 174
Ahmed, Shahbaz, hockey player 197
air travel 158-9, **160**
Akbar, Mughal Emperor 50-3, **51**, 56, 176, 185
al-Biruni, Abu Raihan, 44, 45, 143, 185
Alexander the Great 36, 115, 138, 146
Ali, Chaudri Muhammad, PM 19
Ali, Habib Fida, architect 170, **171**
Ali, Muhammad, Khilafat Movement 64, 67, 73
Ali, Shakir, artist 173, 174, **175**, 184
Ali, Shaukat, Khilafat Movement 64, 67, 73, **77**
Aligarh Muslim University 62, 66, 67
All Pakistan Women's Association (APWA) 167
All-India Muslim League 63, 66-74, 190
Amritsar
  Jallianwalla Bagh massacre 73
  Treaty of 145
Anjuman Mimaran, in architecture 172
Arab rulers 42-4, 185
Arabic language 185
architecture
  ancient civilisations 29-30, **31**, 34, 39, 45, **126**
  British era 121-2, **130**, **131**, **132**, 133
  modern 113-14, **131**, 168-72
  Mughal 51-3, **54-5**, **56**, 145
    in Lahore **52**, **53**, **54**, **56**, **121**, **122-3**, **124**, **125**
  regional styles **116-17**, 129, **138**, 145
armed forces **27**, 133, 199, 202-3
  and British rule 61, 62, 64, 77
  ethnic make-up 77, 116, 138
art
  ancient civilisations 29-31, **32**, 33, 34, **35**, **43**, 48
  paintings 173-5, **176**, **177**, 184
art *see also* Gandharan; Mughal
Aryan rulers 35, 114
Asoka, Mauryan Emperor 37, 38, 114
Atlee, Clement, British PM 69
Aurangzeb, Emperor 53, **54**, 56, 121, 176
Avari, Byram, businessman and yachtsman 197
Awami League, in East Pakistan 21

Ayaz, Sheikh, poet 191, 193
Ayub Khan, General 9, 19, 20, **21**, 152, 165, 198,199
  Islamabad founded by 113, 169
Babur, Zaheeruddin, Emperor 47, 49, 56, 186
Bactrian kingdom 38
Badshahi Mosque, Lahore **54**, **121**
Bahadur Shah I, Mughal Emperor 53
Bahadur Shah II, Mughal Emperor 61
Bahmini kingdom 49, 50
Bahuu, Sultan, poet 117, 191
Bairam Khan, guardian of Akbar 50
Baksh, Ustad Allah, artist 173, **175**
Bala Hisar fort, Peshawar 141
Baloch people, in Sindh 130
Balochistan
  crafts **150**, 151, 180, **181**, 182
  culture in 150, 151, **179**, 190, 193
  feudalism in 148
  geography of 94, 95, **98**, 147-8
  Islam in 146
  livestock in 148, 151
  people/ costume of **15**, **28**, 67, 147, **148**, **149**, 150, 151
  politics of 23, 59, 67, 146-51
  sea fishing 148
  wildlife conservation in 108
Baltistan, mountain region **95**, **99**, **100**, 103, 142
Bangladesh, secession of 20, 21-2
banking 62, 62, **84**, 89, **134**, 153, 154, 162
Barelvi, Sayyid Ahmed 62, 66, 145, 195
basic democracy, system of 20
bazaars 122, **130**, **132**, 141, 142
Beas River, Punjab 102, 104
Beg, Mirza Qalich, writer 191
Bengal
  and the British 57-8, 66
  Muslim majority in 67, 69, 71, 76
Benthamism, and British rule 61
Besant, Mrs. Annie, Home Rule League 71
Bhambore, ancient port 40, 42, **43**, **44**, 184
Bhils, in Sindh desert 131
Bhutto, Benazir, PM 25, 26, 153-4, 167
Bhutto, Zulfikar Ali 20, **21**, 22, 23, 25, 152, **162**, 199
bin Qasim al Thaqafi, Muhammad, 42-3, 125
Bogra, Muhammad Ali, PM 18, **19**
Bolan Pass 59, 95, **146-7**
Borah Muslims 131
Bose, Subas Chandra, and J 76
Brahmin rule 37, 146
bridge construction 42, **49**, **95**, **96**, **105**, **158-9**
bridge playing 197
Britain, modern relations with 199, 203
British rule 57-69
  and art 173, 176
  in Balochistan 146, 148, 151
  in Karachi 132-3
  in Kashmir 144
  in Punjab 116, 121-2
Buddhism
  in Baltistan 142
  Gandharan era 37, 38-40, **41**, 173, 184

  in Kashmir 144
  in Punjab 114
  in Sindh 42
Buddhists, in modern Pakistan 172
Buksh, Colonel Ilahi, physician to J 89-91
Bullhe Shah, poet 178, 191
Bunda, Naseer, wrestler 196
Bundu Khan, Ustad, musician 179
Cabinet Mission 69, 80-1
Caliphates 42-4, 45, 63-4
camels **118**, **125**, 126, **146-7**, **156**, 183
carpet and rug making 122, **150**, 180, 181, **183**
caste system 35, 49
Chach dynasty 37
Chandragupta, Mauryan Emperor 36-7, 114
Charsadda (Pushklavati), Gandharan city 35, 36
Chaukundi tombs, near Karachi 47, **183**
Chenab river, Punjab 102, 104, 114
China, relations with 199, 201, 203
Chishti, Mueenuddin, Sufic Order of 195
Chitral 44, 94, **96**, 107, 136, 138
Christians 37, 65, 131, 172
Chuari Chaura massacre 73
Chughtai, Abdur Rehman, artist 173, **176**
Chundrigar, Ismail Ibrahim, PM 19
Churchill, Sir Winston, British PM 69
cinema, modern developments 194
Clive of Plassey, Baron Robert 57-8, 66
communications, modernisation of 158-61
costume **14**, **15**, **181**, 182-3
cotton production 156, **157**
crafts **14**, **15**, **118**, **119**, 180-3
  in ancient civilisations 30, 33, 34, 35, **44**
cricket **196**
Cripps, Sir Stafford 69, 80
Crow, Nathan, East India Company 132-3
culture
  and British rule 64-5
  modern 13
  Mughal 50-3, 52-3, 56
Curzon, Lord George, Viceroy 59, 63-4, 66
Dada, Nayyam, architect 171
Dahir, King of Sindh 42
Daibul, town of 42, **43**
Dalhousie, Lord James, GG 61
dance
  classical (Khatak) **12**, 194
  folk 194
Dara Shikoh, Prince 195
Darius I, Persian King 35, 146
Darius III, Persian King 36
Data Ganj Baksh al-Hujweri, Hazrat 115, 117, 186, 195
Deccan 49, 50, 53, 56, 186
Delhi 52,53
Delhi Sultanate 48, 49
democracy, development of 9, 10-12, **15**
Dholavira (India), ancient civilisation 29, 30
Dogra rule, in Kashmir 144-5
Dostum, General Rashid, Uzbek leader 201
Doxiades, architect in Islamabad 113, 169

205

Dunham, Sister Phyllis, nurse to J 90-1
Durand Line 136
Durranis (Afghans), in Lahore 121
East India Company 57-9, **60**, 61, 132-3, 145
East Pakistan, at Partition 16-19
economic migrants 112, 137, 153
economy 13-14, 20-1, 152-5, 162, 203
Edhi, Abdul Sattar, social worker 135
education **11**, 14, 20, 21, 164-5
   academic institutions 123, 141, 170-2
   and British rule 61-2
Eighth Amendment 10, 23, 26
energy resources
   buffalo dung **97**
   coal 155
   and deforestation 108
   electricity **12**, 13, 104, 153, 161
   oil 14
Faiz Ahmed Faiz, poet 123, 192
Family Planning Association of Pakistan 165
Faqir Khana museum, Lahore 184
Fariduddin Shaker Ganj, Baba 115, 117, 191, 195
"Fasting Siddartha" **41**, 184
Fateh Ali Khan, Nusrat, musician 178, 179
Fazlul Haq, A.K., politician 69, 76, 78, 79-80
festivals and fairs **45**, **115**, **122**, **123**, 130, 151, **178**
feudal system 128, 148
Firuz Shah, Tughlaq ruler 47
fishing
   economic importance of 157
   inland **101**, **104**, **106**, 125, 128, **137**
   sea **28**, **106**, **129**, 148
   and urban pollution 112
food processing, economic importance of **154**, 155
foreign aid 107, 153, 154
foreign investment 13, 161
forests 108, 110, 157
"Fourteen Points", of J 67, 74
Frere, Sir Bartle 132, 133, 191
fuel, *see* energy
Gandharan era 35, 37
   art of 37, 38-40, **41**, 173, 180, 184
Gandhi, Mohandas Karamchand
   Home Rule League 72
   and J 72, 75, 76, 78, 80
   and Khilafat Movement 72, 73
   on partition 69, 80
   Salt March 75
   satyagraha passive resistance 67
   and separate electorates 64
Gandhi, Indira, and Kashmir dispute 25
gardens, Mughal architecture 52, **56**, **57**, **122**
Ghalib, Asadullah Khan, poet 185, 186, 187
ghazal, poetic form 179, 185, 186, 187, 189, 192
Ghaznavid dynasty 45, 115, 186
Ghulam Ishaq Khan, President 25
Ghulam Muhammad, GG 18, **19**
Ghuri dynasty 45-7
Gilgit Agency, mountain region **15**, 44, 103
glaciers 95, **96**, 103, 104
Government of India Act 67, 72, 76
Greek era 36-7
Gulab Singh, in Kashmir 59, 145
Guljee, artist 173
Gupta dynasty 40
Habba Khatun, Kashmiri poet 145
Hala, Sindh, pottery of **133**, 181
Haleji Lake, Sindh, wildlife in **107**, **112**

Hameed Khan, Dr. Akhtar, sociologist **132**, 135
Hanif Mohammad, cricketer 196
Harappa, civilisation 29-30, 32, 34-5, 105, 184
Hari Singh, Maharajah of Kashmir 24
Hayat Khan, Sikander, politician 79
Hazara, Indus in 94, 111
Hephthalites *see* Huns
Himalayan mountain range 93, 94, 97, 103
Hindi language 68, 76
Hindu Kush mountains 93, 94
Hinduism 37, 40, 42, 43, 45, 114, 143-5
   and arrival of Islam 48-9, 56
Hindus
   in British rule 61, 61-3, 66
   in modern Pakistan 172
hockey 196, 197
Holy Quran, translation of 66, 187, 193
Home Rule League 71, 72
Home Rule (*Swaraj*) movement 70, 71, 72-3
Hudood Ordinances 167
Hujeri, Syed Ali *see* Baksh, Data Gunj
Humayan, Mughal Emperor 49-50, 176, 186
Huns, invaders 37 40
hunting
   and endangered wildlife 107, **108**, **109**, 110, **111**, **112**
   in Sindh 125, **127**, 128
Hunza, mountain area 44, 93
Hyat Khan, Sir Sikander, politian 76
Hyderabad 105-6, 172
Ibn Hauqual, chronicler of Arab rule 43
Ikramullah, Begum Shaista, politician 78, 167
Imran Khan, cricketer and politician 26, 196
Independence, struggle for 66-9, 163
India
   constitutional development 70-5
   culture and early Islam 43-4, 50
   and Kashmir dispute 24-5, 84, 153
   relations with 20, 161, 199, 200, 202-3
   and secession of Bangladesh 2, 21
   and water resources 161
Indian Mutiny (War of Independence) **60**, 61, 66
Indian National Congress
   and British rule 63
   and Independence struggle 66-9
   Muslim demands 70, 76-7
   and Partition 17, 70-3
Indo-Aryan peoples, in the Indus Valley 32, 34
Indus River **49**, 97, 102-6, 114, 125
   sedimentation in 31, 33, 97, 104-5, 111
Indus Valley civilisation 29-33, **43**
industry
   development in 10, 20, 122, 148
   and the economy 152-3, 154-5
   and Indus waters 102
   nationalisation of 23, 152-3
   privatisation of 153-4
International Monetary Fund 153-4
Intizar Hussain, writer 192
Iqbal, Sir Shaikh Muhammad 189-90
   philosopher 63, 187-90
   poet 9, 67, 123, 185, 187-90
   politician 67, 190
   teacher 190, 198
irrigation
   in agriculture 94, 103, 128
   and Indus barrages 104, **105**
   karez system in Balochistan 148, **150**

system, economic needs of 154
Irwin, Lord, Viceroy 74-5
Islam
   arrival of 40, 42-4, 47-8, 115, 146
   and the economy 153
   and Hinduism 48-9
   in Kashmir 143-5
   literature of 185-7
   and Mughal rule 50, 56
   politics and 10-11
   and religious tolerance 42
   scholarship in 43, 44, 45, 48
   Sufism in 195
Islam *see also* All-India Muslim League;
Muslim; Partition
Islamabad 113-14, 169, 184
Ismaili muslims 44, 85
Ispahani, M.A.H., supporter of J 79, 90
Jalaluddin Rumi, mystic 187, 191, 195
Jalib, Habib, poet 123, 192
Jamiat-ul-Ulema, Indian Islamic scholars 73
Jammu and Kashmir 143-5
Jatoi, Ghulam Mustafa, PM 25
Jats, ethnic group 53, 115, 126, 147
Jehangir, Emperor **52**, 53, **56**, 57, 143, 186
jewellery, craftmanship in 33, **43**, 180, **181**
Jhelum River, Punjab **100-1**, 102, 104, 114, 115
Jinnah, father of J 85
Jinnah, Dina, daughter of J 75, **79**
Jinnah, Emi Bai, first wife of J 86, 87
Jinnah, Fatima, J's sister, **79**, 84, 85-91, **131**, 167
Jinnah, Mithibai, mother of J 85, 86, 87
Jinnah, Mohamed Ali
   birth and early life 70, 85-6, 134
   character of 72, **73**, 75, 84
   marriages 75, 84, 86
   ill-health 83, 84, 88, 89-91
   death and mausoleum of 91, **131**
   lawyer 70, **71**, 87-8
   in Bombay 87-8
   in London 70, 75, 76, 86-7
   "Fourteen Points" 67, 74
   and Gandhi 72, 75, 76, 78, 80
   GG of Pakistan 18, 83-4
   politics
      entered 70, 73, 87, 88
      development of 70-5, 78, 88
      Muslim League 67, 69, 70, 72, 75, 76-83
   and the press, use of 163
   vision of 9, 16, 18
Jinnah Poonja family 86
Jinnah, Rattenbai (Ruttie), wife of J 75, 84
Junejo, Mohammed Khan, PM 23, 153
kabaddi, indigenous team game 196, 197
Kabul River **102-3**, 102
Kafir Kalash people, of Chitral 138, **178**
Kalat, Khanate of 146
Kalhana, Pandit, Kashmiri historian 143-4
Kanishka, Kushan ruler 37
Karachi
   airports 159, **160**
   British in 132-3
   communities in 131, 134
   J's birthplace 70, 85
   J's death in 84, 90-1
   modern architecture in 170, 171-2
   Muslim League in 76
   National Museum 184

INDEX

seaports 113, 159-60
theatre in 194
urban pollution in 112
Karakorum Highway 161, 201
Karakorum mountain range 93, 94, 103
Karakota dynasty, in Kashmir 144
Kashmir 143-5
  costume/peoples **14**, **144**, **145**
  crafts of **14**, 145, 180
  culture 144-5, **178**
  dispute over 17, 18, 20, 24-5, 84, 144, 145, 153, 199, 202-3
  Indus headwaters in 102, 103, 111
  Islam in 143-5
Kautilya (Chanakya), political teacher 36
Khaljis rulers 47
Khan family, squash players 196-7
Khariji sect of muslims 44
Khilafat movement 64, 67, 72, 73
Khojah Muslims 70, 85, 131
Khusrau
  Hazrat Amir
    musician 178, **179**
    poet 48, 186, 187, 190, 195
Khyber Pass 93, 95
kite flying 122-3, 196
Kohari, sculptor 173
Kohistan, people of 138, **139**
Kushan era 35-7
Lahore 35, **65**, 121-4, 159
  Congress meeting in 75
  crafts in 122
  culture in **122**, 123, 194
  Ghaznavid rule 45, 121
  Iqbal's tomb **189**, 190
  modern architecture in 171
  Mughals in **52**, **53**, **54**, **56**, 115, 121, **122-3**, **124**, **125**
  museums in 184
  Muslim League in 68-9, 73, 78, 88
  National College of Arts 123, 170, 171
  Sikh shrine in **172**
Lahore Fort **52**, **122-3**, 184
languages
  and Arab rule 43
  and Islamic scholarship 46, 49
  and Mughal rule 52
  and the press 163
  regional 136, 138, 142, 150, 185, 190
Lari, Yasmeen, architect 170
Leghari, Farouk, President 26
Liaqat Ali Khan, Begum Ra'ana 76, 166-7
Liaqat Ali Khan, PM 9, 18, **68**, 76
Linlithgow, Lord, Viceroy, and J 78, 79
literature
  heritage of 65, 185-7
  post-Partition 192-3
  regional 143, 190-1
livestock 128, 148, 151, 156, 157
  buffalo dung as fuel **97**
  and deforestation 108
  goats and sheep **28**, **145**, **156**
  oxen **156-7**
  yak as pack animals **97**
livestock *see also* camels; horse; nomads
Lodhis, Afghan rulers 47, 49
Lucknow, Muslim League in 76, **77**
Lucknow Pact 67, 71, 72
MacDonald, Ramsay, and J 67, 74-5

MacPherson, J. M., and J in Bombay 87
Mahatma Gandhi *see* Gandhi, Mohandas Karamchand
Mahbubul Haq, Dr., Finance Minister 152
Mahmood, Faisal, cricketer 196
Mahmood, Zia, bridge player 197
Mahmud of Ghazni 44, 45, 46[b], 121, 143, 144,185
Makli Hills, Thatta, necropolis **48**, **49**, **126**
Makran, Balochistan 42, 43, 146, **150**
Mangla Dam 110, 161
mangrove forests, and urban pollution 112
Manto, Saadat Hassan, writer 123, 192
Maratha rule 53-4, 58
Marri people 147, **157**
martial law, rule of 19-25, 163
Masud, Ahmed Shah, Tajik leader 201
Mauryan empire 36, 38
medicine
  early knowledge of 37, 44, 145
  modern facilities 164, 165-6
Mehrgarh, ancient civilisation 29, 32, 33
Memon Muslims 131
Memorandum of Nineteen 71
Menander, Greek ruler 37
Miandad, Javed, cricketer 196
mining 28, 155
Mirza, Iskander, President and GG 19
Mirza, Mehdi Ali, architect 170
Mistry, Dr. Mohammad Ali, physician to J 90
Mohajir Qaumi Movement (MQM) 134
Mohenjodaro, civilisation 29-32, 105, 180, 184
Montagu, Edwin, Secretary of State for India 72
Morley-Minto Reforms 63, 70
mosque, first in the subcontinent 42, 42
mosques, Mughal architecture in 52, 53, **54-5**, **56**
mountains, of Pakistan 93-7, 104, 113, 136, 147-8
Mountbatten, Lord Louis, Viceroy 24, **68**, 69, 80, 81-2, 84, 202
Mueenuddin, Khawaja, theatre of 194
Mughal Empire 47, 49-56, 57, 186
  architecture, influence of 169
  art of 51, 52-3, 173, 176, **177**
  crafts of 180, 181
  in Kashmir 144, 145
Mughal Empire *see also* Lahore
Muhammad Gaisudaraz, Sufi 195
Muhammad Shah, Mughal Emperor 52, 53
Mujib ur-Rahman, Sheikh, Bangladeshi PM 20-22
Multan
  architecture in 42, 43, **120**, **168**
  crafts of **45**, **155**, 181, 182, 183
  invaders of 42, 43-4
  treasures of 42
Mumtaz, Kamil Khan, architect 170, **171**
museums 184
music **15**, 65, **119**, **123**, 130, 145, 150, 178-9, 185
Muslim dynasties, in Punjab 115
Muslim League 25, 26, 154
  1997 elections 10
  J as leader 17, 76-83, 88
  Nawaz Sharif as leader 134
Muslim League *see also* All-India Muslim League
Muslims, and British rule 61, 61-3, 65-6,66
Nanak, Guru, Sikh founder 114, 191
Naoroji, Dadabhai, politician 70, 87
Napier, Sir Charles, Governor of Sindh **58**, 59
national parks 107, 110, **112**, 114
Nazimuddin, Khwaja, PM 18, **19**, **77**

Nehru, Jawaharlal
  Congress leader **68**, 69, 75, 76
  on J 73
  and Kashmir dispute 24
  partition rejected by 81, 82
Nehru, Pandit Motilal, Report of 67, 74, 75
Nizam of Hyderabad 58, **63**
nomadic herders 32, 130, **139**, **146-7**, 148, 151
non-governmental agencies (NGOs) 134-5, 164-6
Noon, Malik Feroze Khan, PM 19
Noor Jehan, wife of Jehangir 53
North-West Frontier 23, 97, 136-42
  agriculture **137**, 138
  British India 59
  costume/peoples **14**, 136-8, **139**, **140**, 141
  crafts from 180, **181**, 182
  food stalls **14**, **139**, 141-2
  Islam in 44, 137, 138, 139
  languages 136, 138
  literature of 190, 193
  music in **178**
  Muslim politics in 67, 69, 76
Northern Areas 107, 136, 158, **159**, 166, 180
see also Baltistan; Gilgit; Hunza
nuclear capability 25, 199, 202, 203
Ollivant, Sir Charles, and J in Bombay 87-8
Orangi Pilot Project 112, **132**, 135, 165
Outram, James, British Resident in Sindh 59
Pakistan International Airlines (PIA) 158-9, **160**
Pakistan People's Party **15**, 21, 23, 25-6, 153, 167
"Pakistan Resolution" 69, 78
Parsi community 75, 84, 131, 172, 193, 194
Parthian invaders 37, 38
Partition 16-17, 66-9, 82-3, 202
  events leading to 76-83
  and Kashmir dispute 202 202
  seeds of 61, 63-4, 66-9, 67
passive resistance (*satyagraha*) 67, 72, 73
Patel, Vitalbhai, politician **68**, 75
Pathan people 136-8, 139
see also North West Frontier
Patna, Muslim League in 77, 78
People of the Book, and religious tolerance 42
People's Party *see* Pakistan People's Party
Persian Empire 35-6, 146
Persian language 52, 190
Persian literature 185, 186-7, 190
Pervez, Ahmed, artist 174, **175**
Peshawar 37, 97, 141-2, 171
  J caught chill in 89
physical infrastructure 21, 61, 158-61
  railways 61, 116, 151, **158-9**, 161
  roads 14, 21, 160, 161
pirs, spiritual mentors 117, 195
poetry 65, 116-17, 145, 150, 179, 185-7
pollution, and population pressure 112
Ponti, Gio, architect 113, 169
Poonja, Jinnah Poonja family 85-6
population 94, 114, 148
  growth 10, 14, 134, 165
  and environmental pressure 107, 108, 110, 111, 112
Portuguese, traders 57
Porus, ruler of Jehlum 36, 115
pottery production 130, 133, **155**, 181
press 13, 23, 26, 123, 163
Progressive Movement, in writing 192
publishing 123

Punjab **45**, **46**, 113-124
   agriculture **100**, **116-17**
   costume/people **14**, 115, 116, **118-19**, 120, **122**, **123**
   crafts of **14**, **118**, **119**, 180-3
   culture of **45**, 116-17, **178**
   fishing **101**
   geography of 95-7, 104-5, 113, 114
   languages of 185
   literature of 116-17, 190-1, 193
   Muslim politics in 67, 69, 71, 76
   population of 114
   religions in 38, 40, 114-15
   rulers in 45, 58, 59, 61, 114, 115, 116
   social structure 117-20
Pushklavati (Charsadda), Gandharan city 35, 36
Qadir, Abdul, cricketer 196
Quaid-e-Azam *see* Jinnah, Mohamed Ali
Quetta 89, 90, 151
"Quit India" movement 69, 80
Qureshi, Moeen, PM 26, 153
Rabbani, Burhanuddin, Tajik leader 201
radio 163
Rahman, Colonel, physician to J 89
railway system 61, 116, 151, **158-9**, 161
Rajputs 49, 50, 115, 131
   and art 173, 176
   and the Mughals 53, 56
Ramay, Haneef, artist 173
Ranjit Singh, Maharajah 58, 59, **62**, 116, 121, **172**
Ravi River, Punjab 102, 104, 114, 121
refugees
   Afghan 112, 141, 151, 201, 202
   at Partition 17, 134
religion
   in Mughal era 50-1
   pre-Islamic 38, 40, 42, 126
      Indus Valley civilisation **29**, 31, **32**, **34**
religion *see also* individual religions
religious minorities 172
revenue collection
   British era 61, 66
   Mughal era 51, 53, 56
Rinchan, Kashmiri ruler 144
rivers 93, 94, 148
   transport on 31, 105, 116
Rizvi, Dr. Adeeb, social worker 135, 166
road system 14, 21, 160, 161
Roe, Sir Thomas, ambassador to Jehangir 57
Rowlatt Committee 72
Roy, Raja Ram Mohan, educationalist 62
Russia, British relations with 59
Russia *see also* Soviet Union
Sadequain, artist 174, **175**, 184
Sadiq, Lieutenant Munir, yachtsman 197
Saeed, Anwar, architect 170
Saiful Maluk manuscript 176
Sajjad, Shahid, sculptor 173
Salim, Masood, bridge player 197
Salt Range, Punjab 40, 95, 97, **98-9**
Sapru, Tej Bahadur, politician 74, 75
Sarhadi, Munir, musician **178**, 179
Sassanians, and Kushan era 37
satyagraha, passive resistance 67, 72, 73
Sayyed rulers 47
Sayyid Bilal (Bulbul Shah), Kashmiri saint 144-5
Sayyids, descendents of the Holy Prophet 139
sculpture 39, 40, **41**, 173
Scythians 37, 38, 39

seaports 159-60
Shafi Khan, Unver, artist 174
Shah Abdul Aziz, scholar 185
Shah Abdul Latif Bhitai, poet 130, 178, 179, 191
Shah Alam, Mughal Emperor 57, 58, 66, 187
Shah Faisal Mosque, Islamabad 114, **115**, 169
Shah, Hussain, boxer 197
Shah, Jamal, sculptor 173
Shah Jehan, Emperor **52**, 53, **56**, 56, 176
Shah Waliullah, Sufi 66, 185, 195
Shahabuddin, Sultan, in Kashmir 144
Shahnawaz, Jahanara, politician 167
Shamiri dynasty, and arts in Kashmir 144-5
Sharif, Nawaz, PM 25, 26, 154
Sher Shah Suri, Afghan ruler **46**, 51, 160
Shia Muslims, in Kurram Valley 137
Shigar Valley, Baltistan 103
shipping 159-60
Siachen glacier, and Kashmir dispute 25, **203**
Siddique, Naheed, Khathak dancer 194
Sidhwa, Bapsi, writer 193
Sikander Lodhi, Sultan, and education 185
Sikhs 53, 114, 116, 145, 173, 184, 191
   and the British 58, 59, 61
   in modern Pakistan 172
Simla Conference 69, **77**, 80
Simon Commission 67
Sindh 94, 125-35
   agriculture in 105, **125**, 126, 128
   British India 59
   costume/peoples **15**, 43, 125, 126, **127**, **129**, 130
   crafts of 129, 130, **133**, 180-3
   culture in 129-30
   fishing in 106, 125, 128
   health progammes in 166
   Indus River **104**, 105-6, 125
   language of 185
   literature of 190-1, 193
   music in **15**, **178**, **179**
   Muslim politics in 67, 69, 76
   religions in 38, 40, 42-4, 125
   rulers in 42, 58-9
   social structure 128
   wildlife conservation in **107**
Sindhiani Tehri, women's organisation 167
Siraiki language, literature in 190-1
Sirajudaulah, Governor of Bengal 57
Skardu, Baltistan 103
Slave dynasty 47
snooker 196, 197
social infrastructure 164-6
see also education; medicine; population
social structure 117-20, 136-9, 148
social work projects, in Karachi 135
Sohail and Pasha, architects 171
sports/pastimes **15**, 122-3, 130, **139**, 151, 196-7
squash 196-7
Stone, Edward, architect in Islamabad 113, 169
Sufi movement **45**, 48, 115, 191, 193, 195
Suhrawardi, Bahauddin, Sufic Order of 195
Suhrawardy, Husein Shaheed, PM 19, 81
Sukkur Barrage 128
Sultanate, and arts in Kashmir 144-5
Sutlej River, in Punjab 102, 104, 114
Swaraj (Home Rule) movement 70, 71, 72-3
Swat, mountains 40, 94, **96**, **99**, 136, **138**, 184
Syed Ali Hamdani (Amir-i-Kabir) 145
Tajik people **138**, 139

Taliban movement, in Afghanistan 201
Talpur rulers, in Sindh 58, 59, 132-3
Tamizuddin Khan, Maulvi, president of the Constituent Assembly 18
Tange, Kenzo, architect 169, **170**
Tarbela Dam **13**, 104, 110, 161
tauheed, concept of 188
Taxila, ancient civilisation 35-6, 37, 38, 184
telecommunications 14, 161
television 13, 163
textiles **119**, 130, **133**, 145, 155, 180-2
Tharparkar region, Sindh 111, 166, 180, 183
Thatta, Sindh **56**, **126**, 133
theatre 187, 192, 194
Tilak, Lokmania, politician 70, 73
timber resources **28**, **142**
Timur, Amir (Tamberlaine), invasion of India 47
Tipu Sahib, Sultan Shaheed of Mysore 58
Todar Mal, Raja, Mughal official 51, 52
tombs, craft work **45**, **47**, **49**, **52**, **56**, **123**
tourism
   beaches near Karachi **135**
   in mountain regions 93, **95**, 143
transhumance (nomadic herders) 32, 130, **139**, **146-7**, 148, 151
transport 31, 148, **150**, **151**, 156-7
see also animals; railway; road
Tughlaq dynasty 47, 181
Turkey, fall of Ottoman Empire 66-7, 73
Turks, rule of 45-7, 52, 146
United States, relations with 199, 201, 202
Urdu
   creation of 52, 185
   Holy Quran translated into 66, 187
   literature in 65, 187, 190, 192-3
   poetry in 65, 185, 186, 187, **188**, 189
   replaced by Hindi 68, 76
Urology, Institute of, Karachi 135, 166
water resources **12**, 94, **96**, 97, 102, 161
   and agriculture **116**, 142, 156
   in Balochistan 148
   disputes over 17
   for drinking 165
waterlogging and salinity 97, 111
Wavell, Lord, and Simla conference 80
Wellesley, Lord Richard, GG 58, 66, 132
wildlife, protection of **107**, 107, 108, 110, **112**
wildlife *see also* hunting
women 166-7
   dress of 120, **127**, **138**, **139**, 141
      purdah 120, 141
   education of **11**, 154, **164**, 165
   English, and British rule 61
   J and emancipation of 78
   Muslim League Ladies Committee 78
Women's Action Forum (WAF) 167
Women's Voluntary Service (WVS) 167
wrestling and boxing 123, 130, 151, 196, 197
yachting 196, 197
Yahya Khan, General, 21-2
Yousuf, Mohammad, snooker player 197
Zainul Abedin, Sultan, in Kashmir 144
Zamzamza, Kim's Gun, Lahore **124**
Zardari, Asif Ali, husband of BB 25, 26
Zia ul Haq, General, President 10, 12, 23-5, 153, 167, 194
Ziarat, J's health in 89, **91**
Zoroastrian *see* Parsi